HART CRANE

a reference guide

A
Reference
Publication
in
Literature

Ronald Gottesman
Editor

HART CRANE

a reference guide

JOSEPH SCHWARTZ

G.K. HALL &CO.

70 LINCOLN STREET, BOSTON, MASS.

Copyright © 1983 by Joseph Schwartz

Library of Congress Cataloging in Publication Data

Schwartz, Joseph.
  Hart Crane, a reference guide.

  (Reference guides in literature)
  Includes index.
  1. Crane, Hart, 1899-1932—Bibliography. I. Title.
II. Series.
Z8198.1.S343   1983   016.811'52   82-18725
[PS3505.R272]
ISBN 0-8161-8493-3

This publication is printed on permanent/durable acid-free paper
MANUFACTURED IN THE UNITED STATES OF AMERICA

For my son
Adam

Contents

The Author

Joseph Schwartz (Ph.D. University of Wisconsin 1952) joined the Department of English at Marquette University, where he is now professor of English, in 1950, and served as chairman of the Department from 1963 to 1975. Among his books are Hart Crane: A Descriptive Bibliography (1972-coauthor) which was the first in the series, Bibliographies of American Authors, published by the University of Pittsburgh Press. He is also the author of Hart Crane: An Annotated Critical Bibliography (1970), coauthor of Poetry: Meaning and Form (1969), and The Province of Rhetoric (1965). Two of his essays are of special interest to Crane scholars: "A Divided Self: The Poetic Sensibility of Hart Crane with Respect to The Bridge," an analysis of the composition of the poem, in Modernist Studies; and the forthcoming essay on Crane's contemporaneous reputation to be published in The Visionary Company. His articles have appeared in Christian Scholar's Review, The New England Quarterly, Modern Language Notes, Fiction International, The Nathaniel Hawthorne Journal, Hart Crane Newsletter, The Journal of Popular Culture, College Composition and Communication, Spirit: A Magazine of Poetry, and the new edition of The Catholic Encyclopedia. His book reviews have appeared in America, Chronicles of Culture, Drama & Theatre and Studies in Short Fiction. He is currently a member of the Board of Directors of the Conference on Christianity and Literature and editor of Renascence, a quarterly devoted to literary criticism and scholarship.

Preface

My principal aim in preparing this reference guide has been to be of service to scholars, critics, and students who are interested in Hart Crane and his work. I have tried to make an accurate abstract of the information and point of view, when necessary, for each item annotated. The guide has four parts: (1) Introduction, (2) Writings by Hart Crane, (3) Writings about Hart Crane, 1919-1980, and (4) Index.

The purpose of the Introduction is to give the reader a whole, albeit brief, view of the critical responses to Crane and his work. The principal editions of his work, the data concerning his manuscripts and letters, and his biography are given brief treatment by way of preface to the largest part of the Introduction, that devoted to criticisms of his work. The patterns in the critical writing about him and his work are traced, the emphasis being on his critical reputation. After a review of his contemporaneous reputation, the criticism of his work is divided into decades and presented in chronological fashion. "Writings by Hart Crane" is not meant to be a primary bibliography. Rather, it is a simple checklist of Crane's works and their dates of publication, a handy reference for the user of this guide.

"Writings about Hart Crane, 1919-1980" is by far the longest section of the guide. It is arranged chronologically by years of publication to illustrate the history and development of Crane's reputation. The arrangement within each year is alphabetical by the last name of the author. Numbering is sequential within sections and starts with "1" again in each section. Each entry includes the names of the author, the title, and publication information. The abstract for each item is a brief presentation of the thesis and, when appropriate, its development. Or the abstract may describe the scope, content, and method of the item. All entries have been verified, seen by me, unless an asterisk (*) precedes the number of the entry. Since reprints indicate critical interest in Crane, they are listed within the year of their appearance. Revised publications are noted separately, not treated as reprints. I have attempted to be inclusive in this section. Since I undoubtedly have missed some

items, despite every reasonable effort to be complete, I urge users
of this guide to send me the bibliographical information for items
which are missing.

In my attempt to be inclusive I have included encyclopedia
entries and brief mentions, since fluctuations in critical interest
in Crane are reflected by these items as well as by longer, more
original pieces. I have included "verse appreciations" since these
in a special way reflect an interest in Crane which tells us something about our culture as well as signaling its interest in him.
Finally, I have included recordings, tapes, films, and video cas-
settes dealing with Crane, listing the manufacturer's identifying
number for each item. I have not included the oral interviews which
John Unterecker conducted with many of Crane's friends while preparing his biography, Voyager; these are available in the Hart Crane
Collection at Columbia University. These oral history files were not
abstracted because they have not been formally published. The same
holds true in part for the treatment of doctoral dissertations. I
have entered dissertations for the convenience of users of this
guide, but they are not annotated because they remain unpublished.
If the dissertation is published in part or whole, such items are of
course abstracted. I have omitted textbooks in which Crane's poetry
appears with notes about the poet, unless there was some special
reason to include them.

The single Index is inclusive with authors, titles, and subjects
interfiled. I have not indexed the Introduction or "Writings by Hart
Crane"; only "Writings about Hart Crane, 1919-1980" is indexed.
Since separately published books devoted entirely to Crane have their
own indexes, I have not cited such works repeatedly for topics under
"Crane, Hart" or under particular poems. Titles of Crane's work have
been indexed. Reviews of the separately published books by Crane are
included under the title of the book being reviewed, as are selected
major studies except for separately published works devoted to Crane
as explained above. Reviews of separately published books about
Crane are indexed under each book. Titles of writings about Crane or
his work are indexed, as are the names of the authors of these sec-
ondary writings. Under "Crane, Hart" in addition to "bibliography"
and "biography" there are a number of topics to which one may refer
as starting points for certain kinds of research. References in the
"Index" refer to year (1939) and entry number (.27)--1939.27--not to
pages of the text. Entry numbers are listed in chronological, then
numerical order.

I am indebted to my chairman, John McCabe, for his many kind-
nesses, to the staff of the Marquette University Library for its
diligence in helping me collect materials, to the Committee on Research of Marquette University for its financial support, and to the
staff of G.K. Hall for their fine editing. Needed assistance on
specific occasions was given by Clarence Brown, Stephen Cook, Malcolm
Cowley, Georgia Pappanastos, Thomas Parkinson, Vivian Pemberton,

Preface

Strother Purdy, Robert C. Schweik, Allen Tate, and Jerome Thale--to all of whom I am grateful. My research assistants over the years deserve special mention: William Graczyk, Kevin Harty, Stephen Belden, Theresa Zink, Steven Liszewski, Nae Kang, Joseph Mueller, and Sarah Witte.

Introduction

The many reviews of John Unterecker's <u>Voyager: A Life of Hart Crane</u> (1969.47) confirmed, if such was necessary, the importance of Hart Crane as one of the major American poets. The amount of criticism which his work has generated from 1921 to the present is testimony to the serious effort which critics and scholars have undertaken in the effort to "place" his poetry in the history of American letters. Firmly entrenched in the academic and literary establishments, Crane ranks in the twentieth century with such poets as Robert Frost, Ezra Pound, T.S. Eliot, and Wallace Stevens. Interest in him is active in foreign countries as translations continue to be made of his poetry and as critics abroad respond to his work. He would be pleased with such attention; he wanted fame, and when he was not characteristically depressed, he exhibited the confidence of his (also characteristic) positive self-assessment. Early on in his career he told a high school classmate, William Wright, "I believe I have it in me to become the greatest singer of our generation." When pleading for his father's understanding of his commitment to poetry, he explained that he had no choice but to become a poet, and he added confidently that the Crane name would be known in literature here and abroad as a result of his achievement. Both Allen Tate and Matthew Josephson remembered his desire to be "The Great American Poet." Shortly before Crane's death, H.P. Lovecraft perceptively characterized him as having arrived as a major American poet who lacked the resources to live with the status he had so desperately coveted:

> I take my pen in hand to relate the events of the day in
> usual fashion--Saturday, May 24, 1930. . . . About 8 o'clock
> the bell rang, & there appeared that tragically drink-
> riddled but now eminent fried of Loveman's whom I met in
> Cleveland in 1922, whose new book, "The Bridge," has made
> him one of the most celebrated & talked-of figures of con-
> temporary American letters. . . . Poor devil--he has
> "arrived" at last as a standard American Poet seriously
> regarded by all reviewers & critics; yet at the very crest
> of his fame he is on the verge of psychological, physical,
> & financial disintegration, & with no certainty of ever
> having the inspiration to write a major work of literature

again. . . . His case is surely a sad one--all the more
so because of his great attainments & of the new fame which
he is so ill-fitted to carry for any considerable time
(1965.18).

Editions, Manuscripts, Letters
Although two concordances for Crane's poetry have appeared--
one by Hilton and Elaine Landry (1973.15), the other by Gary Lane
(1972.15)--the projected variorum edition of his poetry has not.
Both concordances use Brom Weber's The Complete Poems and Selected
Letters and Prose of Hart Crane (1966), a generally more reliable
edition than the 1933 Collected Poems edited by Waldo Frank. Both
White Buildings (1926) and The Bridge (1930) have been re-issued by
Liveright exactly as published in Crane's lifetime, White Buildings
in 1972 with an added essay by John Logan and The Bridge in 1970 with
an added essay by Thomas Vogler. Kenneth A. Lohf edited Seven Lyrics
in 1966, and With a Photograph to Zell was published separately as a
broadside in the same year. Poems, fragments, and drafts were
brought together by Lohf in Ten Unpublished Poems in 1972. A small
number of previously unpublished poems have appeared as well in books
and articles. The first collection of Crane's prose appeared as an
appendix to Philip Horton's Hart Crane: The Life of an American Poet
(1937.13). Another collection was included in Brom Weber's Hart
Crane: A Biographical and Critical Study (1948.21), and some pieces
were reprinted in his 1966 edition of the poems. In addition, Weber
edited some prose for Twice a Year (1945.4). Lohf prepared facsimile
editions of some of Crane's prose in "The Prose Manuscripts of Hart
Crane: An Editorial Portfolio" (1972.16).

Kenneth Lohf's The Literary Manuscripts of Hart Crane (1967.21),
as subsequently amended by others, is a carefully edited guide to the
location of Crane manuscripts in various collections in the United
States. It is collated with the 1933 edition of the poems.

Brom Weber's The Letters of Hart Crane, 1916-1932 (1952, and 1965
with corrections) includes around 400 letters. His working collection
from which that selection was made is on file at the Yale University
Library. His projected variorum edition of the letters has not yet
appeared. Five separate collections of letters have been published
since Weber's 1952 edition. Twenty-One Letters from Hart Crane to
George Bryant came out in 1968. A much more important collection was
edited with commentary by Susan Jenkins Brown (1968.8), Robber Rocks:
Letters and Memories of Hart Crane, 1923-1932. Thomas S.W. Lewis
brought together the published and previously unpublished letters to
and from Crane, his mother, and grandmother in Letters of Hart Crane
and His Family in 1974. Once thought lost, Crane's letters to Yvor
Winters were discovered after his death by his widow, Janet Lewis
Winters, edited by Thomas Parkinson, and published as Hart Crane &
Yvor Winters: Their Literary Correspondence (1978.22). Finally,
Warren Herendeen and Donald Parker published "Wind Blown Flames: The

Letters of Hart Crane to Wilbur Underwood," in <u>Southern Review</u>
(1980.4). A number of other letters have been published here and
there as they have come to light, for example the once-thought-lost
letter that Crane wrote to Winters as a result of his review of <u>The
Bridge</u>.

Biography

It has always been difficult to separate the man from his
work. Crane's life was sad and dramatic, perhaps even melodramatic,
and although he resented from the start personal references to his
life in connection with his poetry, the practice remains common in
any assessment of him. Born in 1899 in Garrettsville, Ohio, the only
child of Clarence and Grace Hart Crane, he appears to have been from
the beginning a weapon in his mother's battle with his father. He
was excessively indulged while at the same time rigid demands were
made of him. Instead of finishing high school in Cleveland, he
talked his divorced parents into allowing him to go to New York where
he would study with tutors in preparation for entering Columbia
University. Never interested in going to college, he spent his time
discovering the avenues in poetry that might be open to him. He had
already published his first poem, "C-33," before coming to New York,
and he persisted in sending his poetry to various little magazines.
Between 1916 and 1923 he lived in New York, Cleveland, and Washington, D.C. before taking up residence on a regular-irregular basis in
New York. Until 1925 he worked at various positions for his father
and others, never taking any of them seriously for long. Thereafter,
outside of a brief period when he was secretary to Herbert Wise in
Hollywood, he seemed not to have been regularly employed.

In 1924 the major poem he counted on to confirm his growing reputation as a poet, "For the Marriage of Faustus and Helen," finally
appeared in its entirety in <u>Secession</u>. Just as important during this
time for his growing reputation was the publication of "Voyages" in
the <u>Little Review</u> (1926). By the time <u>White Buildings</u> was published
at the end of 1926, he already had an emerging reputation as a serious
and gifted poet, having placed his poems in some of the better small
journals. <u>White Buildings</u> was widely, and generally well, reviewed,
giving him a place in the literary world. The difficulties with the
composition of <u>The Bridge</u> occupied him until 1930, when it was published by Harry and Caresse Crosby's Black Sun Press in Paris against
his better judgment. By that time, he had a large number of acquaintances and friends among the literary generation that produced so
many luminaries in the American literary sky. His circle included
Allen Tate, Waldo Frank, Gorham Munson, Malcolm Cowley, Kenneth
Burke, Jean Toomer, Eugene O'Neill, James Light, Slater Brown, Kay
Boyle, and Robert Graves, to mention only a few.

During this period he quarreled (never to be reconciled) with his
mother and used an inheritance from his grandmother to spend some
time abroad, mostly in France. The publication of <u>The Bridge</u> was a

major event in modern poetry, and it was extensively reviewed. Crane was as aware of its faults as any of his critics. After the publication of the poem, he found himself unable to write and unable to achieve any kind of social stability. His homosexuality, never a means of bonding with his literary friends, became more aggressively uncontrollable. At a loss for anything else to do, he applied for and received a Guggenheim Fellowship, which he used to spend approximately a year in Mexico to work on a Mexican epic or drama which never developed into anything. His only known heterosexual affair took place there with Peggy Baird, Malcolm Cowley's former wife. The final, brilliant "The Broken Tower" was the only significant poem he completed after The Bridge. Faced in 1932 with a return to the United States without having accomplished anything, disturbed by the death of his father with whom he had been reconciled, and uncertain about everything one must have some certainty about in order to function, Crane leapt into the sea from the deck of the S.S. Orizaba on his return from Mexico to the United States. He was thirty-three years old, our Keats, as some have implied.

Crane's familial and sexual difficulties have loomed large in the attempts to explain and understand him. The psychological difficulties first with his father and then, more aggravated, with his mother, as well as his reluctant homosexuality were connected, it would appear, and together provide partial explanations for his deep depression, his manic enthusiasms, and his ultimate inability to find a stable place for himself personally and socially. The critic interested in Crane's life is fortunate in having three major works to consult. Philip Horton's early, sensitive biography, Hart Crane: The Life of an American Poet (1937.13), remains the best written of the three and the most perceptive with respect to Crane's character. Its early appearance made it impossible for Horton to use the vast amount of material that subsequently became available. In addition to its being incomplete, it shows too much of the influence of Grace Hart Crane, the poet's mother. Brom Weber's Hart Crane: A Biographical and Critical Study (1948.21) had the advantage of greater distance and shows less of Mrs. Crane's influence. Less biographical and more critical than Horton's, Weber's work suffers from the book's dual purpose. Although references to Crane's life in connection with his poetry were made during his lifetime and occasionally after his death, outside of the biographies by Horton and Weber there were few essays showing such an interest until the great explosion of the sixties. In 1969 after ten years of work John Unterecker published Voyages: A Life of Hart Crane (1969.47), a massive text crammed with information. It remains the principal resource text for information about Crane's life. Many reviewers noted, however, that this was also its central problem. Unterecker chose to be complete and comprehensive and paid little attention to Crane's poetry. The vast collection of material exhibited no particular point of view outside of a generally sympathetic attitude toward Crane's troubled life. Although indispensible for any student of Crane's life and work, it may prove difficult to use since the endnotes were published separately

as a pamphlet. Many of the reviews of the book were written by
knowledgeable Crane scholars and critics and are often of interest
for the biographical insights and special information they contain.

   In addition to these three works, the published memories or reflections of some of Crane's friends and acquaintances are now available. One would want to consult, among others, Malcolm Cowley's many
essays, Matthew Josephson, Allen Tate, Waldo Frank, and Gorham Munson.
Additional information on Crane's biography became available with the
publication of the various collections of his letters referred to
previously. In the seventies Vivian Pemberton published her many
short essays about Crane's Ohio background.

   Criticism
   A number of notices of Crane's death dramatized him as a
figure whose tragic career was typical of the unappreciated artist in
America. Often used for their own purposes by various writers, his
career was made to illustrate the point that society had neglected a
great talent. Since he was then, and prematurely, already a legendary
figure, he was made to order for such responses. It is now evident
that his personal agony was caused by familial, personal, and social
tensions with which he could not cope. The response to his poetry is
quite another matter. The facts show that he managed to publish without unusual difficulty almost everything he submitted. He found a
publisher early in his career for his first volume, a publisher who
remained committed to the value of his work, bringing out the two
remaining volumes without delay. His poetry was reviewed regularly
by his contemporaries in those publications where poetry was taken
seriously. He had the further good fortune that among his appreciative contemporaries were some of the most discriminating literary
minds of this century. Many in that group made a special point of
calling his poetry to the public attentive to significant poetry. A
brief survey of the contemporaneous reviews of his work reveals that
his reputation was established during his brief lifetime. Subsequent
critical and scholarly work has confirmed and extended that reputation.

   Crane himself was confident that White Buildings would get "wonderful" reviews. Allen Tate said that it was probably the most distinguished first book of poems ever published in the United States.
There were a few hostile reviews; this was to be expected since the
personal intensity of the poems found expression in a style both demanding and original. Some, therefore, found the poems intensely
mannered, self-conscious, and aloofly intellectual. Even the critics
who took a positive attitude remarked regularly on Crane's obscurity.
Tate's foreword (1926.3) was an exceptional stroke of good luck, because it was used by a number of reviewers, helping to set the tone
for such reviews. Crane's originality was praised and his intellectual quality emphasized. The description of his poems as "intellec-
tualized" puzzled Crane, since he had little formal education, read

stipulatively, and freely confessed his own inadequacies in the intellectual order. It may be that his love of language and his mastery of a personalized vocabulary were misunderstood as intellectualism. That the poetry was willful and that it had discovered a language in which it had nothing to express was noted by a few. Most of the reviews, however, were positive in emphasizing his originality, his visionary quality, even when it overwhelmed his theme, and his ability to accept his age passionately without losing the sensitivity to explore both its strengths and weaknesses. Donald Davidson's comment to Allen Tate that Crane had received a good press for the volume was generally accurate. Some of the major critical approaches to his work were defined by these first reviews: his obscurity (virtue or vice), his personalistic and seemingly cerebral style, his individual vision, and his dazzling diction. On the basis of White Buildings Yvor Winters placed Crane among the five or six greatest contemporary poets. Waldo Frank asserted that he was as original and profound as Whitman.

Publication of The Bridge (1930) was an important event. Poetry: A Magazine of Verse awarded it the Helen Haire Levison Prize. Again the reviews were mixed, but the characteristic tone of almost all of them was clear: Crane was a major poet and The Bridge was a major poem. Although Winters was hostile to the ideological substance (or lack of it) of the poem, even he conceded that he was responding to the work of genius of the highest order. Tate, too, objected to the cosmic intent of a poem that was basically lyrical, but there was no doubt in his mind with respect to Crane's superlative lyrical gift. Because many reviewers had already read those parts of The Bridge which had been published separately as autonomous poems, they had difficulty seeing how the programmatic intention of the poem now expressed in new poems like "Cape Hatteras" could be integrated with the already existing sections. The reviews with reservations regarded it as flawed, but revealing great ability and even greater potential. The majority of reviewers felt that it was a notable contribution: "there is no one writing poetry today with like emotional intensity." Granville Hicks was convinced that it was "as important a poem as has been written in our time." Comparisons to T.S. Eliot's The Waste Land was common, Vincent Hugh claiming that it was "the most remarkable attempt at an orchestrated modern American poem since Eliot's." Even the Saturday Review of Literature, an establishment journal which Crane regarded as hostile, published Louis Untermeyer's positive notice as well as William Rose Benét's serious consideration which contrasted with his earlier satire on White Buildings. Morton D. Zabel, despite his reservations, asserted that Crane was one of the "few authentic poets now writing in English," that the poem "unquestionably displays the vision of a major poet," and that The Bridge "ranks high in the annals of twentieth-century poetry." Again most of the principal lines in the criticism of the poem were articulated in these contemporaneous reviews, especially the still-responded to position outlined by Tate, Winters, and Zabel. Various analyses since that time have returned to the basic points made by these reviewers, either to challenge or confirm them. Because of White Buildings and The Bridge, Crane's poetry became a part of the accepted universe of discourse of those writing criticism at that time. That he was singled out in various essays about poetry as either the extreme representative of unintelligible modernism or of the best in modern poetry are evidence of the attention given to his work.

After his death continuing interest in his work persuaded Liveright to bring out without delay (1933) a collected edition of his poetry. It provided his contemporaries with an opportunity to review what was then regarded as his complete corpus, inviting them to assess and reassess his achievement, and providing an opportunity for "placing" him. Generally, the reviewers took the tone of one making a statement about an established figure. "Almost all the attributes of poetic insight were in him." No new critical issues were introduced. The concerns that surfaced in the reviews of the two earlier volumes remained. There was a good deal of emphasis on his vision as a poet, on his response to the modern technological world, on the problem of being unable to employ traditional forms and beliefs in the modern cultural chaos, and on the question of his own life in his poetry. Babette Deutsch provides a convenient summary. The poet, she said, must shape the chaos in which he finds himself lest it destroy his poetry. He can no longer merely respond to and interpret the world; "he has practically to create it."

In summary the following major and persisting critical points were made in the reviews of the three published volumes. Waldo Frank made the point concerning Crane's mysticism, defending the systematic program to which he thought he had converted Crane. For Frank the major effort to define the myth of modern America with its machine culture appeared in Crane's poetry. Others, too, though in very different ways, commented on Crane's search for an Absolute, the spiritual character of his poetry, on his religion. Allen Tate, Yvor Winters, and Morton D. Zabel wrote with great clarity about the mistake Crane made in attempting to follow Frank's lead, an idea that had its roots in Emersonianism. Crane's supreme lyric gift was noted and praised. The poet as cultural hero was already a subject of contemporaneous responses. The crisis that modernism presented for the sensitive imagination had already become a commonplace in the criticism of the time. His obscurity and the demanding character of his language were mentioned repeatedly. Then, as now, The Bridge tended to deflect critics away from the notable achievement of White Buildings, even though both Crane and Tate felt that the latter was more representative of Crane's genius and style.

The important criticism in the thirties after Crane's death was written by Tate, Frank, and R.P. Blackmur. Tate combined and reworked three earlier essays for Reactionary Essays (1936.9), and the result remains one of the outstanding critical essays on a single poet in our century, one of the seminal essays in Crane criticism. Using his intimate knowledge of the poetry and his personal knowledge

of Crane, but without personal acrimony, Tate "placed" Crane so con-
cisely that every subsequent reading of his poetry has had to take
the estimate into account. He linked Crane to the fundamental ideas
of romanticism, describing him as "the archetype of the modern American poet, whose fundamental mistake lay in thinking that an irrational surrender of the intellect to the will would be the basis of
a new mentality." Frank's introduction to The Collected Poems was
reprinted in his In The American Jungle (1937.10) and should be
referred to specifically at this point because it took a stance so
radically different from Tate's. Frank thought that the challenge
of writing The Bridge gave Crane "the integrating theme" he had been
seeking and gave order to his poetic sensibility if not to his life.
The cosmic vision he encouraged Crane to make his own became the
means for understanding the organic unity of self, man, nature, and
cosmos—à la Whitman. Thus, he was able to form his "Word unaided,"
since there was nothing in the past that could sustain him. He was
"a true culture-child . . . of modern man." Frank praised Crane for
precisely the same reasons that Tate thought were his singular weaknesses. Blackmur's important essay, "New Thresholds, New Anatomies,"
(1957.2) is indebted for its starting point to Tate and Winters. In
contrast to Frank, Blackmur felt that if Crane was a "mystic" visionary what he needed was theology. Of particular importance were his
comments on Crane's language. The language appropriate for his
lyrics was not fitting for the epic intention of The Bridge. "He
used the private lyric to write the cultural epic." Also of note
during the thirties was the identification of Samuel Greenberg and
Crane's indebtedness to him by Philip Horton and James Laughlin. The
many reviews of Horton's biography attest to the significance of
Crane's stature, a circumstance not unnoticed by academe, the first
two Ph.D. dissertations being written at this time.

Criticism and scholarship in the forties were concerned, in part,
with continuing to place Crane in the field of twentieth century
American poetry. It was natural that he should be considered in such
conventional studies as Elizabeth Drew's Directions in Modern Poetry
(1940.3), Henry Wells's two books, New Poets from Old (1940.6) and
The American Way of Poetry (1943.7), Horace Gregory and Marya
Zaturenska's A History of American Poetry: 1800-1940 (1942.2), and
Amos Wilder's The Spiritual Aspects of the New Poetry (1940.7). The
much reviewed Hart Crane: A Biographical and Critical Study (1948.
21) by Brom Weber was one of the major highlights of this decade.
Wallace Fowlie contributed the earliest influence study, "The
Juggler's Dance: A Note on Crane and Rimbaud" (1943.2), a topic that
would continue to interest scholars. Warren Ramsey's "Poesia e
Platonism" in Inventario (1947.10) was the first critical study in a
foreign publication.

The question of Crane's spiritual interests was one of the most
important topics of this time, a topic which still remains lively in
Crane criticism. Amos Wilder thought that as a mystic and pantheist
Crane was "religious" in approaching his art. He was of special

interest to those concerned with the direction the religious spirit takes outside its usual forms. "All his work betrays a search after the Absolute." Henry Wells felt that The Bridge was "the strongest mystical poem" written in America after Whitman and Dickinson, and traced its relationship to The Divine Comedy. His faith was romantic; he awaited the time when America would be "governed at last by a long-awaited spiritual regeneration." Horace Gregory and Marya Zaturenska thought that "in writing The Bridge Crane unwisely sublimated the religious emotion that has a far more complete expression in 'The Broken Tower,'" his best poem because it "reveals the religious impulse that should have been given proper scope in The Bridge." In "Poet of a Mystical Atlantis" and "Religious Elements in Modern Poetry," Babette Deutsch characterized Crane as a religious poet in an irreligious age. In response to the loss of religious feeling in the culture, Crane had to create his own religion by taking the bridge as a symbol of something transcendentally significant. In Sense and Sensibility in Modern Poetry (1948.12) William Van O'Connor described Crane as a myth poet whose culture did not afford him a large and unifying belief. His personal difficulty in the composition of The Bridge is an illustration of a characteristic modern problem--the effect of the confusion of beliefs upon poets committed to long poems.

Articles of special interest were those by Hyatt Waggoner, Frederick J. Hoffman, and especially Yvor Winters. In "Hart Crane's Bridge to Cathay" (1944.3) and "Hart Crane and the Broken Parabola" (1945.3) Waggoner asserted that Crane was the victim of fundamentally confused idealism. "He searched for and sometimes seemed to have found God; but his poems record more of desire than discovery." Taking Whitman as his model, he set out on the ambitious project of synthesizing America, but failed in this because he could not find a system which made his intuitions meaningful. In "The Technological Fallacy in Contemporary Poetry" (1949.6) Hoffman dealt with Crane's view that the poet needed to absorb the machine, "acclimatize it . . . naturally and casually." Although Crane succeeded "more than any other poet of his time" in illustrating the problems of modernism, The Bridge was a failure because he was unable to organize the facts of his subject around the few symbols he collected. The single most important essay was Winters's "The Significance of The Bridge by Hart Crane, or What are We to Think of Professor X?" in In Defense of Reason (1947.13). No subsequent criticism of The Bridge has been able to ignore it. Crane was described as "the saint of a wrong religion," and The Bridge was his attempt to deal with the relationship of the individual American with his country, with God, and "with the religious significance of America itself." To do this he went back to Whitman-Emerson who glorified change for its own sake. Instead of being an epic, the poem is a loosely joined sequence of lyrics, some of which have only the slighest connection with the announced theme. The best of the individual lyrics rank among the most magnificent romantic poetry in English. The poem is seldom at its best, however, because Crane, whose religious passion was so

intense, settled for the fuzziness and triviality inherent in the
ideas borrowed from Whitman-Emerson. Although Crane had the courage
of his convictions, something lacking in Professor X, he lacked the
critical intelligence to understand where his doctrines were in error.
Karl Shapiro in "The Meaning of the Discarded Poem" (1948.17) also
felt that Crane's poetic ancestors had presented him with "a false
vision of life which eventually Crane was to employ for his own self-
destruction." When the myth inherited from Whitman failed him, he
could not live with the consequences. "Cape Hatteras," the Whitman
section, is the weakest part of the poem and "threatens to poison the
whole work." It is the defeated cry of the "demonic poet" not the
cry of a man who had lost his gift. In the early fifties Oscar
Cargill published a full-scale attack on Winters and Tate in "Hart
Crane and His Friends" (1958.6). In "tearing him to bits" they left
a fragmentary picture of the poet.

   The major publishing event of the fifties, however, was Brom
Weber's The Letters of Hart Crane, 1916-1932 with its many reviews.
While a variorum edition of the letters remains critically necessary,
the publication at that time of some 400 letters was a great service
to Crane scholars. Since Crane wrote the first criticism of his own
work, and since he enjoyed speculating about the nature of the poetic
art, the letters proved of special value in studies of his poetics.
Sister Bernetta Quinn used his two published essays plus a few of the
letters in "The Poetics of Hart Crane" (1951.12) in demonstrating
that Crane felt that poetry is something, not that it means something. An experience in itself, it does not depend upon the experience of the maker or the reader. The word stands by itself, possessing substance and accidents. Barbara Herman's "The Language of
Hart Crane" (1950.4) was a significant pioneer study of Crane's
attitude toward words. She picked up the challenge of Tate that
someone should set about isolating the principle upon which Crane's
poetry was organized, and discovered that principle to be his attitude toward words both as metaphysical entities and craftsman's
material. His method of composition "may be termed crosshatching of
reference." His language was his philosophy. As an absolutist, he
sought a mystic vision, and to objectify his mysticism he sought the
Word. The partial failure of The Bridge, seen as a whole, can be
explained by the unsuccessful effort to transfer his personal mysticism
to the creation of a national myth. In "Four Cosmic Poets" James E.
Miller, Jr. (1957.7) emphasized Crane's notion of myth as constituting
his poetics. Deeply religious, Crane discovered his religion by instinct and not in any dogma. The mystic evolution of the poem is
analogous to the mystic evolution of the universe. Crane's poetry
emphasized the romantic view or the organic nature of the poem. In
Achievement in American Poetry, 1900-1950 Louise Bogan (1951.1) also
contended that Crane was trying to create an "essentially religious
myth from the facts of modern man's soaring technical triumphs." It
broke down because of his inadequate faith. Like Tate, she felt that
his best work was in White Buildings. The quarrel he had with himself was far more grievous than his quarrel with the world. For

Introduction

Babette Deutsch (Poetry In Our Time) (1952.5) Crane was a "spiritual
Crusoe," a religious poet without a religion. While The Bridge was a
brilliant tour de force, he did not have the intelligence to handle
the problems he confronted.

Specific studies of The Bridge, as could be expected, continued
to appear in this decade. Hyatt Waggoner rethought his two earlier
pieces for the chapter devoted to Crane in The Heel of Elohim
(1950.9). His myth for the poem could not be crystallized into a
significant form; his ideas were not much more stable than his emotions. He thought of poetry as philosophical, architectural, and
mystical, but he could not synthesize the influences on him of T.S.
Eliot, I.A. Richards, P.D. Ouspensky, Oswald Spengler, and Whitman.
His was the search of "a religious mystic for a system of belief."
While the vision he sought was hinted at and promised in The Bridge,
it was not ennunciated--"the poem itself was not achieved." Henry
Lüdke suggested instead in Geschichte der Amerikanischen Literatur
(1952.10) that The Bridge miscarried because Crane could not attain
"the Olympian balance, the quiet faith of the old master Whitman."
Unable to balance his terror of and admiration for science, the poem
fragmented into a series of parts of unequal quality, possessing only
external coherence. Frederick J. Hoffman's chapter on The Bridge in
The Twenties (1962.11) remains one of the best short treatments of
the poem in the Tate-Winters tradition. The modern poet par excellence, Crane did not want to surrender to what he considered the
pessimism of his time. Unfortunately, he did not have any systematic
body of knowledge through which he could translate his affirmative
convictions into art. The vision was oversimplified while his awareness of the realistic circumstances was compelling: this tension was
never confronted. The analysis of the poem section by section is
careful and detailed. Hoffman concluded that Crane was a man "alien-
ated from his community because (and in the very act of) his search
for an acceptable, believable synthesis of that community."

While many of the reviews of The Bridge when it was published
were generally positive in their endorsement of Crane's achievement,
it was not until the fifties that critics began to take a like
approach. Because the Tate-Winters ideas had dominated studies of
The Bridge, these essays might be termed revisionist. Stanley K.
Coffman's "Symbolism in The Bridge" (1951.4) was the first essay on
Crane to appear in PMLA. Crane attempted to speak "a new word, never
before spoken and impossible to actually ennunciate." The bridge as
object was meant to reproduce all the qualities of experiencing belief
in what the object symbolized. The poem itself was meant to be a
metaphor translating the poet's awareness of this belief. The patterns of language, the symbols, and the images must be examined in
detail to discover this point. Coffman was especially concerned with
light, whiteness, and music. Recognizing weaknesses in the poem,
Coffman asserted that the effectiveness of the imagery wavers whenever
Crane loses his interest in what the passage is meant to say. In
"The Unfractioned Idiom of Hart Crane's Bridge" (1955.6) L.S. Dembo

first made the point he would develop at length in his later book on the poem. He confronted directly the two major charges against the poem: that Crane was a romantic poet and that the poem was "a romantic lyric" with epic implications. The poem, however, was really about the poet as cultural hero and recorded his struggle to remain an affirmative visionary in its modern tragic role. In "The Structure of Hart Crane's The Bridge" (1958.18) and in "Transmutation in Crane's Imagery in The Bridge" (1958.19) Bernice Slote held, contra Tate-Winters, that the poem must be considered as unified by looking at its design on Crane's own terms. It was intended to have a symphonic structure and written in the affirmative tradition Crane came to know through Whitman. The poet was an instrument of divine union, joining the diversity of creation as a whole. The poem was not about science or the machine; it was a drama of achieving a perceived spiritual vision--the myth of God's spiritual action. Transmutation, the poetic technique by which images recur in slightly changed patterns, occurs so often in the poem that it can be considered a unifying device. The reader is required to fuse the "relationships of the metaphor it evolves," the reader, thus, helping to create the poem. Sister Bernetta Quinn in The Metamorphic Tradition in Modern Poetry (1955.4) made the point that the poem found its anchoring symbol in place, and it is a symbol which undergoes "perpetual metamorpheses throughout the poem." The bridge itself is a concretization of God considered in terms of incarnation. Hungry for the Absolute, Crane "saw the bridge as a way of expressing the means of union with his Creator."

Although much of the significant criticism of the poems in White Buildings continued to center around "Voyages," Konrad Hopkins's "Make the Dark Poems Light" (1955.8) was the earliest and fullest criticism of White Buildings. He saw the volume as an integrated and relatively unified whole, gaining its coherence through "recurrent themes, repeated symbols and images," projecting a "uniform representation of the poet's own consciousness. . . ." H.C. Morris followed Crane's own sense of the poem in "Crane's 'Voyages' as a Single Poem" (1954.9). Unity was achieved throughout by the way the theme was presented through poetic devices--syntax, language, and symbol. In "Hart Crane and Moby Dick" (1956.2) Joseph Warren Beach showed how "Voyages II" was influenced by Melville's novel. During this decade Crane's final poem, "The Broken Tower," began to receive the attention it deserved. Herbert Martey's "Hart Crane's 'The Broken Tower'" (1952.11) began with a corrective analysis of what Crane meant by "the logic of metaphor"; plainly Crane meant the illogic of metaphor. "Symbolization and mood become the important facts in Crane's use of language and technique." The poem is carefully explicated as typical of Crane's complexity. That "The Broken Tower" is "an objective and deliberately thought out expression of Crane's literary faith in his last months, and expresses what he learned of his own limitations by writing The Bridge" is the point made by Marius Bewley's "Hart Crane's Last Poem" (1959.1), one of the seminal essays on "The Broken Tower." It may be, Bewley concluded, his most important poem because in it he

finally recognized that an absolute vision must be balanced by the
perspective of a moral vision.

The sixties were characterized by an explosion in Crane criticism
and scholarship. During the decade nine books were devoted exclusively to the criticism of his poetry. Brom Weber's "Hart Crane" in
Fifteen Modern Authors (1969.50) is an excellent survey of the work
done on Crane from the beginnings to 1970. His "apology" I can
easily repeat as my own for this essay. "The vastness of the literary-
cultural problems centered on Crane, and the divergent analyses and
solutions offered, make synthesis in a limited space impossible;
nothing less than a book will do. Summary notice, then, becomes
necessary." The books about Crane represent generally a high level
of critical intelligence, although variant points of view are evident.
Samuel Hazo's Hart Crane (1963.12) viewed him in a light of the
serious and fundamental questions characteristically asked in the
twenties. The answers he reached sustained him for a brief time only;
he could not face the future with "wisdom, confidence, and hope."
Himself a poet, Hazo's explication of individual poems is one of the
outstanding features of the work. His guiding principle is that
Crane was a lyric poet. Vincent Quinn's Hart Crane (1963.18) is an
excellent introduction to the major poems. "The keystone of this
book is the recognition that Crane looked upon poetry as the expression of gratuitous intuition, and that the central theme of his in-
spiration was the desire for absolute beauty and love." Transcendence
is the key word in Quinn's rewarding approach, since he considers
Crane to be in the tradition of the visionary poet. His chief contribution to Crane scholarship is the chapter in which he discusses
the critical position of Jacques Maritain vis-à-vis the positions of
Tate, Winters, and Blackmur. R.W. Butterfield's The Broken Arc: A
Study of Hart Crane's Poetry (1969.11) is an examination of Crane's
growth as a poet in relation to biographical, sexual, social, aesthetic, and religious forces. It is an ambitious book because he accepted Crane not only as a major poet but also as "a central and
absolutely crucial figure in American cultural and intellectual history." If Crane's major work was a failure, it is a good deal more
interesting and awesome than smaller successes. Like Quinn,
Butterfield feels that transcendence is the key to Crane's verse.
Jean Guiget's L'Univers Poetique de Hart Crane (1965.10) is in part a
survey introduction for French readers. The method, however, is
unusual. Guiget isolates the different elements which constitute the
poetic universe of Crane--elements of earth and elements of civilization, and then moves to an overall consideration of his poetry with
an analysis of these elements in mind. There seems to be a modest
general consensus that The Poetry of Hart Crane: A Critical Study by
R.W.B. Lewis (1967.19) is as of now the major critical work on Crane's
poetry. It did, however, generate strong and well thought out negative reviews as well. The student will do well to read such divergent
reviews as those by Dennis Donoghue and Alan Trachtenberg. Lewis considers Crane one of the finest modern poets in English and among the
dozen or so major poets in the history of American literature. His

method is to follow the development of Crane's poetry from the earliest poems through "The Broken Tower," charting the "career of Crane's imagination." Disagreeing with the general position of Tate, Winters, and Blackmur, he claims for Crane "the role of the religious poet par excellence in his generation." Lewis's study is unusual in that the central thesis is asserted but not proved. While there are questionable readings of some poems, his explications are generally valuable, stimulating, and challenging. Monroe Spears's pamphlet-size Hart Crane (1965.21) is one of the better short introductions to Crane. With respect to The Bridge, he wrote, "My own view is that the formulations of Tate and Winters are still accurate." Crane's status as a major poet rests, rather, upon a substantial number of unique, splendid, and powerful lyric poems.

Analyses of Crane's poetics continued to appear. Harvey Gross's Sound and Form in Modern Poetry (1965.8) contained one of the better pieces on the subject. He characterized Crane's style as rhetorical. Having no gift for the "plain" style, Crane sought after the incantatory power of words and for a rich, rhythmic language. Although his rhetoric is self-defeating at times, when Crane can control his rhythms the excesses can be overlooked and one can enjoy his intoxicating use of language. In The Modern Poets (1960.17), M.L. Rosenthal made an extended comparison of Crane and D.H. Lawrence. Crane's real triumph was his ability to register those complex states of feeling in which one is neither wholly confident nor wholly in despair. Hilton Landry identified Crane as "the last Romantic" in America in "Of Poetry and Praise: The Poetry of Hart Crane" (1966.20). He asked for a positive reevaluation of Crane's own critical statements about the nature of poetry. "A transcendental idealist," Crane's vision does not confuse readers; it is, rather, the lack of a traditional vocabulary to express that vision in religious terms. David R. Clark's "Hart Crane's Technique" (1963.7) carefully examined Crane's syntax and his use of metaphor. When both of these are opaque, the reader has a problem with the poetry.

An important influence study that explored the nature of Waldo Frank's influence on Crane--Robert Perry's The Shared Vision of Waldo Frank and Hart Crane (1966.24), appeared during this decade. Whitman finally came through Frank to Crane, enabling him to find a way of reconciling the fact of death with his otherwise basically affirmative attitude toward life. Since the influence of Frank had not been given sufficient attention, Perry's study acted as an important corrective of past attempts to trace the principle influences on Crane and his work.

In addition to the full-scale studies mentioned above, all of which include analyses of The Bridge, many others were published during this time. Both L.S. Dembo and Pietro Spinucci offered book-length critiques of The Bridge. In Il Ponte di Brooklyn (1966.26) Spinucci held that the poem was truly unified, having a coherent structure and theme. This was missed by most critics because they

did not understand Crane's being a part of the new humanism, his indebtedness to Melville, and the importance of the machine to him.
Dembo's Hart Crane's Sanskrit Charge (1960.7) remains one of the most
important of the revisionist studies. The Bridge did not attempt to
create a national myth; it was, instead, an account of the isolated
and exiled poet's search for Logos. It is a romantic lyric with epic
implications. There is disillusionment in the poem, but not enough
attention has been paid to the meaning of reaffirmation, the key to
the poem's meaning. Nietzsche's theory of tragedy, overlooked by
critics, gave Crane a metaphysical argument with which to handle
disillusionment. A traditional romantic, he made the subject of the
poem his own search for the Absolute. That Crane made himself the
hero of the poem is also the thrust of Albert Van Nostrand's "The
Bridge and Hart Crane's Span of Consciousness" (1962.22). In Crane's
theory of poetry a poem is as much about the experiencing as about
the experience itself. "I propose that Crane's involvement in his
poem was such that his struggle to form it became in fact the subject
of the poem, and when the poem is read this way it is a whole docu-
ment whose parts are organic." Robert Andreach's chapter on Crane in
Studies in Structure (1964.1) is valuable because he questioned the
free (and inaccurate) use of the term mystic as applied to Crane.
His religious approach made The Bridge an attempt to give America a
religious epic. How contemporary man can regain his lost faith was
the question Crane faced. Science may have built Brooklyn Bridge,
but by the end of the poem modern man has created a bridge to God.
This movement explains the real unity of the poem. It should be
noted, however, that his basic religious attitude is non-Christian.

Although The Bridge has always had a tendency to deflect interest
away from the other poetry, increasingly during the sixties it, too,
received significant attention. Herbert A. Liebowitz's Hart Crane:
An Introduction to the Poetry (1968.22) is devoted exclusively to the
shorter poems. Faithful to the spirit of modern romanticism, his
most representative poems followed the pattern of an ascent from de-
jection to a moment of vision followed by a descent into "the short-
sightedness of daily life." Four chapters are devoted to Crane's
chronological development through "'Voyages,' his highest achievement." The following five chapters deal with the technical charac-
terisitics of his poetry. L.S. Dembo's short survey of the poetry
before "For the Marriage of Faustus and Helen" ("Hart Crane's Early
Poetry" [1961.9]) is concerned with his continued attempt to define a
role for the poet in a hostile and chaotic world. Until he absorbed
Nietzsche's theory of tragedy, he had a keen sense of the poet's isolation, but then learned that he had a crucial role in society.
Maurice Kramer's "Hart Crane's 'Reflexes'" (1967.17) is also concerned with the earlier poems. In his successful poems Crane em-
bodied the change from suffering to alienation to transcendent wholeness, a constant alternation between hope and despair. The theme
referred to most often in the criticism and scholarship of the sixties
was this "transcendental wholeness," appearing under a variety of
names--the Absolute, spirituality, mysticism, religion.

Introduction

One of the notable advances of the seventies was bibliographical. Joseph Schwartz and Robert C. Schweik's Hart Crane: A Descriptive Bibliography (1972.28) was the first in the important series of bibliographies devoted to American writers published by the University of Pittsburgh Press. It included everything written or drawn by Crane that appeared in published form. Separate editions are listed first and arranged chronologically by the date of publication. This is followed by an alphabetical listing of works not published separately, divided into poetry, prose, and letters. Crane's drawings, translations of his work, adaptations of it, and doubtful attributions are separately listed. Among the appendixes are a chronology of the publication of his poetry and a listing of the periodicals in which his work first appeared. Hart Crane: An Annotated Critical Bibliography (1970.34) by Joseph Schwartz was an alphabetical listing by author of the writings about Crane from 1921 to 1968. Hart Crane: A Reference Guide is an updated, altered in method, and refined continuation of the earlier work repairing its omissions and changing the method of annotation. Bibliographical information, memorabilia, short notes, and brief essays characterized the Hart Crane Newsletter which was published 1977-79 in two volumes (four issues). It served well the traditional function of a newsletter about an individual writer.

The many explications of Crane's shorter poems during this decade cannot be conveniently summarized, except to say that Crane's passionate, borrowed cry "Make my dark heavy poem light" has been responded to repeatedly. The obscurity of his verse continued to generate close readings of his texts and lines from the texts. This habit, fortunately, shows no signs of diminishing; it is a much-needed aspect of the criticism of his poetry. Melvin E. Lyons's The Centrality of Hart Crane's "The Broken Tower" (1972.19) is a good sample. He focuses on the tower, God, Christ, and the lady, showing how each had been used in Crane's other work as a way of understanding their use in this poem. On the one hand, this method is helpful in reading specific images and lines in the poem. On the other, it mistakenly emphasized the sexual notion that the elevation of the spirit must be gained through human intercourse. Philip Yannella's "'Inventive Dust': The Metamorphoses of 'For the Marriage of Faustus and Helen'" (1974.26) analyzes the poem as presenting the diametrical opposition of William Blake and T.S. Eliot, "one of the characteristic dichotomies of 20th century America." Crane combines both. He sees Helen as a symbol of technological culture, discussing the influence of Waldo Frank and Gorham Munson on Crane's conversion to the need for taking the machine into account in his art. The crucial issue of the poem emerges in the conflict between the Newtonian and relativistic conceptions of the universe.

Samples of approaches to The Bridge in the seventies are the essays by Eugene Paul Nassar and Thomas A. Vogler, since both review in some detail past criticisms of the poem. In The Rape of Cinderella: Essays in Literary Continuity (1970.29) Nassar was

particularly interested in responding to the view that the poem was
meant to create a myth of America. He asserted instead that the subject of the poem is the greatness and significance of myth itself,
because it is the myth-making power that sustains man. Crane, he
concluded, was neither a transcendentalist nor a romantic, affirming
rather that the myth-making capacity of the imagination as man's way
of satisfying his hunger for vision. Preludes to Vision: The Epic
Venture in Blake, Wordsworth, Keats, and Hart Crane (1965.28) by
Vogler also examined the position which labelled The Bridge a failure
because it did not achieve its purpose. The elements which were
pointed to as reasons for Crane's failure are precisely the elements
which give the poem its theme and significance. The poem intends to
move from lyric vision to "sustained and comprehensive vision" and
succeeds. The lack of faith, which others point to as failing to
sustain Crane in the composition of the poem, is rather its motivating
force. Crane is searching in the poem itself for a mythic vision,
one that would assure a positive future for the pessimistic present.
He did not come to the poem with a fixed vision in mind. The process
of the composition of the poem also interested Edwin Fussell in
Lucifer in Harness: American Meter, Metaphor, and Diction (1973.11).
Because it was mentioned so frequently in his letters, we have "the
best documented example" of the way in which "a poem of constituting
metaphor may come into being." In contrast to Vogler's view, Fussell
saw the poem as uneven and fragmentary because it got lost somewhere
between its beginning and end. Crane "was trying to write out of the
wrong tradition." Joseph Schwartz identified that tradition in "A
Divided Self: The Poetic Sensibility of Hart Crane with Respect to
The Bridge" (1979.20). By temperament one kind of poet, he undertook
a willful shift to become another kind of poet because of the influence of Waldo Frank. The essay traces how the divided self came about
by examining, first, the essential poetic sensibility of Crane, and,
second, how he came to think of himself as Whitman's heir. Helge
Normann Nilsen was also concerned with Crane's divided self in Hart
Crane's Divided Vision: An Analysis of The Bridge (1980.6). He concluded that the national idealism expressed, the result of the influence of Frank and Whitman, was a central factor of the American character and a continual challenge to the artist. Crane, however, was
never comfortable with the nationalistic, mystic symbolism. The
poem was also the religious myth of America, revealing God in the
works of Americans. Crane's divided responses--wholly optimistic and
blackly pessimistic--were equally real for him. As a drama of faith
and doubt, the poem's importance is in its being a reminder to America
to fulfill its destiny. In Hart Crane's The Bridge: A Description
of Its Life (1976.19) Richard P. Sugg argued that it was a unified
poem because it was the result of the natural organic process in
which intellect and passion are united in the life of the imagination.
Outside of his response to the readings of Tate, Winters, and
Blackmur, he ignored most other readings of the poem.

Of the three full-scale studies of Crane's work published in the
seventies M.D. Uroff's Hart Crane: The Patterns of His Poetry

(1974.24) proved to be the most valuable. She did not see Crane as a poet of the divided self. Instead, his work was of unusual continuity, "of patterns recurring with obsessive frequency." The pattern of violence is seen in his urge to "violate the certainties of the world" which led to suffering but eventually to the "confidence to be won from the violence of art." The pattern of possession flows from the pattern of violence, because to violate the world is to possess its otherwise resistant reality in an imaginative way. Although it is common to separate his lyrics from The Bridge, as Crane himself did, it is impossible to separate Crane's poetry into periods. His work must be read as a unified whole. "He matured as a poet early, and aside from his very early poetry his work is of one piece." Although excessive emphasis on The Bridge has led to the view that he is a visionary poet, no poet of his generation was more sensitive to physical sensations. "Crane went against the grain of his time." In Vision of the Voyage: Hart Crane and the Psychology of Romanticism (1978.9) Robert Combs also objected to the description of Crane as a visionary poet because it led to his being judged on "the efficacy of whatever vision the critic can find." Crane was basically a romantic who opposed any dogmatic way of thinking. His lack of commitment to a single vision is his romantic strength. His poetry is a personal record of a man who struggled and suffered because reality was incomplete. In his review of Sherman Paul's Hart's Bridge (1972.23) L.S. Dembo complained that while Paul acknowledged previous commentators on The Bridge, "he never engages them head-on nor makes clear what he has added to their insights." One's response to the work depends pretty much on how sympathetic he is to the attempt in the final chapter to argue Gordon Grigsby's point that many critics had reservations about The Bridge because Crane did not share their ethical or religious systems. He had the "wrong masters." Paul's careful explications of the poetry depend upon his defense of Crane as a self-liberated romantic.

While a detailed summary is impossible, one can pick out certain major concerns over the years with Crane's work. It is impressive to note that from the beginning his poetry has been given significant attention. The continuing debate as to his place in our literary history will probably not end, since his career dramatizes the larger problem of modernism. He will always be a poet who represents the hard case. Was The Bridge a failure because it celebrated modernism or was that the source of its success? Is Crane a poet of the transcendental whose visionary quality best defines his art, or did he make himself the subject of his poetry by delineating the struggles of one man against hostile and resistant reality? Was his primary gift lyrical and was he the last (even apotheosis) of the romantics, or was his lyricism the phase that led him to the epic in symphonic form, or was he both? How significant is his biography in the reading of his poetry? Explications of the individual poems are an indication of his essential obscurity, an obscurity that has been praised as organic and decried as willful. His language has occupied much space in the criticism because it is so powerful, so stipulative, so anxious to articulate a (the?) Word. Has criticism succeeded in making his "dark heavy" poems "light"? To a striking degree, yes, although that effort has hardly ended. As a poet in his own right and as a representative of the knottiest problems of modernism, Hart Crane's poetry has received on the whole responses worthy of its importance and its difficulties.

Writings by Hart Crane

White Buildings. With a foreword by Allen Tate. New York: Boni & Liveright, 1926.

The Bridge. With three photographs by Walker Evans. Paris: Black Sun Press, 1930.

The Bridge. New York: Horace Liveright, 1930.

The Collected Poems of Hart Crane. Edited with an introduction by Waldo Frank. New York: Liveright, 1933.

Two Letters: Hart Crane to Frederick Clayton. Brooklyn Heights, N.Y., 1934.

The Collected Poems of Hart Crane. Edited with introduction by Waldo Frank. London: Boriswood Press, 1938.

"Prose Writings of Hart Crane." Edited by Brom Weber. Twice a Year Vols. XII-XIII, pp. 424-52, 1945.

The Letters of Hart Crane, 1916-1932. Edited by Brom Weber. New York: Hermitage House, 1952.

Voyages: Six Poems from White Buildings. With wood engravings by Leonard Baskin. New York: Museum of Modern Art, 1957.

The Complete Poems of Hart Crane. Edited by Waldo Frank. Garden City, N.Y.: Doubleday Anchor Books, 1958.

The Letters of Hart Crane, 1916-1932. Edited by Brom Weber. Berkeley and Los Angeles: University of California Press, 1965.

The Complete Poems and Selected Letters and Prose of Hart Crane. Edited with an introduction and notes by Brom Weber. Garden City, N.Y.: Doubleday Anchor Books, 1966.

Seven Lyrics. Preface by Kenneth A. Lohf. Cambridge, Mass.: Ibex

Press, 1966.

With a Photograph to Zell, Now Bound for Spain. Cambridge, Mass.:
    Ibex Press, 1966.

Twenty-One Letters from Hart Crane to George Bryan. Edited by Joseph
    Katz, Hugh C. Atkinson, and Richard A. Ploch. Columbus: Ohio
    State University Libraries, 1968.

Robber Rocks: Letters and Memories of Hart Crane, 1923-1932. Edited
    by Susan Jenkins Brown. Middletown, Conn.: Wesleyan University
    Press, 1968.

The Bridge. Commentaries by Waldo Frank and Thomas A. Vogler. New
    York: Liveright Publishing, 1970.

White Buildings. With an introduction by Allen Tate and a foreword
    by John Logan. Liveright Publishing, 1972.

Ten Unpublished Poems. Introduction by Kenneth A. Lohf. New York:
    Gotham Book Mart, 1972.

"The Prose Manuscripts of Hart Crane: An Editorial Portfolio."
    Edited by Kenneth A. Lohf. In Proof: The Yearbook of American
    Bibliography and Textual Studies. Edited by Joseph Katz. Vol.
    2. Columbia: University of South Carolina Press, 1972.

Letters of Hart Crane and His Family. Edited by Thomas S.W. Lewis.
    New York: Columbia University Press, 1974.

Hart Crane & Yvor Winters: Their Literary Correspondence. Edited by
    Thomas Parkinson. Berkeley and Los Angeles: University of
    California Press, 1978.

"Wind Blown Flames: The Letters of Hart Crane to Wilbur Underwood."
    Edited by Warren Herendeen and Donald Parker. Southern Review
    16, no. 2 (April 1980), 337-76.

Writings about Hart Crane, 1919-1980

1919

1   CHAMBERLAIN, ALICE. "Millionaire's Son Is Clerk in Akron
     Drugstore." Akron Sunday Times, 21 December, p. 3.
        A two-column interview which Crane thought of as a joke,
     but which disturbed his father. Crane is reported to have said
     that the artist cannot stay aloof from business "in an age of the
     most violent commercialism the world has ever known." Contains
     probably the first published photograph of Crane.

1921

1   BROOKS, CHARLES STEVEN. "A Visit to a Poet." In Hints to
     Pilgrims. New Haven: Yale University Press, pp. 92-102.
        Brooks's visit with Crane (although Crane is not mentioned
     by name) when Crane was advertising manager of the Little Review,
     living in a garret above the magazine offices.

1922

1   UNTERMEYER, LOUIS. "The New Patricians." New Republic 33 (6
     December):41-42.
        Crane mentioned in the final paragraph of the essay as
     among the "still younger and unaffiliated" poets.

1923

1   TATE, ALLEN. "Sonnet: To a Portrait of Hart Crane." Double
     Dealer 5 (March-April):123.
        Verse appreciation.

1924

1 BOYD, ERNEST. "Aesthete: Model 1924." American Mercury 1
   (January):51-56.
      Although Crane is not mentioned by name in this essay, he
   probably served as one of the models for the composite portrait
   satirized by Boyd. Crane and his friends appeared to be much
   offended by the piece; their reaction gave it a footnote in
   literary history.

1926

1 COWLEY, MALCOLM. "Hart Crane." Little Review 12 (Spring-
   Summer):34.
      Verse appreciation.

2 MONROE, HARRIET. "A Discussion with Hart Crane." Poetry 29
   (October):34-41.
      The famous exchange of letters between Miss Monroe and
   Crane concerning "At Melville's Tomb." Miss Monroe's second
   letter indicates that she was not convinced by Crane's now famous
   explanation.

3 TATE, ALLEN. Foreword to White Buildings. New York: Boni &
   Liveright, pp. xi-xviii.
      Tate volunteered to write the essay when Eugene O'Neill,
   who had promised to introduce the poems, found he could not do so.
   While primarily laudatory, Tate does take into account Crane's
   limitations. Crane's poetry is ambitious, contemporary, and in
   the grand manner. His themes are confined to an experience of
   the American scene. From the Imagists, Crane learned structural
   economy. From Pound and Eliot he got his sense of what it means
   to be contemporary. "If the energy of Crane's vision never quite
   reaches a sustained maximum, it is because he has not found a
   suitable theme." His present vision of the world is intensely
   personalized; his expression of this theme is necessarily obscure. Reprinted: 1975.23.

1927

1 ANON. Review of White Buildings. Boston Evening Transcript,
   16 April, p. 4.
      One of the many reviews of White Buildings which began by
   responding to Allen Tate's foreword. Crane's themes are obliquely
   presented and cannot be reduced to logical meanings; they must be
   made sense of through intuition. Especially taken with Crane's
   technique. Refers the reader to Crane's correspondence with
   Harriet Monroe (1926.2).

2 ANON. Review of White Buildings. Booklist 24 (November):59.

A review in one sentence: "These poems are restlessly and intangibly mystic—shadowy projections often so personal and obscure in their interpretation of things seen and felt that their thought fails to break through the rigidity of speech, even when words are most deftly chosen and arranged."

3   ANON. Review of White Buildings. Dial 82 (May):432.
     Brief and unfriendly. Although Crane has ability as a poet and makes good phrases, he seldom writes a completely satisfactory poem. "Partly this is due to certain affectations of idiom, to a straining and self-conscious and disingenuous preciosity; partly it is caused by an unreflecting indulgence in what one might call high-class intellectual fakery." Samples of Crane's best work are "In Shadow" and "Voyages II." Tate and Crane suspected that Conrad Aiken wrote this review. In a letter to Tate (27 March 1927) Crane wrote, "I think that you may give good reasons for assuming that Aiken wrote it."

4   ANON. Review of White Buildings. Times Literary Supplement (London), no. 1308 (24 February), p. 130.
     Crane is praised for his structural economy, his objectivity, and his searching and personalized vision of the world. His single lines and some whole poems reveal a profound originality. His obscurity, however, is at times so deep that the effort required to pierce it kills the possibility of an aesthetic response. Crane was pleased that his work was reviewed by a British publication.

5   ANON. Review of White Buildings. Open Shelf (April), p. 51.
     Crane's poetry is at once contemporary and in the grand manner. His themes are abstract, metaphysically conceived, but confined to an experience of the American scene. A three-sentence comment is adapted from Allen Tate's foreword.

6   ANON. Review of White Buildings. Saturday Review of Literature 3 (2 April):704.
     The poetry is highly cerebral, difficult to comprehend. Crane's hieroglyphics do not always indicate subtlety. The poetry is intensely mannered and self-conscious. "It often rapes language under the impression that it is paying expression the highest possible compliment by being almost understandable." The reviewer confesses that he hasn't the slightest idea what a good deal of the poetry means.

7   BROOKS, VAN WICK; KREYMBORG, ALFRED; MUMFORD, LEWIS; and ROSENFELD, PAUL. The American Caravan: A Yearbook of American Literature. New York: Literary Guild of America, pp. 804-6, 836.
     An anthology containing "Ave Maria" and a brief biographical note.

8   DAVIDSON, DONALD. "Hart Crane's Poetry Difficult but Bold and Masculine." <u>Nashville Tennessean</u>, 3 April, p. 7.

Feels that <u>White Buildings</u> is a bewildering and impressive volume; often the meaning of Crane's poems eludes the reader in spite of the extraordinary definiteness of the language. "The practice of telescoping metaphors is theoretically quite unassailable, but how far can the process be carried? He is most successful, I think, in those poems where he is nearest to tradition: 'Praise for an Urn,' 'Stark Major,' and some parts of 'Voyages.'" In a letter to Tate (31 March 1927) Davidson says "nevertheless, I cannot get around an unpleasant effect that I constantly get from his poetry. . . . Part of the unpleasantness comes, no doubt, from the elements mentioned in the reviews; but there is something else I just can't define. I just give up, gasping like a fish." Reprinted: 1963.9.

9   DAVIS, GEORGE. "Hart Crane's Bon-Bons Are Acclaimed." <u>Cleveland Press</u>, 4 June, p. 6.

A casual review of <u>White Buildings</u>. Relies to a great extent on Charles S. Brooks's "A Visit to a Poet" in <u>Hints to Pilgrims</u> (1921.1).

10   FRANK, WALDO. "The Poetry of Hart Crane." <u>New Republic</u> 50 (16 March):116-17.

Crane is the kind of poet who makes his world rather than arranges it. In his successful poems, the reader will find no statements, for statements are judgements. Crane gives us structures, not sequences. His image groups seem to be independent of the normal sequences of time and space and independent of cause and effect. Although some of his poems are mere heaps of rhetorical beauties, when he succeeds, he succeeds magnificently. Some of his best poems are: "For the Marriage of Faustus and Helen," "At Melville's Tomb," "Lachrymae Christi," "The Wine Menagerie," and "Voyages."

11   GORMAN, HERBERT S. "Tradition and Experiment in Modern Poetry." <u>New York Times Book Review</u>, 27 March, p. 2.

One of eight volumes reviewed. Crane's poetry is characterized as original and intellectually concentrated, more esoteric than that of John Crowe Ransom; "indeed, most of the time it is incomprehensible so far as the actual thought-content goes." The structures are so beautiful and the images so vivid, however, that the intelligent reader will still experience pleasure in reading the poems. Concludes with comparison: "Both Mr. Ransom and Mr. Crane belong to that modernistic category of poets that is dubbed intellectual. The emotions they handle have been translated in passing through the brain."

12   JOLAS, EUGENE. "Suggestions for a New Magic." <u>Transition</u> 3 (June):179.

Mentions Crane as among those who are showing the way in

poetry's attempt to find new words, new abstractions, new symbols, and new myths.

13   MARICHALAR, ANTONIO. "La estética de retrosesco y la poesia de Hart Crane." Revista de Occidente 5, no. 44 (February): 260-63.
         In Spanish. Review of White Buildings. For some time, European artists have been incorporating principles of American origin and achieving a style. This style is now heading back to the United States, "reshipped with the approval of Europe. . . . The same thing is happening in literature." Formerly an imagist poet, Crane absorbed European influence, particularly that of Rimbaud. "He is a powerful visionary whose mystical impulse overwhelms his theme."

14   PIERCE, FREDERICK E. "Four Poets." Yale Review 17 (October): 176-78.
         Review of White Buildings. The poets reviewed are Archibald MacLeish, Humbert Wolfe, Edwin Arlington Robinson, and Crane. The reviewer complains that there was so much that he could not understand even after three readings. It is clear to him that Crane has the soul of a poet, although it is not so clear that he has the technique of an artist.

15   RIDING, LAURA, and GRAVES, ROBERT. A Survey of Modernist Poetry. London: W. Heinemann, pp. 46-49, 288-91.
         A reference in passing to the vision of Crane which forced him to react romantically against contemporary classicism. Much of the intensity of his poetry is due to the conflict between the need for discipline and his great originality. "The result is a romantic mysticism of rhetoric." Reprinted: 1971.28.

16   TAGGARD, GENEVIEVE. "An Imagist in Amber." New York Herald Tribune Books, 29 May, sec. 6, p. 4.
         Review of White Buildings. Beginning with Crane's own explanation of "At Melville's Tomb," Taggard is convinced that Crane did not do in the poem what he said he did in the prose explanation. She then proceeds to rewrite the poem as it should have been done. "Mr. Crane is an Imagist in the amber of rich sound. . . . But so far as I can see, he has not yet written a poem." White Buildings is made up of fragments that are not a part of each other; they point back only to their maker.

17   _____ . "White Buildings: The Strange Poetic World of Hart Crane." Boston Transcript, 16 April, p. 4.
         Crane's technique is more important than his vision. His work is interesting and profitable. Compare with her review in the Herald Tribune (1927.16).

18   UNTERMEYER, LOUIS. American Poetry Since 1900. New York: Henry Holt Co., p. 349.

Mentioned once as being too concerned with verbal crafts-
manship.

19 Van DOREN, MARK. "First Glance." <u>Nation</u> 124 (2 February):
    120.
         Review of <u>White Buildings</u>. Poems are formidable and futile.
    He has a powerful and poetic mind, but it strains in its naked-
    ness to express nothing. "I am sure that it is distinguished
    poetry, and I am sure that <u>White Buildings</u> is important."

20 WILSON, EDMUND. "The Muses Out of Work." <u>New Republic</u> 50 (11
    May):319-21.
         Review of <u>White Buildings</u>. Two works emerge as of major
    interest when one looks back on the American poetry of this
    season--<u>The King's Henchman</u> by Edna St. Vincent Millay, and <u>White
    Buildings</u> by Crane. Crane has a remarkably, strikingly original
    style--"almost something like a great style." While we do not
    demand of poetry nowadays that it should provide us with logical
    metaphors, yet with Crane, though he sometimes moves us, it is in
    a curiously vague way. Reprinted: 1952.22.

21 WINTERS, YVOR. "Hart Crane's Poems." <u>Poetry</u> 30 (April):47-
    51.
         The first thirteen poems in <u>White Buildings</u> are relatively
    simple, more or less imagistic. Crane's faults are an occasional
    tendency to slip into vague rhetoric in an attempt to construct
    poems of a series of perceptions so minute and so thoroughly in-
    sulated from each other that little unifying force or outline
    results. His faults are the least interesting phase of his work.
    His best poems are those composed "of a steely tangible imagery
    that crystallizes an infinitude of metaphysical and nervous im-
    plications." He is an unusual poet in that he accepts his age in
    its entirety, accepts it with passion and has the sensitive
    equipment to explore it. "Among the five or six greatest poets
    writing in English." The editor, Harriet Monroe, appends a note
    indicating that Winters is somewhat "overdecisive in the review,
    since it is a bit hazardous to hurl the adjective <u>great</u> at any
    contemporary."

                              1928

1   BENÉT, WILLIAM ROSE. "Mr. Moon's Notebook." <u>Saturday Review
    of Literature</u> 4 (10 March):665.
         An unsympathetic review of <u>White Buildings</u>. The more Benét
    thinks about the poetry, the less he can make of it. Most of the
    review is devoted to parodies of Crane's poetry. The review is
    filled with "O dear, O dear!" and "Yes, <u>I</u> did that. No, that
    wasn't Crane. <u>I</u> did that. Pretty good, eh?"

2   BOYLE, KAY. "Mr. Crane and His Grandmother." <u>Transition</u> 10

(January):135-38.

Considering her later comments on Crane, this review of White Buildings is not very sympathetic. "And it's all doomed to failure because it is false; it is dull and humorless; it's like Wells writing about men like gods; it's a lot of words hiding a human fear." Crane's fervor is described as Baptist or Presbyterian and he is described further as a Rotarian entertaining the American Legion. Superior poets would be Marianne Moore and Robert McAlmon. Compare the review by Laura Riding (1928.5) in the same issue of Transition.

3 JOLAS, EUGENE, ed. Anthologie de la nouvelle poésie américaine. Paris: Simon Kra, p. 46.

Includes "O Carib Isle!" in French only, and a brief biographical note on Crane identifying him as the most discussed poet of his generation.

4 MUNSON, GORHAM. "Hart Crane: Young Titan in the Sacred Wood." In Destinations: A Canvass of American Literature since 1900. New York: Sears, pp. 160-77.

One of the earliest essays on Crane. Describes Crane as the most richly endowed of our younger poets, characterized especially by verbal music, gorgeous and evocative images, and lyrical eloquence. Progressed from a gaudy imagism through an elegant derivation from symbolism, and then through poems "dealing with isolated emotional themes, in which he was discovering his own style." Principal characteristics are his mental range, his weighty vocabulary, and his images used as symbols with their profound overtones. What is unique is "an extraordinary tension of verse structure, of mood, and of thought. The surfaces of his poems are tight and solid and his emotions and intuitions have pulled taut the leash of common sense." Also characteristic is his obscurity, the result of his "highly specialized subjectivity" and his "metaphysical guessing." Although Crane is a poet of great creative force and potentiality, his principal weakness is that "he does not know enough. He has no system; he has an intuitive doubt of the truth of appearances and suspects the existence of intuitions of higher dimensions."

5 RIDING, LAURA. "A Note on White Buildings by Hart Crane." Transition 10 (January):139-41.

A poet's job is to say something, and "being a spokesman of reality is one way the poet has of going about his job." The reader will find the noblest, most strenuous, and most magnificent poetry of this kind appearing in White Buildings. "I do not want to write a god-almighty big-talking review of White Buildings-- you will find one all hot and ready to serve in the preface to White Buildings by Allen Tate." Compare the review by Kay Boyle (1928.2) in the same issue of Transition.

1929

1   ANON. "Poet Seized on 'Left Bank': Now You Must Stay Dry." New York Times, 11 July, p. 5, col. 4.

    After a fight with two policemen, among others, at the Café Select, Crane was sentenced to eight days in prision (sentence suspended) and fined four dollars. The magistrate enjoined Crane not to abuse the liberties of France. Crane promised, amid the joyous laughter of the whole court, to remain dry while he was in France.

2   ANON. "Singers of the New Age." Vanity Fair 33 (September): 89.

    Mentioned as among a group of distinguished young poets who have found fresh material in the American scene. A picture, not often reproduced, of Crane. Liveright selected a portion of it as a blurb for the dust jacket of the second issue of White Buildings. "As aspiring and as clear-cut as the skyscrapers of which he writes are the verses of Hart Crane whose intellectuality and sensibility, as evidenced in White Buildings, his last volume, have made him an acknowledged leader among the younger Americans."

3   DRINKWATER, JOHN; CANBY, HENRY SEIDEL; and BENÉT, WILLIAM ROSE, eds. Twentieth Century Poetry. Boston: Houghton Mifflin Co., p. 572.

    The first book appearance of "The Tunnel" with a brief biographical note of some interest because it was written during Crane's lifetime. Identified as a baffling poet who represents the newest tendencies in poetry. His poetry "reveals, with a new insight, and unique power, the mystic undertones of beauty which move words to express vision."

4   KREYMBORG, ALFRED. Our Singing Strength: An Outline of American Poetry (1620-1930). New York: Coward-McCann, pp. 602-7.

    Crane's first appearance in a history of American poetry. Mentions Crane's connection with Secession and describes his arrival in New York "with a modest sheaf of Imagistic poems." After rereading White Buildings and the poems eventually included in The Bridge, the author confesses that he is now able to see that "Crane is a poet stemming from the major traditions of our soil and literature." Though he came out of Imagism, his real ancestors are Whitman and Melville. Crane has not yet found a theme large enough for his powers, but his next book will reveal that he is pursuing his proper destiny. "It will be an erratic book, but its main march will come out of our best tradition and penetrate the future."

5   TATE, ALLEN. "American Poetry since 1920." Bookman 68 (January):503-8.

    Crane is described as one of the new poets of superior talent. White Buildings is the most distinguished first book

ever issued in this country. His chief defect is the lack of a
system of disciplined values "which could clarify and control
most of the prodigal poetic gift in America." Predicts that the
publication of The Bridge will be an important event in contemporary letters.

6   TAUPIN, RENÉ. L'Influence du symbolisme français sur la
      poésie américaine. Paris: Librarie Ancienne Honoré Champion,
      pp. 240, 266, 272, 294.
           The strict forms employed by Gauthier are used in America
      by Elinor Wylie, Crane, and Archibald MacLeish. Bruno's Bohemia
      in 1913 had the honor to publish Crane's first poem. Crane
      profited from the lessons of T.S. Eliot, and profited also from
      the lessons of the French Symbolists who have experimented with
      brilliant images and harmony of form.
           Taupin's Ph.D. dissertation at the University of Paris.
      Reviewed in 1931.14.

                                 1930

1   ANDERSON, MARGARET. My Thirty Years' War. New York: Covici,
      Friede, pp. 153, 205.
           Passing references throughout to Crane and the critical
      advice which she claims she gave him.

2   ANON. "The Bridge." Boston Transcript, 25 June, p. 2.
           Crane is an intensely modern poet who will befuddle the
      ordinary reader of poetry. One not in sympathy with modern ten-
      dencies may cast the book aside. That would be a mistake, since
      reading The Bridge will repay the mental effort required, and
      give some idea of "what the best of the extreme modernists are
      trying to do."

3   ANON. "Crane, Hart, The Bridge." Booklist 27 (October):58.
           The brief notice is a quotation from Malcolm Cowley's re-
      view in New Republic (1930.8).

4   ANON. "Crane, Hart, The Bridge." Open Shelf 5, no. 2 (Decem-
      ber):153.
           Two sentences, one from William Rose Benét's review
      (1930.7) and one from Louis Untermeyer's (1930.19).

5   ANON. "Hart Crane: Author of The Bridge." Wilson Literary
      Bulletin 5 (October):104.
           Biographical sketch.

6   ANON. "The Helen Haire Levinson Prize." Poetry 37 (November):
      103.
           The prize of $200 for a poem or group of poems published in
      Poetry during its eighteenth year was awarded for The Bridge "of

which one section, Eldorado, appeared in Poetry last April, and another, Cutty Sark, in October, 1927." Poetry varied its usual custom by awarding a prize for the poem as a whole, recently published in book form, rather than specifically for the sections which were printed in the magazine.

7   BENÉT, WILLIAM ROSE. "Round About Parnassus." Saturday Review of Literature 6 (5 July):1176.
    Benét had not been impressed with White Buildings except for the wild talent that made itself articulate now and again. Crane's most apparent characteristics are a gift of imagery, a feeling and sensitivity to mood, and an abundance of rhetoric. The total impression of reading The Bridge is that "the author is an outstanding modern writer." "The River" and "The Tunnel" are especially praised. Although fascinated by the poem, Benét is still disturbed by the haphazardness of its organization and its many moments of banality. "It is a most interesting failure; and it reveals potencies in the author that may make his next work even more remarkable." Reprinted: 1970.6.

8   COWLEY, MALCOLM. "A Preface to Hart Crane." New Republic 62 (23 April):276-77.
    Crane's poetry has always been ambitious, and in The Bridge he has chosen his most ambitious subject in an attempt to create the myth of America. "We might well conclude that such an attempt was foredoomed to failure." Although the poem is an overall failure, it has succeeded to an impressive degree in part. Cowley discusses in detail "The River." Crane's treatment of the subject is oblique; he does not proceed logically, but rather by associations of thought, by successive emotions. His imagination is conceptual, concrete, and constructive. Reprinted: 1967.6; 1970.6.

9   CROSBY, HARRY. Shadows of the Sun. Paris: Black Sun Press, pp. 6-8, 10, 12-15, 36-37, 40-43, 46, 68, 73, 100.
    Tells of meeting Crane, reading parts of The Bridge, and agreeing to publish it. Important for information regarding first (Black Sun Press) publication of the poem, and for Crane's French sojourn. See Caresse Crosby's The Passionate Years (1953.8).

10 D., F.W. Review of The Bridge. Miscellany 3 (July):33-35.
    While Crane attempts to create some sort of new American myth, the poem as a whole is without design. The new grand manner is the result of the poet's attempt to find an appropriate mode of expression for his ambitious themes. The central fault is its obscurity. "The fantastic absurdity of many passages of The Bridge is unequaled in poetry. . . ."

11 GREGORY, HORACE. "Far Beyond Our Consciousness." New York Herald Tribune Books, 20 April, sec. 9, p. 4.

The sensation of living in a large modern city produces
actual emotions which may not be clearly defined, a kind of religious exaltation as well as a terror which one cannot escape.
The Bridge captures this particular emotional crisis, translating
it into esoteric speech. Crane's emotional content is all-
important, since his poems are fundamentally nonintellectual.
The value of The Bridge rests largely on Crane's ability to break
away from the tendencies illustrated by T.S. Eliot. "These are
the obvious elements of the poems that by loose association with
a central image are bound together for the expression of a genu-
inely religious point of view." Crane's promise as an important
American poet is fulfilled. His effort to create a synthesis is
a notable contribution to American poetry. Reprinted: 1970.6.

12   HICKS, GRANVILLE. "Hart Crane Scales New Poetical Heights in
      The Bridge." Book World, 4 May, p. 10.
          Although Crane is unmistakably a modern poet representative
of his time, he stands apart from his fellow poets in that he is
both affirmative and ambitious, neither platitudinous nor weak.
"If it is the essence of poetry to say what cannot be said in
prose, Mr. Crane's rank as a poet is extraordinarily high." The
Bridge is as important a poem as has been written in our time.

13   _____. "The Rediscovery of America." Nation 130 (30 April):
      520-22.
          Although Crane's work is difficult, it is not obscure in
any cheap or wanton fashion. Much contemporary poetry is more
difficult, but there is very little that is so rewarding. The
major part of the review is an outline of The Bridge, with very
little explication. The poem concludes with an ultimate vision
in which the bridge, symbol of all that America may be, is a symbol also of "that union of the individual song with the eternal
reality which is the goal of every mystic's quest." Crane's
affirmative view of things should be contrasted with the elegiac
tone of most contemporary poetry.

14   HUTCHINSON, PERCY. "Hart Crane's Cubistic Poetry in The
      Bridge." New York Times Book Review, 27 April, p. 2.
          No ordinary poem, either in substance or manner. "We
imagine the writer would like to have called [it] a symphonic
poem." In emphasizing the individuality of his poem, has the
poet sacrificed common sense and beauty? At times the effectiveness of the poem seems to lie in its lack of intelligibility.
The cubistic theory of poetry is one which encourages the piling
up of startling and widely disparate word structures so that for
the mind the result is very like the cumulative result of sky-
scrapers for the eye when looked on through a mist. "Since to
the mind of the present writer cubism, whatever value it may have
for painting, is wholly valueless in poetry, The Bridge, nevertheless, remains for him, in spite of its glitter and its seeming
intellectual importance, a piece that is in the main spurious as
poetry."

15　McHUGH, VINCENT. "Crane's Bridge: Mighty Symbol of the
　　Nation." New York Evening Post, 19 April, p. 11.
　　　　"This is perhaps the most remarkable attempt at an orches-
　　trated modern American poem since Eliot's Waste Land. . . . One
　　does not feel that The Bridge has been more than partially suc-
　　cessful in its larger implication. To propose so enormous and
　　complex a mystic synthesis is almost to invite failure. Hart
　　Crane has succeeded at least in catching certain major qualities
　　of the American spirit and tradition. He has welded them in a
　　'swift peal of secular light.' He has honorably advanced the
　　tradition of Walt Whitman."

16　NICHOLL, LOUISE T. "Spring Poetry." Outlook and Independent
　　155 (28 May):146.
　　　　Review of The Bridge. Notes it is a work full of visions
　　and ideas, but Crane does not make them into poetry.

17　SHEPARD, ODELL. "The Bridge by Hart Crane." Bookman 72
　　(September):86-87.
　　　　Crane's ambitious poem attempts to represent the America of
　　the twentieth century. "Recorders ages hence" will do well to
　　use his report upon us with extreme caution. We are not nearly
　　so insane with noise or haste, nor are we so hag-ridden by
　　machinery as Crane would have the future believe of us. In
　　imagination he never gets farther west than Brooklyn Bridge or
　　closer to the twentieth century than Walt Whitman. He seems
　　excited by anything that moves quickly or makes loud noises. His
　　failure to reveal anything about America can be attributed to his
　　preoccupation with his own originality. Although he explicity
　　claims intellectual descent from Whitman, he is a better poet
　　than this would seem to indicate. Had he been true to Whitman,
　　he would not have chosen Brooklyn Bridge as a symbol, but the
　　crowded subway car instead.

18　TATE, ALLEN. "A Distinguished Poet." Hound and Horn 3 (July-
　　Summer):580-85.
　　　　Review of The Bridge in which the poet is commended for his
　　technical proficiency. Subject appears to be a vision of the
　　heroic past and an attempt to envision the spiritual future. The
　　logical meaning is difficult to convey by paraphrase; the emo-
　　tional intensity is simple. If the fifteen poems are regarded as
　　a single poem, it is impossible to discover the overall coherence
　　outside of the personal tone of the author. The theme is an emo-
　　tional oversimplification. "The poem has not observed the dis-
　　tinction between a metaphor and a philosophical idea." The sound
　　impulse of the poem is religious, but the poet by himself cannot
　　create a myth. The form is static. If it can be regarded as a
　　collection of lyrics, one can say that the best of them "are not
　　surpassed by anything in American literature." But philosophi-
　　cally speaking, the poem is a muddle. Crane follows the main
　　stream of romanticism of the past hundred years and may be said

to represent its end.

19   UNTERMEYER, LOUIS, ed. <u>Modern American Poetry and Modern</u>
     <u>British Poetry</u>. New York: Harcourt, Brace & Co., pp. 784-92.
          The 1930 edition of Untermeyer's standard textbook was
     prepared in Crane's lifetime and gives the reader another insight
     into Crane's contemporary reputation. His poetry is incompre-
     hensible to some and extraordinary to others. Although founded
     on rhetoric, it occasionally transcends the author's ingenuity.
     The visions of <u>White Buildings</u> were uncoordinated until Crane
     found his theme in <u>The Bridge</u>, "a highly sophisticated, highly
     syncopated local epic."

20   WEINSTOCK, HERBERT. "<u>The Bridge</u> Rises to Realms of Major
     American Literature." <u>Milwaukee Journal</u>, 12 April, p. 4.
          Crane's poetry brings back to American literature a spacious-
     ness which it has lacked since Whitman and Melville. The poem
     does not have conventional unity; it is a fantasia "taking its
     start from meditations concerned with Brooklyn Bridge." The sec-
     tions of the poem are unevenly good. The difficulties of the
     poem rise from its complexity and the depth of the materials
     used. "Clearly he makes no strained effort toward novelty or
     eccentricity."

21   WINTERS, YVOR. "Poetry, Morality, and Criticism." In <u>The</u>
     <u>Critique of Humanism</u>. Edited by C. Hartley Grattan. New
     York: Brewer & Warren, pp. 301-33.
          Passing references to Crane. Functions best in a limited
     functional range; guilty of intellectual confusion. Crane does
     not try to master and understand the plane of experience from
     which he is trying to escape; this creates a sense of incoher-
     ence. One of the four or five extraordinary poets of his time.

22   _____. "The Progress of Hart Crane." <u>Poetry</u> 36 (June):153-
     65.
          <u>The Bridge</u> cannot be called an epic in spite of its attempt
     to create a national myth because it has no formal framework and
     lacks the formal unity of an epic. Neither is it didactic, nor
     is there a logical expression of ideas. The structure is lyrical,
     but the poem is not a single lyric. It is a collection of lyrics
     on themes more or less related and loosely flowing out of each
     other. The obvious model for the poem is Whitman. The Whitmanian
     basis of the poem makes a hero impossible. The destiny of a
     nation, a vague generality, is hard to get at in the abstract.
     There is no question that Crane is a poet of genius, but "the
     flaws in Mr. Crane's genius are, I believe, so great as to par-
     take, if they persist, almost of the nature of a public catas-
     trophe." Reprinted: 1970.6.

23   ZABEL, MORTON DAUWEN. "<u>The Bridge</u>: a Poem of America."
     <u>Commonweal</u> 13 (24 December):120-21.

"Undoubtedly marks the highest literary achievement of the year in the United States," even though he has failed to realize the implications and the significance of what he is attempting. The weakest point of the poem is his use of symbolism. Because of the many ways the bridge is used, what it symbolizes is never really established.

1931

1   ANON. "Crane, Ohio Poet Wins Fellowship." Cleveland Plain
     Dealer, 30 March, p. 3.
          One of three Ohioans among seventy-seven recipients who
     have been awarded Guggenheim fellowships.

2   ANON. "Viene a escribir una serie de versos sobre Mexico un
     gran poeta" [A great poet is coming to write a series of poems
     on Mexico]. Excelsior (Mexico City), 2 June, p. 2.
          In Spanish. Account of Crane's arrival in Mexico City, in-
     cluding a brief interview with him.

3   ANON. "Hart Crane." Publishers' Weekly 121 (7 May):1952.
          Obituary notice.

4   ANON. "Passenger Notifies Hart Crane's Uncle Here." Cleveland
     Plain Dealer, 28 April, p. 4.
          Brief report on Crane's death at sea.

5   ANON. "Poet Leaped into Sea Ship Reports." Cleveland Plain
     Dealer, 30 April, p. 5.
          Brief article on Crane's death at sea.

6   ANON. "Poet Lost at Sea Is Air Report." Cleveland Plain
     Dealer, 28 April, p. 5.
          Brief article concerning Crane's death at sea.

7   EASTMAN, MAX. The Literary Mind. New York: Charles
     Scribner's Sons, pp. 93-97.
          Assuming as he generally does that poetry is essentially a
     communicative act, Eastman wonders why critics can call The
     Bridge one of the great poems of our generation when they confess
     that they don't know what the poet is talking about. "At
     Melville's Tomb" is an illustration of this problem. Without the
     author's exegesis, his poems seem meaningless. Crane "is in fact
     so brilliant in this process that he always proves beyond a
     glimmer of doubt not only that his poetry when explained by him
     can be understood by anybody, but also that when not explained by
     him it can be understood by nobody."

8   _____. "Poets Talking to Themselves." Harper's 163 (October):
     563-74.

Simultaneously published with 1931.7.

9   FLINT, F. CUDWORTH. "Metaphor in Contemporary Poetry."
     Symposium 1:310-35.
        Crane illustrates the author's idea that the most inter-
     esting recent poetry in America is of the "difficult" variety.
     The Bridge is one of the most notable and obscure of recent poems.
     Despite Herbert Read's notion that it is foolish to ask what the
     poet "means," something can be done by way of explaining the
     meaning of the poem. To illustrate the success of paraphrase,
     the author cites Crane's analysis of "At Melville's Tomb." Con-
     temporary poets have replaced the simile with the metaphor, be-
     cause the metaphor is more poetic. Crane's poetry illustrates the
     notion of multiple reference in which the metaphor consists of an
     identification between an object or an idea and two or more other
     objects and ideas, each of these identifications having a single
     ground or basis. Poets are increasingly employing the psycho-
     logical method as can be seen in Crane's correspondence with
     Harriet Monroe.

10   KUNITZ, S[tanley] J. [Dilly Tante], ed. Living Authors: A
     Book of Biographies. New York: W.W. Wilson Co., pp. 86-87.
        Brief biographical sketch with portrait.

11   MENCKEN, H.L. "Market Report: Poetry." American Mercury 24
     (October):151-53.
        There is "a great dearth of talented newcomers." Since
     Robinson Jeffers, Crane is the poet who seems to have received
     the most serious attention. He is a difficult, even painful,
     poet to read. Although he is earnest, industrious, and patriotic
     "if a new Masters or Frost or Sandburg were to arrive tomorrow,
     Crane would be knocked off the board. He is safe only so long as
     he doesn't have to compete with poets writing in plain English."

12   SCHAPPES, MORRIS U. "Notes on the Concrete as Method in
     Criticism." Symposium 2 (July):315-24.
        The poems of Yvor Winters, Stanley J. Kunitz, and Crane are
     vilified or appreciated--"I have never seen them criticized."
     Criticism means a precise, line-by-line, word-by-word analysis of
     particular poems. Schappes has not taken the risk of muddying
     his own view of Crane's work by making any attempt to look at the
     published work of others. After explaining his critical method
     briefly, he analyzes "Moment Fugue." He objects to the title
     since a series of contrasts "admittedly in the poem" do not make
     a fugue. The purpose of the poem is seen be comparing the first
     line with the final line. "The choice of flowers (like the
     typography) is not guided by any definite purpose. In the first
     line violets is used instead of, say, primroses, for the sake of
     the open vowel and the letter l, which occurs throughout the
     line."

13 UNTERMEYER, LOUIS. "Contemporary Poetry." In <u>American</u>
    <u>Writers on American Literature</u>. Edited by John Macy. New
    York: Horace Liveright, p. 575.
       One paragraph on Crane.

14 WINTERS, YVOR. "The Symbolist Influence." <u>Hound and Horn</u> 4
    (July-September):607-18.
       Review of Renet Taupin's <u>L'Influence du symbolisme fran-</u>
    <u>çaise sur la poésie américaine (de 1910 à 1920)</u> (1929.6). In
    discussing the question of influence, Winters brings up Gerard
    Manley Hopkins. Crane read Hopkins for the first time around
    Christmas, 1927, after borrowing Winters's copy; by that time
    nearly all of <u>The Bridge</u> had been written. Crane told Winters
    that he had never read Hopkins's poetry. If Hopkins did influ-
    ence Crane, Crane doesn't show any trace of the influence. Their
    philosophies and their poetic temperaments are radically differ-
    ent. Further on in the essay Winters discusses Taupin's remark
    that <u>Faustus and Helen II</u> reflects the style of Rimbaud. Since
    Crane was not able to read Rimbaud in the original, Winters sees
    little likelihood of the influence of Rimbaud on Crane. Winters
    finds that the style of the poem reflects the influence of Jonson
    as the passage from <u>The Alchemist</u> as the head of the poem sug-
    gests. Winters is illuminating about the function of this epi-
    graph in the poem. Crane is more like Jonson and Donne than like
    Rimbaud.

1932

1 ANDERSON, FORREST. "For Hart Crane." <u>Contempo</u> 2 (5 July):1.
      Verse appreciation.

2 ANON. "Crane Chose His Death at Sea." <u>Cleveland Press</u>, 30
   April, p. 2.
      Title is self-explanatory.

3 ANON. "Crane Hailed as Great Poet at 32, Drowned." <u>Cleveland</u>
   <u>Press</u>, 28 April, p. 2.
      Brief article about his death at sea.

4 ANON. [COWLEY, MALCOLM]. "Death of a Poet." <u>New Republic</u> 70
   (11 May):340-42.
      "Widely recognized as the first poet of his generation,"
   Crane was not like Poe or Baulelaire, a lyric poet dealing primarily in personal emotions. He tried to see beneath the surface
   of American life and attempted to understand its meaning. Forced
   to doubt that our present society had little meaning whatsoever,
   he sought for some hidden secret but came to doubt that such a
   secret existed in our society. Although he felt that society
   must be changed, he questioned whether poets were the men to
   change it. His death was his poem of action which the world can

interpret as it sees fit.

5   ANON. "Hart Crane." Nation 134 (11 May):531.
        The recent death has a special significance. Despite the
    charges made against his unintelligibility, the perceptive reader
    will continue to recognize Crane as one of the few powerful
    writers of the century. Tate's introduction to White Buildings
    is recommended. "What he wanted to say it was hard to know. The
    way he said it was powerful, memorable, and precise."

6   ANON. "News Notes." Poetry 40 (June):176.
        "Recently he wrote us that he would soon be sailing home,
    and referred to a poem he had sent us, which unfortunately we
    never received."

7   ANON. "Obituary Notice: Hart Crane." Publishers' Weekly 121
        (7 May):1952.
        A conventional obituary note, with this interesting obser-
    vation: "A friend, Marguerite Cowley, wife of Malcolm Cowley,
    accompanied him on the voyage home to prevent a possible attempt
    at suicide. She said he had been grieving because 'there was no
    place in the world today for poetry.'"

8   ANON. "Poet's Death Linked with Loss of Father." New York
        Times, 29 April, p. 4, col. 5.
        Quotes friends in Mexico City to the effect that Crane had
    been severely affected by the death of his father in the previous
    year.

9   ANON. "Report Hart Crane Lost from Ship." New York Times,
        28 April, p. 19, col. 4.
        A report from Warren, Ohio, indicating that relatives had
    received a wireless message about Crane's being lost at sea.

10 CALMER, ALLAN. "The Case of Hart Crane." New Republic 71
        (20 July):264.
        In response to the New Republic editorial on the death of
    Crane, Calmer develops what he thought was the major point of the
    editorial. A corrupt and decadent society has produced a corrupt
    and decadent aesthetic tradition. Crane is an example of the
    artist of integrity who faced the modern dilemma. In the period
    of transition between the decay of the old society and the begin-
    ning of a new society, "where shall the poet find his tradition?"
    Eliot's attempt to find it in the past offers no solution, but
    John Dos Passos "has glimpsed a way out." Like Dos Passos, Crane
    looked to the future for his inspiration rather than to the past
    and found his new artistic symbols in industrialism. But unlike
    Dos Passos, Crane did not "possess the Communist attitude, which
    would have strengthened and clarified his approach to the machine
    and the industrial life."

11   COWLEY, MALCOLM. "The Late Hart Crane." <u>New English Weekly</u> 1
      (14 July):315.
            Cowley takes issue with what he calls several misstatements
      of fact in Gorham Munson's "A Poet's Suicide and Some Reflec-
      tions," which appeared in the <u>New English Weekly</u>, 23 June. Munson
      had stated that "The Broken Tower" had been submitted to various
      editors five years before Crane's death. Cowley asserts that
      "the Broken Tower" was written in Mexico over a period of months
      just before Crane's suicide. See 1932.13, 19, 20, 22.

12   ESLER, R. "At the Grave of Hart Crane." <u>Poetry</u> 41 (November):
      68-69.
            Verse appreciation.

13   FRANK, WALDO. "The Late Hart Crane." <u>New English Weekly</u> 1
      (21 July):338-39.
            A letter answering Gorham Munson's article, "A Poet's
      Suicide and Some Reflections," in the <u>New English Weekly</u>, 23
      June. Frank calls Munson's essay "a shocking and regrettable
      performance," because Munson's analysis will give radically false
      impressions of Crane to readers. A severe rebuttal to both the
      tone and substance of Munson's article. Finally, Frank makes it
      clear that he will edit Crane's poems, not E.E. Cummings. See
      1932.11, 19, 20, 22.

14   KNIGHT, GRANT C. <u>American Literature and Culture</u>. New York:
      R. Long & R.R. Smith, pp. 464, 476.
            Brief reference.

15   KUNITZ, S[tanley] J. [Dilly Tante], ed. "The Death of a Poet."
      <u>Wilson Library Bulletin</u>, 6 (June):690.
            Obituary notice.

16   LEWISOHN, LUDWIG. <u>Expression in America</u>. New York: Harper
      & Brothers, pp. 588-89.
            Crane could occasionaly burst the bonds of disillusionment
      and fright, although Lewisohn does not think very highly of his
      poetry about machinery.

17   MONROE, HARRIET, and HENDERSON, ALICE CORBIN, eds. <u>The New
      Poetry</u>. New York: Macmillian Co., pp. 701-2.
            The two-page biographical note was probably written by
      Harriet Monroe.

18   MUNSON, GORHAM. "The Fledgling Years, 1916-1924." <u>Sewanee
      Review</u> 40 (January-March):24-54.
            Personal reminiscences of the literary aspects of the jazz
      age. Most of the article is devoted to a history of the magazine
      <u>Secession</u>, with a few references to Crane. Munson thought Crane
      was a genius on their first meeting; he was his first steady
      champion, "writing the first essay about his merits."

19   _____. "Hart Crane." New English Weekly 1 (18 August):435.
        After Cowley, Frank, and Simpson had answered Munson's
original article, he wrote this letter. He acknowledges that
Waldo Frank, and not E.E. Cummings, will be the editor of Crane's
final volume. He does say that it had been announced in the
press that Cummings would be the editor. I have been unable to
find any such reference. Munson still insists, despite the evidence, that "The Broken Tower" was in circulation five years before Crane's death. He thinks "that Crane revised last Spring
the original poem." See 1932.11, 13, 20, 22.

20   _____. "A Poet's Suicide and Some Reflections." New English
        Weekly 1 (23 June):237-39.
        The period of the Munson-Crane friendship was from 1919 to
1924. Crane was never able to reconcile his "artiness" and
Bohemianism with the other impulses that made him an avid reader
of the "mystics." "In the end, between Ouspensky's responsible
mysticism and Waldo Frank's private brew of uncheckable assertion
and wild speculation, he chose Frank." The Crane cult that grew
did no service to him. It was too interested in his sexual inversion and tried to picture him as an American Rimbaud. His
life was too romanticized. At his best, Crane is entitled to a
permanent place in the history of American poetry. His weakness
as a poet was that he was too suggestible to literary fashions.
He had been influenced by imagism, E.E. Cummings, Rimbaud, and
the Little Review. "At last the poet was buried in the unproduc-
tive Bohemian." His strong side is the side that was stimulated
by his reading of the Elizabethans and the "mystics." "The
Broken Tower" was not Crane's last poem because it had been submitted to various editors five years before his death. He also
asserts that E.E. Cummings will be the editor of Crane's Collected
Poems. See 1932.11, 13, 19, 22.

21   ROBERTS, MICHAEL. "Hart Crane." New English Weekly 1 (19
        May):113-14.
        "He had been accidentally drowned in the Gulf of Mexico."
The lyrics in White Buildings contain difficulties which are not
found in The Bridge. In contrast to some of his contemporaries,
Crane, with his tremendous energy, joyfully accepted his destiny,
even though he did not know its end. The Bridge is a poem of
immense scope, and nothing of this scale was attempted by any
other American poet of comparative ability. His poetry exhibits
an intense feeling for words, sometimes becoming pure rhetoric
and magnificent ranting. But the faults and achievements of
Crane are those of a major poet.

22   SIMPSON, LESLEY BYRD. "The Late Hart Crane." New English
        Weekly 1 (15 September):531.
        A letter in response to Gorham Munson's original article
in the New English Weekly on the suicide of Crane. Munson's
article is described as ungenerous and written in the spirit of

carping, containing, in addition, one gross misstatement which
Simpson corrects. Munson stated that "The Broken Tower" was submitted to various editors five years before Crane's death.
Simpson recalls that he was with Crane in Taxel, Mexico the
morning of 27 January, when Crane first conceived the idea of
"The Broken Tower." For two months after this, Crane worked
feverishly at the poem, finishing it by the time he left Mexico
late in April. See 1932.11, 13, 19, 20. Compare Simpson's
account of the genesis of this poem with that of Peggy Baird
(1961.2).

23   TATE, ALLEN. "Hart Crane and the American Mind." Poetry 40
      (July):210–16.
          Written in response to the news of Crane's suicide. Crane
wrote Tate that he realized his soundest work was probably in
White Buildings. Because it attempted to be an epic, The Bridge
was a failure, albeit a magnificent one. Pointless as an answer
to Eliot's "pessimism," since Crane was fundamentally in error in
his understanding of The Waste Land. He never succeeded in coming
to terms with the valuelessness at the heart of The Bridge. The
center of his writing was romanticism. He lost his sense of an
individual consciousness; his world had no center. The blind
assertion of the will did not save him. "Crane was the archetype
of the modern American poet, whose fundamental mistake lay in
thinking that an irrational surrender of intellect to will would
be the basis of new mentality." See 1936.9.

24   ____. "In Memoriam: Hart Crane." Hound and Horn 5 (July-
      September):612–19.
          Another reflection inspired by Crane's suicide. While
Rimbaud "achieved" disorder out of the implicit order of his
world, Crane's "disorder was original and fundamental." He had
little education and was probably incapable of the discipline it
implied. His suicide was "the most appropriate end imaginable"
for him. It was the only act of will left to him. His defect
"lay in his inability to face out the moral criticism implied in
the failure to impose his will on experience." The Bridge, intended as an epic, failed because of "the sullen irrationality"
of his romanticism. Yet the poem contains some of the greatest
lyric poetry of modern times. Crane was the kind of man "every
age seems to select as the spokesman of its spiritual organization." The moral value of his poetry is that it reveals the
defects of modernism. He ends the romantic era in his own person
"logically and morally." He had "the most nearly perfect sense
of lyrical form of his time." See 1936.9.

25   WHEELWRIGHT, JOHN. "To Hart Crane." New Republic 71 (8
      June):91.
          Verse appreciation.

26   WILLIAMS, WILLIAM CARLOS. "Hart Crane [1899-1932]." Contempo
      2 (5 July):1, 4.

Two letters by Crane appear as well as his poem "Bacardi
Spreads the Eagle's Wing." Williams's piece is both an obituary
and an evaluation of White Buildings with a few remarks about The
Bridge. He praises Crane's music extensively, but says that he
could be "profound" in the worst sense of the word. "Worse than
that, Crane wanted to be cosmic, I think." As a result, he took
his eye away from the word--"and the word slipped away from him."
He accuses Crane of sentimentality when this happens, "but in his
music Crane was often superb. . . ." Williams dislikes, however,
the rhapsodic element in Crane; in those moments his language is
a step backward to the bad poetry which followed Whitman. He
needed to be more aware of the "objectivity of words in making up
his compositions."

27   ZABEL, MORTON DAUWEN. "Phelps Putnam and America." Poetry 40
      (September):335-44.
          Review of The Five Seasons, by Phelps Putnam. Crane was
planning to review this volume of poems during the last months of
his life. Several of his letters referred to it. After Poetry
sent him a copy for review, Crane wrote from Mexico: "Putnam is
more surprising and magnificent than ever! I am glad to have
such a challenge of a review." Crane later noted that he was
having difficulty coping with Putnam's "assiduous romanticism."
Zabel feels that Putnam's saga of Bill Williams shares with The
Bridge the ambition to transform a critical conception of the
American continent into a lyric idealism seeking its embodiment
in myth and symbol. Both Crane and Putnam exhibit in their work
an urgent desire to discover something upon which an American myth
can be created. Neither is unduly optimistic about this effort,
but Crane is more exalted and messianic in his attitude. "He
attempted to make divine symbols of the instruments whereby that
ruin of America has been compared--the buildings, railways, and
bridges of the American scene." Zabel contends that Crane sur-
rendered too much of his maturing power to formidable literary
influences.

                                1933

1   ANON. Review of Collected Poems of Hart Crane. Booklist 29,
     no. 1. (May):262.
         Identifies this 1933 edition as definitive, the work of "a
poet who had achieved high rank in modern American literature."

2   ANON. "The Collected Poems of Hart Crane." Boston Transcript,
     31 May, p. 3.
         It seems probable that the poetry of Crane will occupy an
exceedingly high place in American literature. His most notable
poem, The Bridge, strove to interpret the conflicting ideals of
twentieth century America. Crane's poetry reflects his life--the
conflict between his temperament and the conditions of his time.

3   ANON. "The Collected Poems of Hart Crane." New Republic 74
     (19 April):289.
         The Collected Poems confirms the impression that Crane was
     the most considerable poet of his generation, as well as the most
     turbulent and unhappy. Waldo Frank's introduction is a longer
     and more satisfying version of the essay which appeared originally
     in the New Republic.

4   DAVIDSON, EUGENE. "The Symbol and the Poets." Yale Review 23
     (September):178-82.
         Review of The Collected Poems. A child of the symbolists,
     Crane imitated them even to the point of automatic writing.
     Crane is a little saddening because he balances words when he
     could be doing better things with them. In writing The Bridge,
     he showed courage, if not the necessary capacity to absorb fully
     his ideas. He had a fine ear and a fine gift for images, but his
     metaphysics ran away with him. His verse seldom has much dis-
     cipline. "Why Crane with his really important talent was not more
     successful is puzzling. Almost all the attributes of poetic in-
     sight and expression were in him."

5   DEUTSCH, BABETTE. "Poetry Out of Chaos." Virginia Quarterly
     Review 9 (1933):620-25.
         Review of The Collected Poems of Hart Crane. The modern
     poet finds himself in a métier in which it is necessary not
     merely to respond and interpret the world, but to practically
     create it. Crane's world is large because he was a mystic, and
     narrow because he expresses himself in such a elliptical and
     idiosyncratic manner. The most significant poem of the collection
     is The Bridge, epical in content, lyrical in feeling, intensely
     personal, and difficult to read. "Yet if it is not to be immedi-
     ately grasped, it is one of those rare performances that reward
     repeated readings." The most obvious influence on his poetry was
     not Whitman, but Laforgue. While Crane could celebrate the
     machine in his poetry, he could not endure a civilization that
     had failed to master its new tool.

6   FRANK, WALDO. Introduction to The Collected Poems of Hart
     Crane. New York: Liveright, pp. vii-xxix.
         See In The American Jungle (1937.10).

7   _____. "An Introduction to Hart Crane." New Republic 74 (15
     February):11-15.
         This is a separate printing of the introduction by Frank to
     The Collected Poems of Hart Crane, 1933 and 1946 editions. The
     introduction by Frank to the 1958 edition, The Complete Poems,
     entitled "Foreword," is a good deal shortened and somewhat
     altered. See In the American Jungle (1937.10).

8   GORMAN, HERBERT [S.]. "Hart Crane and the Machine Age." New
     York Times Book Review, 30 April, p. 2.

Review of The Collected Poems. One does not express the
machine in poetry by simply writing about it. It must be an
integral part of the life-urge from which inspired expression
comes. This is what Crane attempted to do in The Bridge, his
"solitary gesture toward permanence as a poet." White Buildings
and Key West are tentative and striving. In The Bridge alone do
we find a comparative maturity where the machine became "an in-
distinguishable part of the mythos of poetry." While Crane could
grasp the chaotic world about him and unify it in his poetry, he
could do nothing about the chaos in his own life. The two demons
of his personal life exhausted him and left him powerless.

9   GREGORY, HORACE. "The Legend of Hart Crane." New York Herald
     Tribune Books, 2 April, sec. 10, p. 6.
        Review of The Collected Poems. Crane realized intuitively
perhaps, but more profoundly than any other individual of his
generation, the underlying facts of our contemporary existence.
As poet, he attempted to absorb the elements of our machine
civilization into his consciousness. His problem was that of
trying to make a complete synthesis. His vision of the world was
that of a mystic, and he could be satisfied with nothing less
than the absolute realization of his objective. The casual
reader of Crane's poetry is always bothered by its organic obscurity. The reader must always grant Crane his original premise
and accept the elliptical, unfulfilled expression of any full
synthesis.

10   HICKS, GRANVILLE. The Great Tradition. New York: Macmillan
     Co., pp. 291-92.
        Crane's tragedy is that he longed more deeply than anyone
else in his generation to reveal the profound and significant
theme of all that America was and is. The Bridge is a powerful
affirmative poem, depicting the intrinsic worth and majestic destiny of the United States. Despite what he saw of contemporary
life, Crane knew intuitively that there existed forces that could
bring about triumph of everything he celebrated. Yet, he did not
know what these forces were, "and in the end his affirmations
rest only on a vague mysticism." In his early work the strong
Marxian bias of Hicks is apparent.

11   LEWIS, MARY OWEN. "Tropic Seas." Sewanee Review 41 (January):
     63.
        Verse appreciation.

12   PARRY, ALBERT. Garrets and Pretenders: The History of Bo-
     hemianism in America. New York: Covici, pp. 357-58.
        Brief reference to Crane's feeling of loss and despair and
the lack of confidence in his abilities which ended in his
suicide.

13   RICE, PHILIP BLAIR. "The Collected Poems of Hart Crane."

Symposium 4 (October):483-91.

Crane, typical of his generation, is now securely established as one of the four or five best poets of that generation.
He dealt directly with a problem peculiar to that generation:
how to make poetry out of the strange new world of the machine.
Crane assimilated contemporary imagery more thoroughly than any
poet of his time. His particular strengths are his passion and
his brilliant and majestic progression. His particular defect is
bombast. When measured by the test he set for himself, his work
must be judged to be, in large measure, a failure. Whitman had
been preoccupied with America's aspirations; Crane had to be concerned with fulfillment as well as aspiration, and he found fulfillment in contemporary America sadly wanting. While The Collected Poems brings together work not previously assembled, the
new works show no development in fundamental conceptions.

14   TATE, ALLEN. "The Whole Image of Man." Hound and Horn 6
      (January-March):345-49.
          In reviewing Phelps Putnam's The Five Seasons (New York,
1931), Tate discusses it, The Bridge, and Pound's Cantos. "In
all three of these works the structure which supports their
various sorts of objective completeness is superimposed over the
material. With Pound and Crane it represents a forced conclusion--
not the result of long meditation, of long seasoning of the mind
and the subject, but rather an assertive act of the will that
assumes too easily the pretentions of a 'philosophy'; meanwhile
the disorganized vision of the poet warns us that here, at least,
one person has missed salvation." In a further comment on the
symbolic use of Brooklyn Bridge, Tate asserts that its being a
symbol was an immediate intuition for Crane prior to any perception necessary to give it meaning. "The final obscurity of The
Bridge lies in the strain between the arbitrary symbol and the
lagging images."

15   WALTON, EDA LOU. "Hart Crane." Nation 136 (3 May):508-9.
          Review of The Collected Poems. Crane had three problems.
First, he had to learn to perfect his medium. Second, being both
modern and mystic, he had to integrate his own life. Third, he
had the difficult problem of synthesizing through his poetic
vision the world from which he drew the subject matter of his
vision. He did perfect his medium--language, imagery, rhythm.
He never did succeed in integrating his own personal experience,
as indicated by the chaos of his inner life. He did manage to
arrive at a synthesis of his poetic vision and the world from
which he drew that vision. He arrived at his vision intuitively,
subjectively, and economically through the use of symbols. Completely opposed to the philosophy of Eliot, Crane spun his own
faith. "It was mystic, romantic, and utterly modern. He accepted
his America." Not as great a technician as Eliot, he is more
original and more vital.

16   ZABEL, MORTON DAUWEN. "The Book of Hart Crane." Poetry 42
      (April):33-39.
          Review of The Collected Poems. Crane's strength as a poet
      easily surmounted the chaotic conditions of the postwar world.
      Crane's task was not that of a public idealist; he perceived in-
      tensely the spiritual corruption of the time. His master might
      have been Melville, perhaps even Poe. One of the poets to whom
      he is most easily compared is Blake; both were bold enough to
      attempt a synthesis of idealism and disruption. "The comparison
      with Blake is enough to suggest how restricted and deliberate
      was Crane's choice of symbols, and how his symbolism is suspect,
      or spacious, the moment it exceeds the solid boundaries of his
      sensibility and intuition." He was interested in rhetoric and
      symbol from the beginning, hoping to create "the grand style."
      But a grand style implies an equivalent vision and belief. Al-
      though Crane's vision developed rapidly, his belief lagged, be-
      cause "the personal integrity wherewith to grasp and sustain it
      lagged." Crane was not equipped to deal intellectually with the
      discrimination of values implied in the structure of The Bridge.
      "The excellence in his work may emphasize its defect, but in
      itself it makes that defect easy to forgive, for there can be
      little doubt that these Collected Poems contain some of the
      finest poetry yet written in America."

                              1934

1   BIRSS, JOHN H. "American First Editions: (Harold) Hart Crane
      (1899-1932)." Publishers' Weekly 125 (16 June):22-23.
          A short bibliographical note and an incomplete listing of
      Crane's works.

2   COWLEY, MALCOLM. "The Age of Islands." In Exile's Return: A
      Narrative of Ideas. New York: Viking Press, pp. 221-34.
          Includes the famous and often repeated account of Crane's
      method of composition. Cowley describes a typical Sunday after-
      noon tea party on Tory Hill during which Crane composed a typical
      poem. Crane is "the Roaring Boy." While composing, he played
      Cuban rhumbas on the phonograph and typed madly, often stomping
      across the room and declaiming to the four walls. "Hart drank
      to write: he drank to invoke the visions that his poems are in-
      tended to convey." Cowley later discovered that Crane would have
      been meditating over that particular poem for months or even
      years, scribbling lines of it now and again, waiting for the
      moment of genuine inspiration when it would all be put together.
      He would revise new poems painstakingly, trying to clarify the
      images, searching for the right words. "Essentially Crane was a
      poet of ecstacy or frenzy or intoxication. . . ." Later Crane
      drank so much that when the visions came he was incapable of
      writing them down. No American poet was ever so much trouble to
      his friends. The chapter ends with Crane rejecting Cowley's

advice that he devote himself less to literature of ecstasy.
Reprinted: 1951.5. See 1958.9.

3   LIPTON, RITA JOYCE. "Last Letters of Hart Crane: With a Com-
     mentary on the Poet and the Man." Literary America 1 (Septem-
     ber):7-14.
         Crane's closest of kin is Walt Whitman. He bears no rela-
tion to the moderns who practice what has been termed the cult of
unintelligibility. The chief characteristics of his poetry are
exuberance and joy. The four letters reprinted were written to
Samuel Loveman, 12 April 1931; 11 September 1931; 17 November
1931; and Easter 1932. They are chatty and personal, recording
Crane's meeting with Dr. Hans Zinsser, and the arrival of David
Sequiros, the Mexican painter, who stayed with Crane for a while.
A previously unpublished poem, "In A Court, is also printed.

4   LOVEMAN, SAMUEL. "Recollections of Hart Crane." New English
     Weekly 5 (2 August):380.
         Recalls that he first met Crane in the spring of 1919 in
Cleveland and learned from him of the existence of what Loveman
calls the left wing of modern literature: the Little Review,
Gorham Munson, and T.S. Eliot. The description of Charles Brooks
in Hints to Pilgrims gives a fair photographic picture of Crane as
he must have appeared to others in his early days in New York.
Recalls Crane's kindness to him when Loveman came to New York,
shortly after Crane had been there only a few weeks. The description of Crane's famous room at 110 Columbia Heights is rather
complete. While Crane lived in New York, his life became more
complicated by drinking and carousing. In spite of a second
printing, White Buildings fell like lead. Increasingly, Crane
became dependent on the stimulus of drink and music to help him
compose. His experience abroad was a disaster. He returned to
New York, an American to his fingertips, a dévoté of Walt Whitman,
Emily Dickinson, and Isadora Duncan. Evaluates The Bridge as a
poem that approached but never reached a complete unification.

5   RIDGE, LOLA. "The Modern Mystic." Saturday Review of Litera-
     ture 11 (1 September):82.
         Review of The Collected Poems. Like most creative person-
alities, Crane lacked the ability to invent; he could only discover. He had to discover the characteristics of his own vision,
painfully to evolve his own designs. Waldo Frank had recognized
early that Crane was a mystic. A "yea-sayer" to the universe, he
responded to Whitman's affirmative philosophy. Spiritually, however, he was not a disciple of Whitman. Highly individualistic,
he responded with primary emotion to the impact of immediate
experience. All of Crane's poems seen as a whole are like a
bridge. He begins rising in White Buildings, he reaches the top
of the crest in The Bridge, and the Key West poems are the end of
the arc that fell too swiftly to the sea. Among the last poems,
"The Broken Tower" is singled out as superior.

6   ROBERTS, MICHAEL. Critique of Poetry. London: Jonathan
      Cape, pp. 90-91, 147-49, 161, 184-85, 230-35.
         Brief negative interpretation of The Bridge. "The man who
attempts to reject accepted values and yet has nothing sufficient
to replace them is always liable to recur for comfort's sake to
some known sentiment. The Bridge is an attempt at an epic American history, but it is incoherent: the poet has no definite
standpoint. . . ."

7   SCHAPPES, MORRIS U. "Robinson Jeffers and Hart Crane: A
      Study in Social Irony." Dynamo 1, no. 2 (March-April):15-22.
         Wishes to demonstrate how important and representative
poets who have been unbalanced by the individualistic philosophy
of the capitalistic system have reacted in a declining American
civilization. Crane's view of the bridge as a force that will
bind the world is an irrelevant vision. The lesson from Crane's
life and poetry is clear--"he who does not take his place in the
trenches of class warfare dies an ironic death."

8   WOLFF, D. "Remembering Hart Crane." New Republic 81 (28
      November):76.
         Verse appreciation.

1935

1   BLACKMUR, R.P. "New Thresholds, New Anatomies: Notes on a
      Text of Hart Crane." In The Double Agent. New York: Arrow
      Editions, pp. 121-40.
         One of the most significant early articles. The Waste Land,
The Cantos, and The Bridge all have failed in similar ways--in
composition, in independent objective existence, and in intelligibility of language. The reader must supply clues from outside
of the poem in order to apprehend the meaning. In addition there
are passages "which no amount of outside work can illumine."
"These notes intend to examine certain characteristic passages of
Hart Crane's poems as modes of language and to determine how and
to what degree the effects intended were attained." Crane chose
the wrong masters and took the wrong things from them--that which
was personal and idiosyncratic to them. The allowances we make
for Crane are fundamental in that we "agree to supply or overlook
what does not appear in the poems, and whereby we agree to for-
give or guess blindly at those parts of the poems which are unintelligible." Chief example used in the article is "Wine Menagerie." Reprinted: 1957.2.

2   BLAKE, HOWARD. "Thoughts on Modern Poetry." Sewanee Review
      43 (April):187-96.
         Although this is a difficult age, it should still be pos-
sible for a few great poets to write great poetry. Too many of
our poets have devoted themselves to lyric poetry and have

stressed the requirement of "perfection in part." Lyric poetry
is highly personal and an indication of "rabid romanticism." Any
short survey of modern poetry reveals that the poets are much
more concerned with themselves than they are with voicing the
problems of man. What this age needs is epic composition. In
The Bridge, Crane tried to raise Wallace Stevens's theory of the
aesthetic to an epic scale. Crane was not a learned man and did
not possess the intelligence to handle the epic form. His
greatest learning was in "the amassing of a varied and applicable
vocabulary." He sought for some sufficiently great symbol to
integrate the life he experienced and the men he knew. Since,
however, The Bridge itself is the product of Crane's personal
desires rather than the expression of a fulfillment of an era, it
cannot be called a successful epic.

3   DEUTSCH, BABETTE. This Modern Poetry. New York: W.W. Norton,
     pp. 140-48.
         Primarily concerned with some generalizations about The
     Bridge. The poem is interesting because it draws together three
     of the significant elements in American poetry. First, it opens
     up for poetry the democratic vistas of Whitman. Second, Crane
     employs the symbolist method of Poe in order to record his own
     nervous terror. Third, the poem celebrates the inviolable self
     which is so characteristic of Emily Dickinson.

4   EMERSON, DOROTHY. "Poetry Corner." Scholastic 26 (16 March):
     11.
         Reprints "The Hurricane" without any significant comment.

                              1936

1   ATKINS, ELIZABETH. "Man and Animals in Recent Poetry." PMLA
     51 (March):263-83.
         Because of the science of psychology and the experience of
     the relativity of value in human life, the modern poet's interest
     in animal life is significantly different from that of older
     poets. Yet there is a persistent childlike mood of marvel in
     modern poetry. "Even the most esoteric poem of our times,
     'Brooklyn Bridge,'" refers to the seagull in this manner. In "A
     Name for All" Crane seems to express envy of animals who are less
     handicapped than rational man.

*2   BIGELOW, MARGARET FRANCES. "An Evaluation of Hart Crane (with
     Reference to the Munson Correspondence)." Ph.D. dissertation,
     Ohio State University.

*3   BRUNNER, ELSIE M. "Literary Symbolism and Its Influence on
     Three American Poets." Ph.D. dissertation, Ohio State Uni-
     versity.

4   DREW, ELIZABETH. "The Trouble With Modern Poetry." Saturday
     Review of Literature 14 (23 May):3-4, 14.
          Many modern poets are so concerned with density of meaning
     in their poems that they forget the essence of poetic beauty. A
     sense of personal disharmony cannot create a myth or a drama.
     The Waste Land achieves a successful structural pattern even
     though it is "a personal phantasmagoria." Crane tried to do
     something more in The Bridge than Eliot had done. A true poet,
     he had an insight into the architecture of the human conscious-
     ness, and wanted to create a structure of words that would span
     his vision of the contemporary world. "But he was not equal to
     the mastery of the thing." Partially because of his own person-
     ality and his environment, "the poem remains a muddle."

5   HORTON, PHILIP. "The Greenberg Manuscript and Hart Crane's
     Poetry." Southern Review 2 (Summer):148-59.
          Greenberg's manuscripts were among Crane's belongings which
     Mrs. T.W. Simpson sent to him. Horton believes that it must have
     been in Crane's possession from 1920 on, although there is no
     mention in Crane's letters of a Greenberg or of any such manu-
     script. The poems are very curious; their diction is unmistak-
     able. They are characterized by bewildering syntax and extra-
     ordinary use of words. Without question, Crane was influenced by
     these poems, particularly in the use of words and phrases. The
     symbols used by both poets have approximately the same meaning
     for both. Crane seems to have borrowed forthrightly and delib-
     erately from the Greenberg manuscript, especially in "Voyages II"
     and in "Emblems of Conduct." The poems are, however, "indubit-
     ably Crane's own poetry." See 1936.6.

6   _____. "Identity of S.B. Greenberg." Southern Review 2
     (Autumn);422-24.
          A supplement to Horton's article on the Greenberg manu-
     scripts, revealing that the identity of Greenberg has now been
     established. William Muriel Fisher, an art critic who lived
     nearby in Woodstock, New York, gave the manuscript to Crane
     during the winter of 1923-24. Crane kept the notebooks for
     several months and made a copy of the poems he considered best.
     These copies made up the sheaf of poems which were sent to Horton
     and led him to the discovery of this influence. See 1936.5.

7   JOHNSON, MERLE. American First Editions: Bibliographical
     Checklists of the Works of 199 American Authors, 3d ed. New
     York: R.R. Bowker, p. 122.
          Crane appears only in the third edition, not in the second
     or the fourth. Crane's first editions in America are listed as
     well as his appearances in A Pagan Anthology. Crane's essay in
     Sayler's Revolt in the Arts is also noted, as is the fact that
     certain of Crane's poems appeared in the Braithwaite anthologies
     from 1926 through 1929.

8 NELSON, JOHN HERBERT, ed. <u>Contemporary Trends: American</u>
<u>Literature Since 1914</u>. New York: Macmillan Co., p. 499.
Brief biographical sketch.

9 TATE, ALLEN. "Hart Crane." In <u>Reactionary Essays on Poetry</u>
<u>and Ideas</u>. New York: Charles Scribner's Sons, pp. 26-42.
Tate's definitive comment on his close friend. All criticisms of Crane's work have been influenced in one way or another
by this piece. Tate does not see any essential affinity between
Rimbaud and Crane. Rimbaud deliberately cultivated his derange-
ment in order to achieve disorder out of an implicit order; the
special quality of Crane's mind that belongs particularly to our
time was that his disorder was original and fundamental. Crane
is one of the "great masters of the romantic movement," largely
self-educated--"a defect of considerable interest in a poet whose
ambitious work is an American epic." In 1930 he told Tate that
he recognized that his soundest work was probably in the short
pieces of <u>White Buildings</u>. One of his defects was that he could
not face the moral criticism implied "in the failure to impose
his will upon experience." He never had the perfect mastery of
his subject that he had achieved in <u>White Buildings</u>. He undertook the composition of <u>The Bridge</u> as an answer to the cultural
pessimism of Eliot. Since he did not understand Eliot's "pessimism," he had difficulty identifying himself emotionally with
the age of the machine. The bridge as symbol stands for no well-
defined experience. <u>The Bridge</u> lacks coherent structure, either
symbolically or as a narrative. He does not have a pattern of
ideas sufficient to create an epic or heroic work. A great epic
must have the groundwork that is simple philosophically and "the
complete articulation of the ideas down to the slightest detail."
Crane's impulse to look for an American myth was sound because
it allowed him to search for a cultural truth which could win
the "spontaneous allegiance of the people." "The impulse in <u>The</u>
<u>Bridge</u> is religious, but the soundness of an impulse is no warrant
that it will create a sound art form." Crane could not create a
myth unaided. Nevertheless, he is a myth-maker "and in an age
favorable to myths he would have written a mythical poem in the
act of writing an historical one." <u>The Bridge</u> is at best, however, a collection of lyrics, "the best of which are not surpassed by anything in American literature." Whe he is least
philosophical, "when he writes from sensation," the writing is
the most distinguished. See 1930.18; 1932.23-24; 1948.19. Reprinted: 1955.19; 1959.16.

<u>1937</u>

1 AIKEN, CONRAD. "The Atlantic Bookshelf." <u>Atlantic Monthly</u>
160 (August):n.p.
Review of Philip Horton's <u>Hart Crane: The Life of an Amer-</u>
<u>ican Poet</u>. Since Crane's story is tragic, wretched, and sordid,

it is greatly to Horton's credit that he has been able to write a moving biography with such unpromising materials. Aiken wonders if Crane was not a "pseudo-genius." He praises Crane's imaginative and verbal power, nothing the occasional superb line and superb image. What he emphasizes, however, is the failure of Crane's substructure to hold together, either formally or conceptually. "He lacked the will or the courage to discipline his talent, indulged in his weaknesses to excess, whipped up his failing associational powers with alcohol, and came inevitably to the point at which they were exhausted." At his death Crane was a hollow man, a man without beliefs. See 1937,13.

2   ANON. "The Book Forum." Forum and Century 98 (August):4.
     Review of Horton's Hart Crane, an entirely worthy biography produced within a decade of Crane's dramatic suicide. See 1937.13.

3   ANON. "Hart Crane: Erratic Life of an American Poet." Springfield Republican, 28 May, p. 12.
     Brief review of Horton's Hart Crane. See 1937.13.

4   ANON. "Poet's Progress." Time 29 (17 May):97.
     Review of Horton's Hart Crane. A brief Time essay in which the book under review is alluded to once. See 1937.13.

5   ANON. Review of Horton's Hart Crane. Booklist 33 (July):336.
     Brief mention. See 1937.13.

6   ANON. Review of Hart Crane by Philip Horton. Forum 98, no. 2 (August):iv-v.
     "The competence of real scholarship occurs in this book without any of its mannerisms." See 1937.13.

7   CLEATON, IRENE, and CLEATON, ALLEN. Books and Battle: American Literature, 1920-1930. Boston: Houghton Mifflin Co., pp. 185, 189.
     Transition published among other works those of Crane, demonstrating that it "extended far beyond the cult of unintelligibility." S₄N illustrated its belief in "growth through disagreement" by printing, among others, Thorton Wilder, Gorham B. Munson, Crane, and William Lyon Phelps. Hence, the authors described S4N as annoying "at least half of its readers all the time."

8   COWLEY, MALCOLM. "The Roaring Boy." New Republic 91 (June): 134.
     Review of Horton's biography, which is praised. The rest of the material in the review has been incorporated in Exile's Return (1951.5). See 1937.13.

9   FLETCHER, JOHN GOULD. Life Is My Song. New York: Farrar &

Rinehart, pp. 117-19.
"I did not meet Crane in the flesh. From what I heard
about him, as well as from his poetry, I judged that his vast
ambitions to recreate an American myth, his gusty rhetoric, his
combination of enfant terrible of Bohemianism and the disciple of
Whitman, made of Crane far more of a poet, though less sure of
his own ideas, than Tate."

10   FRANK, WALDO. In the American Jungle. New York: Farrar &
     Rinehart, pp. 96-108.
          Among the "portraits" number seven is of Crane. The
material is much the same as his introduction to the Collected
Poems. Agrarian America gave us a common culture which Frank
calls "the great tradition." It inspired an ideological art of
"the golden day," and had a great effect upon the character of
the American people. But society became transfigured by science
and certain economic forces. "The poetry of Hart Crane is a
deliberate continuance of the great tradition in terms of our
industrialized world." Yet, in Crane none of the old securities
survive, and his need to find new words to communicate his vision
is acute. "In his lack of valid terms to express his relationship with life, Crane was a true culture-child . . . he was a
child of modern man." His search for an integrating theme ended
in The Bridge, a product of Crane's deliberately myth-making will.
The Bridge can synthesize the world of chaos, joining the river
and city. In actual life the symbol given to him by the bridge
itself did not sustain him. With the exception of "The Broken
Tower," his later poems reveal a retreat to the mood seen in the
final poems of White Buildings. The Bridge is a superb achievement; the flaw in the poem "lies in the weakness of the personal
crystallization upon which the visions rests." Crane's poetry
will probably be easily comprehensible to future readers rather
than obscure. See 1933.6-7.

11   GREGORY, HORACE. "Guilt-Haunted American Poet." New York
     Herald Tribune Books, 30 May, p. 4.
          Review of Horton's Hart Crane. A combination of tact and
candor makes his book one of the brilliant documents in contemporary American writing. The theme of the book is the guilt consciousness which ran throughout the course of Crane's life. The
center of Crane's poetry is the tension between fear and terror
and his affirmation of a new hierarchy of faith. See 1937.13.

12   HOLMES, JOHN. "The Strange Life of an American Poet." Boston
     Evening Transcript, 3 July, sec. 5, p. 4.
          Review of Horton's Hart Crane. Especially praised is the
clarity and impartiality of the author's approach. Horton makes
it clear that Crane's disintegration was his own and was not
forced on him by his times. See 1937.13.

13   HORTON, PHILIP. Hart Crane: The Life of an American Poet.

New York: W.W. Norton, 352 pp.
  Classic account of Crane's life. Because it was written so
shortly after Crane's death, Horton was unable to take advantage
of many of the documents and letters that have since come to
light. Although the work is primarily biographical, it does contain analyses of Crane's poetry throughout. It is fundamentally
sympathetic to Crane without being maudlin. "His spiritual ambivalence is seen to be a reflection of life as he experienced
it, and must be considered as inevitable in The Bridge as Dante's
completely articulated religious dialect was in The Divine Comedy,
the work so frequently on the lips of Crane's critics." "Together
with Whitman he shares the distinction of serving as a model for
younger poets. And why should he not? In his character as a
national poet he expressed major qualities of the American spirit
which have not been heard in poetry since Leaves of Grass. In
his own work he combined the best traditions of English verse
with innovations and idioms without which poetry would become
formalized, static, and lifeless." The valuable appendix contains Crane's previously unpublished essay "General Aims and
Theories," his famous letter to Harriet Monroe in reply to questions concerning "At Melville's Tomb," a letter to Otto Kahn out-
lining the subject matter of The Bridge, and a letter to Gorham
Munson in reply to the essay in Destinations. Reviewed in
1937.1-6, 8, 11-12, 15-20; 1938.1; 1957.4; 1958.3. See 1965.7.

14   MacINTYRE, C.F. "To Hart Crane." Southern Review 3, no. 3:
     153.
       Verse appreciation.

15   MATTHIESSEN, F.O. "An Absolute Music." Yale Review 27 (Fall):
     173-75.
       Review of Horton's Hart Crane. Horton has found in Crane's
career a symbol of our recent culture. Eliot's early work left
a lasting mark on Crane's own style. In thought, he felt a close
kinship with Whitman's affirmation of American possibilities.
Crane was a symbol of the American temperament in the postwar
decade, with his combination of buoyant aspirations and sudden
bewildered despair. Horton's patience and tact are praised.
Even if Crane did not succeed in The Bridge in competing a whole
poem, parts of it are conceived with magnificent wholeness,
notably "The River" and "Harbor Dawn." Crane "was more greatly
endowed than any other poet in America since Eliot with the essential talent of being able to conceive of his poems not as
'ideas,' nor as expressive lines and passages, but as complete
rhythmical entities." See 1937.13. Reprinted: 1952.12.

16   MUNSON, GORHAM. "An American Tragedy." Saturday Review of
     Literature 16 (29 May):7.
       In this review of Horton's Hart Crane, Munson asserts that
none of Crane's friends understood him as well as his biographer.
He agrees with Horton that the key to Crane's character is his

lack of spiritual and secular security. "Mr. Horton's psychological insight is matched by his good judgement." Munson asserts
that Crane underwent a kind of religious experience several times.
Both in his life and in his poetry he was an incorrigible roman-
ticist. See 1937.13.

17   POORE, CHARLES. "The Turbulent Life of Hart Crane." New
     York Times Book Review, 30 May, p. 4.
         Review of Horton's Hart Crane, describing it as a sound and
     thorough biography. Poore is only a partial admirer of Crane's
     poetry, feeling that he wrote some good poetry, although usually
     one has to go to some trouble to discover it. See 1937.13.

18   RITCHEY, JOHN. "Trophies of the Sun." Christian Science
     Monitor Magazine, 7 July, p. 10.
         The virtue of Horton's Hart Crane lies in its objectivity,
     despite the fact that Horton must have admired his subject tre-
     mendously. The book pictures an unhappy and unsavory life.
     Crane is best understood through his poems and his letters. See
     1937.13.

19   TATE, ALLEN. "A Poet and His Life." Poetry 50 (July):219-24.
         Review of Horton's Hart Crane. Crane brought into the
     poetry of our time a hitherto unknown quality, and made it
     necessary to reevaluate his immediate predecessors. Like Poe, he
     will influence many of his successors out of all proportion to
     his intrinsic merit. Horton is praised for his tact in the
     biography, while at the same time not actually sparing anyone.
     He understood Crane's character. Tate holds the view that given
     Crane's character, he would have been frustrated and destroyed in
     any society. "In order to see in Crane's personal disaster and
     the fragmentary character of his work a full indictment of the
     society in which he lived, one must accept the most extreme tenet
     of romanticism, which ends up by asserting that society ought to
     exist primarily for art." Insecurity is the key to Crane's life.
     Although he professed to believe in the high mission of the poet,
     "he never had any deep confidence in the significance of his own
     work or in the arts as a whole." See 1937.13.

20   WALTON, EDA LOU. "There is a World Dimensional." Nation 144
     (26 January):733-34.
         Review of Horton's Hart Crane, in which he is praised for
     presenting his materials objectively and impersonally. The result
     is a dignified analysis of a complex and tortured mind. Neither
     his family nor the period into which he was born afforded him any
     security. She suggests that one of the reasons he committed
     suicide was that he was returning home without a job during the
     Depression and believed himself too much the individualist to
     accept the current political scene. It is impossible to document
     this opinion. She insists, however, that he is the one poet of
     this period who would have found his greatest poetic convictions

substantiated and his mystic faith posited by the Marxian philosophy. Since there was some disagreement about the date of the composition of "The Broken Tower," Miss Walton quotes a letter from Crane to her dated January 1931, in which he wrote: "Give my greetings to Léonie Adams, and tell her that I think her poem 'Bell Tower' makes me long to do something half so perfect as its delicate and yet majestic overtones achieve." See 1937.13.

21 WINTERS, YVOR. <u>Primitivism and Decadence</u>. New York: Arrow
    Editions, pp. 27-33, 80-85 and passim.
        Passages from <u>Faustus and Helen</u> provide examples of the kind of poetry which maintains grammatical coherence when there is no coherence of thought or very little. "The Dance" illustrates the transference of values from one field of experience to another and unrelated field. The poem deals largely with the death and apotheosis of Maquokeeta, the apotheosis taking the form of the union with Pocahontas. The difficulty of the poem resides in the meaning of the union of the two. "The only possible conclusion is that he was confused as to his own feelings and did not bother to find out what he was really talking about." Winters asserts the impossibility of creating a religion or conception of immortality simply by naming the soil Pocahontas and then by writing love poetry to the Indian girl. If one agrees that experimental poetry in the twentieth century developed in either the direction of primitivism or of decadence, Crane's poetry is an example of decadence.

<u>1938</u>

1 BRADLEY, SCULLEY. Review of <u>Hart Crane: Life of an American
   Poet</u>. <u>American Literature</u> 9 (January):480-82.
        Crane was an example of the artist crushed by the materialism and neglect of his age. The forces which destroyed Crane were within himself and within his family environment. Horton's biography is praised for the vivid description it gives of the literary scene of the period. After MacLeish, Crane is the most modern of the metaphysical poets. The concluding line of the review must be quoted in full; "We shall probably remember a few of Crane's poems always as the evidence of what he might have been." See 1937.13.

2 HORTON, PHILIP. "Death of a Poet." <u>Coronet</u> 3 (January):56-
   60.
        A popular piece that lacks almost all the qualities of Horton's biography. Crane's suicide, a melodramatic and tragic gesture, marks the end of a period not only in literature but in society as well. In a few years he became a powerful current in the mainstream of American letters. The surprising thing, however, is the abuse that has been heaped on him because of his personal life. No American poet since Poe has been more spirit-

ually tormented and morally disordered. Crane's most obvious
obscene and borrish behavior was only the reverse side of his
sense of guilt, his frustration, and his mental anguish. Such
behavior was not characteristic of his life until after 1927.
His critics have forgotten most of his sterling qualities: a
genius of high order, generous, kind, loyal, and rigorously
honest. His almost childlike naïveté was outstanding. Crane was
the kind of man who needed some kind of faith or moral equivalent
of faith. His poetry is spiritual and mystical.

3   SYMONS, JULIAN. "Hart Crane." Twentieth Century Verse, no. 8
     (January-February), pp. 171-74.
          The great romantic poet is inhuman and untouchable. Al-
     though a romantic, Crane was too human, too soft inside. Because
     he was not as tough as Rimbaud or Whitman, he did not become a
     major poet. Because he had the gifts of a major poet, he must be
     judged harshly. On the other hand, a failed genius like Crane
     "is more valuable, and more interesting, than twenty good minor
     poets." Reprinted: 1966.29.

4   _____. "How Wide Is the Atlantic? or Do You Believe in
     America?" Twentieth Century Verse, nos. 12-13 (September-
     October), pp. 80-84.
          Since about 1912, the best American poets have been of two
     kinds--those of a markedly European habit of mind and those of a
     markedly American habit of mind. Crane belongs to the second
     group. He is "the only markedly American poet of the last twenty
     years whom I can read with much sympathy or understanding." Re-
     printed: 1966.30.

                              1939

1   ANDERSON, GEORGE K., and WALTON, EDA LOU. "American Writers
     Observe Social Conditions." In This Generation. Chicago:
     Scott-Foresman, pp. 579-607.
          Crane finding beauty in modern life, especially in machin-
     ery, disliked T.S. Eliot's negative view of life. Crane's first
     task was to create a new language which could express this
     beauty; so he used industrial language to communicate a sense of
     the beauty of the modern industrial world. "Eliot looked back-
     wards; Crane looked forward." In reaction to Eliot, Crane turned
     to Whitman for a mystical statement of belief in America, feeling
     it was the duty of the poet to see beyond chaos to a new synthesis
     of values. The Bridge was meant to "recreate the major forces in
     the development of American civilization." The authors claim
     that some of the most intelligent remarks about The Bridge and
     about Crane's poetry in general were made by Ben Belitt in an un-
     published essay. As far as I know, the comments which they quote
     are the only appearance of Belitt's work. Belitt believes that
     Crane was a miniaturist and never at home in the epic form. The

epic moves in perspectives; the miniaturist works in planes. The
epic is concerned with masses, the miniaturist with facets. Yet
there are portions of The Bridge such as "Ave Maria" and "The
Tunnel" which indicate that Crane had some of the powers of an
epic poet. Belitt states: "Crane's poetry is poetry in which
ideas are caught up and wrenched out of their lodging, subjected
to change in speeds and changing stature." Crane was caught by
his own images and by their double or triple significance and by
all of their associations.

2   BISHOP, JOHN PEALE. "The Myth and Modern Literature."
     Saturday Review of Literature 20 (22 July):3-4, 14.
         See The Collected Essays of John Peale Bishop (1948.3).

3   ____. "The Sorrows of Thomas Wolfe." Kenyon Review 1
     (Winter):7-17.
         See The Collected Essays of John Peale Bishop (1948.3).

4   BROOKS, CLEANTH. Modern Poetry and the Tradition. Chapel
     Hill: University of North Carolina Press, pp. ix-x.
         Explains that he will deal with the poets who are the
     clearest and most significant illustrations of the modern criti-
     cal revolution. Necessarily he has had to exclude many poets
     from consideration. "Hart Crane, for example, possessed one of
     the most brilliant talents of his generation, and some of his
     poems are surely among the most important of our time. His
     omission from this study is based on a general consideration of
     the clarity of the book as a whole--not certainly on his lack of
     importance as a poet."

5   LAUGHLIN, JAMES. "The Greenberg Manuscripts." In New Direc-
     tions in Prose and Poetry. Norfolk, Conn.: New Directions,
     pp. 353-81.
         When Horton was preparing his biography of Crane, he
     searched for the Greenberg manuscripts, found them, and discussed
     the relationship of Crane to Greenberg in two essays. Laughlin
     feels it unnecessary to add anything to what Horton had already
     done. He merely remarks that Crane did more than steal from
     Greenberg--"he recreated, making something entirely new, entirely
     his own, from original materials." Yet, he feels that Crane
     should be strongly censured for his failure to state clearly his
     source. Reprinted: 1967.18.

6   LEAVIS, F.R. "Hart Crane From This Side." Scrutiny 7
     (March):443-46.
         Review of The Collected Poems, the Boriswood edition. If
     the legend of Crane remains significant, it will not be because
     he was a genius. We have been told that his genius is especially
     revealed in The Bridge; however, the poem is "a wordy chaos, both
     locally and in sum." That America in the twenties should have
     produced Crane is not surprising. What is surprising is the

critical respect that he commands. The question is not at what point does he fall short, but rather why should he enjoy any reputation as a poet at all.

7   TOMLINSON, ELIZABETH. "The Metaphysical Tradition in Three Modern Poets." College English 1 (December):208-22.

      Because of the spirit of uncertainty, gloom, and frustration of our age, present-day poets have revived the metaphysical conceit in their effort to write as our age demands. Crane is a metaphysical poet because of his effort to find some continuity between the chaos of the modern world and his mystical conception of order and beauty--"the bridge of fire that links Atlantis and Cathay." The bridge is his symbol of essential unity. Like Eliot, the evidences of personal struggle are strong in his poetry. The airplane and the dynamo offer him the same challenge that the new science offered to Donne.

8   UNTERMEYER, LOUIS. "Prophetic Rhapsody." Saturday Review of Literature 6 (14 June):1125.

      Crane's poetry for all its finesse is founded on rhetoric, but the rhetoric of a new order. Tate had hinted in his introduction to White Buildings that Crane had not yet discovered a theme to embody his vision. In The Bridge the theme has been found. His visions are those of Blake, Dickinson, and Whitman. As a phrasemaker, Crane commands attention; although it is not phrasemaking that chiefly distinguishes his poetry. "It is apostrophic power, the strangely tuned but undeniable eloquence which makes The Bridge an important contribution to recent American poetry." While his allusiveness and allegory make him difficult for "the plain reader," he has written "a highly sophisticated, highly syncopated local epic."

1940

1   ANON. "Adventures in Cooperation: I. Choric Dance--Drama." Theatre Arts 24, no. 7 (July):501-3.

      A record of Bennington School of the Arts presentation of The Bridge with chorus, dance, and dramatic dimension. It was produced without omitting a line or changing the order of words or sections in the poem. "Each episode was conceived as a problem in theatre space." The director was Arch Lauterer; choreography by Martha Hill; Ben Belitt directed the speaking of the lines; Gregory Tucker wrote the musical score. Contains illustrations of the scene designs by Lauterer.

2   ANON. "News Notes." Poetry: A Magazine of Verse 55 (February):284.

      Notes on the production of The Bridge by the Bennington Theatre Studio. Three performances were given on 13, 14, and 15 December 1939.

3   DREW, ELIZABETH. <u>Directions in Modern Poetry</u>. New York:
    W.W. Norton, pp. 212-17.
        "Voyages II" is an example of a method by which the poet
    establishes psychological unity without having a clear logical
    structure. The theme of the poem is a desire that the union of
    the lovers be fulfilled by a mystical union with the sea. There
    is no overt statement of the poet's theme, since there is no ex-
    plicit logical content in the poem. The words and the images
    bear the weight of revealing the theme by their power of sugges-
    tion and reverberation. It communicates much before we under-
    stand the thought, and we understand the thought only after many
    readings.

*4 FOSTER, MARGARET. "Arthur Rimbaud and Hart Crane: An Essay
    in Influences and Parallels." Ph.D. dissertation, Ohio State
    University.

5   MILLET, FREDERICK B. <u>Contemporary American Authors: A Crit-
    ical Survey and 219 Bio-bibliographies</u>. New York: Harcourt,
    Brace & Co., pp. 150, 305-6.
        A conventional biographical sketch. The 1949 edition shows
no change in the listing. Reprinted: 1949.7.

6   WELLS, HENRY W. <u>New Poets From Old</u>. New York: Columbia
    University Press, pp. 116-25.
        Crane's poetry is a combination of old ideas and an old
    technique with the use of old images and some new grafted on
    them. <u>The Bridge</u> is the "strongest mystical poem" written in
    America since the work of Whitman and Dickinson. It is, as well,
    an example of the characteristic features of modern poetry. The
    bridge as symbol is intended to signify the marriage of past and
    present. The poem is most easily compared with mystical, reli-
    gious, and allegorical poems: <u>The Divine Comedy</u>, <u>Piers Plowman</u>,
    and <u>Pilgrim's Progress</u>. Although Crane appears to be the most
    modern of poets, the core of his experience and its guiding sym-
    bolism come from ancient traditions; only his incidental symbol-
    ism is new. The necessity for a bridge between the finite and
    the infinite is one of the oldest of themes. Like the medieval
    poets and philosophers, Crane is concerned with beginning and
    end. His desire to see unity rather than diversity in existence
    is an indication of his religious spirit. Brooklyn Bridge as a
    symbol has the same kind of appeal for Crane that cathedrals did
    for medieval men. "In spirit and technique he stands with Hugo
    of St. Victor, who pictured God in stone, and with Dante, who
    depicted him in words."

7   WILDER, AMOS N. "A Note on Hart Crane As Discussed by Yvor
    Winters and Allen Tate." In <u>The Spiritual Aspects of the New
    Poetry</u>. New York: Harper's, pp. 122-30.
        Crane's work is of special interest to those who are con-
    cerned with the direction a religious spirit takes outside of its

usual forms. A true twentieth century romantic, he fixed his
ardor on the undefined dream of the American future. A mystic
and a pantheist, he was "religious" in his approach to his art.
"All his work betrays a search after the Absolute." Winters and
Tate probed deeply into the error of many modern artists. The
characteristic moral defect of romanticism is its tendency to
spiritual self-aggrandizement, defined by Winters as imposing
one's identity upon, and by Tate as imposing one's will upon, experience and desiring to possess the world. The tendency is self-
destructive. The healthy mystic is one who can face his predicament. Crane gave himself completely to subjectivity; even a
magnificent poem like The Bridge bears the marks of escapism,
"exploiting . . . subjectivity in willful detatchment from
reality."

8   ZINSSER, HANS. As I Remember Him. Boston: Little, Brown &
     Co., pp. 334-39.
          Recalls his meeting with Crane on the ship which took the
     two of them to Mexico. Crane was rarely entirely sober, but he
     was an engaging companion most of the time. He was impressed
     with his intelligence, his literary discrimination, and his
     generous taste. Crane freely acknowledged the abnormalities
     which seem to have been the source of his unhappiness. Zinsser
     recalls the incident in which he had to throw two typhus-infected
     rats overboard. Crane saw this and seemed horrified. Having had
     too much to drink, he was considerably excited by the event and
     started to recite poetically that the doctor had thrown rats into
     the Havana harbor. "Crane had an appealing and lovable nature,
     and was unquestioningly a man of great gifts which might have
     flowered into coherent beauty had he been more stable." See
     1940.9.

9   _____. "More Truth in Poetry." Atlantic Monthly 165 (April):
     563-92.
          See As I Remember Him (1940.8), simultaneously published.

                              1941

1   BROOKS, VAN WYCK. Opinions of Oliver Allston. New York: E.P.
     Dutton, pp. 173, 264.
          Crane is mentioned as an example of the majority of modern
     American writers who are romantic in grain: "His broken romantic
     bridge to the future." Crane serves also, oddly enough, as a
     sample of one of Brooks's favorite theses, that when Crane was at
     home in the West at his father's inn (the West being Cleveland),
     the "strained, egotistical, violent man became the natural human
     being."

2   CARGILL, OSCAR. "The Decadents." In Intellectual America:
     Ideas on the March. New York: Macmillan Co., pp. 274-81.

A poet of less emotional depth than Eliot, Crane gave freer play to his feelings. However, The Bridge is not the product of creative frenzy in the ordinary understanding of the term. It was composed very deliberately; although his life may have been chaotic, his manuscripts were not. The ramifications of decadent influence on Crane is significant, but the single greatest influence was that of Rimbaud. The late poems in Key West continue to show his great interest in the decadents. The Bridge, an architectural poem, not the symphonic poem he writes of later, is one of the greatest poems in contemporary American literature; a magnificently conceived idea which contains all the strands of experience that are woven into the American consciousness. It is a poem of hope and affirmation, based on "a deeply submerged faith" producing the "first Decadent poem to turn definitely away from Decadence."

3 COWLEY, MALCOLM. "Remembering Hart Crane." New Republic 104
   (14 April):504-6.
      Yet another version of Crane's method of composition. This piece is a good deal closer to the material as presented in Exiles Return (1951.5), but uses some of the same specific data as the article in Esquire (1958.9).

4 DEUTSCH, BABETTE. "Religious Elements in Modern Poetry."
   Menorah Journal 29 (January):24-28.
      The religious consciousness is repeatedly expressed in traditional English poetry, but as one comes closer to contemporary times, he finds poets disturbed over the fact that there is nothing for them either to believe or to doubt. Mythology is essential to the poet; hence, the fact that the myth that created organized religion has failed is of significance. The modern poet's response to the loss of religious feeling has varied with his own temperament. In an attempt to create his own religion, Crane took as a symbol the bridge, a triumph of modern engineering. The Bridge is a religious poem and a deeply American poem. His chief American predecessors are Whitman, Dickinson, and Poe. The poem is heavily rhetorical, the product of a man whose imagination is excited both by his material and by the words with which he seeks to describe it. But it is rhetorical in the perjorative sense as well, since Crane often uses language to conceal the poverty of his feeling. His religion was essentially an artifact.

5 GREGORY, HORACE. "American Poetry: 1930-1940." Accent 1
   (Summer):213-28.
      A listing of the works published by important American poets (including Crane) during the ten-year period mentioned in the title, along with some of the more important reviews of these works.

1942

1   BARBOUR, JOSEPH. "Hart Crane Considered as an Oyster." In
    Princeton Verse Between Two Wars. Edited by Allen Tate.
    Princeton, N.J.: Princeton University Press, p. 36.
        Verse appreciation.

2   GREGORY, HORACE, and ZATURENSKA, MARYA. "Harold Hart Crane:
    Death and the Sea." In A History of American Poetry: 1900-
    1940. New York: Harcourt, Brace & Co., pp. 468-81.
        Of all of the poets who came into prominence in the 1930s,
    Crane is most likely to achieve immortality even though he is a
    great poet of the second class. His poetry has closer affinities
    to the prose of Melville than it does to the poetry of Whitman.
    From White Buildings, the authors select the following poems as
    among Crane's best: "Black Tambourine," "Praise for an Urn,"
    "At Melville's Tomb," and "Voyages II, V." The Bridge is Crane's
    "never quite completed major book." The poem was conceived as
    multiple levels of meaning and experiences. It was probably too
    deliberately planned, but at the same time too dependent upon the
    notion of "intoxication" so important to Crane. "It could almost
    be said that in the writing of The Bridge Crane unwisely sub-
    limated the religious emotion that has far more complete expres-
    sion in 'The Broken Tower,'" his best poem because it most com-
    pletely realized the religious impulse that should have been
    given proper scope in The Bridge.

3   HORTON, PHILIP. "Of Resolution." In Princeton Verse Between
    Two Wars. Edited by Allen Tate. Princeton, N.J.: Princeton
    University Press, p. 42.
        Verse appreciation.

4   LEWIS, JAMES FRANKLIN. "In Memoriam." In Three Young Poets.
    Denver, Colo.: Swallow Press, p. 18.
        Verse appreciation.

5   LUNDKVIST, ARTUR. "Hart Crane." Ord Och Bild: Illustresrad
    Manadsskirft (Stockholm) 51:411-14.
        In Swedish. A conventional, brief survey of Crane's life
    and work for Swedish readers.

6   SAVAGE, DEREK S. "The Americanism of Hart Crane." Horizon 5
    (May):302-8.
        Crane is "the unofficial laureate of modern America" be-
    cause of his relationship to our bustling industrial American
    society. Although an impressive poet, he is obscure in a very
    real sense and his collected work appears fragmentary. Judged by
    his own aspirations, he must be regarded as a glorious failure.
    While objecting to the commercial spirit that was so much a part
    of the American scene, he accepted the spirit of industrialism
    unquestioningly. "For Crane, modern progress was a reality." He

wished to give spiritual significance and meaning to the mechanized society of America. While some of Crane's literary asso-
ciates turned for their salvation to social criticism in the late
twenties and early thirties, Crane rejected this path and continued his aesthetic examination of the machine age. Since the
distinguishing mark of the "great" poet is his ability to dominate, as a poet, the society of his time, we cannot grant Crane
the title he wanted--"the greatest singer of my generation."
Reprinted: 1944.2.

7   SYMONS, JULIAN. "Hart Crane." Poetry 59 (February):248.
        Verse appreciation.

*8   WAGGONER, HYATT H[OWE]. "Science and Modern American Poetry."
        Ph.D. dissertation, Ohio State University.
            See 1950.9.

                              1943

1   BURKE, WILLIAM, and HOWE, WILL D. "Crane, Hart." In American
        Authors and Books, 1640-1940. New York: Grammercy, p. 181.
            Brief biography. Reprinted: 1962.2; 1972.6.

2   FOWLIE, WALLACE. "The Juggler's Dance: A Note on Crane and
        Rimbaud." Chimera 2 (Autumn):3-14.
            The poetry of Rimbaud and Crane need neither narrate nor
        celebrate love because it condenses passion into an image. Since
        the experience of the poem is love itself, the poem need not talk
        about it directly. Various sections of The Bridge use images and
        phrases that recall the cult of the Virgin. The clown, the
        juggler, and the poet are one. The poet identifies himself as
        buffoon in "Chaplinesque." "Hart Crane, in the poems he wrote
        between the ages of twenty and thirty, saw himself as the artist
        in the midst of the normal bourgeois Chicago and New York, and
        was in reality the clown among the sailors and the tough boys of
        the waterfront bars. But both Crane and Rimbaud, in their art,--
        and herein lie the signal greatness and transcendency of the
        homosexual--attain purity, a Platonic purity, unknown to the
        ordinary artist. A change which transforms a man into an artist
        takes on for the homosexual a fervor and religious profundity
        akin to the transformation of a man into a priest, because in the
        change are all hope and justification for himself as a man." Re-
        printed: 1950.3. See 1965.7.

3   LARRABEE, ANKEY. "Three Studies in Modern Poetry." Accent 3
        (Winter):115-21.
            An analysis of the symbol of the sea in "Voyages." These
        poems celebrate the interrelationship of passion and death; the
        sea is the principal symbol for this union which is developed
        through a pattern of sea imagery. The first poem is introductory,

in which the poet tells himself that "the bottom of the sea is cruel." In the second poem, Crane turns away from the freshness and brilliance of childhood to his major erotic chord. The third section is a variation of Eliot's "Death by Water" section of The Waste Land. Immersed by love, one manages to escape death. The fourth poem mingles the sea and flower imagery introduced in the second poem. Both the sea and flowers suggest eroticism. The fifth poem depicts "the sea as a cradle of forgetfulness." The image of sleep is important. The sea as lover is given a human aspect. "The last of the 'Voyages' is a tone poem of places and forms." In the final poem the sea is a source of passion and re-birth. It points to the future, since Belle Isle is a place of hope.

4   MOSS, HOWARD. "Disorder as Myth: Hart Crane's The Bridge." Poetry 62 (April):32-45.
    The Bridge, written out of a desperate need to reintegrate the chaos of modern society "into some sort of symbolic continuum with the past," is a failure because Crane is unable to comprehend the true nature of his celebration. The essential ambiguity at the heart of Crane's major symbol cannot be concealed by metaphysics or metaphor; Crane was unable to explore the social and economic values implied in the symbol. "The second serious failure is the essential nonfertility of the symbol." The "Cape Hatteras" section is crucial to the poem because in it we should see the turning point between reality and mysticism. Instead, "the myth loses contact with the earth and begins to impinge on metaphysics." In this section the earth is perceived in two ways: as Whitman's rural reality, and as Crane's superstructure of urban society. The eagle and the serpent are no longer space and time; instead we have the radio and the camera as the new symbols for time and space. In attempting to make the airplaine his Icarus symbol, Crane hopes for a way out of his dilemma. It fails. Here then is the precise falsification of the symbol of the bridge. Crane has finally found an industrial symbol which is no longer static, "but the problem of consciousness is still vested in the body of Pocahontas. . . . To capture one it is necessary to forego the other."

5   SHATTUCK, ROGER. "Hart Crane's Other Bridge." Yale Literary Magazine 19 (Winter):9-10, 18.
    That Allen Tate referred to Crane's poetry as religious and that Waldo Frank called him a mystic point toward a very important truth about Crane; he never left for an instant the artist's realm of experience. He was a poet in his writing and in his life. The tone of powerful celestialism is characteristic of his best poetry. Although The Bridge did not realize its purpose of myth-making, every section contains "a verse of unerring, in-spirational imagery—inspirational in the rudimentary sense of causing a catch in the breath." "For the Marriage of Faustus and Helen" is, however, a more illuminating poem for both critic and

reader. "The idiom of the work does not follow the academic title, but the subject matter does." The true richness of this poem is seen in that Crane subordinates all of the themes in the poem to the central theme of all of his poetry--the pursuit of artistic expression.

6   STOVALL, FLOYD. *American Idealism*. Port Washington, N.Y.: Kennikat Press, pp. 204-5.
        Three contemporary poets who derive from Pound and Eliot are Archibald MacLeish, Horace Gregory, and Crane. Crane tried to build a philosophical foundation for his life out of American materials, but did not wholly succeed, since he really had no faith in which to anchor his bridge.

7   WELLS, HENRY W. "American Rhapsody." In *The American Way of Poetry*. New York: Columbia University Press, pp. 191-204.
        Begins with a comparison of Stephen Vincent Benét's *John Brown's Body* and Crane's *The Bridge* as epic celebrations inspired by Walt Whitman. Benét was influenced by Whitman's democracy, Crane by his mysticism. Crane's poem is more philosophical, metaphysical, and religious. "It is also more poetic in its intrinsic quality, sustaining a lyric intensity and an extraordinary handling of metaphysical imagery throughout its brief scope." Despite numerous French and British influences on his work, the spirit and direction of *The Bridge* are most influenced by Whitman, Poe, Dickinson, and Melville. Among his contemporaries, he is most indebted to T.S. Eliot, even though he is consciously writing to refute Eliot's position. He wished to be regarded as the spokesman of American civilization. Crane's poetry other than *The Bridge* is minor. His extreme egoism and self-expression come out in the personal lyrics which are "crabbed, obscure, distressing, and of small human significance." He was seldom able to free himself from his sense of personal disaster. Only in *The Bridge*, "a noble and basically impersonal poem of epic vision," was he able to liberate his soul and art from confusion.

8   WINTERS, YVOR. *The Anatomy of Nonsense*. Norfolk, Conn.: New Directions, p. 246.
        Crane's best poems are "Repose of Rivers" and "Voyages II."

1944

*1   RAIZISS, SONIA. "The Relation of Certain Modern Poets to the Metaphysical Poets of the Seventeenth Century." Ph.D. dissertation, University of Pennsylvania.
        See 1952.15.

2   SAVAGE, DEREK S. "The Americanism of Hart Crane." In *The Personal Principle*. London: Routledge, pp. 113-20.
        Reprint of 1942.6.

3   WAGGONER, HYATT H[OWE]. "Hart Crane's Bridge to Cathay."
     American Literature 16 (May):115-30.
        Although Crane embraced Whitman, the America of the 1920s
     was very different from the America of the nineteenth century.
     Whitman's transcentental faith allowed him to accept science.
     Crane had Whitman's urge to synthesize but was fearful of science.
     Crane thought Whitman had synthesized science and faith in his
     day and had announced a vision that transcended experience. Crane
     wanted to do this for his own time, but did not have the educa-
     tion or ideas for this endeavor. Ouspensky's work confused Crane
     and gave him the illusion of having found some kind of faith.
     While such works buoyed him superficially, his natural propensity
     to doubt was encouraged by Spengler's Decline of the West. "Thus
     Crane alternated between faith and doubt, both equally non-
     rational so far as he was concerned." His merits and defects are
     typical of the jazz age, although no poet has been so harmed by
     his environment. His principal faults are his obscurity and his
     "combined subjectivity and sentimentality." The chief cause of
     his obscurity is the example of the French symbolists. He found
     Ouspensky's "logic of ecstacy" a rationalization for his practice.
     The nihilism that results from looking steadily at chaos often
     leads to sentimentality. "He searched for, and sometimes seems
     to have found, God; but his poems record more of desire than
     discovery."

                              1945

1   CARTER, ELLIOTT. "'Voyage' (Hart Crane)." In A Musical Com-
     position for Voice and Piano. Mount Holyoke College, South
     Hadley, Mass.; Smith College, Northampton, Mass.: Valley
     Music Press.
        The composer provides a commentary on "Voyages III" to help
     the singer in forming his interpretation of the text. The poem
     has three protagonists: the sea, love, and the poet. The poet
     petitions love to allow him to go safely through an ordeal which
     will bring him under love's power. The sea is an obstacle to be
     voyaged through to reach love. Love seems to be both an actual
     person and a principle of power.

2   TATE, ALLEN, and CHENEY, FRANCIS. Sixty American Poets, 1896-
     1944. Washington, D.C.: Library of Congress, pp. 18-19.
        An incomplete list of works by and about Crane.

3   WAGGONER, HYATT H[OWE]. "Hart Crane and the Broken Parabola."
     University of Kansas Review 11 (Spring):173-77.
        Taking Whitman as his model, Crane set out to accomplish
     the most ambitious possible project--"synthesizing" America, but
     failed to achieve this goal. Crane had the poetic gifts to carry
     out his grand project; his failure lay not in technique or in
     sensibility but in doctrine. He had many intuitions about the

unity of science and faith, America's past and its future, but he
was unable to find a system which could make the intuitions meaningful. He was hurt especially by his reading of I.A. Richards
and P.D. Ouspensky. Richards's theory of poetry as emotive language reinforced a dangerous tendency already present in Crane.
And Ouspensky's emphasis on the logic of estacy was a further
dangerous and damaging conception. Crane was unable to see the
difference between the creative act itself and the finished poem.
This may be the cause of his obscurity. Finally, his philosophical inadequacy is revealed in the sentimentality into which he
was led by his persistent nihilism relieved fitfully by intui-
tional faith. "Though the prose paraphrase is not the poem, few
poems have ever lived for which some prose paraphrase, however
inadequate to express the total or even the essential meaning,
has not been possible. That Hart Crane did not know or was persuaded to disbelieve this is our loss."

4   WEBER, BROM. "Introduction for Prose Writings of Hart Crane."
     Twice a Year 12-13:424-52.
          Brief introduction to a reprinting of the reviews, letters,
     and articles of Crane that had not been readily available. Of
     special interest are the pieces written before Crane was twenty-
     five. They reveal the attitudes of his formative years which do
     not appear in his later poetry. Weber claims that the collection
     of eleven pieces comprises all of Crane's published prose works.
     These early prose pieces reveal that "Crane was not a sentimental
     or simple being, childlike in character, who lost his balance
     upon meeting with the world's harshness and brutality." The
     pieces printed are "The Case Against Nietzsche," "Joyce and
     Ethics," "The Ghetto and Other Poems by Lola Ridge," "Minna
     and Myself," "Sherwood Anderson," "A Note on Minns," "Eight More
     Harvard Poets," "A Discussion With Hart Crane," "From Haunts of
     Proserpine," and "Modern Poetry."

1946

1   FLETCHER, JOHN GOULD. "The Builders of the Bridge." In The
     Burning Mountain. New York: E.P. Dutton, pp. 88-91.
          Verse appreciation. See 1966.22.

2   HOFFMAN, FREDERICK J.; ALLEN, CHARLES; and ULRICH, CAROLYN F.
     The Little Magazine: A History and a Bibliography. Prince-
     ton, N.J.: Princeton University Press, passim.
          Incidental references to Crane, noting the appearance of
     his poems in little magazines.

3   KAZIN, ALFRED. "Brooklyn Bridge." Harper's Bazaar (Septem-
     ber):204-5, 296-97.
          History and description of Brooklyn Bridge. Mentions Crane
     and his poem.

4   McMANIS, JACK, and HOLDEN, HAROLD. "Poet from Oblivion."
     Mademoiselle 24, no. 1 (November):162-63, 265-70.
          Crane is mentioned as one who was influenced by Greenberg's
     poetry.

5   MILES, JOSEPHINE. Major Adjectives in English Poetry: From
     Wyatt to Auden. Berkeley and Los Angeles: University of
     California Press, pp. 318-21, 400-3, 406-7.
          Considers Crane's likenesses and differences to other poets
     in epithet tradition. Considers the proportion of adjective
     types, the stress on the active participle, the emphasis on sen-
     sory qualities, and the manufacturing of adjectives from nouns.
     Looks specifically at Crane's use of "white" as well as some
     other of his major adjectives. Crane shares the modern method of
     mixing the sensory and the conceptual for an evaluative effect
     with emphasis on the sensual.

6   STAUFFER, DONALD. The Nature of Poetry. New York: W.W.
     Norton, p. 48.
          Crane was experimental in the use of rhythm.

7   WALCUTT, CHARLES C. "Crane's 'Voyages.'" Explicator 4 (May):
     Item 53.
          "Voyages" is concerned with love, death, and eternity,
     mystically fused by the symbol of the sea. The most puzzling as-
     pect of "Voyages IV" is "its union of classical myth and Northern
     setting." Reads the poem in the light of the myth of Orion who
     was blinded by Oenopion of Chios for having ravished his daughter,
     Merope. Aided by Eos, goddess of the dawn, Orion goes to the
     seaside and recovers his sight when the rays of the rising sun
     strike his eyes.

                                 1947

1   BEACH, JOSEPH WARREN. "The Cancelling Out: A Note on Recent
     Poetry." Accent 7 (Summer):243-51.
          Is concerned with what he calls the strongest feature of
     contemporary poetry--"the rich complexity of its imaginative tex-
     ture." Jean Garrigue's "Dialogue for Belvedere" and Randall
     Jarrell's "Love in Its Separate Being" serve as examples for his
     thesis. When this complexity is carried to extremes and unmas-
     tered by a central poetic "idea," the result is the poetic failure
     one sees in Crane. His imagination was subject to "freakish
     association of ideas, together with a penchant for vocabulary
     traditionally associated with poetic effusiveness as in his poem
     addressed to Brooklyn Bridge." There are certain lines for which
     "no amount of imaginative readjustment will suffice to disentangle
     the snarled meanings." Beach modifies his judgement in part:
     "Still in Crane, one can generally apprehend somehow, through the
     violence and barbarity of figures and illusions, the substance of

the aesthetic experience which the poem aims at."

2   FRANK, WALDO. The Re-discovery of America. New York: Duell,
     Sloan, & Pearce, pp. 140, 141, 142.
         Incidental references to Crane. For a tragic artist in the
     twentieth century there remains only the apocolyptic method--
     "this direct recreation of a formal world from the stuff within
     us." This is seen in the dancing of Isadora Duncan, the sculpture
     of Gaston Lachaise, the paintings of Arthur Dove, the music of
     Leo Ornstein, and the mystical verse of Crane.

3   GREGORY, HORACE. "Robbed from Pain and Existence." New York
     Times Book Review, 20 July, p. 4.
         Crane is mentioned as being influenced by Greenberg.

4   HOLDEN, HAROLD, and McMANIS, JACK. Introduction to Poems by
     Samuel Greenberg. New York: Henry Holt & Co., p. xxi.
         Incidental reference. Crane's flow of language is not un-
     like Greenberg's. The editors refer to Horton's description of
     Crane's excitement upon first reading Greenberg's work at Mr.
     Fisher's house in Woodstock, New York in 1923. The Greenberg
     influence is seen particularly in "Emblems of Conduct" and
     "Voyages." See 1947.11.

5   LAUGHLIN, JAMES, ed. "The Greenberg Manuscripts." In Spear-
     head: Ten Years' Experimental Writing in America. New York:
     New Directions, pp. 150-71.
         Specific attention is paid to Crane's borrowing of lines,
     words, and ideas from Greenberg's works, mostly for Crane's
     "Emblems of Conduct."

6   LOVEMAN, SAMUEL. "Hart Crane." Bodley Bookshop Catalogue,
     no. 92, pp. 63-64.
         Although this is listed by both Rowe and Leary, I have been
     unable to discover a copy. It is supposed to contain Loveman's
     personal reminiscences of his friendship with Crane from 1919 to
     1932.

7   MATTHIESSEN, F.O. "American Poetry, 1920-1940." Sewanee Re-
     view 55 (January-March):24-55.
         Written for The Literary History of the United States; some
     references to Crane, notably the influence of T.S. Eliot on Crane.
     See 1953.18.

8   PEYRE, HENRI. "American Literature Through French Eyes."
     Virginia Quarterly Review 23 (Summer):421-38.
         Crane is cited as an example of tragic pessimism. Although
     known in France, his popularity is not great.

9   PUTNAM, SAMUEL. Paris Was Our Mistress. New York: Viking
     Press, pp. 25, 107, 111, 225, 238-39.

Crane is mentioned in passing, with particular emphasis upon the tragic character of his life in Paris.

10   RAMSEY, WARREN. "Poesia è platonismo." Inventario 1 (Fall-Winter):78-88.
     In Italian. To understand The Bridge is to understand Crane. In the poem, he attempts to make a mystic synthesis of America. In Ouspensky's Tertium Organum, Crane had learned that the aspirations of neo-Platonism were about to be realized through science. This may be the source of some of his exotic and indigenous symbolism. Tate's analysis of The Bridge is ultimately correct. Comments on "For the Marriage of Faustus and Helen," "Voyages," and other poems in White Buildings. In spite of everything, Crane was a religious man, a kind of Platonic mystic. He loved everything near him, and had concurred with Ouspensky that "love is the force which moves and guides creative activity." First article in a foreign publication.

11   TATE, ALLEN. Preface to Poems by Samuel Greenberg. Edited and introducted by Harold Holden and Jack McManis. New York: Henry Holt & Co., p. xiii.
     Records that Crane grew to dislike "Emblems of Conduct" because so much of it had been borrowed from Greenberg and that he wanted to leave it out of White Buildings, but Cowley and Tate persuaded him to include it. See 1947.4.

12   TAYLOR, FRAJAN. "Keats and Crane: An Airy Citadel." Accent 8 (Fall):34-40.
     Crane was attracted to the concept of the generative power of extrasensual love which he had discovered in Ouspensky's Tertium Organum. This idea is also found in Keats's "Endymion." Besides sharing a belief in the power of this sort of love, Crane and Keats were both romantics, both indebted to the Elizabethans, both died young in tragic deaths, and both had written ambitious poems successful only in part. There is a striking difference: Keats had a sense of "Negative Capability," while Crane admitted his inability to heed the negative. Taylor illustrates this by comparing "The Wine Menagerie" with "Ode to a Nightingale." Both poems have the same theme, a desire for renewal and escape from the burden of identity. The two poems are superb examples of Nietzsche's description of the Apollonian poet and the Dionysian poet.

13   WINTERS, YVOR. "The Significance of The Bridge by Hart Crane, or What Are We to Think of Professor X?" In In Defense of Reason. New York: Swallow Press, William Morrow, pp. 575-603.
     In speaking of the significance of The Bridge, Winters is talking about its content and its moral. The first question dealt with is "What is The Bridge about?" Most of Crane's thought was derived from Emerson, "or could easily have been."

We see in Emerson and Whitman the glorification of change for its
own sake and this is one of the most important ideas of The
Bridge. After this preliminary lengthy analysis, Winters mentions his friendship with Crane, concluding that the doctrines of
Emerson and Whitman if really put into practice would naturally
lead to suicide. The Bridge is a poem which endeavors to deal in
some measure with the relationship of the individual American to
his country and to God, and "with the religious significance of
America itself." The two climaxes of the poem are "The Dance"
and "Atlantis." "The Bridge is a loosely joined sequence of
lyrics, and some of the individual pieces have only a tenuous
connection with the principal themes." The "Proem" is itself a
bridge joining past and present, present and future, life and
death, the old world and the new. Because of Crane's absolute
seriousness, Winters describes him as "a saint of the wrong
religion." Although he had the courage of his convictions and
the virtue of integrity, he did not have the critical intelligence
to see what was wrong with his doctrine. Reprinted: 1959.21.

1948

1   ALLEN, CHARLES. "The Advance Guard." Sewanee Review 51
    (Summer):410-29.
         Principally concerned with the little magazines and their
    influence since 1912. Crane's work appeared in a number of these
    magazines.

2   ANON. "Life of an Unhappy Poet." Time 51 (22 March):102-5.
         Review of Weber's Hart Crane. Crane's fame rests not so
    much on his work as on his becoming a classic example of the
    frustrated American genius. "The legend of life--the misunder-
    stood poet throwing away his gifts and at last his life in a
    gesture of futile defiance--is less an intellectual tragedy than
    a sort of Greenwich Village Uncle Tom's Cabin." Weber's book is
    highly praised, not only because it includes new material made
    available by Crane's mother, but because Weber is lucid, level-
    headed, and candid. See 1948.21.

3   BISHOP, JOHN PEALE. The Collected Essays of John Peale
    Bishop. Edited by Edmund Wilson. New York: Charles
    Scribner's Sons, pp. 127-28, 131-32.
         Crane is mentioned at the end of the essay, "The Myth and
    Modern Literature." Along with Thomas Wolfe, Crane is regarded
    as one of the most conspicuous failures in American letters.
    Both wanted to write about the greatness of America, the world of
    the machine and its promises of progress. The bridge became for
    Crane a symbol of man's undaunted desire, but his faith in it was
    arbitrarily enforced. When the myth of the greatness of America
    failed him, he attempted to make myths of his own. "And that, I
    am inclined to think, is something no one man can do. Crane

failed." This essay appeared originally in the <u>Saturday Review</u> <u>of Literature</u> for 22 July 1939. The second mention of Crane occurs in "The Sorrows of Thomas Wolfe." Again, Crane and Wolfe are linked together as artists. Both were geniuses who felt they must celebrate the greatness of their country. Wolfe, like Crane, was unable to give coherence to his work, and found, like Crane before him, that the America he longed to celebrate did not exist. See 1939.2-3.

4   DEUTSCH, BABETTE. "Poet of a Mystical Atlantis." New York Herald Tribune Books, 2 May, p. 3.
        Review of Weber's <u>Hart Crane</u>. <u>The Bridge</u> is generally recognized as a superb failure. Crane was a religious poet in an irreligious age. His American antecedents are Whitman, Poe, and Dickinson. It is unfortunate that <u>The Bridge</u> was not strong enough to bear the weight which Crane wanted to give it, nor were Crane's powers sufficient to the task he had set for himself. The disorder in the world around him prevented him from having more than fragmentary glimpses of his vision. Perhaps his greatest problem was the extreme confusion of his own inner world. Weber is not able to deal coherently with Crane's failure. His study is valuable chiefly for the new materials it includes, especially the hitherto unpublished verse of Crane, and some of his work sheets. See 1948.21.

5   F., L. "Hart Crane." <u>Antioch Review</u> 8:246-48.
        Review of Weber's <u>Hart Crane</u>. One of the intellectual dif-ficulties of our time has been the wall separating the reader from the poet. Poets have been partially responsible for this wall and even ridiculous on occasion; we have come to expect them to be incomprehensible. Crane is a particularly interesting example of this tendency because of the great respect in which he has been held by a wide variety of critics, despite the fact that so little illumination has been shed upon what he is saying or trying to say. Crane has been fortunate in having Horton writing about him. Weber, too, writes from deep knowledge and interest, presenting some fresh material. The trouble is not in what Weber tells us, but in what he does not tell us or trouble to learn about. He speculates about what Crane meant to do, and should have attempted to do, but the meaning of Crane's approach to America remains cloudy or uninvestigated. If Crane is the major poetic talent Weber insists he is, why don't his poems speak to us? See 1948.21.

6   FERRIL, THOMAS HORNSBY. Review of <u>Hart Crane</u> by Brom Weber. San Francisco Chronicle, 13 June, p. 18.
        A generally complimentary brief review, although Weber is faulted for trying to place Crane among those poets who will en-dure. See 1948.21.

7   FYELDE, ROLF. "<u>Hart Crane</u> by Brom Weber." <u>Yale Poetry Review</u>

8:34-36.

Since Crane's suicide, the reputation and influence of his poetry has grown remarkably, beyond the extent that critical attention would seem to indicate. Crane's strongly marked style can be successfully reproduced in its outlines by lesser poets. "It is easier to write bad Crane than bad Pound." But the major factor in the growth of his influence is the drama of his life-- a life of tragic economy and inevitability that is symbolic of the major contradiction of our time, critical hope and paralyzing despair. It is difficult to estimate his ultimate significance because he is too near us. Weber has, however, written a highly conscious book that is sound and responsible in its judgment. Although frequently not well written, it is a better book than Horton's for a study of the poetry. See 1948.21.

8   HONIG, EDWIN. "Review." New Mexico Quarterly 18:370-71.
      Review of Weber's Hart Crane. Calls it an ambitious book which will undoubtedly become the standard guide to the life and work of the poet, although it is poorly organized and somewhat illogically chaptered. Its most notable deficiency is its defensive tone. The critical section is more unified and illuminating than the biographical section. See 1948.21.

9   MEYER, GERARD PREVIN. "Poète Maudit." Saturday Review 31 (24 April):26.
      Review of Weber's Hart Crane. Because the book is a mixture of criticism and biography it is neither a full-scale biography "nor as sensitive a critical study" as Crane deserves. The principal fault is an insensitivity to language which makes his value judgments of Crane's poetry somewhat questionable. See 1948.21.

10   O'CONNOR, WILLIAM VAN. "The Influence of the Metaphysicals on Modern Poetry." College English 9 (January):180-87.
      Crane's description of the sea as "this great wink of eternity" is cited as a modern instance of a metaphysical conceit.

11   _____. "The Employment of Myths." In Sense and Sensibility in Modern Poetry. Chicago: University of Chicago Press, pp. 18-25 and passim.
      A peculiar modern problem is the effect of the confusion of belief upon poets committed to long poems. Some aspects of the problem can be seen in contrasting the method of Eliot with that of Crane. Eliot's symbols support his myth, The Waste Land as symbol being the true center of his poem. Crane's bridge is not. Crane's apparent theme finds readier acceptance than Eliot's; however, Crane's inability to find a moral focus, in Tate's terms, is paradoxical proof of the major contention of Eliot's poem. "The confusion in the structure of The Bridge is ultimately derived from Crane's inability to examine his world in terms of a defined set of values and to accept the consequences." The theme

53

of the poem demands that the machine be our salvation; however, all the evidence Crane presents substantiates the fact of the opposition of the person to the age of the machine. Although Crane comes closest to stating his view of what can save those in the demonic city in "Cape Hatteras," he is not able to specify the idea or ideal he has in mind. Whitman's version is not enough. The defect of The Bridge is not only in the formulation of its symbols, but in the fact that the parts do not live within the life of the major symbol. The bridge would have been a better symbol for the medieval world than it is for ours. Men cannot will themselves a significant myth; the symbols that really matter are not chosen, they are given. Instinctively, Crane was a mythic poet but his culture did not afford him a large and unifying belief. Hence, he did not create the poem he was, in a sense, meant to create. See 1948.12.

*12   _____. "Sense and Sensibility in Modern Poetry." Ph.D. dissertation, University of Chicago.
     See 1948.11.

13   PEYRE, HENRI. "Hart Crane's Poems." New York Times Book Review, 4 April, pp. 4, 26.
     Review of Weber's Hart Crane. "Hart Crane may well remain as the greatest poet produced by America since Walt Whitman and Emily Dickinson." Weber's book is a distinguished piece of literary criticism. Steering clear of blind adoration and not repeating too much of Horton, Weber's main concern is wisely with the poems themselves. See 1948.21.

14   RAGO, HENRY. "Review." Commonweal 48 (16 April):638-39.
     Review of Weber's Hart Crane, described as no considerable addition to what we already know about Crane because the intentions of the study are unclear. Crane's psychological problems are simply blurred, and so is Weber's reading of the poetry. His analysis of The Bridge "is fairly consistent, but consistently pedestrian." See 1948.21.

15   ROSKELSKO, HARRY. "Atlantis--Hold Thy Floating Singer Late!" Voices: A Quarterly of Poetry 134 (Summer):62-63.
     Review of Brom Weber's Hart Crane, an important book about an important poet; it is scholarly, keen, and contains much new information. See 1948.21.

16.   SCHWARTZ, DELMORE. "Raw Genius, Self-delusion, and Incantation." Partisan Review 15 (October):1135-36.
     Review of Weber's Hart Crane, praising it as a collection of materials for the study of Crane, but marred by poor writing, poor thinking, and an inadequate knowledge of other kinds of poetry. In Crane we are dealing with a poet who simply misuses words. The dominant tendency, however, of his work is to achieve a kind of "hallucination of meaning" produced by the misuse of

words. Crane is not obscure in the sense that most good modern
poetry is obscure. In going beyond any meaningful statement, he
hopes that "the very concussion of false meanings" will produce
the proper emotion of exaltation. This may be the result of his
ignorance, but it is also the result of an infatuation with language and a mastery of versification, and the true possession of
such emotions as exaltation. His complicated feeling for the
connotations of words makes this poetry of incantation possible.
Crane's poetry can be compared to music, if one keeps in mind
that it is not the sound of the words so much as the associations
of meanings which the words evoke that justify a musical comparison. "This kind of poetry is an extreme made possible by raw
genius, ignorance, and self-delusion. Ignorance and self-delusion alone would not have sufficed, of course. But if this were
the only kind of poetry, most poetry would not be worth reading."
See 1948.21.

17   SHAPIRO, KARL. "The Meaning of the Discarded Poem." In Poets
      at Work. Edited by Rudolph Arnheim. New York: Harcourt,
      Brace & Co., pp. 111-18.
         Crane seems to have been a poet possessed by a demon.
      Among his poetic ancestors--Poe, Baudelaire, Rimbaud, and
      Whitman--Whitman "presented him with a false vision of life which
      eventually Crane was to employ for his own self-destruction."
      When the myth inherited from Whitman disintegrated, the disap-
      pointment was too great to live with. By the time he came to
      the composition of "Cape Hatteras," he already knew the futility
      of his effort. Hence, this is the weakest section of the poem.
      The "hymn to Whitman . . . threatens to poison the whole work."
      Shapiro compares the final version of the poem with the work
      sheet manuscript owned by Peter Blume. Crane does not succeed in
      assimilating the machine imagery into his poetry. The sentimen-
      tal conclusion of "Cape Hatteras" is the defeated cry of a
      "demonic poet" who has lost his way, not the cry of a man who has
      lost his gift, "which was the weak construction Crane chose to
      put upon his dilemma." Reprinted: 1970.6.

18   SPILLER, ROBERT E. et al., eds. Literary History of the
      United States. New York: Macmillan Co., pp. 1344-45, 1387.
         See 1953.18; 1963.20.

19   TATE, ALLEN. On the Limits of Poetry. New York: Swallow
      Press.
         See Reactionary Essays (1936.9).

20   WAGGONER, HYATT HOWE. "Review." American Literature 20
      (November):345-47.
         Review of Weber's Hart Crane. The value of the book is in
      the last 150 pages, Weber's explication of The Bridge, and the
      appendix. The rest of the book is thin and perfunctory. It is
      worth little as biography and is not impressive as criticism

aside from the section on The Bridge. This may be because Weber
is uneasy when handling ideas. See 1948.21.

21   WEBER, BROM. Hart Crane: A Biographical and Critical Study.
      New York: Bodley Press, 452 pp.
         Both biography and criticism, because Weber feels that one
      cannot be separated from the other if we are to understand either.
      Appearing some years later than Horton's book, it was not as much
      under the influence of Mrs. Grace Hart Crane. (Weber has since
      discovered that the appendix listing uncollected poetry is no
      longer accurate because he used a faulty typescript.) Deals with
      Crane's poetry in the order in which it was composed, but does
      not deal with the poetry written after The Bridge. It is less a
      biography than Horton's work, but more a critical study. Weber
      pays attention to the people who were a strong influence on
      Crane, such as Ouspensky and Frank. Reviewed in 1948.2, 4-9, 13-
      16, 20, 22; 1949.1, 3; 1970.42. Reprinted: 1970.42.

22   WEST, RAY B., Jr. "Portrait of the Artist as American."
      Western Review 12 (Summer):247-51.
         Review of Brom Weber's Hart Crane, more concerned with
      Crane's poetry than with his life. Weber does not, however,
      recognize completely the symbolic nature of Crane's life, a qual-
      ity which Tate observed and called attention to. Weber agrees
      with Winters and Tate that Crane's major works were, on the whole,
      failures, though containing excellences of technique and sensi-
      bility. West emphasizes Crane's need to affirm, which was
      stronger than his own disgust with the Philistine life of the
      twenties. Crane knew that "to accept the material world was as
      dangerous as death, yet he never seemed to have lost the hope
      that it could be accomplished with honor." See 1948.21.

                                   1949

1   FRANK, JOSEPH. "Hart Crane: American Poet." Sewanee Review
      57:152-59.
         Review of Weber's Hart Crane, an indispensible book for
      students of Crane's work. Applauds Weber's point that Crane's
      development was determined by the contrasting literary attitudes
      associated with T.S. Eliot and Sherwood Anderson—the major
      literary influences on Crane. Frank quarrels with Weber's inter-
      pretation of "Faustus and Helen." He also questions the reasons
      for Weber's judgment that The Bridge is a failure, albeit a
      superb one: "he is proving merely that Crane was not a scientific
      historian, but he does not thereby prove that this lack of knowl-
      edge has anything to do with the poetic failure of The Bridge."
      See 1948.21.

2   GHISELIN, BREWSTER. "Bridge into the Sea." Partisan Review
      16 (July):679-86.

"The River" is the major achievement of The Bridge. The
hoboes, although referred to by Crane as "blind fists of nothing,"
are significant because they are, like other figures in the poem,
pioneers. Columbus as the first pioneer opened the way to a new
continent; Crane tried to discover a new Cathay. The hoboes find
their significance in that they lead the reader across space and
time into the legendary depths of the American continent. Crane's
encounter with the chaos of the sea is the most compelling theme
of The Bridge, because it reveals the theme of order that has
been destroyed. Most of what seems confusing in The Bridge is
clarified if the reader understands the "consequence of the
vacillation produced by Crane's central longing and revulsion"
for the sea. Basically, the author offers a Freudian explication
of The Bridge, seen partly in the light of Crane's inversion.
Ultimately in The Bridge the poet was unable to find fulfillment
in "death by water." The Orizaba became finally "his bridge into
the sea." "What he could not do directly and fully as an artist,
he did in his symbolic death: he found his way to the waters.
But it was an imperfect attainment." Reprinted: 1970.6.

3   GLIXON, NIEL. "The Education of Hart Crane." Kenyon Review
    11, no. 11 (Winter):152-55.
        Review of Brom Weber's Hart Crane. Praised for the material
    assembled and the sometimes excellent exegesis of individual
    poems. The book is finally "sloppy," because of its disorganized
    overall structure. See 1948.21.

4   GRAVES, ROBERT. The Common Asphodel. London: Hamilton, pp.
    78-79.
        Brief mention of "Passage," with a technical analysis of
    the opening lines. "Strangely enough, when we come upon an ex-
    ample of free verse which shows clarity, restraint, and propor-
    tion, we do not think of it as free verse, though on the other
    hand we do not think of it as poetry of a traditional form. And
    this is as it should be."

5   HEATH-STUBBS, JOHN. "Hart Crane." In The Charity of the
    Stars. New York: William Sloane, p. 71.
        Verse appreciation.

6   HOFFMAN, FREDERICK J. "The Technological Fallacy in Contem-
    porary Poetry: Hart Crane and MacKnight Black." American
    Literature 21:94-107.
        When they were conscious of "the machine" at all, the
    writers of the twenties saw it either as a perfect and concrete
    demonstration of the ingenuity of man or as the final symbol of
    the evil which science had created. Poems which attempted to
    realize the machine in poetic terms failed because they remade
    the machine "into an object directly available to human emotions."
    Crane felt that the poet needed to absorb the machine in order to
    "acclimatize it as naturally and casually as trees, cattle,

galleons, castles, and all other human associations of the past."
The poet can write about the machine only if he refuses to con-
sider it as "merely an efficient and abstract modus operandi of
the intellect, by endowing it with the very qualities which in its
construction were most conscientiously omitted, or by speaking of
it only in terms of its effect upon human experience." The technological fallacy is "a failure of emotional grasp of the meaning
implicit in a machine's purpose in nature." In attempting to
present an imaginative record of America in The Bridge, Crane
felt he had to include the facts of the machine world and its
effects upon the human consciousness. The structure of the poem
failed because he was unable to organize the historical and
spatial facts of his subject around the few symbols he selected.

7   MILLET, FREDERICK B. Contemporary American Authors: A Crit-
     ical Survey and 219 Bio-bibliographies. New York: Harcourt,
     Brace & Co., pp. 305-6.
        Reprint of 1940.5.

8   REXROTH, KENNETH. The New British Poets. Norfolk, Conn.:
     New Directions, pp. xviii-xix.
        Brief references to Crane's influence on Dylan Thomas.

9   RUKEYSER, MURIEL. The Life of Poetry. New York: A.A. Wyn,
     pp. 183-85.
        Brief explication of the images in "The Broken Tower."

10   SHOCKLEY, MARTIN STAPLES. "Hart Crane's 'Lachrymae Christi.'"
     University of Kansas City Review 16 (Autumn):31-36.
        Crane's famous obscurity may be explained in that he
     attached more importance to intense feeling than he did to logical
     thought, conceiving of language (under the influence of Richards
     and Ouspensky) as evocative symbolism. Granting this, Shockley
     attempts to show that "Lachrymae Christi" is an intelligible poem
     and that it has "some merit" beyond mere intelligibility.
     Shockley's critical method is prose paraphrase, very difficult to
     apply to many of Crane's poems. Christ and Dionysius are brought
     together as images of resurrection and used interchangeably to
     indicate "that life though constantly sacrificed is constantly
     renewed." The identification shows that Crane considered his
     theme universal, not merely Christian. The "smile" in the last
     line survives everything. The poem gives us a body of ideas con-
     cerned with the beauty of the world, the identity of man with
     nature, the universality of human suffering and human sympathy,
     the transcendent and eternal quality of love and life above suf-
     fering and beyond death—all symbolized in the tears of Christ.

11   SWALLOW, ALLAN. "Hart Crane." The University of Kansas City
     Review 16 (Winter):103-18.
        "Self-destruction ended the greatest poetic talent ever
     seen in America." Crane's influence has been second only to that

of Eliot. Crane is an excellent example of a poet who inherited
a society so shoddy and chaotic that it could not nourish his
artistic talent. He inherited as well "a group of shoddy ideas
about poetry and art" which made it difficult for him to throw
off the shackles of his society. He was subject to the influences of the sophisticated Eliot group who were influenced by the
metaphysical poets and French symbolists, and the indigenous
American group that traced its ancestry to Emerson, Whitman, and
Melville. Of all the poets at that time, he attempted most and
achieved a synthesis of the two groups. Crane explored the ideas
coming out of these two groups more fully than any other poet with
the exception of Pound. "What is the result? Pound is now in a
mental institution, and Crane destroyed himself, the forces of
these ideas were sufficient to destroy him." The three efforts
in modern times to write major poems in English (Cantos, The
Waste Land, and The Bridge) reveal three very faulty poems. The
Bridge was conceived as Crane's effort to play the role of
Whitman. He intended to write a poem about the spirit of America,
but he needed a myth in order to do this and "thereby lay one of
his troubles." Since a myth is never created by the assertion of
the poet's will, the bridge remains a symbol, not a myth of America's development. Reprinted: 1962.19; 1967.35.

12   VIERECK, PETER. "The Poet in the Machine Age." Journal of
     the History of Ideas 10 (January):88-103.
          See 1950.8.

13   WILBUR, RICHARD. "Between Visits." Poetry: A Magazine of
     Verse 74, no. 2 (May):115.
          Brief reference to Crane's ability to write well even when
his mind was in a state of chaos.

<u>1950</u>

1   BERGLER, EDMOND. The Writer and Psychoanalysis. Garden City,
    N.Y.: Doubleday & Co., pp. 108-12.
         Psychological interpretation of Crane. Writing, alcoholism,
homosexuality "cope from different angles with the same oral conflict." Bases his analysis on Horton's life. Feels that Crane
saw his mother as the cause of his problems. His drunkenness was
one of his "oral tendencies" and could not be separated from his
"masochistic ones."

2   BROOKS, CLEANTH, and WARREN, ROBERT PENN. Understanding
    Poetry, 2d ed. New York: Henry Holt & Co., pp. 332-36.
         "At Melville's Tomb" is included in this anthology (with
three other poems by Crane) along with most of the correspondence
between Harriet Monroe and Crane. The editors' comment on the
correspondence and the poem is of interest, particularly with
reference to the rather common student question: "But the poet

couldn't have been thinking of all this when he wrote the poem."

3   FOWLIE, WALLACE. "Rimbaud et Hart Crane." Arts e Lettres
     17:5-13.
         Reprint of 1943.2.

4   HERMAN, BARBARA. "The Language of Hart Crane." Sewanee Re-
     view 58 (January-March):52-67.
         Takes up Allen Tate's charge that someone should set about
     isolating the principle upon which Crane's poetry is organized.
     The principle is Crane's attitude towards words--words as meta-
     physical entities and as craftsman's materials. Crane's language
     was his philosophy. He was both an absolutist, who sought some
     kind of mystic vision, and a pantheist who wanted reassurance of
     an absolute and permanent reality behind a chaotic world of
     appearances. To objectify his mysticism, he sought the Word.
     Because he had no religion, he found this to be little more than
     "a verbal concept." Thus he sought, as well, "a vague apotheosis
     of the national ethos," the values discovered by Waldo Frank and
     Gorham Munson, the American mystic group. In language, the ob-
     ject and the work could be combined, since it is the instrument
     by which heterogeneous experience can be selected and ordered
     into a coherent whole. It is the very vehicle through which "the
     magic properties of the artist's material" can be managed. Words
     were to Crane what geometric form was to the abstract artist.
     The need to manipulate them as if they had fixed values in them-
     selves arose from his desire for some kind of stable order. In
     Crane's own language, images which are ordinarily not associated
     can be joined "in the circuit of a particular emotion located
     with specific relation to both of them," bringing great vividness
     and accuracy of statement in defining a particular emotion. His
     principles were two: first, distortion or syntactical displace-
     ment, and second, the packing of meanings by juxtaposition,
     either through compression or contiguity. "His chief method may
     be termed crosshatching of reference."

5   HEWITT, JAMES ROBERT. "Rimbaud and Hart Crane: A Comparative
     Essay." ID (Paris) 1:60-71.
         Examines the general similarities in the work of the two
     poets, finding them alike in that "both sought to destroy the
     conventional idioms and ideologies, and their instructive work
     entailed reconstruction of values, esthetic, moral and metaphysi-
     cal." Both were creators of myth, but Rimbaud's myth was more
     cosmic.

6   RAMSEY, WARREN. "Crane and Laforgue." Sewanee Review 58
     (July-September):439-49.
         Noticing a rude but healthy irony in some of the poetry
     written after April 1921, Ramsey notes that this poetry was
     written after Crane had ordered and received from Paris the works
     of Laforgue. The Laforguian quality could also have come to

Crane by way of Eliot's poems in 1917. Although there are fundamental dissimilarities between the two poets, it must be noted
that Crane liked Laforgue's poetry, that he imitated him, and
that he translated him during the decisive years in which his own
style was being formed. Three of Laforgue's poems--"Locutions de
Pierrot"--were translated by Crane in 1921 and published in the
Double Dealer in May 1922. Under the impact of Laforgue and
Chaplin's The Kid, Crane wrote "Chaplinesque." The influence of
Laforgue is also seen in "For the Marriage of Faustus and Helen."
In it Crane is looking for something which Laforgue had given
up--"a point of view which can only be described as religious."
Beginning with "Faustus and Helen" Crane's poetry moved toward a
structure and style radically different from that of Laforgue.
See 1953.16.

7   SOUTHWORTH, JAMES G. "Hart Crane (1899-1932)." In Some
    Modern American Poets. Oxford: Basil Blackwell, pp. 159-75.
        Since maturity was impossible for Crane, he became a poet
of a single short theme--"the search for security." The facts of
his tortured life explain the immeasurable waste of talent "by
one of the most richly endowed of American poets." He was, however, a careful craftsman. Most of his obscurities are resolved
by a second or third reading. Since he felt that love and mercy
issued from the experience of pain, it is evident that "he de-
rived a degree of sensuous ecstacy" from the experience of pain.
Southworth sees a curious connection between his need for security
and the fact that he is identified as a mystic. The search for
love and unity (to overcome his insecurity) is the major note of
his poetry. Many critics have complained that Crane did not know
enough; this is not the problem. He was incapable of the discipline that leads to knowledge, because he preferred to plunge
himself into experience. His great error was that he mistook
sensation for experience. Continual submission to his emotions
was disastrous. The problems in Crane's poetry are his concern
with form, which he sometimes confused with mere outline, his
rhetoric, and his imagery. His greatest failures were caused by
"his lack of ability to sustain an intellectual discipline." The
Bridge is the chief illustration of his virtues and his defects.

8   VIERECK, PETER. Strike Through the Mask. New York: Charles
    Scribner's Sons, pp. 66-70.
        The most exciting promechanist among poets was Crane, who
rightly called himself "the Pindar of the Machine Age." The
Bridge is an extraordinary example of the impact of mechanization.
Viereck contrasts Brooklyn Bridge and the New York subway as two
motifs of Crane's poem. At times the poem treats machinery as
"the third hand of man," but at times it seems that man is but
another appendage of machinery. The figure of Poe in the subway
symbolizes the lover of beauty who is trapped in the urban
jungle of steel. One must understand, however, that the subway
supplies the modern means to our new goal--whatever it is the

bridge symbolizes. There is "irrefutable good sense" in certain
of Crane's comments in 1929 on the function of art in a machine
age. The reflections that interest Viereck are those which deal
with acclimatizing the machine naturally into poetry. See
1949.12.

9   WAGGONER, HYATT H[owe]. "Hart Crane: Beyond All Sesames of
     Science." In The Heel of Elohim: Science and Values in
     Modern American Poetry. Norman: University of Oklahoma
     Press, pp. 155-92.
        Contains much of the material included in his 1944 and
1945 articles; there is, however, considerable elaboration and
some changes. "I myself have added to the extensive literature
analyzing Crane's failure in two essays which I have come partially to regret, though most of their content still seems to me
true." Crane's glorious attempt was a failure because his myth
could not be crystallized into a significant form. His effort,
however, resulted in some of the finest poetry of the century.
It is difficult to be specific about Crane's ideas, because his
ideas were not much more stable than his emotions. A few things
about The Bridge, however, are clear. Crane's bridge was meant
to join mystical and historical America in a synthesis. "Cape
Hatteras" is the key to the meaning of the poem. Crane's education and temperament made it unlikely that he would be able to
forge a new myth synthesizing America's past and present, "fact
and ideal, science and religion, man and God." Crane needed the
influence of Ouspensky and Richards in approaching the composition of the poem. While "Modern Poetry" is confusing, a knowledge
of its chief ideas are a necessary preliminary for analyzing the
failure of The Bridge as myth. The confusions in the essay, as
well as the difficulties in the poem, can be explained in part by
the influence of Richards, Eliot, Ouspensky, and Whitman. The
bridge moves as a symbol "from concrete to abstract, from physical to spiritual, from limited to infinite suggestiveness." "The
myth has not been enunciated, it has been hinted at, glimpsed,
promised. Strictly speaking, the poem itself has not been
achieved." The central concept of love in the poem is not love
in any sense of the word caritas. "It is not a Christian poem."
The Bridge is not a single poem; it is a group of poems on various
aspects of a single theme.

                              1951

1   BOGAN, LOUISE. "Ideology and Irrationalism, 1930-51." In
     Achievement in American Poetry, 1900-1950. Chicago: Henry
     Regnery, pp. 82-86.
        Crane was the first important talent in America "to be
drawn into a close relationship with the operation of idealistic
materialism," but his poetry in no way reflects Marxian dogma.
He did try, however, to absorb the machine into his poetry and to

find symbols in our urban and mechanized society. The Bridge was his major attempt to create "an essentially religious myth from the facts of modern man's soaring technical triumphs." Although this myth was originally intended to be loaded with hope for the future, Crane's symbol broke down because his faith in his inadequate vision was never steady. It contains flashes of poetic insight, but a good deal of the poem is inflated with romantic rhetoric. Crane's real success was in his short lyrics, especially in those dealing with primitive surroundings. Crane, in spite of the tone of some parts of The Bridge is primarily a poet of "acceptance and celebration." Unlike Rimbaud, he never fully explored his anguish and thus was not able to pass beyond it.

2   CAMPBELL, ROY. Light on a Dark Horse. London: Hollis & Carter, pp. 311-12.
        "The famous American poet, Hart Crane, came to visit us, too. He was an extraordinary, tragic creature, who appeared in those classical surroundings [Marseilles and environs] like a mad howling dervish, always weeping, or exalted beyond himself. He could neither hold his drink nor control his abnormal, 'queer' nymphomania: he made himself a public laughingstock everywhere among the sailors and fishermen, by making advances to them, so that we had to send him away. He was charming when sober, which was seldom: he read his wonderful poems like an angel, and we were very fond of him, but he needed a keeper. He had only one religion, the Almighty power of the U.S.A.--he believed in Whitman's vision of it, altogether. When drunk, this puny, flat-footed fellow would boast for hours about how with seventy American marines he could conquer Europe. I think the realization of the slump must have broken his heart and contributed to his ultimate suicide."

3   COFFMAN, STANLEY K., Jr. Imagism. Norman: University of Oklahoma Press, p. 224.
        One mention of Crane as removed from the immediate sphere of imagism. Although two or three of his early poems clearly follow imagist models, The Bridge has a style which would make it pointless to trace imagist technique in it.

4   _____. "Symbolism in The Bridge." PMLA 66 (March):65-77.
        Significant article in which The Bridge is examined in light of Ezra Pound's definition of the image: "that which presents an intellectual and emotional complex in an instant of time." The language of the poem, however, as it creates, in Crane's terminology, "a new word, never before spoken and impossible to actually enunciate," has never been adequately examined. The Bridge as an object was meant to reproduce all of the qualities of experiencing the belief which the object symbolized. The poem dominated by this symbol was to have become a metaphor translating the poet's consciousness of this belief. One pattern of language that conveys the poet's exhiliration grows

from Crane's mysticism, seeing the bridge as vaulting the sea, leaping, striding, straddling, spanning. "He abstracts, then, from the bridge properties of motion (implicit) and of configuration." The uses of motion evoke with some directness the feelings which accompany the function of the symbol. The more one penetrates into the use of the symbol and its properties of motion, the more one understands how deeply indebted to Whitman Crane was. Coffman discusses the images of light and whiteness in the poem, noting that the light of The Bridge is predominantly the light of dawn. The color is seen in man's world as well as in nature's world. Light as color seems to be used in two ways in the poem: as cool or chill whiteness and as fire. "The effort of The Bridge is to express the conquest of space and time, which is accomplished symbolically in 'The Dance,' and show the common source of the two kinds of light, sanctified white and earthly red, to go beyond the materialistic half-truth of the hoboes who simply attribute change and destruction to 'fire and snow.'" The bridge is a symbol not in a conventional sense, but conceived of as the French symbolists did, with correspondences worked out between the object and other phenomena in the natural or civilized world, and between the object and the state of consciousness of the poet. A third kind of imagery is especially dominant in "Atlantis"--music, fusing the other patterns and giving them intensity. Reprinted: 1970.6.

5   COWLEY, MALCOLM. Exile's Return: A Literary Odyssey of the
     1920's. New York: Viking Press, pp. 227-34.
          Reprint of 1934.2. See 1958.9.

6   _____. "Twenty-five Years After: The Lost Generation Today."
     Saturday Review of Literature 34 (2 June):7-8, 33-34.
          Crane is mentioned but once in this biographical survey.
     The fates of Crane and Fitzgerald appear alike in that both
     writers were deeply involved in the frenzy of the boom years with
     the result that the economic collapse also meant the end of their
     careers.

7   ELATH, M. "In Another Direction." Intro (Winter), pp. 112-
     34.
          A response to the New Criticism; mentions Crane when
     attacking Allen Tate. Crane tried to find integration in the
     "by-products of early 4th dimensional specualtion." The Bridge
     was prophetic; "anyone who says [it] fails shows the sensibilities
     of a horseman."

8   FITZELL, LINCOLN. "The Sword and the Dragon." South Atlantic
     Quarterly 50 (April):214-32.
          Crane's central vision is of the will that made the imagi-
     nation an intense organ with which to feel as well as perceive.
     "Always available to Crane in his moments of best creation was
     the right word complementary to the grand as well as to the

homely vision."

9   FRIAR, KIMON, and BRINININ, JOHN MALCOLM, eds. Modern Poetry:
     American and British. New York: Appleton-Century-Crofts,
     pp. 427-28, 449-56.
          The notes on Crane in this anthology are worth looking at.
     "The Broken Tower" is interpreted as the poet's need to build a
     spiritual tower, healed and pure, which may plumb the womb of the
     heart and purify the poet's vision. In "O Carib Isle!" the con-
     trast between death and fertility is essential. There are notes
     on "To Brooklyn Bridge," "Ave Maria," "The Harbor Dawn," and
     "Atlantis." "Voyages" invokes the sea as the womb and tomb of
     life, as the source and end of love and passion, as an eternal
     imperturbability in which man finds his visions, yet in which he
     is wrecked and drowned.

10   ISSACS, J. The Background of Modern Poetry. London: G. Bell
     & Sons, pp. 80-83.
          "At Melville's Tomb" and a portion of Crane's letter about
     the poem to Harriet Monroe. He offers the poem not because it is
     one of the best, but because of what Crane says about it. "I
     wish this kind of comment were more accessible in this country.
     We want more inside information, even if the poet sometimes
     proves that our guess is as good as his. It frequently should be
     as good, if the right kind of communication has been established.
     It can only be better than his when the poem has had time to
     reverberate in the civilisation of which it is one of the roots
     as well as one of the flowers. It is the poet who must tell us
     the direction in which he is going, and the more signposts on the
     road the more grateful we are."

11   QUINN, ARTHUR HOBSON, ed. The Literature of the American
     People. New York: Appleton-Century-Crofts, pp. 861, 968-69,
     974.
          Three very general paragraphs on Crane, quite conventional
     in the points which they make: his obscurity, the dissipation of
     his private life, and his failure to provide a structure for his
     poetry.

12   QUINN, Sister M. BERNETTA. "The Poetics of Hart Crane."
     Perspective 4 (Spring):81-88.
          A summary of Crane's poetics using his two published essays
     and a few of his letters. The principal poem analyzed is
     "Legend," although there are general references to other poems.
     For Crane there were three aspects to the role of the poet:
     seer, magician, and comedian. The artist as prophet is hardly a
     new concept; Crane agrees with the traditional notion that a
     prophet and only a prophet can interpret humanity to itself. The
     poet is a magician of the Faustian type, one who makes a bargain
     wherein he receives supreme lordship over words. Finally, the
     poet is a comedian as represented by Chaplin in "Chaplinesque."

"By his very nature, then, the poet is a prophet; by a cosmic
necessity he is a magician who must bargain with the agents of
darkness for mastery; but by avoidable and artificial obstacles
as they exist in present-day society he is reduced to the laughed-
at exile, the tolerated comedian." Crane accepts the aesthetic
notion that poetry is something, not that it means something.
The poem is not dependent upon the experience of its maker nor
even upon the use to which the reader may put it. Imagination
constructs a better world than reality, and one paradoxically
more real than reality. The poem is an experience in itself.
Crane's practice as a poet is explained by the fact that he conceived language "in a manner different from that of any other
writer." Just as a poem stands by itself, so did Crane think of
the world as possessing substance and accidents, standing by itself, calling up the rich symbolism which gives one insight into
reality.

13 SANDERS, THOMAS E. "Crane's 'The Return.'" Explicator 10
    (December):Item 20.
        The poem paints an impressionistic picture of the tropical
    typhoon romantically conceived. Beginning with a detached feeling
    of observation, it soon plunges into the sweep of a tropical
    storm. Sanders is especially impressed with the punctuation.
    Examining the poem from a Freudian point of view he describes it
    as "a sexually visualized poem," beginning serenely and building
    rapidly to a crashing climax.

14 STRAUMANN, HEINRICH. American Literature in the Twentieth
    Century. London: Hutchinson's University Library, pp. 132-
    35.
        Although it is not usual to connect Carl Sandburg with
    Crane, the two poets have a number of essential qualities in
    common. Both were concerned with a vision of the fundamentals of
    America, past and present; both wished to accept the reality of
    the machine age; and both were indebted to Walt Whitman. In
    tone, however, Crane differs profoundly from Sandburg.

15 Van DOREN, MARK. Introduction to Poetry. New York: William
    Sloane, pp. 102-7.
        An explication of "Praise for an Urn," praising the poem
    for its mixture of precision and imprecision. It illustrates a
    type of modern poem whose content is complicated almost beyond
    the reach of words, but a poem also in which the effort is made
    to make the words do all they can. Like a typically modern poem,
    it begins more confidently than it can end. It illustrates the
    tendency of modern art to delight in frustrating its own form.

16 WILLIAMS, WILLIAM CARLOS. The Autobiography of William Carlos
    Williams. New York: Random House, pp. 171, 313, 318.
        Although he never met Crane, he knew of his work and once
    accepted a short poem by him for Contact.

1952

1   ANON. "The Letters of Hart Crane." Booklist 49 (15 October):
     66.
         Review of The Letters of Hart Crane. Not only do the
     letters provide an interpretive key to such major poems as The
     Bridge but they are, sometimes, poems in themselves.

2   BEVINGTON, HELEN. "The Letters of Hart Crane." South Atlantic
     Quarterly 52:310-11.
         Review of The Letters of Hart Crane. Although one could
     hardly discover from his letters that Crane was a remarkable
     poet, one would inevitably conclude that he was a disturbed, un-
     stable, and unhappy man. He simply did not bother to write well
     in a letter.

3   BLACKMUR, R.P. "New Thresholds, New Anatomies." In Language
     as a Gesture. New York: Harcourt, Brace & Co., pp. 301-16.
         Reprint of 1935.1.

4   CAHOON, HERBERT. "The Letters of Hart Crane." Library Journal
     77 (1 September):1395.
         Review of The Letters of Hart Crane. Although the letters
     reveal the changing literary judgments and personal experiences
     of Crane on the long road he travelled, rarely do any of them
     achieve literary excellence.

5   DEUTSCH, BABETTE. "Alchemists of the Word." In Poetry in Our
     Time. New York: Henry Holt & Co., pp. 312-30.
         Crane is characterized as a "spiritual Crusoe," a religious
     poet who had no religion. She feels that Crane understood this
     problem more clearly than Yeats and dealt with it more overtly
     than Eliot. Noting Crane's likenesses to Dickinson, Whitman,
     and Poe, the author suggests that Rimbaud was an influence on
     Crane's idea that the poet must be a visionary. While The Bridge
     is affirmative in tenor, Crane also takes into account the ugly
     aspects of a mechanical age, feeling a deep sense of alienation
     from commercial society. After a brief consideration of "Voyages
     II," Deutsch presents a cursory analysis of The Bridge as a
     brilliant tour de force fundamentally faulty in structure. Crane
     did not have the intelligence to handle the problems which he con-
     fronted.

6   FRIEDMAN, PAUL. "The Bridge: A Study in Symbolism." Psycho-
     analytical Quarterly 21:49-80.
         Crane is a classic example of the creative homosexual in
     conflict. The bridge is really the bridge of love. Antagonism
     and attraction characterize his relationship with his father, and
     this ambivalence appears to be the underlying principle of Crane's
     poetry. The bridge itself is not an accidental metaphor, since
     seas, rivers, and bridges are the primary symbols in his work.

"Thus the bridge failed him as the sea had betrayed him." Crane's tensions were such that he could not erect the bridge of love. "The psychoanalyst may add that this deep narcissism caused the total collapse of Crane's sublimational striving and brought about his failure both as man and poet."

7   GEIGER, DON. "Hart Crane." <u>University of Kansas City Review</u> 18 (Spring):198.
      Verse appreciation.

8   GREGORY, HORACE. "The Best of Hart Crane's Poetry Improves With Time." New York <u>Herald Tribune Books</u>, 9 November, p. 3.
      Review of <u>The Letters of Hart Crane</u>. Crane's best poetry has improved with time. There can be no doubt that he deserves the recognition that he has received. Weber's careful, sympathetic editing of the letters has resulted in a book that closely resembles an autobiography. Crane was not a great letter writer, bu he was voluminous and self-revealing. To the psychologist, Crane's letters are likely to suggest details of a tortured psyche who ended as a suicide. To the moralist, his suicide may offer proof that his dissipations led to his death. Neither is able to explain the presence of his poetic genius. The critics are incorrect when they conclude that his accomplishment was overwhelmed by failure. Although his intention in the writing of <u>The Bridge</u> was not completed, the design of the poem remains secure and its major passages cannot be ignored. "The Broken Tower" and many of the poems in <u>White Buildings</u> are now "beyond critical patronage."

9   HORTON, ROD W., and EDWARDS, HERBERT W. <u>Backgrounds of American Literary Thought</u>. New York: Appleton-Century-Crofts, pp. 322, 359.
      The twenties could never be written off as a sterile decade because it produced such a figure as Crane. The imagist movement, imported from Europe, attracted adherents as "unlike each other as Ezra Pound, Amy Lowell, Carl Sandberg, T.S. Eliot, and Hart Crane."

10   LÜDEKE, HENRY. <u>Geschichte der Amerikanischen Literatur</u>. Bern: A. Francke, A G Verlag, pp. 555-66.
      In German. After a brief biographical sketch, the author mentions the effect of Crane's unsuccessful trip to Mexico, his growing emotional instability, and "a disabling discrepancy between Crane's powerful poetic endowment and his inability to find a clear path in the spiritual confusion of the twenties" as conspiring to "darken his spirit and his poetry." The poems in <u>White Buildings</u> already show that he mastered the language, the open form, the associative links, the rhythms, rhymes, and assonances of the new technique, and could handle distinctive melody. The more ambitious <u>Bridge</u> miscarried because Crane lacked the "Olympian balance, the quiet faith of the old master

Whitman." In the oscillation between terror and admiration before
the power of science, which drove him to an exaggerated confidence
in unbridled imagination, his work fell apart into a series of
parts of unequal quality and only external coherence. "What remains, however, gives witness to an extraordinary poetic power,
and even his final failure speaks for the integrity of Crane's
art."

11   MARTEY, HERBERT. "Hart Crane's 'The Broken Tower': A Study
      in Technique." University of Kansas City Review 18 (Spring):
      199-205.
          Begins with an analysis of what Crane meant by his famous
      phrase "logic of metaphor." Crane's word choice is inept in that
      his explanation is unsatisfactory in the famous passage from
      "General Aims and Theories." The passage must mean that the
      words employed in the poem are selected primarily for their
      associational meanings and not for their logical significance.
      They operate on a metaphorical plane, stimulating the extension
      of thought on the reader's part. The main trouble with Crane's
      theory is the confusion with which it is expressed, since it is
      apparent that he is speaking of the illogic of metaphor. In his
      letter to Harriet Monroe defending "At Melville's Tomb" he re-
      phrased this theory, emphasizing the illogical impingements of
      the connotations of words on the consciousness. His theory of
      language involves the very manner in which he uses language in
      the creation of symbols and moods which disclose the meaning of
      the poem. "Symbolization and mood become the important factors
      in Crane's use of language and his technique." "The Broken
      Tower" is analyzed because it is typical of Crane's complexity.
      The subject of "The Broken Tower" is love. The ten stanzas of
      the poem are clearly divided into three parts: part I, stanzas
      1-4; part II, stanzas 5 and 6; part III, stanzas 7-10. Each
      deals with a different aspect of love.

12   MATTHIESSEN, F.O. "An Absolute Music: Hart Crane." In The
      Responsibilities of the Critic. New York: Oxford University
      Press, pp. 103-5.
          Reprint of 1937.15.

13   PORTER, KATHERINE ANNE. The Days Before. New York: Harcourt,
      Brace & Co., p. 74.
          Miss Porter's significant memories of Crane appear in
      Horton's biography. In this work, she simply makes reference in
      passing to Crane and her reading of Pavannes and Divisions by
      Ezra Pound. Crane burst out saying, "I'm tired of Ezra Pound!"
      When Miss Porter asked him who else there was, "he thought a few
      seconds and said: 'It's true there's nobody like him, nobody to
      take his place.'" The reader interested in the relationship be-
      tween Crane and Porter should consult Horton's biography (1937.13)
      pp. 283-87. Crane accepted her invitation to make his temporary
      quarters at her home in Mixcoac, a suburb of Mexico City. His

stay with her was not a success. It is not clear if Horton includes the entire text which Miss Porter had written, nor is it
clear when he is simply paraphrasing her.

*14   QUINN, Sister M. BERNETTA. "Metamorphosis in American Poetry."
       Ph.D. dissertation. University of Wisconsin.
           See 1955.14.

15   RAIZISS, SONIA. "MacLeish-Wylie-Crane." In The Metaphysical
      Passion. Philadelphia: University of Pennsylvania Press,
      pp. 230-41.
          Crane is a remarkable synthesis of Rimbaud and Laforgue;
      he inherited the Donne tradition; he borrowed from Edith Sitwell,
      Wallace Stevens, and T.S. Eliot. He has the impulses of Whitman,
      and the New England habits of Emily Dickinson. His rhetoric is
      like Marlowe and the Elizabethans, with the nervous quality of
      Donne's tension, although he is closer to Crashaw in temperament
      than to Donne. He is like D.H. Lawrence and Robinson Jeffers,
      but bears a resemblance to the obsessed visionary, Blake. He has
      mastered the spirit and style of George Herbert, Gerard Manley
      Hopkins, and Samuel Greenberg. Crane is a metaphysical poet in
      vision and technique. He manifests this especially in his attempt
      to use the artifacts of our mechanical age. His failure is ex-
      plained by the diversity of his literary inheritance and the
      agonies of his personal life. A sense of the prophetic and the
      rhapsodic are persistently challenged by the ironic predicaments
      of modern society. Nevertheless, his scenes and symbols are
      based on some form of hope. No modern poet in America has brought
      together with the intention of synthesis "a more sumptuous imagery
      of contrasts." See 1944.1.

16   RODMAN, SELDEN. "A Tragic Conflict." New York Times Book Re-
      view, 19 October, p. 32.
          Review of The Letters of Hart Crane. The classic figure of
      the mad poet was revived in our time in the person of Crane. His
      reputation is more firmly established by the shorter poems than
      by the high-pitched The Bridge. The best of his letters are
      "destined for . . . immortality." As a poet, he could not write
      out of a tradition but had to be possessed. What saved Crane as
      a poet from the irresponsibility of his life as a sensation
      seeker was an artistic integrity that never wavered. The letters
      reveal his poise, philosophical detachment, and clear thinking.
      It is the tragic conflict between Crane the artist and Crane the
      man, the embodiment of the neuroses of his time, that makes the
      letters moving and dramatic.

17   SCOTT, W.T. "Great and Wretched." Saturday Review 35 (18
      October):27.
          Review of The Letters of Hart Crane. The tragedies in
      literary history are those of writers who had genius and nothing
      else; Crane was one of them. His story is a terrifying one of

self-destruction, told earlier by Philip Horton and now revealed
by Crane himself in his letters. Because of the omissions, the
letters will probably have to be edited again. The valuable
letters are those that reveal the soundness of his aesthetic
judgments. He had amazing good sense about his contemporaries.

18   SHAPIRO, KARL. In Defense of Ignorance. New York: Random
         House, pp. 13, 191, 269, 303.
         Brief references, including the comment that The Bridge is
      "one of the few modern poems worth reading more than once."

19   TATE, ALLEN. "Crane: The Poet as Hero." New Republic 127
         (17 November):25-26.
         Review of The Letters of Hart Crane. It is a painful chore
      to review the desperate and melancholy life of Crane again. What
      astonishes Tate in the early letters is "Crane's moral as well as
      intellectual precocity." His moral deterioration came more
      slowly. Between 1917 and 1926 he became confirmed in his homo-
      sexuality and cut off from any secure relationship. It is signif-
      icant that Crane was "an extreme example of the unwilling homo-
      sexual." Tate emphasizes his sexual deviation in this essay be-
      cause "beneath it lies the mystery of the disintegration, at the
      age of thirty-two, of the most gifted poet of his generation."
      The curious relationship with his mother was crucial; he was still
      trying to "explain" himself to her at the end of his life. "None
      of us was capable in the end of taking the place of his family,
      and that was what he demanded of us." Out of Crane's central
      conflict emerged "modernism" in its extreme development. Crane
      even spoke to himself towards the end as the "last romantic."
      Tate wishes to make it clear that Crane was never alienated. "He
      did not reject, he simply could not achieve, in his own life, the
      full human condition; he did not for a moment suppose that there
      was a substitute for it." Crane's deepest friendships were not
      with homosexuals but with men with whom he could live the life of
      the mind and the imagination. The circumstances of his life, the
      character of his poetic sensibility, and the body of lyric poetry
      he produced make him eligible to be named "our twentieth-century
      poet as hero." See 1953.20. Reprinted: 1955.20.

20   TINKLE, LON. "Year of the Long Autumn (A Reviewer Wanders
         Through 1952)." Saturday Review 35 (27 December):9.
         Notice of The Letters of Hart Crane.

21   WILDER, AMOS [N.]. Modern Poetry in the Christian Tradition.
         New York: Charles Scribner's Sons, pp. 5, 11, 233-34.
         Brief references. Crane does not use the Christian tradi-
      tion; rather he attempts to construct his vision from the myth
      and legend of the American scene and "make a religion of his art."

22   WILSON, EDMUND. "The Muses Out of Work." In The Shores of
         Light. New York: Farrar, Straus & Young, pp. 197-211.

Reprint of 1927.20.

23   WINTERS, YVOR. "The Anniversary: To Achilles Holt." In
     Collected Poems. Denver, Colo.: Swallow Press, p. 81.
          Verse appreciation. Reprinted: 1960.22.

24   WOLF, LEONARD L. "Hart Crane--A Note (December, 1948)."
     University of Kansas City Review 18 (Spring):198.
          Verse appreciation.

25   WOOD, FRANK. "Three Poems on Whitman." Comparative Litera-
     ture 4 (Winter):44-53.
          At least three modern poets have contributed a poem of
     merit on the subject of Whitman: Stephen Vincent Benét, Garcia
     Lorca, and Crane. The "Cape Hatteras" section is virtually an
     ode to Whitman. In this section Crane attempted to synthesize
     three levels of American experience--industrial, agrarian, and
     historical. The critics are unanimous in their opinion that
     Crane made the major effort of our day to span the world of
     Whitman and our own. Since this section is the turning point of
     the poem, it was important for Crane's purposes that the Whitman
     theme be introduced there.

1953

1   ANDERSON, SHERWOOD. The Letters of Sherwood Anderson. Edited
    by Howard Mumford Jones and Walter B. Rideout. Boston:
    Little, Brown & Co., pp. 52, 63, 70, 73.
         In a letter dated 17 December 1919, Anderson refers to
    Crane as one of the "brothers buried away beneath all this roaring
    modern insanity of life." In a letter of 1920, Anderson is grate-
    ful for Crane's sympathetic understanding of Poor White. The
    letter of 4 March 1921 praises "Black Tambourine," with a criti-
    cism of the last lines of the second and third verses. The letter
    of 2 April 1921 comments on the same poem, Crane having sent a
    revised copy to Anderson. "Your poem has now real charm and
    meaning."

2   ANON. "The Letters of Hart Crane." New Yorker 28 (7 Feb-
    ruary):95-96.
         Was fundamentally robust and sanguine. A true picture of
    him comes through in spite of the disorganizing flaws of his
    temperament.

3   ANON. "The Letters of Hart Crane." United States Quarterly
    Book Review 9 (June):113.
         The letters are of value mainly as a picture with dramatic
    clarity of Crane's personal and aesthetic development. The col-
    lection of letters would have been improved, however, by fuller
    annotation.

4   ARNAVON, CYRILLE. L'Histoire littéraire des États-Unis.
    Paris: La Libraries Hachette, pp. 373-75.
        In French. Brief note, emphasizing his likenesses with
    Pound, the early Eliot, Melville, and Waldo Frank.

5   BROOKS, VAN WYCK. "Beyond Adolescence." In The Writer in
    America. New York: E.P. Dutton, pp. 79-82.
        Crane was mistaken in following Rimbaud when he wished to
    write a poem in the tradition of Whitman. Being torn between
    Rimbaud and Whitman was a fatal conflict for a poet who wished to
    sing of the American myth, for he could not reconcile these two
    opposing influences. Faith in the future was the essence of his
    theme, but his poem fell apart into fragments before it was
    finished. Crane being influenced by Rimbaud "is emblematic of
    many other cases in which Americans, unsure of themselves and un-
    sure of their tradition, have literally followed strange gods to
    their own undoing." Crane should have lived deeply in harmony
    with the whole context of his theme and turned a deaf ear to dis-
    believers in Whitman's idea.

6   BURFORD, WILLIAM. "Religious Poet in America." Southwest
    Review 38 (Summer):261-64.
        Review of The Letters of Hart Crane. What the letters make
    clear is that Crane is a religious poet without a religion.

7   CARRUTH, HAYDEN. "The Crane Legend." Nation 176 (February):
    151.
        Review of The Letters of Hart Crane. American poets are
    seldom elevated to mythological status as rapidly as Crane. Un-
    fortunately it may be true that he is more useful to American
    letters as a myth than he was or would have been as a working
    poet. It is unfortunate as well that this volume will do little
    to reestablish the memory of the poet "on a more effable plane."
    The fact is that Crane believed himself to be a myth. One cannot
    read the letters without receiving the impression that Crane was
    more than half-mad almost all the time. The main objection to
    the volume is that it may be premature, since there are so many
    omissions.

8   CROSBY, CARESSE. The Passionate Years. New York: Dial Press,
    pp. 237-45.
        The Crosbys published The Bridge at the Black Sun Press.
    This is an account of April 1929, in Paris with Crane. He was
    put up in their daughter's room and brought a chimney sweep home
    for the night. All the dainty objects were covered with the
    "blackest footprints and handprints I've ever seen, hundreds of
    them." She tells how they took Crane to the mill where he was
    supposed to be shut up to do some composing. He was very diffi-
    cult to handle, managing to seduce the chauffeur. There are two
    other brief references, one to Crane's signing the manifesto in
    Transition, and a record of the party he gave in New York after

the publication of The Bridge.

9   CUMMINGS, E.E. i: six non lectures. Cambridge, Mass.: Harvard University Press, p. 65.
     One passage from Cummings's Soviet Russian diary, EIMI, is reprinted in full. The passage concludes, "the poet Hart Crane was able to invent growth's likeness." Each reader, after surveying the rest of the passage, will have to interpret what that line means for himself.

10   EDWARDS, JOHN. "Letters of One Poet--and Verse of Another." San Francisco Chronicle, 18 January, p. 21.
     Review of The Letters of Hart Crane. Praises Crane's genius but says little about the letters.

11   GERBORE, PIETRO. "La libertà del subcosciente." Libri Nuovi 1 (1 May):284-86.
     In Italian. Review of The Letters of Hart Crane, using the occasion to present a number of details of Crane's life.

12   HARDING, WALTER. "Erratic Genius of 1920's Revealed in His Letters." Chicago Tribune, 18 January, p. 2.
     Very brief review of The Letters of Hart Crane.

13   HARDWICK, ELIZABETH. "Anderson, Millay, and Crane in Their Letters." Partisan Review 20 (November-December):690-96.
     Since letters are a useful means of expressing one's ideal self, there is some point in looking carefully at the letters of Sherwood Anderson, Edna St. Vincent Millay, and Hart Crane. We can get some idea of how the person saw himself over a period of time. "These letters are marvelous, wonderful simply to read, important in what they add to our notion of Crane." They remind one of the letters of Keats, and give an inadvertent but accurate picture of America itself from 1916 to 1932. Although Crane was annoyed by his parents, he was also fascinated by them. He seems to have "enjoyed" his homosexuality and his addiction to alcohol. Unlike Fitzgerald, Crane does not seem to have felt that he was heading for destruction. "The sheer power of mind they reveal is dazzling." The only way to account for the joy in the letters is to suspect, a "disturbing possibility," that Crane led a happy life. Reprinted: 1962.10.

14   KIEFAR, H.C. Review of The Letters of Hart Crane. Arizona Quarterly 9, no. 1 (Spring):73-74.
     Discusses Crane's life more than the letters.

15   MARITAIN, JACQUES. Creative Intuition in Art and Poetry. Bollingen Series 35. New York: Pantheon Books, 505 pp. passim.
     Seven references to or quotations from Crane. "I do not think that Brooklyn Bridge is built with any intention of beauty;

and it was able to stir the deepest emotions of Hart Crane, and is bound forever to his lines."

16   RAMSEY, WARREN. <u>Jules Laforgue and the Ironic Inheritance</u>. New York: Oxford University Press, pp. 213-22. See 1950.6.

17   SMITH, GROVER. "On Poets and Poetry." <u>New Mexico Quarterly</u> 23 (Fall):319-21.
        Review of <u>The Letters of Hart Crane</u>. It is obvious that Crane, "that pitiable anarch," was grievously disordered. The neurotic irresponsibility of his private life is revealed directly in the undisciplined fancy of his poetic images. One is appalled to realize that he did not know the difference between a random and a logical mode of association. Since Crane observed no rules of conscious order, he was incapable of the metaphysical conceit. He was a deadly example to his imitators. "What is true of his poetry is true of his life. He knew no pattern; he was himself a kaleidoscope, a disintegrated personality." His letters do not show the intensities of a great man. They reveal his curiosity, eclecticism, and caprice. While they do show his many interests and his talent, they proclaim no detachment from the hurly-burly of everyday affairs, from the efforts of greed and sensuality. "There is no concentration of alert feeling; there is no style."

18   SPILLER, ROBERT E. et al., eds. <u>Literary History of the United States</u>. Rev. ed. New York: Macmillan Co., pp. 1344-45.
        The most striking illustration of the influence of T.S. Eliot can be seen in <u>The Bridge</u>. Crane's life was a record of the disintegration that can result from modern rootlessness. <u>White Buildings</u> revealed the extent to which he was affected by the French poets. In "The Marriage of Faustus and Helen" he composed a poem in the manner of Eliot, using myth to interpret the past and present. In contrast to Eliot, however, he was more concerned with a positive goal. The result was <u>The Bridge</u>. Much of it was, however, a mere "act of the will and not the product of his deepest consciousness." Despite his admiration for Whitman, he was much more like Poe. Crane's failure is the failure of the romantic ego. "His 'vision' had degenerated into sensationalism." Contains a short bibliography. See 1947.7; 1948.18; 1963.20.

19   ____. <u>Bibliography: Literary History of the United States</u>. New York: Macmillan Co., pp. 457-58.
        Brief bibliography. Incorrect on primary works.

20   TATE, ALLEN. <u>The Forlorn Demon: Didactic and Critical Essays</u>. Chicago: Henry Regnery, pp. 61-62, 152-56.
        Reprint of 1952.19.

21   _____. "The Self-made Angel." New Republic 129 (31 August):
        17, 21.
             Concerned with the problem of morals and metaphysics in
        literature, Tate compares two short passages from Dante and
        Crane: Dante's "And in His Will is perfected our peace. . . ."
        and stanza seven of "The Wine Menagerie." Like most modern poets,
        Crane has "underwritten" his poems. "It is half-poetry. It is
        sometimes called the poetry of sensibility." Crane's poem is
        obscure. Through magic the poet is trying to find a new thres-
        hold; the only threshold that "we are likely to know are those
        that God has already given us." Personal sensibility and magic
        will not produce new ones. This standard romantic self-pity in
        which the poet is a "self-made angel trying to cheat the condi-
        tion of man." In sum, magic cannot replace a religious belief.
        Despite this analysis, "he was probably as great a poet as a
        magician can be."

22   THORPE, WILLARD. "The Letters of Hart Crane." American
        Literature 25 (May):240-42.
             A desire for personal freedom was characteristic of Crane
        and his contemporaries. Yet his recklessness is more often a
        form of courage than mere defiance. In their vividness and in
        their style, Crane's letters are much superior to those of Edna
        St. Vincent Millay. The chaos of his private life contrasts
        strangely with the artistic control evident in his poetry. One
        is struck, as well, by the immaturity of his life in contrast
        with the maturity of his judgments of people. Weber's editing
        is satisfactory. This volume greatly enriches the small body of
        primary materials having to do with the literary life of the
        twenties.

23   TINDALL, WILLIAM YORK. "The Literary Twenties." Yale Review
        42 (March):452-53.
             Review of The Letters of Hart Crane. One can get an im-
        mediate sense of the twenties from Weber's careful edition of the
        letters. The letters, no less fascinating than the poems and
        more important than some of them, are splendid and pathetic
        memorials to the defeat of youth. For critics of Crane's poetry,
        the value of the letters is enormous. His own explanations of
        his better poems help to make the obscurities plain.

24   UNGER, LEONARD, and O'CONNOR, WILLIAM VAN. Poems for Study.
        New York: Rinehart, pp. 637-41.
             Although a textbook, the discussion of "Voyages II" is
        worth reading.

25   VIERECK, PETER. "The Poet in the Machine Age." In Dream and
        Responsibility: Four Test Cases of the Tension Between Poetry
        and Society. Washington, D.C.: University Press of Washing-
        ton, D.C., pp. 47-65.
             Crane rightly called himself "the Pindar of the Machine

Age," because he was the most exciting "pro-machinist" poet of
his time. His attempt to answer Eliot's The Waste Land with The
Bridge was a failure.

26   WEST, RAY B., Jr. "Money and the Arts." Western Review 17
     (Winter):158.
         Review of The Letters of Hart Crane. In comparing the
     letters of Crane and Sinclair Lewis, West is struck by the im-
     portant role money plays in both volumes. He demonstrates this
     by reference to Lewis's letters, but he does not make the point
     with respect to Crane. Crane wanted desperately to succeed as a
     poet. His letters are revealing documents of despair, frustra-
     tion, and conflict with himself and with others, presenting a
     somewhat different perspective on Crane than one gets in the ex-
     cellent studies of Horton and Weber. The letters mirror his
     astuteness and his naïveté, his poetic genius as well as his
     personal failure, "a document of a poet's almost willful struggle
     to destroy that which he prizes most highly--his talent."

*27 WILLINGHAM, JOHN R. "The Whitman Tradition in Recent American
     Literature." Ph.D. dissertation, University of Oklahoma.

                                1954

1   CAMBON, GLAUCO. "Hart Crane, Icaro della parola." Aut Aut 23
     (September):414-27.
         In Italian. See 1963.6.

2   CHAPLIN, CHARLES. My Autobiography. New York: Simon &
     Schuster, pp. 248-49.
         Refers to meeting Crane through Waldo Frank. Chaplin has
     no taste for modern poetry, finding The Bridge "too shrill."

3   COWLEY, MALCOLM. The Literary Situation. New York: Viking
     Press, pp. 37, 86, 114.
         Incidental references to Crane.

4   DEUTSCH, BABETTE. "The Waste Remains." Poetry 83 (March):
     353-57.
         Review of The Letters of Hart Crane, which gives us a more
     complete portrait of the poet than we have had, revealing the
     interplay between the circumstances of his life and his own
     nature, the struggle that went on in him to bring his work closer
     to his vision of what should be. "From first to last it is a
     story of divided loyalties." The early letters reveal the per-
     ceptiveness of an untutored young man from the provinces. The
     letters correct an impression given readers by Weber in his study
     of Crane that Crane knew the work of Dante and Hopkins rather
     early. The letters indicate that he did not know Dante until
     after the completion of The Bridge, and it was not until 1928

that he received a copy of Hopkins's poetry from Yvor Winters.
(Weber has replied to this charge in 1954.13.) From reading the
letters one gathers that his best work was left undone in spite
of the memorable lyrics and the magnificence of his failure in
The Bridge. The most painful thing about the letters is to
recognize that Crane, a person capable of mature tenderness,
responsibility, and dignity, was undone by destructive forces
with which he had never been disciplined to grapple.

5   GREGORY, HORACE. "The Romantic Heritage of Dylan Thomas."
     Yale Literary Magazine 22 (November):30-34.
         Brief reference to Crane's influence on Thomas's lyricism.

6   GRIFFITH, BEN W., Jr. "Crane's 'Paraphrase.'" Explicator 13
     (October):Item 5.
         "Paraphrase" is an excellent example of Allen Tate's idea
     that "the finest passages in his [Crane's] work are single moments
     in a stream of sensation." The word winking in line one is of
     interest because of its connection with the first line of "Voyages
     II." While Rimbaud, an influence on Crane, cultivated the notion
     of deliberate disorder, this poem attempts to present "the actual
     chaos of the stream of sensation in as orderly a manner as is
     possible."

7   LEARY, LEWIS. Articles on American Literature, 1900-1950.
     Durham, N.C.: Duke University Press, pp. 60-61.
         A list of thirty-nine items with four volume numbers listed
     incorrectly.

8   MOORE, JEFFREY, ed. The Penguin Book of Modern American
     Verse. London: Penguin Books, pp. 17, 22, 28, 199-209.
         Much of the negative criticism of The Bridge is classical
     criticism of a romantic poet. Crane was the "first New Romantic."
     Although a poet of the Whitman type, his sensibility was much
     more akin to that of Wallace Stevens.

9   MORRIS, H.C. "Crane's 'Voyages' as a Single Poem." Accent 14
     (Autumn):291-99.
         Crane regarded the six poems as part of a sequence, yet the
     six are presented together as a single work only in White Build-
     ings and Collected Poems. Crane achieved unity through theme and
     through the use of poetic devices. The theme interweaves love,
     sea, voyage, and death; syntax, language, and symbol bind these
     elements together. Poems I and II introduce the twofold nature
     of the sea as symbol as it will be used in the poems; the sea
     symbolizes paradoxically love and death. Further, all of the
     parts in direct address are to a specific lover. On the literal
     level a voyage is being made; on another level the lover is
     making a voyage to his beloved. The lover loves the sailor and
     the sea, the sailor loves the sea and the lover, and the sea
     loves the sailor. "Voyages IV" offers greater difficulties than

other parts of the poem. The movement is from the lover on the shore to the beloved at sea. In "Voyages V" the beloved and the lover are together. To the lover, the sea means death and separation; to the beloved the sea means life and love. In "Voyages VI" we are to assume that the lover has irrevocably lost his beloved--either because the sailor has returned to the sea or because the sea has swallowed him in death. The love theme in the sequence as a whole is paramount.

10   SIMON, ADELAIDE. "Apples and Dust." Free Lance 2 (Last Half): 3-6.
     Description of the "Cleveland Renaissance," the center of which was William Sommer's studio just outside Cleveland. Members of the group who gathered for "inquiring, buoyant and robust" talk were Ernest Nelson, Sam Loveman, Willy Lescaze, and Hart Crane. The poets that congregated at Sommer's were thrust into the main currents of American thought, not inhibited by the regal notions that dominated the circles of Berenson or Gertrude Stein, and not inhibited by the "genteel sentimentality" of the Chicago school dominated by Harriet Monroe and Mrs. William Vaughn Moody. Both Crane and Sommer felt strong affection for Whitman, who was the spiritual guardian of the group.

11   TATE, ALLEN, and CHENEY, FRANCIS. Sixty American Poets, 1896-1944. Rev. ed. Washington, D.C.: Library of Congress, Reference Department, General Reference and Bibliography Division, p. 24.
     Selected bibliography.

12   UNTERMEYER, LOUIS. "Poets Without Readers: The Sad State of Poetry in the United States." Americas 6, no. 9 (September): 3-5, 26.
     Mentions Crane as one of the most original poets of his generation, The Bridge is described as "a malformed epic" with some of the "richest writing" of the period.

13   WEBER, BROM. "Communication." Poetry 84 (July):245-46.
     Weber's reply to Babette Deutsch's review of Crane's Collected Letters. Deutsch claimed that Weber was misinformed when he wrote that Carl Schmitt had analyzed the work of Dante, Hopkins, and other poets, interesting Crane in their ideas and techniques. She asserted that Crane had not read Hopkins or Dante until 1928. Weber claims that nothing in The Letters substantiates Deutsch's assertion. Crane seems to have had a bad memory in his letters dating his reading of certain poets. There is conflicting evidence. The external evidence came to Weber in his interview with Schmitt. He finds no reason to distrust Schmitt's memory or his integrity. He welcomes, however, any new factual information. See 1954.4.

14   WILLIAMS, WILLIAM CARLOS. Selected Essays of William Carlos

Williams. New York: Random House, pp. 261-62.
    Williams has certain reservations about Crane. Crane ex-
hausted his method, but the method itself was "never more than an
excrescence." It didn't seem to make much difference how he used
his method; when he came to the end of it, he felt there was no-
where for him to turn. "Peggy [Baird] said that in the last
three hours he beat on her cabin door--after being deceived and
thrashed." He had tried in Mexico merely to write, to write anything, but he couldn't.

15 ZIGERELL, JAMES. "Crane's 'Voyages II.'" Explicator 13
    (November):Item 7.
    Zigerell disagrees with a reading of "Voyages II" offered
by William Van O'Connor in Sense and Sensibility in Modern Poetry
(1948.11). O'Connor suggests that the sea as symbol of eternity
suggests the relationship of man to the flux of nature into which
he will be reabsorbed. Zigerell feels that theme is of little
importance to the poem because theme indicates an ideational
structure. He attempts a close reading of the poem to demonstrate
that it is an aesthetic experience. The sea is the dominant symbol, but it is not a unitary one since Crane wishes to exploit
the connotative power of words. The sea is related to the eternity, he suggests, as a "wink" is related to time--"a fleeting
Platonic reflection of the reality." See 1956.9.

                                1955

1   BELL, MILLICENT. "The Black Sun Press: 1927 to the Present."
    Books at Brown 17 (January):2-24.
    While the article is concerned primarily with the history
of the Black Sun Press in connection with an exhibit of its books
at Brown University, it includes a brief note on Crane's relationship with the Crosbys, first publishers of The Bridge.

2   BOGAN, LOUISE. "Hart Crane." In Selected Criticism: Prose,
    Poetry. New York: Noonday Press, pp. 40-44.
    A two-page tribute to Crane, poet of genius. The dis-
tinguishing mark of his poetry is seen in that the quarrel he had
with himself was far more grievous than his quarrel with the
world. This inner feud also explains his quarrel with the world
and his suicide.

3   BURKE, KENNETH. A Rhetoric of Motives. New York: George
    Braziller, p. 203.
    One mention of Crane that should be noted because Burke
uses a phrase in connection with Crane that is important in subsequent criticism--"esthetic myth." A passing reference on the
same page to the figure of the "religious gunman" as a mythic
figure who might stand for ambiguous or unconscious sexual motives.
Burke's suggestion, in passing, that an esthetic myth might become

a substitute for a religious myth has influenced a number of Crane's critics.

4   CAMBON, GLAUCO. "Il 'Bridge' di Hart Crane arco voltaico della poesia americana." Paragone 70 (October):7-51.
    In Italian. Reprinted: 1956.3; translated 1963.6.

*5   DEMBO, LAWRENCE [S.]. "The Poetry of Hart Crane." Ph.D. dissertation. Cornell University.
    See 1960.7; 1961.9.

6   DEMBO, L[awrence]. S. "The Unfracturer Idiom of Hart Crane's Bridge." American Literature 27 (May):203-4.
    Reprinted in 1960.7.

7   HOFFMAN, FREDERICK [J.]. "The Text: Hart Crane's The Bridge: The Crisis in Experiment." In The Twenties. New York: Viking Press, pp. 222-39.
    The Bridge reveals the true meaning of experiment in modern American literature. Crane, exposed to all the movements in modern literature that were of any consequence, discovered how extreme his need was to be self-sufficient. Every critic has acknowledged his extraordinary native lyric power. Just as obvious is the fact that his mind was shaped by modern influences; even in using the past, he put it to a modern use. He is the modern poet par excellence. Crane did not want to surrender to what he thought was the pessimism of his time. Since he saw the important positive qualities in the age of the machine and in urban society, he decided to "set the modern to right." Unfortuantely, he did not have any systematic body of knowledge through which he could translate his convictions into art. Hoffman details the history of the composition of The Bridge, emphasizing Crane's indebtedness to Whitman, the "divine and mythical spirit" who would lead him to safety to "Atlantis." The "Proem" contains all "the essential metaphors through which the entire poem is unified." In summary, the ultimate knowledge of the bridge, with its curveship, unites all patterns of curve both mundane and divine. It is the culmination of Crane's search for a secular myth, "not dependent upon past dogmas but 'intrinsic' containing its certainties and its symbology within itself." The bridge as object takes the place of what was the "Hand of God." That the poem concludes with questioning and doubt indicates that Crane is where he began--uneasy and uncertain. "The poet of The Bridge is a man alienated from his community because of (and in the very act of) his search for an acceptable, believable synthesis of that community." See 1962.11.

8   HOPKINS, KONRAD. "Make the Dark Poems Light: A Study of Hart Crane's White Buildings." Florida State University Studies in English and American Literature 19:125-42.
    Allen Tate agreed with Crane that "his soundest work was in the short pieces of White Buildings." This early work is inte-

grated and unified. It gains its coherence through the use of
recurrent themes, repeated symbols and images, and through a uniform representation of the poet's own consciousness. The confusion in his poetry results from his personal confusion about
America. On the one hand, he was inspired by Whitman and Waldo
Frank to accept the profound belief in the potentialities of this
country. On the other hand, Ouspensky caused him to doubt the
ideal of progress and material well-being. The basic duality of
Crane's character made it difficult for him to make intellectual
choices, and his ambivalence carried over into his art. This
duality is found in the poems in White Buildings in various ways.

9   KORETZ, JEAN; MOSELY, VIRGINIA; and WILLINGHAM, JOHN R.
      "Crane's 'Passage.'" Explicator 13 (June):Item 47.
         Mosely and Willingham read the poem as "an attempt to sug-
gest the nature of the aesthetic moment." The poet must shed
memory for the achievement of vision. The voyage becomes, however, a round trip. In stanza one the protagonist hopes for and
courts a rebirth. Stanzas two and three relate the preparation
of the protagonist for his voyage at the beginning of his experience. In stanza four the protagonist reaches the summit of the
mountain on his way to the sea. He must reconcile the experience
of his vision with the phenomenological world. Koretz reads the
poem as "almost a précis of the major psychological conflicts" of
Crane's life, a prophecy of "his final suicide." On one level
the poem is a parable of the predicament of the artist in modern
society, but on another level it relates the protagonist's search
for innocence and mystical purity. The journey in the poem is
the life journey of the poet. Within the wasteland he cannot
find the spiritual purity and innocence for which he sought. In
the final stanza the poet attains the death which he desired.
The sea reappears as the eternal principle in which time is re-
united with its divine source.

10   KUNITZ, STANLEY. Twentieth Century Authors: First Supple-
      ment. New York: H.W. Wilson, p. 243.
         Biographical sketch.

11   LeBRETON, M. "The Letters of Hart Crane." Études anglaises
      8:277.
         In French. A true revelation, giving the reader the best
and worst aspects of his nature. He was essentially an unstable
person, and this seems to be explained by the conditions of his
life and education. Many of the letters are admirable and dis-
cerning in their report on the New York literary scene of that
time. Of the greatest value are the letters concerned with The
Bridge; the allusions of Crane himself constitute an excellent
commentary on the poem and they also help to clarify his inten-
tions as an author.

12   LeCLAIR, MARGARET FOSTER. "Hart Crane, Poet of the Machine

Age." In <u>Lectures on Some Modern Poets</u>. Carnegie Series in English, no. 2. Pittsburgh: Carnegie Institute of Technology, pp. 4-23.

"I should like to take you back this morning to the spring of 1924. The time is dawn; the scene is a room in downtown Brooklyn--a room with a view of the East River. At the window stands a tall young man watching the last star turn in the waking west and go to sleep. . . . To understand even in part what Brooklyn Bridge meant to Hart Crane--the young man at the window on that spring morning--we must travel backward through many springs to the 1870's when, from the same window, Washington Roebling, paralyzed, his sight and hearing impaired, supervised the building of the bridge . . . and insofar as one may say poets are born, I think he [Crane] was born a poet."

13 PRESS, JOHN. <u>The Fire and the Fountain</u>. New York: Barnes & Noble, pp. 82-83.
    Brief reference. Contends that Hart Crane's best poetry was written to the accompaniment of music, and claims that he habitually wrote in a room through whose open windo drifted the noise of traffic and the strains of jazz from a radio or victrola. Distinguished poets have often had recourse to stimulants.

14 QUINN, Sister M. BERNETTA. "Eliot and Crane: Protean Tech-niques." In <u>The Metamorphic Tradition in Modern Poetry</u>. New Brunswick, N.J.: Rutgers University Press, pp. 144-67.
    <u>The Bridge</u> and <u>The Waste Land</u> resemble each other in that both find their anchoring symbol in place, and it is a symbol which undergoes "perpetual metamorphoses throughout the poem." Crane presents the bridge as a concretization of God, considered in terms of incarnation. This method can be seen in the thir-teenth century <u>Dialogues</u> of St. Catherine of Sienna (Sister Bernetta is indebted to Caroline Gordon for this suggestion). "Proem" provides a synopsis of most of the later uses of the bridge as a Christ-symbol. He did not deliberately select Christ as the subject of his metaphor, but, hungry for the Absolute, his mind saw the bridge as a way of expressing the means of union with his Creator. The most important subsidiary symbols metamor-phosized in the poem are those of the serpent and the eagle as figures of time and space. The metamorphosis of these symbols reaches its climax ("The Dance") in the merging of the protagonist and Maquokeeta. The bridge itself binds together time and space in America (Atlantis)--"the kingdom of perfection." "It would hardly strain this definition to consider Cathay as Crane here employs it as a synonym for salvation." Metamorphosis is natural to the work of Crane and Eliot. "They use metamorphosis rather as a means of unifying their difficult insights into modern reality, through constantly shifting <u>personae</u> and images." See 1952.14.

15 ROBINSON, JETHRO. "The Hart Crane Collection." <u>Columbia</u>

Library Columns 4 (February):3-7.
    Contains illustrations of Crane, his father, and his
mother. Claims some uniqueness for the collection of Crane
materials at Columbia, especially since the first biography, "the
source of nearly all that is known about his life," was written
far too much under the influence of Mrs. Crane. The traditional
story will have to be altered and many prejudicial details aban-
doned.

16   ROSENTHAL, M.L., and SMITH, A.J.M., eds. Exploring Poetry.
      New York: Macmillan Co., p. 335.
          A brief analysis of "Passage."

17   ROWE, H.D. Hart Crane: A Bibliography. Denver, Colo.:
      Allan Swallow, 30 pp.
          At best, a checklist, listing the principal editions of
Crane's work, but not always accurate in its description of each.
There are notable omissions. "Source Material" includes the
principal biographies, a selected list of books, and a selected
list of articles in periodicals. See 1955.18.

18   _____. "Hart Crane: A Bibliography." Twentieth Century
      Literature 1:94-113.
          See 1955.17.

19   SPILLER, ROBERT E. The Cycle of American Literature. New
      York: Macmillan Co., pp. 213-14.
          Crane is identified as a more American poet than T.S. Eliot
because he remained at home. He began to write poetry under the
strong influence of Eliot, but did not follow him into "the
farther reaches of his conservatism." In The Bridge he sought to
discover an American tradition of unity and faith in a series of
complex symbols, "but the poem remained an expression of a brilliant and confused personality rather than of a united people."

20   TATE, ALLEN. "Hart Crane." In The Man of Letters in the
      Modern World. New York: Meridian Books, pp. 283-98.
          Reprint of 1936.9; 1952.19.

21   TINDALL, WILLIAM YORK. The Literary Symbol. New York:
      Columbia University Press, pp. 138-39, 154-55.
          In The Bridge, the central image seems at first to be a
happy device for uniting the parts of the poem. Crane's intention, however, was better than his choice. "A bridge that connects the Navy Yard with the borough of Manhattan may not connect
the Far Rockaway with the Golden Gate." His bridge, moreover, is
so alien to Columbus, Pocahontas, and covered wagons (though all
crossed something), that it fails to embody them, and the poem,
full of such excellent things, falls apart. A central image,
however exciting in itself, must be chosen for its power to function in a structure where it takes back what it gives for its own

enlargement and the enlargement of what surrounds it. The "curve-ship" of the bridge fails in that, but the failure is splendid. Crane's best poem is "Voyages," strongly influenced by his reading of <u>Moby Dick</u> and Rimbaud.

22   WILLIAMS, STANLEY T. <u>The Spanish Background of American Literature</u>. 2 vols. New Haven: Yale University Press, 1:211, 254, 387, 407; 2:279.
      In Volumes 1 and 2, Williams makes passing references to Crane's interest in ironic use of Spanish-American subjects.

23   WILLINGHAM, JOHN R. "'Three Songs' of Hart Crane's <u>The Bridge</u>: A Reconsideration." <u>American Literature</u> 27 (March): 62-68.
      Deals with the difficulty of justifying the "Three Songs" in the structural pattern of <u>The Bridge</u>. The "Three Songs" have a structural function if we keep in mind the rest of the poem. The ending of "Cutty Sark" and the beginning of "Cape Hatteras" dramatize the contradiction the protagonist has discovered between the vision of the pioneers and the material facts of modern times. It only seems that the change in mood from "Cape Hatteras" to "Three Songs" is damaging; it is intentional. Crane has been influenced by the critical theories and the writing of Waldo Frank. Frank's novels attempt to use the structure of the symphony--theme followed by countertheme with the whole resolved in a final movement. The protagonist is trying in "Southern Cross" to apply the lesson of Whitman to the sailor's night journey in "Cutty Sark." The protagonist discovers the lack of satisfaction in love of the sailor in "Southern Cross" and next considers "National Winter Garden." The modern Magdalene is the striptease dancer, but like the Magdalene of the New Testament, she could "become a means to show men the way to spiritual redemption, in spite of what men thought she was." Our lust and our faith can never be completely separated, and the degeneracy and cheapness which she seems to symbolize is another test of Whitman's vision and faith. Magdalene is the bridge which leads from "Southern Cross" to "Virginia." In "Virginia" the protagonist still seeks his vision and attempts to reclaim the importance of the female principle of mystic America which had been suggested earlier in the poem in the figure of Pocahantas. The full importance of Eve and Magdalene is seen in Mary who takes on the full spiritual significance of the Virgin. "Eve as thesis, through Magdalene as antithesis, to Mary as synthesis." "Far, then, from marring the structure of <u>The Bridge</u>, these three songs provide a bridge between the apparently disparate American worlds of Pocahantas and of Dickinson, Duncan, and Hart Crane." Reprinted: 1970.6.

1956

1   ALVAREZ, A[LFRED]. "The Lyric of Hart Crane." <u>Twentieth</u>

Century 160 (December);506-17.
 Although Crane wrote some good and original poems, he is
clearly not a great epic genius. The main element of his life
was confusion. The Bridge is only a symbol of the poem that
Crane wanted to write. The poetry is original, although it has
no clear argument. His lyric poetry is superior to his faults as
a poet. His achievement is to be measured in "a handful of obscure, powerful lyric poems." In short, a fine minor poet. Reprinted: 1958.1.

2 BEACH, JOSEPH WARREN. "Hart Crane and Moby Dick." Western
    Review 20 (Spring):183-96.
 Concerned with "Voyages II" primarily. All of the poems
entitled "Voyages" would be better understood if we apprehended
how much they owe to the imagery and phrasing of Moby Dick.
Crane was an assiduous reader of Melville, borrowing ideas and
language from him. What Beach notes as the religious theme of
"Voyages II" may also have been borrowed from Moby Dick. "It is
clear that Crane thought of these poems as not merely love-poems
but also as journeys in supernal truth."

3 CAMBON, GLAUCO. "Il 'Bridge' di Hart Crane areo voltaico
    della poesia americana." In Tematica e sviluppo della poesia
    americana. Rome: Edizioni di Storia e Letteratura, 227 pp.
 In Italian. Reprint of 1955.4; translated 1963.6; 1970.6.

4 COWLEY, MALCOLM. "Hart Crane: A Memoir." In A Second
    Flowering. New York: Viking Press, pp. 191-215.
 An anecdotal portrait of Crane as he and other friends knew
him. Describes Crane's search for approval and fame, his kindness, his exuberance and outrageousness, his snobbishness, his
travels, his ailments, his conflict with the Tates, his attempts
to find models for The Bridge in other authors. Given Crane's
family troubles and his literary attitudes and methods, his suicide was inevitable. His poetic process had four steps and could
take years. This worked only in the years 1923-27 and worked well
for only five weeks of 1926 when he composed the lion's share of
The Bridge.

5 GREGORY, HORACE. Introduction to In the American Grain, by
    William Carlos Williams. New York: New Directions, pp. ix-
    xx.
 The Bridge, published five years after In the American
Grain, shows how deeply Williams's book left its impressions on
Crane's mind. Borrowings can be seen in the quotation reproduced
on the title page of "Powhatan's Daughter," in "Ave Maria," and
in the treatment of Poe in "The Tunnel."

6 LOCHE, E. "Note on Hart Crane." Saturday Review 39 (18
    August):28.
 Verse appreciation.

7   LOWENFELS, W. "Hart Crane." Nation 183 (15 September):225.
Verse appreciation.

8   SCHLAUCH, MARGARET. Modern English and American Poetry:
Techniques and Ideologies. London: Watts, pp. 72-73.
Analysis of "O Carib Isle!" This one sentence poem is an
excellent example of the periodic and intricately arranged sentence. The action word is the very last one, and it is unmodi-
fied. The poem is diagrammed. The single word at the end of the
poem, "mourns," bears the weight and impact of the long and elab-
orately inverted subject.

9   SCHULZ, MAX F. "Crane's 'Voyages,' 1-5; 21-25." Explicator
14 (April):Item 46.
A response to James Zigerell's reading of Crane's "Voyages
II" in which Zigerell inadequately explained why the "lovers ask
to be swallowed up" by the sea. Because the sea fascinated Crane,
one should not feel free to interpret the sea as being the actual
object of his love in the poem. The sea comes to symbolize "the
permanent transcendence of time and space, first through the
fertile consummation of desire and finally through death." It is
clear Crane did not mean for his lovers to sink literally into
the sea. Because of their surrender to passion, the lovers hope
to be united for eternity and to be allowed to retain this communion throughout their lives until by their death "they gain the
absolute key to paradise." See 1954.15.

10 SMITH, GROVER. T.S. Eliot's Poetry and Plays. Chicago:
University of Chicago Press, p. 276.
Reference to "The River" as influencing Eliot's description
of the Mississippi in Four Quartets.

11 TAYLOR, WALTER F. The Story of American Letters. Chicago:
Henry Regnery, pp. 300-1.
Crane is one of the many who attempted to come to grips
with industrialism by absorbing the rhythm and energy of the
machine into his poetry.

1957

1   ANZILOTTI, ROLANDO. Storia della letteratura americana.
Milan: Casa Editrice Dr. Francesco Vallardi, pp. 96-97.
In Italian. Brief mention.

2   BLACKMUR, R.P. "New Thresholds and New Anatomies." In Form
and Value in Modern Poetry. Garden City, N.Y.: Doubleday,
pp. 269-85.
Reprint of 1935.1.

3   BLOCK, HASKELL M. "Furor Poeticus and Modern Poetry." Trans-

actions of the Wisconsin Academy of Sciences, Arts, and Letters 45:77-90.
     Crane is part of a radical experiment in structure and language--the widespread effort in our time to reconstruct the foundations of poetic art. The doctrine of furor poeticus, creation under the direct impulse of a divine inspiration and in a momentary condition of delerium or frenzy which deprives the poet of his reason, had played a major role in shaping the attitude of the poet toward his art in recent years. Such poetry takes on the force of prophecy. It does not merely glorify, but predicts the future because of a divinely inspired vision. The great ancient poets and philosophers saw no conflict between the poet's madness and his concern with historical or moral truth. This idea is set forth fully in Plato's Ion. Crane is the most representative of the American poets in this tradition in both theory and practice. The Platonic view of poetic inspiration affected his poetics and his poetry throughout his career. He found additional inspiration for this view of poetry in Blake, Whitman, Nietzsche, and Rimbaud. "General Aims and Theories" is an attempt to provide a conscious rationalization of an art founded on the exploration of the unconscious and irrational. Crane regards it as the poet's province to affirm the power of vision and to transform reality. The doctrine of furor poeticus has "served in our time as a reassertion of the poet's primitive authority and spiritual power, the liberation of the ecstasy and wonder of the poet's universe."

4   BRUFORD, WILLIAM. "Avis aux amateurs." Poetry 91 (November): 117-20.
     Review of Horton's biography. Crane's story is a familiar one typical of the thousands of talented Americans who set out every year for New York. Crane was not mistaken in writing a poem like The Bridge, despite what many critics say. It is a splendid poem, the most energetic poetry written in America since Song of Myself. One of the principal figures in the story of America is the man like Crane: footloose, rootless though loving the land, a stranger. See 1937.13.

5   COWLEY, MALCOLM. "A Weekend with Eugene O'Neill." Reporter 17 (5 September):33-36.
     Cowley spent a weekend with O'Neill and Crane in November 1923, at O'Neill's Brook Farm in Ridgefield, Connecticut. O'Neill, Crane, and Cowley tap a barrel of raw cider.

6   LOMBARDO, AGOSTINO. Realismo e simbolismo: saggi di lettera-tura americana contemporanea. Rome: Edizioni di Storia e Letteratura, pp. 20, 58, 122, 159.
     In Italian. Brief references.

7   MILLER, JAMES E., Jr. "Four Cosmic Poets." University of Kansas City Review 23 (June):312-20.

Walt Whitman, D.H. Lawrence, Crane, and Dylan Thomas constitute the main line of a tradition which has been ignored because critics have been so preoccupied with the tradition represented by T.S. Eliot and The Waste Land. From the poetry of
these four poets a coherent view of the universe and man's place
in it emerges. For them the universe is not chaotic but schematic
in a mystic evolutionary sense, coherent and purposeful in the
unfolding of time. A mystic life force impels itself onward in
the paradox of mystical materialism. Great importance is given
to the here and now, the focal point of all time past and the
origin of all time future. Whitman, Lawrence, Crane, and Thomas
are deeply religious poets, although they subscribe to no formal
religion. Their religion is discovered by instinct and not em-
bodied in any dogma. Characteristically they speak not of the
creation of a poem but of its growth, emphasizing the organic
theory of peotics characteristic of romanticism. This can be
seen in Crane's theory of poetry, especially in the crucial distinction he makes between "ordinary logic" and the "logic of
metaphor." They are religious poets in the sense that they see
the universe as pervaded by mystic evolution, and they are in-
stinctive poets because they envision poetry as impelled by some
kind of "emotional evolution."

8   NORMAN, CHARLES. e.e. cummings. New York: E.P. Dutton, pp.
     108, 138, 208.
     Crane attended parties at the home of Paul Rosenfield, then
music critic of the Dial. Crane lived on the top floor of the
Little Review building. When Cummings was asked what he thought
of World War II, he replied: "Well, let's see. The word war re-
minds me of a poet named Hart Crane. He said there had always
been three kinds of people--warriors, priests, and merchants."
Not just one kind; not just merchants. And I think he was right."

9   TATE, ALLEN. "Reflections on American Poetry, 1900-1950."
     Sewanee Review 64:59-70.
     Crane is one of a handful of the best American poets who
tried to discover new and precise languages by which poetry gives
us knowledge of the human condition. An imperfect genius, his
profound honesty drove him to suicide after years of debauchery
had stultified his mind. Among the greatest poets of our time
are Frost and Stevens at the beginning, Crane and E.E. Cummings
in the middle, and Robert Lowell towards the end.

1958

1   ALVAREZ, A[LFRED]. "The Lyric of Hart Crane." In The Shaping
     Spirit: Studies in Modern English and American Poets. London:
     Chatto & Windus, pp. 107-23.
     Reprint of 1956.1.

2   _____. Stewards of Excellence. New York: Charles Scribner's
       Sons, pp. 107-23.
           American printing of 1958.1. See 1956.1.

3   ANON. "A Review of Horton's Hart Crane." College English 19
       (December):152.
           Horton's biography is more rewarding than the subject,
       "telling us all we want to know about that sad symbol of the
       1920's, Hart Crane." See 1937.13.

4   BRADBURY, JOHN M. The Fugitives. Chapel Hill: University of
       North Carolina Press, pp. 21, 52, 57, 64, 73, 103, 124.
           Recounts how Crane and Allen Tate got to know each other
       and how Crane introduced Tate to Eliot's work. During the period
       when Tate was in closest relationship with Crane, his poetry shows
       greater density, complexity, and a richer and sometimes more
       strained vocabulary.

5   BROWN, ASHLEY. "On Hart Crane." Nation 186 (29 March):264.
           Writes to the Nation protesting a number of features in
       Oscar Cargill's attack on Allen Tate and Yvor Winters in an
       earlier issue of the Nation. Tate had held Crane in high esteem
       for thirty-five years, going out of his way to uphold this judg-
       ment. Crane has never been a forgotten poet. Winters, too, has
       always been fascinated by Crane, rating him higher than most
       poets of the twentieth century. See 1958.6-7.

6   CARGILL, OSCAR. "Hart Crane and His Friends." Nation 186 (15
       February):142-43.
           An attack on Yvor Winters and Allen Tate; "His Friends" in
       the title is used with irony. Great enthusiasm, according to
       Cargill, existed for Crane's poetry in the late twenties. Within
       the next decade, "his friends" left us a picture of Crane as a
       fragmentary poet at best--"they tore him to bits." Tate was
       wrong in his criticism of Crane, because Crane never attempted to
       establish the greatness of America as the theme of The Bridge.
       Further, Crane's symbolism was not irrational, at least in the
       sense that Tate meant the word. Winters unfairly used statements
       from Crane's personal letters to him. Cargill asserts that there
       has been no adequate examination of The Bridge. The Bridge should
       be examined as a symphonic composition, rather than as an epic.
       If this were done and if "the author's original principles were
       kept in mind" we would discover it to be a genuine poem of a
       superior kind. Crane wrote some of the most sympathetic and
       imaginative lyrics of his generation. See 1958.5, 7, 21.

7   _____. "On Hart Crane." Nation 186 (29 March):264.
           Brief reply to Ashley Brown in the same issue defending his
       original attack and hoping that the controversy will not obscure
       his chief point--that The Bridge is built on an analogy with sym-
       phonic music. See 1958.5-6.

8   CIARDI, JOHN. "The Epic of Place." Saturday Review 41 (11 October):37-39.
      William Carlos Williams's Paterson, is an epic in intent, if by "epic" one is willing to understand "the sustained handling of a society-enclosing subject matter." If this is true, Paterson is related to Pound's Cantos, Eliot's The Waste Land, and Crane's The Bridge. The modern epic is symphonic in its development, orchestrating multiple themes of the human condition.

9   COWLEY, MALCOLM. "The Leopard in Hart Crane's Brow." Esquire 50 (October):257-60, 264-71.
      Rewrite of the chapter in Exile's Return. Crane's method of composition is made quite specific. Instead of a typical Sunday, it is a specific Sunday, 5 July 1925. Instead of a typical poem, it is specifically "The Wine Menagerie." This essay should be compared carefully with the chapter in Exile's Return (1951.5).

*10   DODGE, STEWARD CHARLES. "The Use of Evolutional Theory by American Poets." Ph.D. dissertation, University of Illinois.

11   GIUDICI, GIOVANNI. "Vita inquieta di Hart Crane: poeta dei Caraibi." Mondo Occidentale (March); pp. 47-52.
      In Italian. Brief review of the "uneasy and restless" life of Crane.

12   JUMPER, WILL C. "Crane's 'For the Marriage of Faustus and Helen,' Part III, Stanza 5." Explicator 17 (October):Item 8.
      Stanza 5 continues the argument of stanza 3--"experience takes on no values unless leavend by the yeast of what I shall call, for want of a better term, the personal imagination." When direct sensuous pleasure and the pleasures of the spirit are "transmuted into personal values of the individual imagination, they will serve as a bulwark against nothingness."

13   LEWIS, R.W.B. "Contemporary American Literature." In Contemporary Scholarship: A Critical Review. Edited by Lewis Leary. New York: Appleton-Century-Crofts, pp. 201-18.
      Mentioned in passing.

14   LOWELL, ROBERT. "Words of Hart Crane." Nation 186 (22 March): 186.
      Verse appreciation.

15   MATTHIESSEN, F.O. "Crane, Harold Hart." In Dictionary of American Biography. Edited by Harris E. Starr. Vol. 21. New York: Charles Scribner's Sons, pp. 206-8.
      Typical entry.

16   McLAUGHLIN, JOHN C. "Imagemes and Allo-images in a Poem by Hart Crane." Folio 22 (Spring):48-63.

Using terminology developed by Harold Whitehall, McLaughlin
applies to "Lachrymae Christi" by analogy the methods developed
by modern linguistics. "An imageme is a class of images which
are conceptually related; its limits are defined by the specific
members of the class (allo-images), each of which has a physical
representation." A number of images in the poem are loosely related by the vague concepts of purification and cleansing. These
can be considered allo-images of a single Imageme I. This imageme
can be further divided into subgroups--the first (Imageme Ia) indicates purification through disillusion and restraint, and the
second (Imageme Ib), purification through distillation and release. Seen in this light the imagemes themselves must be rede-
fined. Imageme Ia is a false purification based on the denial of
the humanity of man. Imageme Ib contains the idea of a revital-
ized flesh transformed by the earth itself. Following the implications of the title, McLaughlin establishes a new class of
images--Imageme IIa, and Imageme IIb, two sets which imply the
pagan-Christian contrast, the contrast between Dionysius and
Christ. Imageme Ia implies a misrepresentation of Christ, and
Imageme IIa defines the true Christ. In the poem itself Imageme
IIa is completely assimilated into Imageme IIb, forming a single
new imageme. "The Nazarene brings to mankind not a new message,
but a reaffirmation of an older faith in the power of the human
emotion to transform the spirit. He thus becomes a part of the
Dionysius-wine complex." Finally the author sets up a third
imageme, of which the allo-images are all related to the concep-
tualized situation of modern man.

17   ROSENTHAL, M.L.   "Irreverence in Poetry."   Nation 186 (17 May):
       450-52.
       Views Crane in a long poetic tradition of the impersonal
spirit of irony and negation. "Crane, notoriously and openly
homosexual, desperately aware of the hostility of our culture to
everything he was and stood for, and nevertheless anxious to find
symbols of affirmation within the real and the necessary, had the
negative strength that only adversity can create." Thus his own
life helps us to understand the meaning of "the higher aesthetic
amorality."

18   SLOTE, BERNICE.   "The Structure of Hart Crane's The Bridge."
       University of Kansas City Review 24 (March):225-38.
       Critics following Tate and Winters assert that The Bridge
is a failure as a whole, a shape without a form. The poem should
be reconsidered from the point of view of its unity by looking at
it as a design on Crane's own terms. First, Crane thought of The
Bridge as a symphonic structure with intricate repetition in
which "motives and situations recur." Second, Crane knew that he
was writing in an affirmative tradition and preferred to identify
himself with those who were aware of a "new vitality." Third, in
his affirmative tradition Crane was strongly influenced by
Whitman, using his point of view, his poetic theory, and some of

his specific patterns. The key to the poem is Crane's identification with Whitman at the end of "Cape Hatteras." "If Whitman is
seen as a bubbling exploiter of American chauvanism, The Bridge
will seem like a hapless panegyric of American history and science, with many of the individual poems obviously unconnected.
If, however, Whitman is seen as a deeply spiritual thinker, a
mystic of cosmic consciousness . . . the pattern in The Bridge
has a chance to come into focus." In Crane's hope to lend a myth
to God from the curveship he found the essential symbol and the
form of the poem. Reprinted: 1960.18.

19 _____. "Transmutation in Crane's Imagery in The Bridge."
    Modern Language Notes 123 (January):15-23.
        Defines transmutation as a poetic technique in which images
    recur in slightly changed patterns or patterns are repeated in
    somewhat different images. Since this occurs so often in The
    Bridge, it can be considered as a device for attaining unity in
    the poem. Refers specifically to "Three Songs" which anticipate
    rather remarkably the pattern of the last three sections of the
    poem--"Quaker Hill," "The Tunnel," and "Atlantis." Crane himself
    noted one of the central transmutations of the poem; the bridge
    becomes ship, world, woman, and harp. Starting with John
    Willingham's "Three Songs of Hart Crane's The Bridge," which pre-
    sents an analysis of the unity of the songs, Slote extends his
    demonstration of their unity by showing their transmutations in
    the last sections of the poem. Reprinted: 1960.18.

20 Van DOREN, MARK. The Autobiography of Mark Van Doren. New
    York: Harcourt, Brace & Co., p. 156.
        Brief mention of his contact with Crane.

21 WEBER, BROM. "Allen Tate, Yvor Winters, and Hart Crane."
    Poetry 92 (August):332-35.
        Weber's answer to Oscar Cargill's attack on Tate and
    Winters. This letter was sent originally to the Nation where
    Cargill's charge first appeared. When the literary editor of the
    Nation decided he could give no more space to the controversy,
    Weber sent it to Poetry. Taking issue with Cargill on almost
    every point, Weber asserts that Tate and Winters firmly bulwark
    the reputation of Crane and defends their right to find weak-
    nesses in Crane's poetry. In concluding, he mentions a curious
    fact of interest to scholars. He encourages Cargill to "mete out
    justice" to Samuel Loveman. Loveman had given Weber several
    typescript manuscripts which he represented as being original
    manuscript versions of Crane's unpublished poetry when Weber was
    doing his book on Crane. Waldo Frank also seems to have been
    duped by these transcripts. The alleged manuscripts provided by
    Loveman were faulty transcriptions of Crane's genuine manuscripts
    which Weber discovered when he edited the letters. See 1958.6.

22 WILLIAMS, WILLIAM CARLOS. I Wanted to Write a Poem. Boston:

Beacon Press, p. 43.
    Felt that his essay, "Soto and the New World," <u>Broom</u>, October 1923, which later appeared in <u>In the American Grain</u>, had been used by Crane in writing <u>The Bridge</u>.

1959

1   BEWLEY, MARIUS. "Hart Crane's Last Poem." <u>Accent</u> 19 (Spring): 75-85.
    An explication of "The Broken Tower." Although the poem may be deeply personal, "it is also an objective and deliberately sought out expression of Crane's literary faith in his last months, and expresses what he learned of his own limitations by writing <u>The Bridge</u>." Accepts Lesley Simpson's account of the beginning of the composition of the poem. An explication of the poem stanza by stanza follows. "Crane had learned that the tower of absolute vision was much too high for him to climb in his poetry, and he realized this with peculiar clairvoyance at the close of his life when he seemed to be running down in a frenzy of neurotic debauchery." The statement made by the poem is central to Crane's life and to his view of poetry. Thus, it may be the most important title in the <u>Collected Poems</u>. Crane finally recognized that an absolute vision must be balanced by the perspective of a moral vision. Reprinted: 1970.3.

2   COWAN, LOUISE. <u>The Fugitives: A Literary History</u>. Baton Rouge: Louisiana State University Press, pp. 64-66, 128, 138-39, 206, 238.
    Crane wrote to Allen Tate after he saw Tate's poem "Euthanasia" in the issue of the <u>Double Dealer</u> in which Crane's three translations of Laforgue appeared. He suspected that Tate had read T.S. Eliot. As a matter of fact, Tate had not read Eliot at that time. The correspondence continued. Crane sent Tate various numbers of the <u>Little Review</u>. Tate's study of Crane's poetry was very close. In his letter to Davidson, 12 July 1922, he speaks of Crane quite naturally as the sort of poet one accepts as a master. Tate discovered T.S. Eliot, Laforgue, and Crane at approximately the same time. Crane's "Stark Major" was entered in the Nashville Poetry Contest. Gorham Munson ranked Crane's poem first; the other two judges ranked it last. Tate described "Paraphrase" as "one of the most intense poems on death I have ever seen."

3   COWLEY, MALCOLM. <u>After the Genteel Tradition</u>. Gloucester, Mass.: P. Smith, pp. 31, 34, 176, 178, 182.
    If Sinclair Lewis were giving his Noble Prize address today, he would probably include the name of Crane. Crane's suicide illustrates what happened to the writers of the twenties when their personal philosophies crashed like banking houses. "Only Crane and John Dos Passos . . . tried to measure themselves

against the great poets or novelists of other ages."

4   ____. "Two Winters With Hart Crane." <u>Sewanee Review</u> 67
(October):547-56.
     More memories of Crane, this time in connection with Allen
Tate, recounting the attempt of Crane to move in with the Tates
at Addie Turner's house near the Slater Browns. "I am not trying
to tell the whole story of the literary friendship between Allen
and Hart, but merely to clarify two or three episodes that have
been misrepresented by some recent commentators." Although the
experiement of living together was a failure, in some ways it can
be counted as a success. "Without those months--and without
Allen's generosity--his <u>Bridge</u> might never have been built."

5 CUNLIFFE, MARCUS. <u>The Literature of the United States</u>.
London: Penguin Books, pp. 318-20.
     The poem in <u>White Buildings</u> point toward <u>The Bridge</u>, a
remarkable achievement with some superb passages, but not a unified
achievement. The rhetoric is unconvincing. "Though he invokes
Whitman, it is the haunted and homeless figure of Poe that charac-
terizes much of his work."

6 DREW, ELIZABETH. <u>Poetry: A Modern Guide to Its Understanding
and Enjoyment</u>. New York: Dell Publishing Co., pp. 20, 73,
215.
     Three mentions of Crane as an illustration of the misuse of
rhetoric.

7 DREW, FRASER. "What Cypher-script of time . . . of hart crane
. . . a memory." <u>Trace</u> 30 (February-March):40-42.
     An impressionistic recreation of the memory of Crane while
the author stands on Brooklyn Bridge.

8 GALPIN, ALFRED. "Memories of a Friendship." In <u>The Shuttered
Room and Other Places</u>, by H.P. Lovecraft and Divers Hands.
Edited by August Derleth. Sauk City, Wis.: Arkham House,
pp. 191-201.
     References to "Crane's early associates" in Cleveland:
Samuel Loveman, Gorham Munson, and Galpin. Crane was interested
in Galpin because of his knowledge of French and his interest in
French poetry.

9 HEMPHILL, J. "Allen Tate." In <u>Seven Modern American Poets</u>.
Edited by Leonard Unger. Minneapolis: University of Minne-
sota Press, pp. 230-35, 242-43, 252-53, 260-63.
     Fruitful in considering the relationship between Tate and
Crane. "Crane stands mostly as an object lesson to Tate."

10 LINK, FRANZ H. "Über das Geschictesbewusstein einiger ameri-
kanischer Dichter des 20. Jahrhunderts: Hart Crane's <u>The
Bridge</u>, Steven Vencent [<u>sic</u>] Benet's <u>Western Star</u> and Robert

Penn Warren's Brother to Dragons." Amerikastudien 4:143-60.
In German. Spends most time on "Proem" because it reveals
all of the principal themes of The Bridge. Concludes that romanticism is a significant element in Crane's poetry.

11 LOEB, HAROLD. The Way It Was. New York: Criterion Books,
pp. 236-37 and passim.
Description of Crane's personality. He "found Crane difficult: when he was down he was very, very down, and when he was
up he smashed furniture. But he had an eloquence - and while
writing he played the same tune over and over on the phonograph.
Best of all, he perceived the wonder around him and wasted little
time weeping over the imaginary glories of other times and
places."

12 LUDWIG, RICHARD M. Bibliography supplement to Literary His-
tory of the United States. Edited by Robert E. Spiller et al.
New York: Macmillan Co., pp. 99-100.
Brief bibliography.

13 MILLER, JAMES E., Jr. "Walt Whitman and the Secrets of History." Centennial Review 3 (Summer):320-26.
A brief reference to Crane as a poet who celebrated Whitman
as a fellow exiled comrade-poet.

*14 QUINN, VINCENT GERARD. "Transcendence in the Poems of Hart
Crane." Ph.D. dissertation, Columbia University.
See 1963.18.

15 SPAIR, EDWARD. "A Letter to Ruth Benedict." In An Anthro-
pologist at Work. Edited by Margaret Mead. Boston: Houghton
Mifflin Co., p. 185.
He does not understand what he calls "the nervous excite-
ment" of Crane. "Can you tell me what he wants?"

16 TATE, ALLEN. "Hart Crane." In Collected Essays. Denver,
Colo.: Allan Swallow, pp. 310-23, 324-28.
Reprint of 1936.9.

*17 TRISOLINI, ANTHONY GEORGE. "An Analysis of the Structure of
Hart Crane's The Bridge." Ph.D. dissertation, Northwestern
University.

18 UNTERMEYER, LOUIS. Lives of the Poets. New York: Simon &
Schuster, pp. 711-14.
A brief mixture of criticism and biography. Crane's de-
votion to "the logic of metaphor" is mentioned. The personal
unhappiness of his life is stressed. Lack of discipline "colors
(or discolors) his poetry."

19 WEST, PAUL. "Symbol and Equivalent. The Poetry of Industrial-

ism." Essays in Criticism 9 (January):61-71.
    Insofar as a poet is interested in the contemporary scene,
he encounters difficulties in writing his poetry. In attempting
to create a new myth, many modern poets reject or evade treatment
of modern industrial life and "substitute for the ideal of honesty
that of a merely narrow beauty by writing about certain subjects
which are time-honored and not a little worn." Eliot, Whitman,
and Crane have occasionally attempted and attained a comprehensive
modern vision. Despite Eliot's sententiousness and Crane's al-
ternately clogged and flooding style, West hopes that the modern
mysticism of these writers "will blossom in a satisfactory following which ignores their idiosyncracies and perpetuates their
real achievement."

20 WIDMER, KINGSLEY. "Crane's 'Key West.'" Explicator 18
       (December):Item 17.
       "Key West" is the key to Crane's final collection of poems,
as well as to his final "hard view" of Western civilization and
the dream of paradise somewhere in the mythic West. The difficulties in the poem are related to a structural metaphor that
Widmer puts in the form of a question: "What is the 'key' to the
West, and of what metal is it made?" After a passionate rejec-
tion of the modern world, the speaker of the poem is shown to be
in self-made accord with the benign indifference of the universe.
"His state stands in emphatic contrast with the Christian-anthro-
pomorphic-personalized view of the cosmos." The final two
stanzas develop the idea that the speaker will not accept a false
faith of mass society in some crude dream of urban order. The
unique and rare saving key for the individual is gold, not steel.
Commercialization is suggested by the base transmutation of the
rare metal into tin, and by the confining of the conscience.
Hence, the "key" to the West exists no longer. The speaker remains at the end of the poem "without community and without
vision of a further shore."

21 WINTERS, YVOR. "The Significance of The Bridge by Hart Crane,
       or What Are We to Think of Professor X?" In On Modern Poets.
       New York: Meridian Books, pp. 120-43.
           Reprint of 1947.13.

1960

1 ANON. "Crane (Harold dit Hart)." In Grand Larousse encyclo-
       pédique. Vol. 3. Paris: Librarie Larousse, p. 621.
       In French. Typical entry.

2 BARBER, ROWLAND. The Night They Raided Minsky's. New York:
       Simon & Schuster, pp. 210-12.
       Many intellectuals and artists in the mid-twenties were
enthusiastic members of the typical Minsky audience: John Dos

Passos, John Erskine, Robert Benchley, George J. Nathan, E.E.
Cummings, Edmund Wilson, and Crane. "There was always a shrill,
flask-passing contingent from Greenwich Village. The only quiet
ones in it were a hungry-looking poet named Hart Crane; a heartier-
looking poet who signed himself 'e.e. cummings' and who filled
pads with pencil sketches of Jack Shargel, his favorite; and
Reginald Marsh, an artist who worked swiftly with crayon whenever
a chorus galumphed onstage."

3   BASLAR, ROY P., ed. A Guide to the Study of the U.S.A. U.S.
     Library of Congress, General Research and Bibliography Division.
     Washington, D.C.: U.S. Government Printing Office, pp. 51,
     101, 122, 213, 218-19.
        Brief references.

4   BERTHOFF, WARNER. American Literature: Traditions and
     Talents. Oberlin, Ohio: Press of the Times, pp. 19, 22-23.
        Our greatest writers are Melville, Whitman, and Emerson.
     Immediately after them are Crane and Henry Adams--"The first for
     the precocious authority with which he pursued the artist's
     classic objectives of 'analysis and discovery,' and coincidentally
     redefined them for his age. . . ."

5   CREELEY, ROBERT. "Hart Crane and the Private Judgment." Free
     Lance:5 (First Half):3-17.
        Everyone reading Crane's poetry should judge for himself
     its value rather than accept the predominant opinion (the 1960s)
     that Crane was a failure as a poet. The Bridge attempted to
     direct our attention to what was historically and mythically sig-
     nificant to the American experience. Crane hoped that his method
     of juxtapositions would be appropriate for dealing with this
     material. Crane moved away from his dependence on irony to lan-
     guage attached to an emotion. Reprinted: 1970.8.

6   DEMBO, L[awrence]. S. "Hart Crane and Samuel Greenberg: What
     is Plagiarism?" American Literature 32 (November):319-21.
        Considers Crane's "Emblems of Conduct" and the three son-
     nets by Samuel Greenberg from which it is supposed to be adapted.
     Dembo concludes that the poem is something more than a copy of
     Greenberg and describes what Brom Weber called Crane's "mosaic
     method of composition." Greenberg's optimism was very appealing
     to Crane even though the poem itself, "Emblems of Conduct," is
     not an optimistic poem.

7   _____. Hart Crane's Sanskrit Charge: A Study of "The Bridge."
     Ithaca, N.Y.: Cornell University Press, p. 137.
        An attempt to answer the most serious charges raised against
     The Bridge: (1) if The Bridge is meant to be an epic poem, it
     does not deal meaningfully with the significant events in Amer-
     ican experience; (2) Crane lost faith in his subject in the course
     of the composition of the poem, destroying the logic of his plan;

and (3) the imagery and diction of the poem are often incomprehensible. These objections can be met. Crane faced Whitman's problems but did not adopt Whitman's solutions. The Bridge does not attempt to create a national myth based on technology; it is an account of the isolated and exiled poet's search for "a logos in which the Absolute that he has known in his imagination will be made intelligible to the world." The Bridge is a romantic lyric with epic implications. Crane was right when he said "the poem, as a whole, is, I think, an affirmation of an experience, and to that extent is 'positive' rather than 'negative' in the sense that The Waste Land is negative." There is disillusionment in the poem, but not enough critics have paid attention to the meaning of the reaffirmation. Nietzsche's theory of tragedy gave Crane a metaphysical argument with which to meet disillusionment. The Apollonian artist who reads and unmasks his dreams must be reconciled with the Dionysian artist who regards life with awe and wonder inspired by a "narcotic draught." The notion that resurrection follows suffering and death is what he borrowed from Nietzsche. "Crane's real purpose in writing The Bridge was to create an environment in which the poet was able to transcend the impotent clown image that was his only face in a nontragic, nonheroic world. Only in a blind but redeemable society--a society in which tragedy was possible--could the poet acquire what Crane thought a befitting role." In short, Crane is traditionally romantic in a definable way. The poet attempted to present "American history as an enlarged or collective version of the romantic poet's biography." Dembo's careful explication makes no significant reference to biographical facts or the conditions of the time. Dembo's conclusion: "victimized by himself and by the world--he still wrote optimistic, visionary poetry." See 1955.5, 7; 1961.5-6, 27-28; 1962.3, 14. Reprinted: 1970.6.

8   DOYLE, JOHN R., Jr. "Experiment in Early Twentieth-Century American Poetry." English Studies in Africa 3:131-45.
      A brief consideration of the contributions of T.S. Eliot, Ezra Pound, Wallace Stevens, E.E. Cummings, and Crane to the development of twentieth century poetry in America.

9   FRIEDMAN, JUDITH S., and PERLMUTTER, RUTH. "Crane's 'Voyages II.'" Explicator 19 (October):Item 4.
      The contrast between the infinite nature of the sea and the finite quality of human love is important. The sea is seen as a flirtatious woman because of the imagery. However, the sea is given other identities in the poem. Although the sea has the ability to destroy everything, she cannot separate the lovers or sully their devotion. The lovers ask not to be returned to reality until they have experienced the essence of their love. They wish to remain afloat on the sea of eternity like islands and like the seal. Having been able to view the sea from this vantage point, they have witnessed part of "paradise."

*10   GRIGSBY, GORDON K.   "The Modern Long Poem: Studies in The-
       matic Form."   Ph.D. dissertation, University of Wisconsin.
          See 1962.8; 1963.10.

 11   HONIG, EDWIN.   "American Poetry and the Rationalist Critic."
       Virginia Quarterly Review 36:416-29.
          Although his language suffers from overcompression, Crane
       represents the tradition of the English metaphysicals and the
       French symbolists.   He could be indignant in his poetry as Auden
       is.   The sea is the private place where the poetic vision redis-
       covers its source and from which it goes forth to do its work.
       This is seen in "Voyages."

 12   KLOUCEK, JEROME W.   "The Framework of Hart Crane's The Bridge."
       Midwest Review 2 (Spring):13-34.
          The difficulty in understanding The Bridge is the same
       difficulty characteristic of most symbolist poetry.   In The
       Bridge we have a sequence of individual poems dramatic or lyric
       in form.   The implicit narrative line is a mystic quest.   Crane
       used the traditional three-stage pattern of the quest described
       in Joseph Campbell's The Hero With A Thousand Faces.   Like the
       higher myths, this quest involves a mystic experience in the
       poet's attempt to transcend the limits of his world, in his
       attempt to discover the divine power imminent within the self and
       the world.   All the variations occur in The Bridge.   The general
       pattern corresponds to this monomyth.   Kloucek analyzes each poem
       as it occurs within the sequence of The Bridge, emphasizing the
       details of the quest, showing how each conforms to it in order to
       describe the narrative structure of the poem in its unity.   Be-
       cause of his symbolist method, Crane could not produce a closely
       woven narrative.   The fifteen individual poems, however, because
       they depict states of consciousness, together with the narrative
       clues given within the dramatic situations, reveal a sequential
       development and a coherent structure.

 13   KUSPIT, D.B.   "Some Images and Themes in Hart Crane's The
       Bridge."   Jahrbuch für Amerikastudien 5:164-74.
          Frank Lloyd Wright remarks in his Autobiography that
       Roebling's Brooklyn Bridge ushered in a new era in architecture
       because of the use of tenuity, a quality of steel--the quality of
       pull in a building.   This essay attempts to relate Wright's era
       of steel with Crane's era of art.   His stylistic procedures give
       tenuity and pull to his poems as Wright's use of steel gives
       these qualities to his buildings.   Crane may have destroyed him-
       self as a man, but not as a poet.   He found inspiration in his
       industry and ecstasy in his civilization.   This point is made
       clear by studying the imagery, particularly a few images in The
       Bridge.   The gull and all it suggests in the poem is the principle
       image studied.

 14   LEARY, LEWIS.   "An Unpublished Hart Crane Poem."   Columbia

Library Columns 10 (November):24-26.
    The first printing of "The Moth that God Made Blind"
written when Crane was sixteen. Discovered by Jethro Robinson in
the Crane Papers at Columbia.

15   LUND, MARY GRAHAM. "Lewis' 'In Memoriam.'" Explicator 18
      (January):Item 23.
    An explication of a poem about Crane, who gave himself over
entirely to the mystique rooted in his being, "to the existential-
ist's choice which had to be followed by death." Since Crane
felt that the period in which he lived was without direction or
philosophy, he wanted to implement thought by a new synthesis of
the machine. Although he was incapable of organizing the historical and spatial elements of science, he tried to incorporate the
machine into poetry by a sort of biological process.

16   LUTYENS, DAVID BULWER. "Order Wrested from Chaos." In The
      Creative Encounter. London: Secker & Warburg, pp. 98-127.
    Crane's poetry is not susceptible to detailed analysis; "it
has to be absorbed through the heart and the emotions rather than
the intellect." As a result, the chapter is a series of general-
izations and impressions. "Crane writes in a kind of inspired
telegraphese." Crane tried to achieve in his poetry the pattern
of order that he could not achieve in his life. His poetry is of
a visionary quality, the metaphors being drawn from his own experience. Crane's emotions surge up and take possession of him.
As a result, the relationship between imagination and reality
often becomes blurred. This obscurity is not merely willful, but
the outcome of an emotional and psychological compulsion. A survey of Crane's poetry, beginning with the early poems, with their
characteristics of loneliness, pain, and yearning.

17   ROSENTHAL, M.L. "New Heaven and Earth." In The Modern Poets.
      New York: Oxford University Press, pp. 168-82.
    An extended comparison of Crane to D.H. Lawrence. Crane
was especially appreciative of Lawrence's sensuousness; but apart
from direct influence, there is a simple convergence of interests.
Crane was not a thinker or a didactic poet; he was best at metaphor and the revelation of what was deeply inward. He sought to
exploit the machine culture, looking to this culture for signs
indicating the ultimate creativity of modern man--"his ability to
bring his splintered life to a new, harmonious whole." The protagonist of The Bridge wishes desperately to have confidence in
the triumph of his civilization over his own inadequacies, and
this triumph would indicate his ability to overcome the aliena-
tions deep within himself. If The Bridge failed, it is because
the fifteen individual poems are somewhat uneven in quality, not
because it expresses "the agonized duality of the human condition"
so honestly.

18   SLOTE, BERNICE. "Views of The Bridge." In Start With the

Sun. Edited by James E. Miller, Jr., Carl Shapiro, and
Bernice Slote. Lincoln: University of Nebraska Press, pp.
137-65.
    Reprint of 1958.18-19. See 1960.21.

19   THORP, WILLIAM. American Writing in the Twentieth Century.
     Cambridge, Mass.: Harvard University Press, pp. 38, 40, 196,
     216-18.
         Imagism was a brief though useful episode in his apprentice-
     ship. White Buildings is described as one example of the new
     style of verse that puzzled critics. Had poetry become an in-
     tellectual parlor game? None of the younger writers were more
     talented than Crane. He was a romantic and a primitive poet who
     was intoxicated with words, able to write only when he was at
     fever pitch. Since he lacked a god to believe in, he sought a
     myth to unify his long poem about America--he worshipped heroes.
     The Bridge is the one long poem of the times which challenges
     comparison with Eliot's The Waste Land. In spite of Crane's
     efforts, however, the parts of The Bridge do not cohere.

20   VIERECK, PETER. "The Crack-up of American Optimism: Vachael
     Lindsay, the Dante of Fundamentalists." Modern Age 4 (Summer):
     269-84.
         In dealing with Lindsay and the crack-up of the Utopian
     American myth, Crane is mentioned incidentally. This myth cul-
     minated in The Bridge, a representative example of the romantic
     and progressive tradition in American literature which affirms
     our democratic and material progress. The aesthetic breakdown
     of myth-making is seen in the poetry of Crane and Lindsay. Crane
     attempted to affirm industrial America, but The Bridge is an un-
     successful attempt "to contrive an untragic myth of affirmation
     out of our modern industrial progress." Because of an innate
     pessimism, Crane had to force himself into these affirmative
     beliefs.

21   WHITE, GERTRUDE M. "Must We Choose Between Whitman and
     Eliot?" Walt Whitman Review 6 (December):76-78.
         Review of Start With The Sun, by Miller, Shapiro, and
     Slote. While praising the book, White suggests that perhaps the
     authors have gone too far in asserting that only Lawrence, Crane,
     and Thomas have preserved the song and magic of poetry. "Even
     Miss Slote's erudition and eloquence can hardly persuade us to
     prefer the intricacies and paradoxes of The Bridge to a single
     stanza of 'On Wenlock Edge.'" See 1960.18.

22   WINTERS, YVOR. "The Anniversary, to Achilles Holt." In The
     Collected Poems of Yvor Winters. Denver, Colo.: Swallow
     Press, p. 81.
         Verse appreciation. Reprint of 1952.23.

23   _____. "Orpheus, in Memory of Hart Crane." The Collected

Poems of Yvor Winters. Denver, Colo.: Swallow Press, p. 85.
Verse appreciation.

24 YOUNG, PHILIP. "Fallen from Time: The Mythic Rip Van Winkle."
Kenyon Review 22 (Autumn):547-73.
In a discussion of the myth of Rip Van Winkle, with its
parallels in other times and cultures, a few lines are devoted
to Crane. Among all authors using the Van Winkle story, Crane
alone has given him serious and extended attention. In the "Van
Winkle" section of The Bridge, he is used as "the guardian angel
of the trip to the past," a figure evoked from the recollection
of the poet's childhood and the nation's. Since this is a
thoughtful and promising way to use the mythic figure, it is un-
fortunate that not much is done with him in the poem.

1961

1 AARON, DANIEL. Writers on the Left. New York: Harcourt,
Brace & World, pp. 80, 242, 272, 441.
Brief references.

2 BAIRD, PEGGY. "The Last Days of Hart Crane." Venture 4:21-
46.
Gives her own version of the story of Crane's last days in
Mexico and aboard the Orizaba. She went to Mexico in the fall
of 1931, while Crane happened to be there, to get a divorce from
Malcolm Cowley. A love affair seems to have developed: "That
night, or what was left of it, we slept in my bed, the clamor of
bells our wedding music." Since this is Crane's first experience
in making love to a woman, Baird records his sense of the excite-
ment of the event. Marriage seems to have been discussed and
plans made. His desperate extravagances did not seem to be
altered by this new experience. The actual moments leading up
to the suicide are touchingly presented. Re "The Broken Tower":
"Teasing, I asked if he thought he could concentrate on writing
the poem. And so he began, phrases scribbled on paper, voiced
in words to test the sound, discarded completely, or held for a
later trial." The frenzy of composition is supposed to have
gone on for three days without any respite; at the end of that
time there were supposed to be three stanzas. Compare this
account of the beginning of "The Broken Tower" with that of
Lesley Simpson (1932.22). Reprinted: 1968.8.

3 BRAUN, HENRY. "Hart Crane's 'The Broken Tower.'" Boston
University Studies in English 5 (Autumn):167-77.
The central image "evidently sprang from an actual exper-
ience in the bell-tower of a Mexican church." The theme of "The
Broken Tower" is concern with poetic sterility and the regenera-
tion of creative power through the experience of love.

4   BURTIS, MARY ELIZABETH, and WOOD, PAUL SPENCER. "(Harold) Hart Crane, 1899-1932." In Recent American Literature. Patternson, N.J.: Littlefield, Adams, pp. 75-79.
     Biographical sketch.

5   CARGILL, OSCAR. "The 'Unfractioned Idiom' of The Bridge." Poetry 98 (June):190-92.
     Review of Dembo's Hart Crane's Sanskrit Charge: A Study of "The Bridge," "the bravest effort in recent criticism." Against the prevailing opinion of major critics, Dembo has demonstrated the unity and artistic completeness of the poem. Since Dembo writes solely about The Bridge, not about Crane's life, no personal contact with the poet gets in the way of his study of the poem. While accepting Dembo's thesis that Nietzsche was a powerful influence on Crane, Cargill notes Eliot's influence as well. Dembo goes too far in trying to dissociate Crane from Whitman. "I rejoice in Dembo's book, for it beckons in an era in which Hart Crane will get his just due as one of the three great poets of the Renaissance of the twenties, the three most likely to survive--Eliot, Crane, and Wallace Stevens, in that order." See 1960.7.

6   CASPER, LEONARD. "Drowned Voyager." Prairie Schooner 35 (Spring):85-86.
     Review of Dembo's Hart Crane's Sanskrit Charge: A Study of "The Bridge." While his analysis of The Bridge makes it appear that the poem often seems to duplicate rather than refute The Waste Land, Dembo is silent on the many affinities the two poems have, not taking into account a parallel dualism in The Bridge. The volume is finally described as "too casual a consideration of critics and of Crane." See 1960.7.

7   COFFIN, TRISTRAM P. "Folklore in the American Twentieth Century." American Quarterly 13 (Winter):526-33.
     The Bridge is a poem which attempts to fuse the dissident elements of America, using Paul Bunyan and Rip Van Winkle "with the implication that Bunyan and Van Winkle are true folklore."

8   COWLEY, ROBERT. "Blume's Oak." Horizon 3 (July):75.
     Crane lived for a time in the same house as the painter Peter Blume.

9   DEMBO, L[awrence].S. "Hart Crane's Early Poetry." University of Kansas City Review 27 (Spring):181-87.
     Deals with poems written before "For the Marriage of Faustus and Helen" (1923). The early poems reveal Crane's continuing preoccupation with his attempt to define some kind of role for the poet in a hostile and chaotic world. Until he absorbed Nietzsche's theory of tragedy (leading to the production of "Faustus and Helen" and The Bridge), he had a keen sense of the isolation of the poet in the world. Dembo considers "In

Shadow," "My Grandmother's Love Letters," "Black Tambourine,"
"Pastorale," "Chaplinesque," "Praise for an Urn," and "Sunday
Morning Apples." Crane gradually learned that the poet serves a
crucial role in society, for without him the world itself would
be destroyed. His imagination is able to comprehend redemption
and take him a step beyond tragedy. "At its very least, this
vision is the creation of a man who desperately wanted to be a
valuable part of the world in which he lived, no matter how hostile that world seemed." See 1955.5.

10 FRIEDMAN, ALBERT D. The Ballad Revival. Chicago: University
    of Chicago Press, pp. 353-54.
        Discusses briefly what he regards as Crane's unsuccessful
attempt to combine jazz rhythm and trained rhythm in "The River"
section of The Bridge.

11 GINESTIER, PAUL. The Poet and the Machine. Chapel Hill:
    University of North Carolina Press, pp. 60-62, 71, 72, 113.
        Crane is representative of the type of poet who accepts and
deplores technological and mechanical civilization. He symbolizes
the sensitive man who can do nothing more than surrender to this
society, although he reserves the right to protest. Crane is a
failure as a poet, albeit a great one.

12 GINSBERG, ALLEN. "Death to Van Gogh's Ear." Kaddish and
    Other Poems 1958-1960. San Francisco: City Light Press, pp.
    61-65.
        Verse appreciation.

13 HALL, DONALD. "The Battle of the Bards." Horizon 4 (Septem-
    ber):117.
        "Crane is in the Eliot stream of American poetry in con-
trast to that represented by the Pound and Williams group."

14 HAMMOND, MAC. "Our Almost Forgotten Poet." Cleveland Plain
    Dealer, 12 November, p. 4.
        Nostalgic biographical feature article.

15 JENNINGS, ELIZABETH. "This Great Wink of Eternity: The
    Poetry of Hart Crane." In Every Changing Shape. London:
    Andre Deutsch, pp. 223-33.
        An easygoing, casual study of the relationship between
poetry and mysticism. Offers no theories but tries to disclose
the real union, the similarity of experience, between the activity
of the poet and the activity of the mystic. Crane is a poet who
made poetry "not simply a channel for mystic experience but the
means to attain it." Although Crane is like Rimbaud, there is
one significant difference: whereas Rimbaud managed to control
and even organize his life, seeking out experience in an analytical way, Crane's life was his poetry and poetry was first of all
sensation and later vision. It was not possible for Crane to

create an ordered world; he could only release into words, occasionally into rhetoric, his inner world--and "this world was a
world of torment." A true descendent of Whitman, Crane, however,
lacked the intellectual stamina and the ability to select and
arrange, the qualities essential for the creation of an epic.
Since the mystic by nature seeks the total surrender of his self
to God and the poet by necessity exploits himself, it might be
thought that Crane is the very opposite of a mystic. In fact,
only his means are different, not his end. He hoped to attain
the kind of experience that mystics know. Although some of his
early work is "Romantic" in the worst sense, his best work seeks
its meaning and unity through entirely contemporary symbols.

16   LOWELL, ROBERT. "The Art of Poetry III: An Interview with
     Robert Lowell." Paris Review 7 (Winter-Spring):57-95.
        Has read a good deal of Crane, but his difficult style has
not influenced him. "Tate was somehow more of a model." Crane
is the great poet of that generation because he got more out of
it than anybody else. Somehow he managed to capture New York:
he was at the center of things in a way that no other poet was.
"He was less limited than any other poet of his generation." Although his wildness and power appeals to Lowell, he cannot write
poems in Crane's manner. He is intrigued by Crane's obscurity.
"You can have a wonderful time explaining a great poem like
'Voyages II' and it all can be explained, but in the end it's
just a love poem with a great confusion of images that are emotionally clear; a prose paraphrase wouldn't give you any impres-
sion whatever of the poem."

17   MILES, JOSEPHINE. "The Poetry of Praise." Kenyon Review 23
     (Winter):120-21.
        Crane is cited as a sample of the twentieth century poet
who has a sense of the American sublime. Central in this tradition is "Voyages II." Reprinted: 1964.15.

18   MOORE, MARIANNE. "Interview with Donald Hall." In A Marianne
     Moore Reader. New York: Viking Press, pp. 267-69.
        Reprint of 1961.19.

19   _____. "The Art of Poetry IV." Paris Review 7 (Winter):41-
     66.
        The interviewer questions Moore concerning the famous case
of her revisions of "The Wine Menagerie." Moore admits that the
Dial had an inflexible rule of not asking for changes of any
kind, but she felt she had to disregard that rule out of compas-
sion. Crane was so desperate to be published, that his gratitude
to her was "ardent." She does admit that "it was lawless of me
to suggest changes." She knew Crane before this event in connection with the people who published Broom. "He was so diffident
and modest and seemed to have so much intuition, such a feel for
things, for books--really a bibliophile--that I took special

interest in him." The Bridge is a poem with a grand theme but it
might have been firmed up. "I think it is a terrible thing when
a writer is unable to be hard on himself." Reprinted: 1961.18.

20   OPPENHEIMER, JOEL. "Not Even Important or The Case of the
      Embryo Rimbaud." Kulchur 3 (Summer):21-25.
         Brief reference to Greenberg's influence on Crane.

21   PEARCE, ROY HARVEY. "The Long View." In The Continuity of
      American Poetry. Princeton, N.J.: Princeton University
      Press, pp. 101-11.
         Like William Carlos Williams, Crane discovered that he was
      in danger of falling under Whitman's spell. The record of his
      struggle to break free is The Bridge, a poem in which Whitman's
      hero tries to come of age. Crane hoped to prove to himself that
      America was worthy of being spoken of if the poet could discover
      the right words, and become convinced "that the power of poetry
      derived from the fact that it was the means of freeing words to
      register a sense of things beyond the life of the mind." Des-
      pite his many references to myth, Crane was really interested in
      magic--the magic of the word. His own role as poet in this
      attempt was passive; he had only to bring to realization the
      potential already in words. He was unprepared to discover that
      making poems involves making linguistic innovations. "He con-
      fused innovation with revolution." He tried to manipulate lan-
      guage so as to tear from it the secret of the meaning of meaning.
      His quest is not for a myth which implies discipline and ritual,
      but for some kind of sheer creativity. Because of his deep de-
      sire to transform things, technology and the machine become all-
      important for him. "The Bridge, as a poem, is meant to be such
      a machine: one which, if the Prodigal sets it right, will surely
      take him home. Only, home is where he has been, but without
      knowing it." Crane used the word "myth" incorrectly, since there
      is no essential story behind the reality which concerned him. He
      is a "adamic" poet, not a mythic poet; his "myth" is the magic of
      the word.

22   REXROTH, KENNETH. Assays. New York: New Directions, pp. 39,
      164.
         "Voyages" is "by far the best transmission of Rimbaud into
      English that exists," a difficult feat considering that Crane
      never learned French.

23   RUNDEN, JOHN [P.]. The Poetry of Hart Crane. Monarch Notes
      and Study Guides. New York: Monarch Press, 90 pp.
         A not always reliable guide for the undergraduate to Crane's
      poetry.

24   SCANNEL, VERNON. "The Ecstatic Muse: Some Notes on Hart
      Crane." Comtemporary Review 199 (May):231-37.
         Complains that no English publisher has published Crane's

poems, ignoring the Boriswood edition. Acutely aware of his own
time and place, Crane was an explorer moving through and beyond
the machine age. While his excesses may seem to have been in
some degree fruitful, they are symptoms of a spiritual sickness
"over which he had no more control than any victim of such a
sensibility scarred by such an environment." The value of Crane's
poetry is in its ability to project the consciousness of the
twentieth century man who struggles to orient himself to an
urban environment dominated by the machine. The bridge, however,
fails as a unifying symbol. "It is an intellectual concept, un-
related to the passionate imagination, and its presence seems
irrelevant to the viable movements of the poem." The poems in
Key West and some of the earlier lyrics in White Buildings are
better examples of Crane's work.

25   SMITH, CHARD POWERS. "Semi-classical Poetry in the Great
      Tradition." Massachusetts Review 3 (Autumn):41-61.
         Crane and T.S. Eliot are identified as "semi-classicists";
   in their "memorable work" one can detect the "glow of subjectivity, actually the romantic quest."

*26   TAKUWA, SHINJI. "Some Impressions of Henry Adams, Hart Crane,
      E.E. Cummings, and Others." Studies in English Literature
      and Language (Kyushu University, Japan), no. 11, pp. 19-53.

27   UNTERECKER, JOHN. "The Bridge Explained." Sewanee Review 69
      (Spring):345-48.
         Review of Dembo's Hart Crane's Sanskrit Charge, which is
   described as the fullest and best study that has been made. One
   of the limitations of the study is an attempt to impose a plot on
   The Bridge--the story of the young man in pursuit of the Absolute.
   The real foundation of Crane's poem may be simpler and more obvious. It is probably an architectural rather than a philosophical poem. Crane saw the bridge as a bridge. He corrects Dembo's
   assertion that Crane is not known to have read Latin, pointing
   out that Crane attended a good academic high school in Cleveland
   and part of his work in the classical course meant three years
   study of Latin. See 1960.7.

28   WEBER, BROM. Review of Hart Crane's Sanskrit Charge: A Study
      of "The Bridge," by L.S. Dembo. Modern Philology 59, no. 2
      (November):149-51.
         Dembo's attempt is to secure the acknowledged importance of
   Crane with proofs of clarity and success in The Bridge. The
   book is satisfactory only as "an approximate insight" into The
   Bridge. Dembo has unconsciously rewritten the poem under the
   guise of criticizing it. Weber feels that the effort of The
   Bridge was to encompass "things irreconcilable" rather than to
   reconcile them by means of a system. See 1960.7.

1962

*1   BULLARO, JOHN JOSEPH. "The Dantean Image of Ezra Pound, T.S.
       Eliot, and Hart Crane." Ph.D. dissertation, University of
       Wisconsin.

2   BURKE, WILLIAM J., and HOWE, WILL D. American Authors and
       Books, 1640 to the Present Day. Augmented and revised by
       Irving R. Weiss. New York: Crown Publishers, p. 203.
          Reprint of 1943.1.

3   COX, H. MORRIS. Review of Dembo's Hart Crane's Sanskrit
       Charge. American Literature 34:126-27.
          "Though Professor Dembo finds more unity in The Bridge than
    most readers will, his extensive explication is useful and per-
    suasive." See 1960.7.

4   CREELEY, ROBERT. "Hart Crane, for Slater Brown." In Four
       Love Poems, 1950-1960. New York: Charles Scribner's Sons,
       pp. 15-16.
          Verse appreciation.

5   EVERSON, WILLIAM. "Our Modern Sensibility." Commonweal 77
       (26 October):111-12.
          Beginning with Tate's distinction between the symbolic
    imagination and the angelic imagination, the author finds that
    Tate's criticism is not borne out in a consideration of Crane.
    The Bridge has an imperfect structure because of Crane's meta-
    physic, but the imaginative attempt is valid. He does not have
    Dante's grasp of the concrete image, but he lives in a different
    era. Because of the deficiencies of his culture and the "mal-
    formation" of his youth, he is deficient in his apprehension of
    the concrete. However, he has a vivid sense of the tremendous
    authenticity of the abstract.

6   FALLEDER, ARNOLD. "In Brandywine (Hart Crane)." Midwest
       Quarterly 3:264.
          Verse appreciation.

7   GELB, ARTHUR, and GELB, BARBARA. O'Neill. New York: Harper
       & Brothers, pp. 542-43.
          Mentions one occasion on which Crane was a houseguest of
    the O'Neills and a drinking partner for Eugene.

8   GRIGSBY, GORDON K. "The Photographs in the First Edition of
       The Bridge." Texas Studies in Literature and Language 4
       (Spring):5-11.
          For the Black Sun Press edition of The Bridge, Crane wished
    to use a reproduction of Joseph Stella's painting of Brooklyn
    Bridge as the frontispiece. Since the press was unable to repro-
    duce the painting, Crane substituted three photographs by his

friend, Walker Evans. These three photographs have never been
included in later editions, but they should have been since they
enrich the quality of the poem. The photographs are placed in
the Black Sun Press edition at the beginning, middle, and end of
the poem. The photographs themselves and their placement in the
text reflect what Crane was trying to do in the poem, both physi-
cally and symbolically, adding a major dimension to the meaning
of the poem. "The Bridge, then, is, as few poems are, 'icono-
logical.'" See 1960.10.

*9   GUIGUET, JEAN. "L'Univers poetique de Hart Crane." Ph.D.
      dissertation, University of Paris.
          See 1965.9.

10   HARDWICK, ELIZABETH. "Anderson, Millay, and Crane in Their
      Letters." In A View of My Own: Essays on Literature and
      Society. New York: Farrar, Strauss & Cudahy, pp. 3-13.
          Reprint of 1953.13.

11   HOFFMAN, FREDERICK J. "The Text: Hart Crane's The Bridge:
      The Crisis in Experiment." In The Twenties. Rev. ed. New
      York: Viking Press, pp. 257-74.
          No significant changes from 1955.7.

12   HOWARD, N.R. "Hart Crane Sought Death 30 Years Ago." Cleve-
      land Plain Dealer, 23 July, p. 2.
          Biographical reminiscences.

13   JOSEPHSON, MATTHEW. Life Among the Surrealists. New York:
      Holt, Rhinehart & Winston, pp. 34-38, 262-65, 289-300.
          Met Crane when he was nineteen and had first come to New
      York. Found his early verses old-fashioned and Swinburnian. Did
      not know the kind of sexual torment Crane was going through.
      There was nothing obviously effeminate about him; used to call
      him "Bully Boy." The sense of isolation in America that artists
      of the period were undergoing was well reflected in the letters
      which Crane wrote to Josephson from Ohio. Tells the famous story
      of the proposed meeting between the writers from Broom and Seces-
      sion at a tavern in "Little Italy." Asserts that Boyd's article
      "Aesthete: Model 1924" was based in part on Crane. While he
      admired Crane's poetry, he was disturbed by his extravagant be-
      havior. He seemed to be two people, driven at times to the under-
      world region of the Brooklyn docks and then coming back to the
      company of his literary friends. The Bridge was his most daring
      work, an epic in intention. "It remains, after all, a ruin even
      if a magnificent ruin, for we know it contains only a part of
      what the poet endeavored to say."

14   MOTTRAM, ERIC. "Review." Modern Language Review 58 (October):
      601-3.
          Review of Dembo's Hart Crane's Sanskrit Charge. Like

Patterson, the Cantos, Eliot's long poems, and The People, Yes, The Bridge is part of an American effort to create poetic struc- tures that unify modern experience. The short epic has become characteristically American. Dembo's book is a great help in aiding the reader to unravel the cross-related images and themes presented in elliptical forms. Yet many difficulties remain. Crane's affirmations, intended as a reply to The Waste Land, appear as ecstasy. If one believes that an epic poem should have a philosophy, the criticism of Tate and Winters remains true. The poem, however, is characteristic of this century because it creates its vision out of the poet's experience, "a Paradiso of light without intellect." See 1960.7.

15   MUNSON, GORHAM. "The Greenwich Village that Was: A Seedbed
     of the 1920's." Literary Review 5, no. 3 (Spring):313-35.
        Discusses Crane's relationships with The Pagan and its
     editor, Joseph Kling.

16   RIBNER, IRVING, and MORRISS, HARRY. Poetry: A Critical and
     Historical Introduction. Chicago: Scott-Foresman, pp. 440-
     41.
        His style was a violent reaction to the ornate diction of
     the Victorians. He preferred the method of the French symbolists.
     An explication of "The Merman," an "interesting though ultimately
     unsuccessful experiment" in structure.

17   RICHMAN, SIDNEY. "Hart Crane's 'Voyages II': An Experiment
     in Redemption." Wisconsin Studies in Contemporary Literature
     3 (Spring-Summer):65-78.
        Because Crane demonstrated even better than Eliot that "the
     spirit kills," in his poetry we may eventually find the most ap-
     propriate symbol of our age. Crane's poetry gives us "an exor-
     bitant and utterly insupportable affirmation of the present and
     the future." The thing we know best about Crane's poetry is that
     it failed. In some ways his very gifts--lyrical vitality and
     dynamic imagination--are the prime ingredients of his failure.
     He had no structure to body forth his compelling intensity. What
     remains of value in The Bridge are the sections of lyric beauty
     that one must accept as complete in themselves. "In short, the
     poem 'lends' no 'myth to God.' If anything, it lends a myth to
     our own Godlessness." It is obvious that Crane is deficient as
     a myth-maker, but perhaps critics shouldn't obstinately focus on
     this point. The Bridge is not solely the creation of a myth, it
     is devoted primarily to the theme of "man's transfiguration" that
     Crane found in Whitman. "Voyages II" is an example of Crane's
     desire to find within disorder itself a "new reality." The best
     single clue to interpreting the poem is supplied by Crane himself
     in his 1925 essay written to clarify the design of White Build-
     ings. It was his desire "to go through the combined materials of
     the poem, using our 'real' world somewhat as a springboard, and
     to give the poem as a whole an orbit or predetermined direction

of its own." He did this on the principle of "the logic of meta-phor."

18 RUPP, RICHARD H. "Hart Crane: Vitality as Credo in 'Atlan-tis.'" Midwest Quarterly 3:265-75.
       Crane's central problem in The Bridge was to create a living symbol of the American dream, seen most dramatically in "Atlantis." Supplies a stanza-by-stanza paraphrase of "Atlantis," emphasizing its constant movement in space and time, the intensity of the images, the alternating pictures of the actual world, the tremendous amount of energy it contains, and the interplay of the symbolic patterns. The movement of the poem parallels the arche-typal birth of the hero as well as the Judaeo-Christian promise of redemption. Traces some of the symbolic patterns in "Atlantis" emphasizing the archetypal pattern of the hero and the archetypal voyage which the hero takes. The fulfillment of the hero's role comes in his prophecy, and from that prophecy will spring a new nation. Crane has recalled God's promise to Noah. He discusses the rich and varied musical symbolism in the poem, and the various symbolic bird patterns, an indication of the care with which Crane wrote the poem. "What principle, one may ask, guided Crane to shape his material in just this way?" It was Crane's belief in vitality. "In order for the symbol to have ultimate validity, it had to be vital." The final pattern expressing Crane's credo is that "of vital compression." The important links in the poem are between an animate and an inanimate object.

19 SWALLOW, ALLAN. An Editor's Essay of Two Decades. Seattle and Denver: Experimental Press, pp. 160-93.
       Reprint of 1949.11.

20 TINDALL, WILLIAM YORK. A Reader's Guide to Dylan Thomas. New York: Noonday Press, pp. 14, 212.
       "Of American poets, [Dylan] Thomas singled out Stevens for dispraise and Hart Crane, some of whose lines (those of 'Recita-tive,' for example) seemed agreeable, for praise."

21 UNTERECKER, JOHN. "The Architecture of The Bridge." Wisconsin Studies in Contemporary Literature 3 (Spring-Summer):5-20.
       The principal difficulty in appreciating The Bridge is that one reads it too carefully. Reading the poem straight through without interruption will clear up many difficulties. The poem only seems to be disorganized; it has a mosaic structure com-pounded from seemingly independent sections, constructed like Moby Dick, The Waste Land, and Ulysses. The plot of The Bridge is a digest of Joyce's Ulysses; Crane had read Joyce's work care-fully. Although the Whitman influence is real, perhaps Crane learned more from William Carlos Williams. Crane is especially indebted to The American Grain and an early Williams poem "The Wanderer." These writers helped provide him the material he needed for his mythic structure. Unterecker pays special atten-

tion to the way in which each section of The Bridge is linked to
other sections; he is also concerned with the temporal and spatial
schemes of the poem. While these structural links are obvious to
the reader, of most interest is the subtle use of the full development of the pair of symbols essential to the poem: the serpent
of time and the eagle of space. All of the river imagery, stream
imagery, and the winding imagery of the poem are connected with
time; all of the strategically placed bird associations with the
eagle of space. The plot of the whole poem takes place in
twenty-four hours, and this chronological pattern recurs in each
of the major divisions. There is also the January to January
linking scheme.

22   Van NORSTRAND, ALBERT. "The Bridge and Hart Crane's 'Span of
     Consciousness.'" In Aspects of American Poetry. Edited by
     R.M. Ludwig. Columbus: Ohio State University Press, pp. 171-
     202.
          The majority holds that he failed to carry out his design
     of an American synthesis because the concept itself was faulty.
     This opinion does not reflect the whole truth. "Understanding
     Crane's attempt to render a doctrine is of course crucial to
     understanding the poem, but the subject of The Bridge lies as
     much in the poet's attempt as it does in the doctrine itself."
     Regards the following by Crane as very important: "Poetry is
     simply the concrete evidence of the experience of a recognition
     (knowledge if you like)." The process by which Crane attempts to
     apprehend his subject is the vital principle of the poem. Crane
     begins with a vision of The Bridge as the apotheosis of human
     experience, but had to work backwards and then forwards toward
     the vital center of his experience. The record of his corres-
     pondence dealing with the composition of the poem indicates that
     he was working toward a center of some sort "which might finally
     define the poem's dialectic." In Crane's theory of poetry a poem
     is as much about the experiencing as about the experience. "I
     propose that Crane's involvement in his poem was such that his
     struggle to form it became in fact the subject of the poem, and
     that when the poem is read in this way, it becomes clear that it
     is a whole document whose parts are organic." Van Norstrand dis-
     cusses Crane's attempt to form a theory based on some kind of
     mysticism and his search for a dramatic form to define his de-
     clared subject. "As Crane's self was the subject of The Bridge,
     how then was he to organize within it those voices which would
     echo him?" In the process of composing the poem, he had become
     the hero. "The organizing technique of the poem is the speaker's
     repeated questing for unity." "Crane's letters made it abundantly
     clear that the central, living principle in The Bridge is the on-
     stage consciousness, contemplating the Bridge and trying to
     generate a new significance about it. Without this vital prin-
     ciple the Bridge would have no nature apart from its mere actuality
     as a magnificent engineering structure." The great importance of
     this poem in the history of American literature is that it is one

of the most important documents in "the American domestication of
Romanticism." Reprinted: 1968.35; 1970.6.

23   WHEELRIGHT, PHILIP. "From Metaphor to Symbol." In Metaphor
     and Reality. Bloomington: Indiana University Press, pp. 99-
     104.
         "To Brooklyn Bridge" illustrates the concept of a presiding
     image of a single poem. The bridge is a symbol that did not have
     any literary or cultural ancestry. Its meaning had to be drawn
     from the many images associated with bridging in the poem.
     Wheelright illustrates the paradox in the bridge as symbol by ex-
     plaining how it is a symbol of both freedom and enchainment.
     "Praise for an Urn" is also discussed under this category, being
     a poem with a presiding image that seems to have a double focus.
     The presiding image is both the urn itself and the memory of the
     dead friend whose ashes the urn holds. This poem shows how dif-
     ficult it is to draw "suitable boundaries around the scope of a
     symbol," since the urn derives much of its symbolic power from
     associations independent of the poem. Crane, who Wheelright de-
     scribes as "America's finest lyricist," also uses a second kind
     of symbol--"the personal symbol," the Atlantis symbol in "Cutty
     Sark."

24   YOUNG, PHILLIP. "The Mother of Us All." Kenyon Review 24
     (Summer):319-415.
         Crane raises Pocahantas "to full mythic stature" in The
     Bridge.

                                1963

*1   ANDREACH, ROBERT JOSEPH. "The Spiritual Life in Hopkins,
     Joyce, Eliot, and Hart Crane." Ph.D. dissertation, New York
     University.
         See 1964.1.

2   ANON. "Crane, Hart 1899-1932." In The Columbia Encyclopedia.
     3d ed. Edited by William Bridgewater and Seymour Kurtz. New
     York: Columbia University Press, p. 506.
         Typical entry.

3   ANON. Review of Hart Crane by Samuel Hazo. Commonweal 79,
     no. 7 (8 November):200.
         "A brief but thorough and perceptive examination of the
     poet's work." See 1963.12.

4   BLOOMINDALE, JUDITH. "Three Decades in Periodical Criticism
     of Hart Crane's The Bridge." Papers of the Bibliographical
     Society of America 57 (July-September):364-71.
         An incomplete but useful listing of articles on The Bridge
     since its date of publication. A brief introductory essay notes
     shifts in the criticism of The Bridge. For a group of critics in

the 50s and early 60s, Crane's magnificent failure is coming to be regarded as his authentic achievement. See 1964.18.

5   BOYER, PETER. "Hart Crane: The Past in The Bridge." Osmania Journal of English 1:34-41.
        Emphasizes Crane's interest in the myth of America and the nineteenth century ideals on which the myth was based. "My intent is to demonstrate the relationship between the interpretation of American belief in the age of Whitman and in the age of Hart Crane, and Hart Crane's allegiance to the former rather than the latter." While he had no intention of denying the reality of the twentieth century, his conclusions were "based on a society which no longer existed."

6   CAMBON, GLAUCO. "Hart Crane's The Bridge." In The Inclusive Flame. Bloomington: Indiana University Press, pp. 120-82.
        Crane was the symbol of his age, and was influenced by his close friends Waldo Frank and Gorham Munson to rediscover America, reacting to Eliot with a strong will of affirmation. The Bridge is a poetic expression of this ambitious affirmation. The co-herence of The Bridge is better understood if one thinks of it as a rhapsody in the musical sense of the term, a network of thematic links and recurrences and developments connecting the various parts of the poem. A lengthy and conventional analysis of The Bridge follows. The Bridge should be grasped from the very start as a voyage, understood in the light of Einstein's space-time theories, spatially realized, a perpetuated temporal gesture. It is an existential poem in which the poet imaginatively rehearses the ritual of death and resurrection. Cambon examines "Chaplin-esque," "For the Marriage of Faustus and Helen," "Recitative," "Passage," "Voyages," and others. See 1954.1; 1955.4. Reprinted: 1970.6.

7   CLARK, DAVID.R. "Hart Crane's Technique." Texas Studies in Language and Literature 5 (Autumn):389-97.
        More than most poets, Crane distorted accepted idiom and syntax. When successful, his experimentation is significant. Unfortunately, however, he is often simply obscure. Like most modern poets, he uses incomplete or amorphous syntax to give the contemporary sense "that in our lives choice has surrendered to chance." "Voyages II" is used to illustrate this point. The in-complete syntax gives the impression of something started, but not finished. Crane uses a chain-reaction series of metaphors which can be effective without being analyzed in terms of ordinary concrete reference. The metaphorical reference which may have been in the poet's mind has disappeared so completely in the poem that the reader can only deal with the implications derived from the word itself as used. "Atlantis" illustrates this technique. When both syntax and metaphor are opaque, the reader has a genuine problem. This is seen especially in "The Broken Tower" which does not seem to have a consistently developed image.

Reprinted: 1972.7.

8   COWLEY, MALCOLM.   "Laforgue in America: A Testimony."
     Sewanee Review 71 (January–March):62–74.
          Discusses the influence of Jules Laforgue, the French sym-
     bolist poet, on various American poets.   Although Crane owned a
     copy of Laforgue, he could not translate him very well.

9   DAVIDSON, DONALD.   "Hart Crane's Poetry: Difficult but Bold
     and Masculine."   In The Spyglass: Views and Reviews, 1924–
     1930.   Edited by John T. Fain.   Nashville, Tenn.:   Vanderbilt
     University Press, pp. 106–9.
          Reprint of 1927.9.

10   GRIGSBY, GORDON K.   "Hart Crane's Doubtful Vision."   College
     English 24 (April):518–23.
          Biographical information on Crane has not been an aid to
     the criticism of The Bridge.   It has been customary for thirty
     years to accuse The Bridge of two contradictory faults, but this
     contradiction has gone unnoticed: (1) The Bridge is too simple
     in its vision; and (2) it is not simple enough.   "In one breath
     Crane is charged with a mindless optimism or idealism; in the
     next he is charged with including ugly realities and negations
     that conflict with his idealism and 'confuse' the poem."   The
     ugly realities in the poem are intended as an integral part of
     Crane's vision.   The dialectic between optimism and pessimism is
     one of the chief sources of strength in the poem.   The most im-
     portant biographical document is the long letter to Waldo Frank,
     20 June 1926, after he had read Spengler's Decline of the West.
     That the poet must accept darkness as part of the realization of
     his vision is essential to Crane's conception of The Bridge.
     Another mistaken notion concerning The Bridge is that it was
     supposed to be some kind of "nationalistic paean to America."
     Crane never felt that America had reached its ultimate develop-
     ment; rather he thought that its unique history as the "New
     World" made it the place where new ideals and new spiritual qual-
     ities might arise.   See 1960.10.

11   GUNN, THOMAS.   "Hart Crane."   In The Concise Encyclopedia of
     English and American Poets and Poetry.   Edited by Stephen
     Spender and Donald Hall.   New York: Hawthorne Books, pp.
     101–2.
          More interesting than the typical entry because of the
     author.

12   HAZO, SAMUEL.   Hart Crane.   New York: Barnes & Noble, 146 pp.
          Views Crane in the light of the problems created by the
     twenties, an era in which serious and fundamental questions were
     asked.   Crane was able to solve his problems as an artist in a
     few poems.   The answers he reached sustained him for a brief
     time only.   Since he was unsuccessful in solving his personal

problems, he could not face the future with "wisdom, confidence, and hope." Begins with a brief review of Crane's life, emphasizing the essentially self-destructive character of his vices. Emphasizes his versatility and success as a lyric poet. The apogee of Crane's lyric gift can be seen in "For the Marriage of Faustus and Helen" and "Voyages." Hazo stresses the thematic unity of "Faustus and Helen." "Voyages" is a series of poems dealing with love, which grows out of the concept of the poet as voyager. The theme of "Voyages" permeates The Bridge--"the need to seek as something important and indispensible in itself, regardless of, and even despite, discovery." The search in The Bridge, however, is for the real American past. If the first half of The Bridge dramatizes the poet's quest into the American past in order to find a synthesis that reconciles the world of time and space, the poems in the second half are concerned rather specifically with relating the synthesis discovered through the world of the future he imagined. The concluding chapter discusses the handful of poems in Key West: An Island Sheaf and "The Broken Tower," Crane's last will and testament, "containing that moment of sudden brightness that came to him before his suicide." Reprinted: 1977.12. Reviewed in 1963.19, 21; 1964.7, 21-22.

13   HENDRICK, GEORGE. "Hart Crane Aboard the Ship of Fools: Some
      Speculations." Journal of Twentieth Century Literature 9
      (April):3-9.
            A piece in which Hendrick speculates that Katherine Anne
      Porter incorporated Crane's characteristics in some of the char-
      acters in Ship of Fools. Crane and Porter, together in Mexico
      for a brief time, had an altercation because Crane was very dif-
      ficult to get on with. Bits and pieces of Crane's correspondence
      and Porter's memoir in Horton are traced to various characters
      in the novel. Crane referred to Lysol in one of his letters and
      a character in the novel is concerned with disinfectant. Eche-
      garay drowns trying to rescue the fat bulldog deliberately thrown
      overboard by Ric and Rac, and this reminds Hendrick of the inci-
      dent in which Crane observed Doctor Zinsser throwing some rats
      overboard. Echegaray carves small animals with a knife, and sits
      crying after the knife is taken away from him "just as Crane,
      his·artistic powers declining, often cried." Herr Baumgartner
      drinks excessively as Crane did. "In The Ship of Fools Miss
      Porter expresses--if these speculations connecting the relation-
      ship between her and Hart Crane with the novel are correct--a
      sharply ambivalent attitude toward the poet."

14   JARRELL, RANDALL. "Fifty Years of American Poetry." Prairie
      Schooner 37 (Spring):1-27.
            Asserts that The Bridge does not succeed as a unified work
      of art because some of the poems are bad or mediocre, and because
      "Crane took for his subject an ambiguous failure and tried to
      treat it as a mystical triumph." Although parts of The Bridge
      are wonderful, Crane's poetry is hurt most by rhetoric and sen-

timentality. "His automatic ecstatic mysticism, often of a
Whitmanesque kind, is a form of sentimentality."

15   LEWIS, R.W.B. "Hart Crane and the Clown Tradition." Massa-
     chusetts Review 4 (Summer):745-67.
        Of the poems before "Faustus and Helen" Crane discussed
     "Chaplinesque" the most. It is the most finished of the early
     poems that deal with the posture of the poet in America. The
     central image of the poet as clown or fool has a long European
     history and a continuing American history. The figure of the
     poet as clown is particularly appropriate in an industrial and
     scientific world which turns human beings into grotesques.
     "Crane's 'Chaplinesque' thus participates in a comic tradition at
     once ancient and specifically American--and which, indeed, has
     reached the point where it is probably the most vital aspect in
     American writing today." Written shortly after Crane had seen
     Chaplin's The Kid, the "we" in the poem indicates the poet's
     identification with the comic Chaplin figure. The image of the
     closing lines shows that the clown figure can transcend his
     shabby environment; however, the main burden of the poem is still
     the image of the poet as "a shabby and antic tramp, a meekfaced
     comedian on the run." Crane reached his maturity when he was
     able to see that the poet is "a clown perhaps, but an inspiring
     clown." See 1964.10.

16   MORGAN, H. WAYNE. "Hart Crane: Spokesman of Vision." In
     Seven Americans. New York: Hill & Wang, pp. 105-26.
        Crane was drawn to the different qualities of Matthew
     Josephson and Sherwood Anderson. Ultimately found balance in his
     art but not in himself. He was always in search of some positive
     attitudes; the bitterness so evident in Crane was transitory, not
     permanent, "and the sum of his poetry is wrought of light, not
     darkness." He perceived early in his career that the machine
     civilization would pose a threat to the artist and to society in
     general; his bitter rejection of machine civilization was not
     accompanied by a nostalgic desire for a return to the past. As
     time passed, he came to look upon the machine in a different
     light. Love could break the power of the machine and bring order
     to the world of chaos. Although he worked hard at the composition
     of The Bridge, he was finally dissatisfied with its form. The
     great truth that Crane perceived was that "chaos, like order, can
     be used to define itself."

17   MOTTRAM, E[ric].N.W. "American Poetry." In The Concise En-
     cyclopedia of English and American Poets and Poetry. Edited
     by Stephen Spender and Donald Hill. New York: Hawthorn
     Books, pp. 27-28.
        Mentioned as one of the poets who attempted to create an
     epic for America, The Bridge, the first self-consciously major
     poem to express the specific aspects of modern culture.

18   QUINN, VINCENT [Gerard]. Hart Crane. United States Authors
     Series, no. 35. New York: Twayne Publishers, 141 pp.
        Concerned with Crane's principal themes as well as Crane's
     attitude towards the act of poetry itself. He analyzes the major
     poems only and discusses the judgments of some of Crane's critics.
     "The keystone of this book is the recognition that Crane looked
     upon poetry as the expression of gratuitous intuition, and that
     the central theme of his inspiration was the desire for absolute
     beauty and love." Crane is in the tradition of visionary poets.
     Crane is also used as a figure in the debate between the conten-
     tion of the logical positivist that science alone can make mean-
     ingful statements about reality and the insistence of the humanist
     upon the autonomous and equally valid contribution of art. Since
     Crane's principal desire was for absolute beauty and love, Quinn
     is concerned with the themes that spring from this desire. Dis-
     cusses the critical positions of Yvor Winters, Allen Tate, and
     R.P. Blackmur. Quinn's contribution to Crane scholarship is seen
     in the chapter where he balances against their critical view the
     position of Jacques Maritain in Creative Intuition in Art and
     Poetry. Maritain emphasizes the power of the creative experience
     which enables it to penetrate reality to a depth beyond, but not
     incompatible with, reason. See 1959.14; 1964.22.

19   SMITH, J. HAROLD. "American Author and Critic Series." Amer-
     ican Bookcollector 14, no. 1 (September):4-5.
        Review of Hazo's Hart Crane, "a carefully ordered study in
     which Hazo is sympathetic without being apologetic." See 1963.12.

20   SPILLER, ROBERT E. et al., eds. Literary History of the
     United States. New York: Macmillan Co., pp. 99-100, 457-58;
     Supplement 2:132-34.
        See 1948.18; 1953.18.

21   TUSIANI, JOSEPH. "Symbolic Mazes." Spirit 30, no. 3 (July):
     85-86.
        Review of Hazo's Hart Crane, a good, well-balanced book
     without getting trapped between the two extremes of Crane criti-
     cism. See 1963.12.

22   WASSERSTROM, WILLIAM. The Time of The Dial. Syracuse, N.Y.:
     Syracuse University Press, pp. 46, 81, 89-95, 117-18, 131, 150.
        Crane complained to Allen Tate that the Dial was not print-
     ing work of the younger American writers. However, Crane's
     poetry, which had been published in one of the earliest numbers
     of the magazine, continued to appear in it throughout the 1920s.
     Crane "decided that Miss Moore was a tyrant." In a letter to
     Tate, he made the much-quoted statement, "How much longer [will]
     our market . . . be in the grip of two such hysterical virgins
     as The Dial and Poetry!" While Crane had seriously objected to
     Marianne Moore's alterations of "The Wine Menagerie," Crane wrote
     his thanks for her suggestions.

23   WHITE, WILLIAM. "Hart Crane: Bibliographical Addenda."
     Bulletin of Bibliography 24 (September-December):35.
          Although Hazo did not mean his list of critical materials
     in Hart Crane: An Introduction and Interpretation to be complete,
     White lists thirty-six pieces which were not included in his
     bibliography, those published since Rowe's Hart Crane: A Bib-
     liography.

24   YOUNG, JAMES DEAN. "Hart Crane's 'Repose of Rivers': What's
     the Evidence? A System for Critics." Xavier University
     Studies 2:121-37.
          A critic must formulate an adequate hypothesis of the value
     of the subject matter, then he must apply a rigorous objective
     analysis to the object (the poem); and finally he must correlate
     the observed evidence with "each single hypothesis of value." Of
     the numerous possible existing value definitions, Young selects
     four which will be applied to the poem: mechanism, contextualism,
     organicism, and formism. "Repose of Rivers" is used as the text
     to illustrate the general critical procedures he has outlined.

                                1964

1   ANDREACH, ROBERT J[oseph]. "Hart Crane." In Studies in
     Structure. New York: Fordham University Press, pp. 102-39.
          Crane is a representative modern author who writes within
     a spiritual frame of reference, both a mystic and a pantheist,
     religious in his approach to art. The Bridge is an attempt to
     give America a religious epic. The first half of The Bridge is
     analyzed to demonstrate the order of the first three stages of
     the spiritual life. An awakening is followed by an illumination.
     In the second half of The Bridge, the protagonist must test his
     illumination, which unites him with the past, in the world of the
     present. The goal of the mystic is the unitive way, and the pro-
     tagonist must undertake the dark night of the soul in order to
     achieve it. Finally, we must credit Crane with creating a uni-
     fied, coherent poem "that strikes directly at the core of the
     fundamental problem in the twentieth century, or in any century
     for that matter." Science may have built Brooklyn Bridge, but by
     the end of the poem modern man has created a "bridge" to God.
     Using the traditional stages in the growth of spiritual life
     should not confuse the reader with respect to Crane's religious
     disposition. His basic religious myth is non-Christian, since
     it lacks the essence of Christianity. God is identified as the
     union of self and all of life. Crane's thesis is that if man
     chooses to grow spiritually, he can discover the imminent reality
     of God in himself, as well as in all men, and in all that is out-
     side of himself. See 1963.1.

2   ANON. Creative Century: Selections from the Twentieth Cen-
     tury Collections at the University of Texas. Humanities

                                120

Research Center. Austin: University of Texas Press, pp. 16-17.
    Briefly describes some Crane manuscripts: a corrected carbon type script of The Bridge; a group of unpublished letters to his mother and grandmother; and the first edition of White Buildings (with galley proofs) with Allen Tate's name misspelled on the title page.

3   BAYLEY, JOHN. The Romantic Survival. London: Constable, pp. 7-8.
    Comments on his ambitious attempt to absorb the world of machines into his poetry.

4   BLAIR, WALTER et al. American Literature: A Brief History. Chicago: Scott-Foresman, pp. 277-78.
    Brief biographical notes.

5   COWLEY, MALCOLM. The Dream of the Golden Mountains: Remembering the 1930's. New York: Viking Press, pp. 51-55.
    His farewell to Crane in March 1932. Suggests he go to Mexico with the Guggenheim money. Some insights into the affair in Mexico of Peggy Baird Cowley and Crane, using her letters. Details of Crane's suicide as recounted by Peggy. Reprinted: 1980.2.

6   FIEDLER, LESLIE A. Waiting for the End. New York: Stein & Day, pp. 185, 199, 207-8, 226-27.
    In The Bridge Crane attempts to keep alive side-by-side the myths of Poe and Whitman as well as their actual influences. Poe is the ghost who haunts him, but it is Whitman he honors as his inspiration and guide. Although The Bridge is characterized by occasional momentary successes, it is an incoherent failure throughout. His whole relationship with Whitman was ambiguous in the extreme. Tate, Blackmur, Winters and others have seen the failure of The Bridge not as Crane's failure but as Whitman's. They insist that Crane used his real powers for the wrong reason. Fiedler disagrees with this judgment.

7   GRIGSBY, GORDON. Review of Hart Crane by Samuel Hazo. College English 25, no. 4 (January):306.
    Brief complimentary review. See 1963.12.

8   GUIGUET, JEAN. "'To Shakespeare' de Hart Crane: Le Peintre et son modele." Études anglaises 17 (October-December):586-90.
    In French. An analysis of the poem, showing that an autobiographical portrait of Crane emerges from close study of the lines.

9   INGALLS, JEREMY. "The Epic Tradition: A Commentary." East-West Review (Kyoto), pp. 173-305.

Discusses briefly Crane's use of the epic form, although Crane is not in the main current of the epic tradition but influenced by Whitman.

10   LEWIS, R.W.B. "The Aspiring Clown." In Learners and Discerners: A Newer Criticism. Selected and edited by Robert Scholes. Charlottesville: University Press of Virginia, pp. 61-108.
See 1963.15.

11   LOVEMAN, SAMUEL. Hart Crane: A Conversation With Samuel Loveman. Edited by Jay Socin, Kirby Congdon, and Ray C. Longtin. New York: Interim Books, 74 pp.
Opens with a two-page essay on "The Alert Pillow," a previously unpublished poem by Crane from the Crane collection at Columbia University. Congdon feels that the poem is of special importance because it presents us with the two sides of Crane as poet--the interior, close feelings of the poet as he lies awake in his bedroom, and the exterior life forces that surround him in the landscape which he recalls to mind. This is followed by another two-page essay by Ray C. Longtin, which serves as a general introduction to Hart Crane. The important section of the book is the conversation with Samuel Loveman. The interviewer is not specifically identified. The discussion begins with some comments on the Crane collection at Columbia. Loveman notes that Crane worshipped his mother and says there was definitely "an Oedipus complex there." The circumstances of Mrs. Crane's life after Crane's death are detailed. Loveman recalls visiting her when she was dying in the hospital. Loveman recalls further that Crane tried to commit suicide in his presence. He asserts that Crane reached a horrible impasse and could no longer write without the aid of music or of liquor. The Browns and Cowley were, along with Loveman, Crane's closest friends. Although Peggy Baird has written that she was to marry Crane, she said later that the marriage would not have taken place because she couldn't take him from a temperamental point of view. Crane proposed to her because he had to have somebody. One of his last affairs with the young Norwegian was especially disastrous. "The entire body of The Bridge was written in a state of drunkenness and revised during periods of sobriety." Other nonsequential recollections.

*12   McMAHON, WILLIAM E. "The Rationale of Hart Crane." Ph.D. dissertation, University of Chicago.

13   MEAKER, M.J. "The Roaring Boy." In Sudden Endings. Garden City, N.Y.: Doubleday & Co., pp. 108-33.
Popular biography emphasizing the chaos and disturbances of Crane's life. There is a bit of psychoanalysis at the end of the article where Meaker fits Crane's suicide into Emile Durkheim's theory of suicide of the egotistic type.

14   METZGER, DEENA POSY. "Hart Crane's Bridge: The Myth Active."
     Arizona Quarterly 20 (Spring):36-46.
          Crane was well acquainted with two middle-American myths:
     (1) that of Quetzalcoatl, the Toltec god of civilization; and (2)
     that of the serpent and the eagle which involved the founding of
     Tenochtitlan. These two myths are important to "The Dance." The
     two myths are related in that each deals with the origin of cul-
     ture. The serpent and eagle myth explains the actual physical
     establishment of civilization; Quetzacoatl, the returning god of
     civilization, explains the complex organization of a people.
     These myths are incorporated in the underlying theme of The
     Bridge: the idea of the returning god who would be aware of the
     mystic possibilities of America as the new world. Crane learned
     much of this from Waldo Frank and from Padriac Colum, as well as
     from D.H. Lawrence and William Prescott.

15   MILES, JOSEPHINE. Eros and Modes in English Poetry. Berkeley
     and Los Angeles: University of California Press, pp. 243-44.
         Reprint of 1961.17.

16   NYREN, DOROTHY. A Library of Literary Criticism, 3d ed. New
     York: Frederick Unger Publishing Co., 1964.
          Five pages of selected reviews on Crane and The Bridge
     specifically.

17   RAMSEY, WARREN. "Exiles and the Seven Arts Group: An American
     Dialogue." International Comparative Literature Association
     Proceedings, pp. 237, 242, 244.
          One of the important voices between 1916 and 1930, particu-
     larly because of the importance he gave to the themes of national
     self-consciousness and alientation. He writes under the strain
     of a divided literary inheritance: the romantic strain which
     holds that the important is probably unsayable and the strain of
     ordering symbolism.

18   TANSELLE, G. THOMAS. "A Further Note on Hart Crane's Critics."
     Papers of the Bibliography Society of America 58 (Second
     Quarter):180-81.
          Corrects and amends Judith Bloomingdale's checklist of
     criticism of The Bridge. See 1963.4.

19   TRACHTENBERG, ALAN. "The Rainbow and the Grid." American
     Quarterly 16, no. 1 (Spring):3-19.
          History of Brooklyn Bridge with a brief mention of Crane's
     interest in it.

*20 VOGLER, THOMAS A. "Preludes to Vision: The Epic Venture in
     Blake, Wordsworth, Keats, and Hart Crane." Ph.D. dissertation,
     Yale University.
          See 1965.26.

21 WAGGONER, HYATT H[owe]. "Review." American Literature 35
    (January):544-45.
        Review of Samuel Hazo's Hart Crane. The modest aim of the
    book is well-achieved, although Hazo is unwilling or unable to
    explore the ultimate significance of Crane's poems, and ignores
    the fact that Crane "was a mystic in the Whitman tradition, the
    tradition of the affirmation of images." See 1963.12.

22 WEBER, BROM. "Review." American Literature 36 (May):228-29.
        Review of Vincent Quinn's Hart Crane, and Samuel Hazo's
    Hart Crane. Quinn's book is judged to be the best short general
    introduction to Crane, sensibly placing Crane in the tradition of
    Emerson and Whitman. Also of note is Quinn's argument that The
    Bridge is "a series of lyrics intended to quicken an affirmative,
    idealistic viewpoint" rather than a unified work demonstrating
    that viewpoint. Hazo's major contribution is his demonstration
    that Crane's most difficult lines can be read by those who will
    bother to understand Crane's poetic method. Because he is a
    stimulating reader of poetry, his critical interpretations are
    good. His attempt to read all of Crane's poetry in some general
    pattern of tragedy leads him to some questionable readings of the
    poetry. See 1963.12, 18.

1965

1   ARMS, GEORGE. "American Poetry." In Encyclopedia of Poetry
    and Poetics. Edited by Alex Preminger et al. Princeton, N.J.:
    Princeton University Press, p. 28.
        Mentions Crane's relationship to Whitman, and the despair-
    ing overtones of his poetry that come from society as well as the
    existential awareness of the poet himself.

2   BAKER, JOHN. "Commercial Sources for Hart Crane's 'The
    River.'" Wisconsin Studies in Contemporary Literature 6
    (Winter-Spring):45-55.
        Although Crane worked for advertising firms, he doesn't
    seem to have drawn the imagery for "The River" from any of the
    advertising copy he wrote. Most of the images are from the
    common fund of advertisements generally in circulation. Baker
    identifies the products and slogans in the poem and asks the
    question, "What then redeems Crane's genre imagery?" He tries
    to answer this question by a very thorough analysis of each of
    the items mentioned, attempting to show how each advances the
    theme of the poem.

3   CARGILL, OSCAR. Toward A Pluralistic Criticism. Carbondale
    and Edwardsville: Southern Illinois University Press, pp.
    154-62.
        A short afterword is of interest. "I do not repent me of
    'Hart Crane and His Friends,' despite the pain I may have in-

flicted." See 1958.6 and 1961.5.

4   DAY, ROBERT A. "Image and Idea in 'Voyages II.'" <u>Criticism</u>
    7 (Summer):224-34.
        An explication of "Voyages II," "one of the richest lyric
    poems of the twentieth century, and . . . a major achievement of
    symbolist poetry." The poem makes conventional poetic statements
    "which Crane enriched by reversing the 'normal' relationships of
    things in space and time according to the principle of relativity
    which he observed in so much of his work, by presenting the re-
    sults of processes of thought and emotion after leaving out, for
    the sake of condensation, several links in the chain of thinking."
    This is the fundamental and indispensible principle to be used in
    analyzing the poem. While it should be considered in relation to
    the other poems of the sequence, "it stands by itself as a clear
    and coherent 'speech,' or dramatic monologue." Day has consulted
    the manuscript drafts of the poem.

5   DAVIS, CHARLES T. "Poetry: 1910-1930." In <u>American Literary</u>
    <u>Scholarship: An Annual/1963</u>. Edited by James Woodress.
    Durham, N.C.: Duke University Press, pp. 165-83.
        A survey of the works on Crane for 1963.

6   DUDEK, LOUIS. <u>Poetry of our Time</u>. Toronto: Macmillan Co. of
    Canada, pp. 17-18, 131-34.
        <u>The Bridge</u> fails because the definition of its final pur-
    pose "seems inflated and unconvincing."

7   FOWLIE, WALLACE. "Man: Rimbaud and Hart Crane." In <u>Love in</u>
    <u>Literature: Studies in Symbolic Expression</u>. Bloomington:
    Indiana University Press, pp. 128-38.
        He is a bit more explicit about three phases of Crane's
    development. In the first phase, the poet as understood by Crane
    seeks the love of God because he is incapable of loving a woman.
    In the second phase, he acknowledges the pure void of lust. In
    the third phase, the poet attempts to transcend simple lust in
    his desire for purity and platonic love. See 1943.2.

8   GROSS, HARVEY. "Hart Crane and Wallace Stevens." In <u>Sound</u>
    <u>and Form in Modern Poetry</u>. Ann Arbor: University of Michigan
    Press, pp. 215-25.
        Crane's prosody, meter, and rhythm are discussed. Although
    Stevens and Crane are very different in technique and temperament,
    they do approach one another in that neither had a gift for the
    "plain style." Each sought after the "incantory" power of
    words--for a rich and rhythmic language. Characterizes the style
    of both as "rhetorical." The rhetorical poet must be a master of
    rhythm, but Crane's rhetoric is often "self-defeating." When he
    can control his rhythms, we can overlook his rhetorical excesses
    and enjoy his intoxicating use of language. Crane was strongly
    influenced by Eliot's prosody, but did not assimilate the influ-

ence well. He could not master the freer rhythms which he had
discovered in Eliot's work. While Crane claimed that he could
use Eliot's technique to express his own purposes, he did not
understand that metrical techniques reflect a poet's temperament.
The techniques of Eliot were not suited to Crane's emotional make-
up or to Crane's subject matter.

9   GUIGUET, JEAN, ed. Le Pont de Brooklyn et autres poémes de
     Hart Crane. Paris: M.J. Minard Lettres Modernes, 63 pp.
          In French. The introduction is a short biography of Crane
     with a brief mention of his principle themes. The English version
     of the poems reprinted appears on one page and the French trans-
     lation on the corresponding opposite page. The edition includes
     "To Brooklyn Bridge," "Ave Maria," "Harbor Dawn," "Southern
     Cross," "At Melville's Tomb," "Voyages II," "Voyages IV," "Voyages
     VI," and "The Broken Tower." See 1962.9.

10   GUIGUET, JEAN. L'Univers poétique de Hart Crane. With a
     preface by Maurice LeBreton. Paris: M.J. Minard Lettres
     Modernes 5, 149 pp.
          In French. Concerned with the difficult problem of poetic
     creation which the author sees exemplified in the work of Crane.
     Emphasis is put upon Crane's rich and vibrant sensibilities. A
     survey introduction for French readers. The mode of criticism is
     to analyze the different elements which constitute the poetic
     universe of Crane--the seasons, the times of day, nature, civili-
     zation, colors, the meaning of the word; certain key words or
     phrases such as "train" or "ship" are traced in Crane's work.
     After analyzing the various elements of the earth as they appear
     in Crane's poetry, certain aspects of civilization, such as
     cities and bridges, and the concept of movement itself, the
     author then moves in the second half of the book to an overall
     consideration of Crane's poetry with an analysis of these elements
     in mind. The conclusion of this general section emphasizes the
     various ways in which Crane has been called a "mystic" and the
     meaning of that term in reference to Crane's poetry. The author
     notes that Caroline Gordon used Crane as a model for one of the
     leading characters in her novel The Malefactors. See 1962.10.

11   HART, JAMES D. Oxford Companion to American Literature, 4th
     ed. New York: Oxford University Press, p. 192.
          Biographical sketch.

12   HÖLLERER, WALTER. Theorie der Modernen Lyrik. Munich:
     Rowoholt, p. 401.
          In German. Incidental reference, noting Crane's interest
     in the word as substance.

13   JACOBSON, ELIZABETH. "Many Poets of the Past Found Success
     Here." Cleveland Plain Dealer, 13 June, p. 1AA, 5AA,
          Feature article mentioning Crane as one of the famous poets

to come out of Cleveland.

14   KAZIN, ALFRED. "The Bridge." New York Review of Books 4,
        no. 12 (15 July):6-8.
           Review of Alan Trachtenberg's Brooklyn Bridge: Fact and
     Symbol. Crane is mentioned as one who was influenced by the idea
     of Brooklyn Bridge.

15   KRAMER, MAURICE. "Six Voyages of a Derelict Seer." Sewanee
        Review 73 (July-September):410-23.
           The six poems in "Voyages" should be regarded as a single
     poem, "the only one of his poems in which Crane manages to ex-
     press a sense of being at peace with himself." Although "The
     Broken Tower" tries to do the same thing, that experience was too
     new and uncertain. A very careful reading of each poem as a part
     of a sequence.

16   KRONENBERGER, LOUIS. Atlantic Brief Lives: A Biographical
        Companion to the Arts. Boston: Little, Brown & Co., p. 193.
           Typical entry.

17   LOPEZ, HANK. "A Country and Some People I Love, An Interview
        with Katherine Anne Porter." Harper's 231 (September):58-68.
           Reminiscences principally about her Mexican experiences.
     Crane was in Mexico at that time. "I tried to take care of him."
     He told her that he wished he had come to Mexico in the first
     place instead of going to Paris. She quotes Crane as saying,
     "Here I feel that life is real, people really live and die here.
     In Paris they were just cutting paper dollies." Crane is referred
     to three times as "poor Hart." ". . . what a terrible time we had
     with him. He was doomed I think. His parasites let him commit
     suicide. He made such a good show and they had no lives of their
     own, so they lived vicariously for his, you know. And that, of
     course, is the unpardonable sin." Compare with the information
     she gave Horton (1937.13).

18   LOVECRAFT, H.P. Selected Letters, 1911-1924. Edited by
        August Derleth and Donald Wandrei. Sauk City, Wis.: Arkham
        House Publishers, pp. 282, 349, 351-54, 357-58.
           Crane is mentioned in the letter of 8 January 1924.
     Lovecraft and Samuel Loveman were friends in Cleveland and he
     noticed at a gathering that a certain Gordon Hatfield, identified
     by Weber as a composer, and Crane were "mortal enemies." It was
     "amusing to watch them when they met by accident, each trying to
     humiliate the other by veiled thrusts and conversational subtle-
     ties hardly intelligible to an uninitiated third person." Crane
     is mentioned again in the letter of 29 September 1924, after
     Lovecraft came to New York and visited Loveman who had a room
     across the hall from Crane, "an egotistical young aesthete who
     has obtained some real recognition in the Dial and other modernist
     organs, and who has an unfortunate predilection for the wine when

it is red." He records they had some enjoyable conversation and
that Crane's room was in excellent taste, containing "a choice
collection of modern books, and some splendid small objects
d'art, of which a carved Buddha and an exquisitely Chinese ivory
box are among the high spots." Crane is mentioned again in a
letter dated 4-5 November 1924, as sober but boasting of a two-
day drunken spree from which he was rescued by E.E. Cummings.
"Poor Crane! I hope you sober up with the years, for there is
really good stuff and a bit of genius in him. He is a genuine
poet of a sort. . . ."

*19   NEWMAN, ARNOLD EUGENE. "The Romantic Image in the Poetry of
      Hart Crane." Ph.D. dissertation, University of Wisconsin.

20   SLATE, JOSEPH EVANS. "William Carlos Williams, Hart Crane,
      and 'the Virtue of History.'" Texas Studies in Language and
      Literature 6:486-511.
          Some parts of Paterson can be related to the life of Crane.
      Although the two never met, Crane and Williams knew of each other
      and of the work each was doing. Crane was critical of Williams
      "fastidious" style, and Williams thought that Crane wanted to be
      cosmic, avoiding the problems inherent in his environment. Par-
      ticularly in the area of religion, their values and beliefs were
      far apart. However, The Bridge and In the American Grain are
      clearly related. Both works seem to be answers to The Waste Land.
      In both works Edgar Allan Poe represents the American artist's
      fear of failure; both refer Poe's failure to themselves and to
      their time. The spirit of Whitman is seen both as a figure of
      hope for the present and the future. Both use Whitman's technique
      of the mask which imaginatively linked the poet in the present to
      the person of some hero in the past. Both use the figure of
      Columbus as the carrier of the message of the New World. Both
      present the land as a female figure, and both use the Indian past.
      The spirit of Crane finds itself in Book I of Paterson where
      Williams concerns himself with the failure of the American poet
      as his major theme.

21   SPEARS, MONROE K. Hart Crane. American Writers Series, no.
      47. Minneapolis: University of Minnesota Press, 48 pp.
          "Crane's talent was astonishing indeed to survive the ex-
      treme disorder of his life and all the forces inimical to it and
      enable him in spite of everything to produce poetry of lasting
      value." We should not miss, however, Crane's constant effort to
      educate himself; his critical comments show great penetration.
      Begins his analysis of the poetry with a discussion of "Chaplin-
      esque," a poem about the nature of poetry and the past, "Black
      Tambourine," and "Praise for an Urn." The major poems of the
      next few years follow a new line and method of composition--the
      attempt to capture ecstasy. The essence of later poetic is seen
      in "The Wine Menagerie." Considers some of poems that exemplify
      this poetic: "Recitative," "Passage," "Paraphrase," "Possessions."

"Voyages" is Crane's best long poem. "For the Marriage of
Faustus and Helen," is considered a relation to The Bridge, "to
which it is precursor and parallel." After summarizing the
diverse criticism of The Bridge, concludes that the unity of the
poem is very loose and that some parts are very much better than
others. Tate has put his finger on the trouble with the symbolism
of The Bridge. Crane's poems raise a question of belief in an
urgent form, because he is a typification of the neo-romantic.
"My own view is that the formulations of Tate and Winters are
still accurate." See 1967.29; 1969.45.

22   SPINUCCI, PIETRO. "T.S. Eliot e Hart Crane." Studi Americani
     11:213-50.
         In Italian. Crane's reaction to The Waste Land is one in-
stance of the many misunderstandings with which Eliot's poem was
greeted. It may seem disrespectful to Italian readers to place
these two names side-by-side, since Eliot is so well-known in
Italy and Crane is so relatively unknown. Compares The Waste
Land with "For the Marriage of Faustus and Helen," because the
latter poem was intended as a direct answer to The Waste Land.
By examining these two poems, one is able to analyze the reasons
and the sentiments of the ideological divergence not only of
these two poets but of a whole poetic generation. Crane's refu-
tation of Eliot's Calvinistic vision of reality may have been a
turning point in American culture.

23   STEWART, JOHN L. The Burden of Time. Princeton, N.J.:
     Princeton University Press, p. 46.
         The influence of Crane on Tate is mentioned, "a friendship
of critical importance in Tate's development." He read the
writers mentioned by Crane and "soon afterward Crane and Eliot
became his principal mentors."

24   TRACHTENBERG, ALAN. "The Shadow of a Myth" and "Epilogue."
     In Brooklyn Bridge: Fact and Symbol. New York: Oxford
     University Press, pp. 142-70.
         Because of his commitment to "visionary" poetry and because
of the influence of Whitman, Crane attempted to compose the myth
of America--especially as an answer to the renunciation in The
Waste Land. Eliot used London Bridge as a passageway for the
dead; Crane projected his myth of affirmation upon Brooklyn
Bridge. The bridge was not like the Grail, an object to be found,
but something to be created through the internal process of consciousness. Hence, the bridge is not "found" in "Atlantis," but
created by the poet, protagonist, and reader throughout the poem.
The Bridge is not an historical poem in the ordinary sense of the
term; its mode is myth. "In this regard the importance of Walt
Whitman requires our special notice." History culminates in
self-discovery; the poet can lead man from his bondage in time
and space to participation in the mythic consciousness. "Cape
Hatteras" raises the central questions of the poem: "What are

the grounds for hope that modern history will not destroy itself?"
"Where lies redemption?" Reprinted: 1970.6.

*25 UROFF, MARGARET DICKIE. "Hart Crane's White Buildings." Ph.D.
     dissertation, Brown University.
          See 1974.24.

26 VOGLER, THOMAS. "A New View of Hart Crane's Bridge." Sewanee
    Review 73 (July-September):381-408.
         Most early recent criticism of The Bridge asserts that it
    is a magnificent failure. Even though more recent favorable
    estimates of the poem have appeared, these comments share with
    earlier ones an emphasis on Crane's statement of purpose. Vogler
    approaches the poem without considering Crane's statement of
    theme, and finds a theme which gives the poem a high degree of
    organic unity. "The poem is a search or a quest for a mythic
    vision, rather than the fixed, symbolic expression of a vision
    firmly held in the poet's mind." Despite the fact that there
    were few hopeful signs in the world as Crane knew it, he had a
    knowledge of a glorious past and provided a bridge from the past
    to a future of hope. The quest was basically personal because
    the poet found a vision that satisfied himself. If he could dis-
    cover vision for himself, it would have social consequences be-
    yond his own private life. See 1964.20.

27 WEISS, KLAUS. Das Bild des Weges. Bonn: H Bouvier Verlag,
    pp. 57-58.
         In German. A long footnote dealing with the images of
    dance, river, and road in the poetry of Crane. A brief compari-
    son between T.S. Eliot and Crane.

28 WILLIAMS, GYN. "The Drowned Man in English Poetry." Litera:
    Studies in Language and Literature (Istanbul) 8:82-90.
         Examines the sea as a symbol of love, security, and mother,
    while associating Crane's love of the sea and suicide with his
    family problems. Crane was aware of the symbolic meaning of the
    death he chose and was poetically moving towards this point from
    the beginning.

                              1966

1 BARTA, AUGUSTÍ. "New York: Two Poetic Impressions."
   Américas 18 (October):14-22.
        The first half of the article is about Crane, the second
   half about Federico García Lorca. Although Crane wished to make
   of The Bridge a transcendental myth, he managed to achieve only
   a resplendent symbol and to express the anguish provoked by the
   contradictions of his own life which happened to coincide with a
   moment of crisis in the United States in the post-World War I
   years. Conceiving of poetry as having a religious function, he

had a clear understanding of the demands of the new revolutionary
notion of poetry as modern myth. The Bridge was written out of
the tension resulting from two antagonistic forces clashing within Crane.

2   BEACH, JOSEPH WARREN. Obsessive Images. Edited by William
     Van O'Connor. Minneapolis: University of Minnesota Press,
     pp. 72-74, 118-21, 190-91, 254.
          Crane is described as having a strong influence on the
     poetry of Horace Gregory. "Voyages" are described as desperate
     love poems, brilliantly imaginative, in which human love is con-
     ceived of as carrying through death into a mystical paradise in
     which all mortal grief and evil are caught up into the good that
     is the final truth of things. Muriel Rukeyser's greatest in-
     spiration was presumably Crane; she was as eager as Crane to in-
     corporate the products of the machine age into the body of her
     faith.

3   BLOOM, H[arold]. "The Central Man: Emerson, Whitman, Wallace
     Stevens." Massachusetts Review 7 (Winter):25-42.
          Incidental mention. Emerson is the immediate begetter of
     Whitman and the ultimate forebearer of Crane, "a strain of
     visionary irony that is not yet worked out, and may indeed be
     the future as it has been the past of what is most central in
     our poetry." Stevens and Crane are the synthesis of the two
     violent strains (Emerson and Whitman) that have made American
     poetry so romantic. The last word in this tradition beginning
     with Emerson belongs to Crane.

4   BOYLE, KAY. "Hart Crane." New York Review of Books 6 (31
     March):30-31.
          This letter to the editor is a response to Edward Dahlberg's
     review of Crane's letters. Miss Boyle calls it "the finest
     piece on Crane I have ever read." The "castle" to which the
     Crosbys invited Crane (where they hoped he would finish writing
     The Bridge) was actually a mill. Questions Dahlberg's conclusion
     that Crane committed suicide because he couldn't face the reality
     of being penniless once more in New York. Suggests that Crane
     may have committed suicide because he had been unable to complete
     or even start the poem he had hoped to write in Mexico. See
     1966.7.

5   CAHEN, ALFRED B., and FRENCH, DAVID B. "On Finding a Hart
     Crane Poem." American Weave 30 (December):1-3.
          The first publication of a poem Crane wrote for his Aunt
     Alice inscribed on the flyleaf of a copy of The Complete Poetical
     Works of Robert Burns which he gave her for Christmas 1914. The
     discovery was announced in the Cleveland Plain Dealer on 12 Sep-
     tember 1966, but this is the first appearance of the poem in
     print. Contains, as well, a previously unpublished photograph
     (circa 1914) of Crane and his family. See 1966.12; 1969.22.

6   COLUM, MARY. <u>Life and the Dream</u>. Dublin: Dolmen Press,
       pp. 222-25.
          Among the writers who gravitated toward Padraic and Mary
Colum was "a raw western boy first sent to us by Harriet Moody--
a gangling, semi-literate youth of about seventeen"--Crane. He
visited the Colums about twice a week for a short period and discussed poetry with them. Mary Colum confesses that she was not
enthusiastic about his poetry. As he made new literary friends,
he saw the Colums only at long intervals and then by accident.

7   DAHLBERG, EDWARD. "Hart Crane." <u>New York Review of Books</u> 5
       (20 January):19-22.
          In a generous burst of enthusiasm, Kay Boyle calls this the
best thing on Crane. Dahlberg remembers Crane since "there were
some similarities in our lives which . . . teased the blood in
the veins." He was asked to read the manuscript of <u>The Bridge</u>.
"Both of us were overwhelmingly alone, castaways of American
letters." The two of them were also "part of a senseless babble
of economics." His poetry is difficult to understand, since "he
could be a syntactical zany as is apparent in some of the passages I have culled from <u>The Bridge</u>." See 1966.4.

8   DEMBO, L[awrence].S. "Hart Crane: The 'Nuclear Self' and the
       Fatal Object." In <u>Conceptions of Reality in Modern American</u>
       <u>Poetry</u>. Berkeley and Los Angeles: University of California
       Press, pp. 129-50.
          Considers Waldo Frank's argument that Crane is a mystic
poet. The central problem in Crane's poetry is the essential
problem in contemporary poetry in general--that is, the relation
of the subject and object in the universe in which objects are
recognized as being absolutes. The realistic poet tries to seek
"continuity" with the world outside; the idealistic poet seeks to
"transfigure" the world to conform to his idea. Crane's central
idea was to become the kind of poet with a "nuclear self" at one
and the same time continuous with and yet free from the chaos
outside of the self--that is, the self "both passive to reality
and generating order." Includes an extensive analysis of "For
the Marriage of Faustus and Helen." <u>The Bridge</u> also can be
interpreted in the light of this tension that runs though Crane's
poetry. Ultimately for Crane the nuclear self does not attempt
to transfigure the world; instead, he renounces it. Thus, he is
not in Frank's sense a mystic determined to perceive and transfigure the chaos of reality.

9   GOODWIN, K.L. <u>The Influence of Ezra Pound</u>. London: Oxford
       University Press, pp. 164-71.
          As an imitator of Pound, Crane was less intelligent and
less independent than William Carlos Williams or Marianne Moore.
Crane imitated Pound on the basis of his works, since he did not
know him personally, although they did correspond after Pound
saw Crane's poem, "In Shadow," in the <u>Little Review</u>. Over a

five-year period (1917–1923), Crane became interested in Pound, became somewhat of a disciple, and then forsook him in favor of Eliot. It was through Pound that Crane became interested in Laforgue and the French symbolists. There is as well the influence of imagism on Crane, although it is impossible to find any poem of his that is wholly imagistic. The greater influence of Eliot is seen in the ideogrammic structure of The Bridge, influenced by that structure in The Waste Land. Since Pound may have given this structure to The Waste Land, perhaps one can say that the structure of The Bridge was influenced by Pound. Apart from the structure, the two clearest examples of Pound's influences are to be found in "The River" and the seafaring sections of The Bridge.

10   GREENBAUM, LEONARD.   The Hound and Horn: The History of a
        Literary Quarterly.   The Hague: Mouton & Co., pp. 57, 68, 72,
        129–31, 139–40, 166.
        Brief mention of the articles about Crane published in the
journal.

11   GURIAN, JAY.   "The Possibility of a Western Poetics."
        Colorado Quarterly 15 (Summer):85.
        Used western materials successfully in "The River." The
Bridge is relevant to a discussion of western poetics, because
Crane was interested in the westward movement as continuing the
frontier of the common man. His use of Indian materials is also
significant.

12   HIRSHFELD, MARY.   "Mary Hirshfeld Hears. . . ." Cleveland
        Plain Dealer, 12 September, p. 17.
        An unpublished poem by Crane has been found on the flyleaf
of a book belonging to Loring Williams, whose wife was Crane's
aunt. The book is in the possession of Alfred B. Cahen, who has
followed Williams as editor of American Weave, the literary
journal. The poem, "A Song for Happy Feast Days," is reprinted
in American Weave 30 (December). See 1966.5; 1969.22.

13   HOLDER, ALAN.   Three Voyages in Search of Europe.   Philadel-
        phia: University of Pennsylvania Press, p. 354.
        The mood of alienation did not characterize much of Amer-
ica's cultural life in the 1930s. That decade exhibited interest
and pride in America's past. The Bridge "published at the start
of the decade and exhibiting a massive interest in the national
past was, in this sense, a prediction of much to come."

14   HURNER, JOY A.   "Old Thresholds, Old Anatomies: A New Approach
        to the 'Voyages' of Hart Crane." New Campus Review 1 (May):
        10-17.
        It is texture--"made up of the connotations, echoes,
nuances, and rhythms of words, born moment by moment within the
poem"--which gives order to Crane's poetry, especially "Voyages,"

rather than form. "Voyages" is the quest of a seer for universal truth, beauty, and love.

15   HURWITZ, LEO, and DAVIS, CURTIS. <u>U.S.A.: Poetry Number Four-teen--In Search of Hart Crane</u>. CA-2-41. A ninety-minute film produced by National Education Television, cassette no. CA-2-41. Broadcast originally the week of 18 September.
      A series of interviews with people who knew Crane, including Malcolm Cowley, Waldo Frank, Gorham Munson, Peggy Baird, and Samuel Loveman. An accurate and moving film without being senti-mental. Curtis Davis was the producer for NET and Leo Hurwitz the producer of the program itself.

16   JOHNSON, THOMAS H. <u>Oxford Companion to American History</u>. New York: Oxford University Press, p. 220.
      Typical entry.

17   JUMPER, WILL C. Review of Robert L. Perry's <u>The Shared Vision of Waldo Frank and Hart Crane</u>. <u>Poet and Critic</u> 3 (Fall):42-43.
      Positive review of Perry, noting that its chief value is in Chapter 4 "which invites the reader to use Waldo Frank's prose as a gloss on Hart Crane's poetic symbolism." See 1966.24.

18   KAHN, SY. "The Slender Fire of Harry Crosby." In <u>The Twenties: Poetry and Prose</u>. Edited by Richard E. Langford and William E. Taylor. Deland, Fla.: Everett Edwards, pp. 1, 3.
      Mentioned as a friend of the Crosbys.

19   KARANEKASS, ALEXANDER. <u>Tillers of a Myth</u>. Madison: University of Wisconsin Press, pp. 163, 191.
      Crane's attempt to create the American myth is mentioned in reference to Allen Tate's analysis of the value of myth. Because he was divided in sensibility, Crane could not overcome the paradox that his age presented to him. Therefore, he failed in his attempt to make a myth for America.

20   LANDRY, HILTON. "Of Prayer and Praise: The Poetry of Hart Crane." In <u>The Twenties: Poetry and Prose</u>. Edited by Richard E. Langford and William E. Taylor. Deland, Fla.: Everett Edwards Press, pp. 18-24.
      Crane is "the last Romantic" in America. A careful study of Crane's theory as well as comparisons with I.A. Richards, Croce, Coleridge, and Maritain indicate that we cannot deny in-tellectual respectability to the view which Crane holds. <u>The Bridge</u> is "a series of lyric poems loosely held together by cer-tain unifying features." The most obvious unifying feature is the theme of the journey that begins with Brooklyn Bridge and takes the protagonist backward and forward in history and time and ends with the bridge again in "Atlantis." The object of this quest is clearly some kind of Absolute. "There is no coherent

myth in The Bridge, only proliferating symbols groping towards
myth, but these symbols exert a second unifying influence on the
poem." Although Crane embraced no formal religion, he pursued
the Absolute and the equivalent of God. "By nature and nurture"
he was "a transcendental idealist." It is not his vision which
confuses readers but the lack of a traditional vocabulary to express that vision in religious terms.

21   LEWIS, R.W.B. "Crane's Visionary Lyric: The Way to the
     Bridge." Massachusetts Review:7 (Spring):227-53.
        Discussion of the poems written in 1925. "Passage," al-
though complex and mysteriously ceremonial, can introduce the
reader to the cycle of imaginative experience that was increasingly becoming the fundamental subject of Crane's poetry. Crane
descended into the ravine of life during the autumn of 1925. His
situation was close to desperate; he was drinking more frequently.
"The Wine Menagerie," one of his most consummate lyrics, depicted
the condition through which Crane was passing in his determination to emerge from it. "At Melville's Tomb" is an "extraordinarily beautiful visionary elegy." It demonstrates Crane's
increasing command of his subject matter and method and testifies
to the importance of Melville for Crane. The "hauntingly beautiful" "Repose of Rivers," a poem about the failure of creativity,
should be compared to "The Broken Tower," since it deals with
Crane's recollection of the phases of his imaginative life. The
period of writing these visionary lyrics prepared him for the
brilliant fit of creativity during July and August 1926, in which
Crane had written or revised almost all of the main sections of
The Bridge and had composed several of his best lyrics.

22   LUND, MARY GRAHAM. "John Gould Fletcher: An Anachronism."
     Southwest Review 51 (Winter):37-45.
        The Bridge haunted Fletcher, who thought Crane the greatest
among the modern American poets. He mourned his death as "the
greatest loss American poetry has ever sustained." A decade
later, he wrote again of The Bridge in "The Builders of the
Bridge," which was reprinted in his last volume of poems, The
Burning Mountain. He called The Bridge "the one major work of
affirmation of the future published in America in this century."
See 1946.1.

23   ONG, WALTER J. "Evolution, Myth, and Poetic Vision." Com-
     parative Literature Studies 3, no. 1:1-20.
        Crane's vision is the result of his sense of his moment in
history, the dawn of the machine age. Like Whitman, he had faith
in the future of the American machine age, but his sense of
history is more intuitive than is Whitman's. He is "typically
American in his determination to try to make poetic sense of
history."

24   PERRY, ROBERT L. The Shared Vision of Waldo Frank and Hart

Crane. University of Nebraska Studies, n.s., no. 33. Lincoln: University of Nebraska Press, 73 pp.

Explores the nature of Frank's influence upon Crane. Delineates the body of ideas that Frank expressed and tries to distinguish which of these ideas was important to Crane. Frank was the single most important influence on Crane, who developed sympathy for his ideas by 1923. Crane was an ideological-religious, manic-depressive. The core of his character was his extremely subjective romanticism, induced by his sensitivity and his isolated, unhappy childhood. Emphasizes the early influence of Nietzsche on Crane. It was reading Frank's "Hope" and Ouspensky's Tertium Organum that brought Crane to the eventual acceptance of Frank's ideas. Crane learned a good deal of Whitman from Frank. The conclusive proof for this is in The Bridge, especially in "Cape Hatteras." Frank suggested the directions that Crane should take, either through his books or by personal contact. The theme of mystic evolution in The Bridge came to Crane from Whitman through Frank. See 1966.17.

25   RIDDEL, JOSEPH. "Hart Crane's Poetics of Failure." Journal of English Literary History 33:473-96.

"The Broken Tower" depicts the failure of vision. Although the poet wills a new tower, the poem ends not be creating that tower, but by "reconfirming his role as a poet, hence affirming the future possibility of creating" that new tower. The poem depicts the poet in his act of being a poet, "pursuing the dream that lies always before him." His method is a quest through words; but the visionary poet is destined to fail because he must repeat the process incessantly. This is the central paradox that explains Crane's limitations.

26   SPINUCCI, PIETRO. Il Ponte di Brooklyn: "The Bridge" di Hart Crane e la poesia americana degli anni benti. Milan: Pubblicazioni Dell'Università Cattolica del Sacro Cuore, Serie Terza, Czinze Filologiche e Letteratura 11, Società Editrace Vita e Pensiero—Largo a Gemelli, 1, 277 pp.

In Italian. Interest in The Bridge began when he became aware of the diverse criticisms, some claiming it as Crane's greatest achievement and others regarding it as a failure. Deals with the criticism of The Bridge, The Bridge seen as an epic poem or quest, the principle themes and poetics of Crane, his own interpretation of The Bridge, emphasizing structure, symbolism, and language, and the relationship of The Bridge to the general tradition of American poetry. Using the phrase "poetry of tomorrow" to describe the work of Crane, he emphazises Crane's willingness to adapt poetry to the modern scene and his attempt to discover a modern idiom for this scene. Suspects that Crane has broken new ground of which poets in the next hundred years will be more appreciative. Too much attention has been paid to the relationship between Crane and Whitman and to the tradition of transcendentalism out of which Whitman grew. Melville's

influence was greater. The machine makes all the difference between Crane and Whitman. Because of the machine, Crane had to
find a new poetic expression to handle it. Although seemingly
fragmentary, The Bridge is truly unified, since it has a coherent
structure and a coherent theme. Part of our difficulty in reading the poem is that a visionary poet uses visionary language.
He is in the tradition of the "Everlasting Yes," and, in this
tradition, he stands for a new humanism. What he was really
trying to do has been missed by most of his critics.

27   STANFORD, ANN. "Poetry: 1910-1930." In American Literary
      Scholarship: An Annual/1964. Edited by James Woodress.
      Durham, N.C.: Duke University Press, pp. 179-94.
         The principal articles appearing in 1964 are mentioned and
      summarized.

28   STONE, EDWARD. Voices of Despair. Athens: Ohio University
      Press, pp. 206-7.
         It was Crane's hope in The Bridge to assert the mastery of
      the American spirit over the voices of defeat and despair. He
      tried to confront what he thought was the sickness of his time,
      but he became more doubtful of the possibilities inherent in the
      myth of America. The Bridge ends without the completeness that
      he hoped his "great affirmation" would have. "Yet it was a
      heroic passage to Cathay, after all. . . ."

29   SYMONS, JULIAN. "Hart Crane." Twentieth Century Verse, no.
      8 (January/February 1938). New York: Krause Reprint, pp. 171-
      74.
         Reprint of 1938.3.

30   _____. "How Wide Is the Atlantic? or Do You Believe in
      America?" Twentieth Century Verse, nos. 12-13 (September/
      October 1938). New York: Krause Reprint, pp. 80-84.
         Reprint of 1938.4.

31   TOLSON, MELVIN B. "An Interview With Melvin B. Tolson." In
      Anger, and Beyond. Edited by Herbert Hill. New York: Harper
      & Row, p. 37.
         Along with Walt Whitman, Crane is a seer--the poet as a
      barometer of his society.

32   UNTERECKER, JOHN E. "A Piece of Pure Invention." Columbia
      Library Columns 15 (May):42-44.
         A letter he wrote to his mother and grandmother (21 October
      1924) contains one of his few occasional poems, "With a Photograph
      to Zell, Now Bound for Spain." It shows his facility for light
      verse, a facility that shows up in his unpublished limericks.
      "With a Photograph to Zell" has been published as a Broadside by
      the Ibex Press. Reprinted: 1967.38.

33 VICKERY, JOHN B. <u>Myth and Literature</u>. Lincoln: University of Nebraska Press, p. xi.
     Brief reference to Crane's "effort to attain poetic vision through jazz-ridden intoxication."

34 WALCUTT, C.C., and WHITESELL, J. EDWIN, eds. "Hart Crane." In <u>The Explicator Cyclopedia</u>. Chicago: Quadrangle Books, pp. 23-34.
     A listing of seven poems with assorted quotations of various criticism of each.

35 WHITE, ROBERT L. <u>John Peale Bishop</u>. New York: Twayne Publishers, pp. 47-48, 124, 129.
     Brief comments. <u>The Bridge</u> failed because Crane was unable to discover or invent "a myth adequate enough to infuse his work with meaning."

36 WILBUR, RICHARD. "On My Own Work." In <u>Poets on Poetry</u>. Edited by Howard Nemerov. New York: Basic Books, p. 171.
     Describes <u>The Bridge</u> as "a magnificent botch of a poem" because of the attempt to find new philosophical, religious, and/or intellectual structures.

<u>1967</u>

1 ADAMS, ROBERT MARTIN. "Myth and Achievement." <u>New York Times Book Review</u> 22 (28 October):28, 30.
     Although a generally complimentary review of R.W.B. Lewis's <u>The Poetry of Hart Crane</u> noting the importance of both Crane's poetry and myth, Adams is critical of Lewis for his "impressionistic" handling of literary evidence and his dependence upon his own responses to the poems. Aware of the obstacles in dealing with Crane, Lewis has "stated the difficulties with admirable precision and frankness, and he has met them head-on." The book is the most ambitious critical effort yet made in the study of Crane's poetry. See 1967.19.

2 AMANUDDIN, SYED. <u>Hart Crane's Mystical Quest and Other Essays</u>. Narayanquda, India: Kauyalaya Publishers Mysore 4, pp. 17-23.
     The organic unity of "Voyages" is seen in the way theme is intimately related to the three stages of the mystic way; awakening (I, II, III), the Dark Night of the Soul (IV, V), and the Unitive Life (VI). "The predominate theme . . . is the relationship between the self and the non-self, that is, a quest for the absolute and timeless concept of imagination, mystical unity and continuity of the soul and the spirit."

3 ANON. "Crane, Harold Hart (1899-1932)." In <u>Chamber's Encyclopedia: New Revised Edition</u>. Edited by M.D. Law and M. Vibart. Vol. 4. London: Pergamon Press, p. 212.

Typical entry.

4   ARPAD, JOSEPH J.   "Hart Crane's Platonic Myth: The Brooklyn
    Bridge." American Literature 39:75-86.
         A striking feature of The Bridge is Crane's unorthodox con-
    ception of myth. The nature and extent of the Platonic influence
    has not been adequately studied. Crane had been influenced by
    Plato's Ion, although he came later to reject the validity of
    Plato's analysis. In articulating his notion of "logic of meta-
    phor" Crane began to equate the poet's acquisition of knowledge
    as identical with that of the Platonic philosopher--perceiving
    universal forms or ideas. Crane's use of the word myth in
    "Proem" is very much like Plato's sense of myth. His inspiration
    is found in the two Platonic myths: the Atlantis myth, which is
    used in the final section of the poem, and the myth of the cave,
    which forms the basis of the prologue to the poem. In order to
    escape the difficulty of celebrating the glory of America in a
    physical symbol, he adapted Plato's myth of the cave.

5   BUTTERFIELD, R.W.   "Transcender."   New Statesmen 73, no. 1884
    (21 April):550.
         Review of Weber's Letters of Hart Crane. In addition to
    the information they provide about Crane, the letters are an
    indispensible document of literary life in America in the 1920s.
    Although in matters not dealing with literature, his thought was
    confused or nonexistent, the letters provide excellent evidence
    of a fine literary intelligence and of critical ability in
    judging literature.

6   COWLEY, MALCOLM.   Think Back On Us. . . :   A Contemporary
    Chronicle of the Nineteen Thirties by Malcolm Cowley.   Edited
    by Henry Dan Piper.   Carbondale and Edwardsville: Southern
    Illinois University Press, pp. 199-202.
         Reprint of 1930.8.

7   DONOGHUE, DENNIS.   "Moidores for Hart Crane."   New York Review
    Books 9 (9 November):16-19.
         Review of R.W.B. Lewis's The Poetry of Hart Crane. The gist
    of the case against Crane was made in a letter William Carlos
    Williams wrote to Horace Gregory. Williams complained that he
    was "stumped" by Crane's verse, because Crane was searching for
    something inside himself, while Williams was dedicated to the
    "sharp use of materials." It is well to keep Williams's comment
    in mind while reading Lewis's book, because Lewis takes for
    granted that Crane is one of the finest modern poets of our lan-
    guage. The most serious fault of the book is that it does not
    take up the challenge of trying to demonstrate that assumption.
    Crane's virtues are genius, an excited sensibility, and a keen
    sense of the English language. But it must be noted that he cul-
    tivated intensity at the expense of every other poetic value. The
    book lacks a sense of scale: "The poems that count are not suffi-

ciently distinguished from poorer work." "Crane still seems to me . . . a poet whose reach far exceeded his grasp; greater in short poems than in long poems; greater in stanza than in poem, in line than in stanza." See 1967.19.

8   ESHLEMAN, CLAYTON. "Meditation Out of Hart Crane." Hanging Loose 3 (Summer):n.p.
    Verse appreciation.

9   _____. "To Crane." Poetry: A Magazine of Verse 3 (November): 78.
    Verse appreciation.

10 FRIEDMAN, NORMAN. "From Victorian to Modern: A Sketch of a Literary Reappraisal." Victorian Newsletter 32 (Fall):24-25.
    The problems Tennyson faced in In Memoriam are still facing modern poets. The attempt to combine the public and the private, the epic and the lyric, can be seen in Eliot, Crane, Pound, and Williams.

11 GALLOWAY, DAVID. "Optimism Lost." Listener 28, no. 1997 (6 July):25.
    Favorable review of Weber's Letters of Hart Crane. The letters most recommend themselves as a spiritual autobiography of the poet. Shows his concern with nineteenth century inheritance which shaped the humanistic idealism that found its ultimate expression in The Bridge.

12 HAHN, EMILY. Romantic Rebels: An Informal History of Bohemianism in America. Boston: Houghton Mifflin Co., pp. 246-51.
    Crane is typical of the person who refused to conform to convention but was never happy in a state of defiance. Because of his emotional difficulties and his alcoholic problems, he represents the popular view of the Greenwich Village Bohemian.

13 HOFFMAN, FREDERICK J. "Symbolisme and Modern Poetry in the United States." Comparative Literature Studies 4:193-98.
    Although Crane has Mallarmé's trust in the magically transcendant quality of words, his debt to symbolisme is not very impressive. He did not make "the Verb into a deity."

14 HOLTON, MILNE. "'A Baudelairesque Thing': The Directions of Hart Crane's 'Black Tambourine.'" Criticism 9 (Summer):215-28.
    "Black Tambourine" marks the change from poetic adolescence to artistic maturity. The poem begins, ends, and is dominated by a single image--a Negro in a cellar. The image is vertical, this being the first poem in which the vertical arrangement of image appears. Although the poem has a social theme, it is not a poem of social protest. The Negro is really a figure for the poet, and the poem is about Crane himself and about the creative process.

15   KERMODE, FRANK. "Strange Contemporaries: Wallace Stevens and
      Hart Crane." Encounter 28, no. 5 (May):65-70.
          Lengthy review of Weber's Letters of Hart Crane and Holly
      Stevens's Letters of Wallace Stevens, with more emphasis being
      given to the letters of Stevens. Weber's edition would be im-
      proved if it had been better annotated.

16   KÖHRING, KLAUS HEINRICH. Die Formen des "Long Poem" in der
      Modernen Amerikanischen Literatur. Beihefte Zum Jahrbuch Für
      Amerikastudien, 21. Heidelberg: Karl Winter Universitäts-
      verlag. 292 pp.
          In German. How the long poem is like and unlike the epic.
      Sixteen characteristics commonly associated with the long poem
      are used to judge the poems considered. Crane was consciously
      seeking an American equivalent of the traditional epic. Although
      influenced by Whitman, he was conscious of the Aeneid. Crane's
      personality is intertwined throughout the poem; the persona is
      the masked poet in search of a vision of America which is finally
      realized in "Atlantis." Crane's experience is too personal to be
      of consequence to modern man.

17   KRAMER, MAURICE. "Hart Crane's 'Reflexes.'" Twentieth Cen-
      tury Literature 13 (October):131-38.
          A study of earlier poems in order to demonstrate the exis-
      tence of two essential motions of mind--"reflexes" in Crane's own
      words. One, Crane is at times talking to himself so the reader
      should be prepared for sudden leaps in association and fluid
      motions of interior dialogue. Two, no matter what the dominant
      theme or image of a lyric might be, the reader should expect cer-
      tain typical responses to make themselves felt. In his success-
      ful poems, Crane is concerned with some aspect of the theme of
      change from suffering alienation to transcendent wholeness.
      Suffering and death are endured by the poet because of his faith
      in some ultimate union with absolute beauty. By accepting suf-
      fering, he could bring out what was essentially valuable in his
      experience.

18   LAUGHLIN, JAMES. "The Greenberg Manuscripts." In New Direc-
      tions in Prose and Poetry, no. 4. New York: Krause Reprint,
      pp. 353-81.
          Reprint of 1939.5.

19   LEWIS, R.W.B. The Poetry of Hart Crane: A Critical Study.
      Princeton, N.J.: Princeton University Press, 426 pp.
          Considers him to be one of the finest modern poets in our
      language and one of "the dozen-odd major poets in American his-
      tory." Does not attempt to prove this thesis directly; his pur-
      pose is to follow the development of Crane's poetry from the
      earliest poems around 1916 to "The Broken Tower" in 1932. "I
      have tried to chart the career of Crane's imagination--of his
      vision, his rhetoric, his craft." Concerned with relating Crane

to the romantic tradition in England and in America, he uses a
minimum amount of biographical material. Crane is the type of
visionary poet who is able to see the actual world transfigured.
"I claim for Crane the role of the religious poet par excellence
in his generation." The first part of the book analyzes the
poetry written before White Buildings and the poetry in White
Buildings. The second section is devoted to an explication of
The Bridge. After a general introductory chapter, considers the
poem section by section. The main point is that The Bridge was a
continuing attempt to realize the implications of the visionary
legacy of America by invoking a national and original archetype--
the bridge itself. "To bring back Cathay, to renew that attitude
of spirit by the resources of poetry, would be to liberate the
American consciousness in an age of iron." Although we are
temporarily blind, this poem shall gradually restore us to sight.
Even though the visionary imagination is periodically defeated
throughout the poem, it is always self-renewing, and it is this
visionary imagination which is the true hero of the romantic epic.
The third and shortest section is devoted to a consideration of
the poems in "Key West" and others. Concludes with an analysis
of "The Broken Tower." Although clearly written with a thesis in
mind, the thesis is not pursued at the expense of an adequate
interpretation of the complexity of Crane. Reviewed in: 1967.1,
7, 20, 37; 1968.2, 4-5, 9, 27, 29, 34, 37-38; 1969.9, 39; 1971.20.

20   LEIBOWITZ, HERBERT [A.]. "Hart Crane's Orphic Songs." Hudson
      Review 20, no. 4 (Winter):598-701.
          Review of Lewis's The Poetry of Hart Crane. The figure
      that emerges from this study is less incoherent than the one we
      usually find. His poetic development was orderly in distinct
      stages. He is properly placed in the romantic tradition. The
      finest section is devoted to a study of The Bridge. Sees Lewis's
      fault in his unclear handling of "myth." See 1967.19.

21   LOHF, KENNETH A. The Literary Manuscripts of Hart Crane.
      Columbus: Ohio State University Press, 141 pp.
          A considerable body of Crane's manuscripts and letters are
      preserved in sixteen repositories throughout the United States.
      In the collections there are 278 manuscripts, 805 pieces of
      correspondence, and 455 letters written to Crane. The collection
      at Columbia University is the largest and most significant
      archive. Lohf gives the following descriptive information for
      each manuscript:
      A. Citation: published title, type of manuscript
      B. Title: transcription of the title as it appears on the manu-
          script
      C. First line. transcription of the first line of the poem, or
          the first two lines in the case of brief lines
      D. Collation: number of sheets, type of paper and color, size
          of paper, numbering of sheets, etc.
      E. Date: specific or approximate date of composition

F. Contents: identification of the class of manuscript as
      draft, worksheet, notes, or typescript
Reviewed in: 1968.2, 3, 5, 10, 29, 34. See 1972.27.

22   LOVEMAN, SAMUEL. Preface to The Hart Crane Voyages by Hunce
       Voelcker. New York: Brownstone Press, n.p.
         Mostly factual and biographical remarks.

23   LYON, MELVIN E. "Crane's 'The Mango Tree.'" Explicator 25
       (February):Item 48.
         Crane's two comments on the poem in his letters help us to
   understand it better. The poem assumes the form of a tree on the
   page, and Crane's reference to it as "the original Eden apple
   tree" provides the key that unlocks the sense of the poem. The
   tree, however, is the source of Paradise rather than its destruction, because Paradise is a state after the fall when man knew
   love. The tree is associated with light and love and continues
   to suggest a promise of life. "The Biblical allusion is used
   with anti-Biblical meaning."

24   McCLINTOCK, PATRICIA. "A Reading of Hart Crane's 'For the
       Marriage of Faustus and Helen.'" Massachusetts Studies in
       English 1:39-43.
         Although the three sections of the poem were originally
   written as separate poems, McClintock reads them as a tightly
   unified poem with a series of images in constant flux. While
   Crane is disturbed by the images of modern life, he is not pessimistic. The protagonist is purged by his experiences in part two
   and three and persists in holding on to a positive final vision.

25   MUNSON, GORHAM. "Chaplinesque." Forum 5:20-26.
         Mostly about the figure of Charles Chaplin, but some of the
   discussion is relevant to Crane. "Chaplinesque" was inspired by
   Chaplin's The Kid, and Crane and Munson had an extensive correspondence about the poem. Munson secured publication for it in
   Gargoyle. Munson insists that Crane was a hero-worshipper of
   Chaplin before this meeting and implies that he hoped for a
   "beautiful friendship with Charlie."

26   NOON, WILLIAM T., S.J. Poetry and Prayer. New Brunswick,
       N.J.: Rutgers University Press, pp. 67, 68-69, 96, 103-4,
       232, 319.
         References to Crane in passing, but his discussion of Crane
   as a nonreligious poet is important. While Crane appreciated the
   imaginative resources of religious symbols rooted in Christian
   culture, he was avowedly secular.

27   ONG, WALTER J., S.J. In the Human Grain: Further Explorations
       of Contemporary Culture. New York: Macmillan Co., pp. 110,
       114-15, 126.
         Crane does not successfully handle cosmic time. His faith

in the future of industrial America "hints at a feeling for
linear, evolutionary time." He was driven toward cyclic views to
fulfill his need for a pattern in his attempt to create the American myth. "Crane is typically American in his determination to
try to make poetic sense of history."

28   RAGO, HENRY. "The Vocation of Poetry." Poetry 110 (August):
      328-48.
          Most contemporary poetry reveals something of the inward
      transformation of the metaphor. This is seen especially in
      Crane's "Voyages." The metaphors are not only "telescoped"
      (Crane's word), but "they move in a ritual of transformation, in
      which love and death and the sea are constantly metamorphosed
      into one another, in 'The Silken Skilled Transmemberent of Song.'"
      In Crane's poetry, the words not only say something "but more
      than that do something, even . . . turn into something." Beyond
      the symbol there is a sign that is called a sacrament. Caroline
      Gordon told Rago that towards the end of his life Crane said to
      her that he longed "to taste blood." Reprinted: 1967.29.

29   _____. "The Vocation of Poetry." In Essays in Divinity.
      Edited by Nathan A. Scott, Jr. Chicago: University of Chicago
      Press, pp. 239-60.
          Reprint of 1967.28.

30   RUSSEL, H.K. Review of Hart Crane by Monroe K. Spears. South
      Atlantic Quarterly 66, no. 2 (Spring):275-78.
          Brief review of 1965.21. Spears gives the reader "intelli-
      gently balanced statements of Crane's defects and accomplishments."

31   SCHWARTZ, ALLAN HOWARD. "The British Ghost of Crane's The
      Bridge." American Notes and Queries 5:150.
          Both the English Catalogue of Books for 1926-30 and H.D.
      Rowe's Hart Crane: A Bibliography list an English edition of The
      Bridge published by E. Goldston. No such edition exists. Schwartz
      speculates that Goldston imported some copies of the Black Sun
      Press edition and pasted his label on the text. "The English
      edition is a non-existent ghost--haunting Crane scholars because
      of one inaccurate entry."

32   SPRATLING, WILLIAM. "Extraordinary Friends." In File on
      Spratline: An Autobiography. Boston: Little, Brown &
      Company, pp. 97-102.
          Had been introduced to Crane by Waldo Frank, and he wrote
      a recommendation for Crane when he applied for a Guggenheim. Got
      to know Crane better during his stay in Mexico. "Hart Crane,
      like Faulkner, a constant drinker, loved to drink. Hart was a
      complete extrovert. He was friendly with everyone, but he had a
      particular fondness for young boys." Peggy Baird appears as Mrs.
      X. "Actually, Mrs. X laid her proposition on the table. A
      forthright woman, highly-sexed, she bluntly proposed to instruct

Hart in the physical joys of male and female relations. Since
their relationship did not involve love in its romantic sense,
and since Hart saw in her skinny little, non-voluptuous, even
boyish person, an ally rather than an amorous entanglement, he
proceeded to receive instructions."

33   STANFORD, ANN. "Poetry: 1910-1930." In American Literary
       Scholarship: An Annual/1965. Edited by James Woodress.
       Durham, N.C.: Duke University Press, pp. 204-19.
            Review of the 1965 work on Crane.

34   SYMONS, JULIAN. "Hart Crane's Letters." London Magazine 6,
       no. 12 (March):99-104.
            Although never popular in England because of his unabashedly
       romantic rhetoric, "Crane was always trying to struggle through
       rhetoric to some absolute truths about the modern world, the
       human spirit, America." There is a tragic tone to the letters
       which illustrates the painful course of his life. Crane's char-
       acter was shaped by the dissension between his parents; the in-
       creased brutality of his sexual encounters was related to his
       decline as a poet. In The Bridge, a "magnificent failure," some
       poems demonstrate masterful control of style while others are
       overwritten and incoherent.

35   SWALLOW, ALLAN. "Hart Crane." Denver Quarterly 2 (Spring):
       93-118.
            Reprint of 1949.11.

36   TANNER, TONY. "The Myth of America." Spectator 218, no. 7233
       (10 February):170.
            Positive and enthusiastic review of Weber's Letters of Hart
       Crane. He became one of the major American poets of this century
       by the amazing brilliance with which he transformed a disinte-
       grating life into "a vital, disciplined art."

37   TRACHTENBERG, ALLAN. "The Plight of Romanticism." Kenyon
       Review 39 (November):712-19.
            Review of R.W.B. Lewis's The Poetry of Hart Crane: A Crit-
       ical Study. What Lewis's excellent book makes clear is the para-
       doxical nature of Crane's work and its relation to his time.
       Crane's visionary quest--the effort to see the ideal in the frag-
       mented and confused reality around him--provides the basis for
       Lewis's interpretation of Crane's poetry. The "brilliantly con-
       ceived arguments" of Lewis are persuasive. He demonstrates that
       Crane's true epic purpose was the celebration of poetry itself,
       of its capacity for ever-renewing hope. Lewis has not carefully
       clarified the role of American culture in the poem, nor is he
       fully persuaded that Crane himself effects the reconciliation of
       the actual and the ideal, of history and myth, in "Atlantis."
       Concludes that this book is the most important study of Crane we
       have. See 1967.19.

38 UNTERECKER, JOHN E. "A Piece of Pure Invention." Forum 5:42–44.
   Reprint of 1966.32.

39 VOELCKER, HUNCE. The Hart Crane Voyages. New York: Brownstone Press, 68 pp.
   Attempts to re-create the imagination of Crane when composing "Voyages," generously mixing the nonliteral with the literal. See 1967.22; 1968.34; 1969.9.

40 WEBER, BROM. "Crane, (Harold) Hart." In Encyclopedia Britanica. Edited by Warren E. Preece. Vol. 6. Chicago: Encyclopedia, p. 695.
   Typical entry, but of more than passing interest because it was written by Brom Weber.

41 WINTERS, YVOR. Forms of Discovery: Critical and Historical Essays on the Forms of the Short Poem in English. Denver, Colo.: Alan Swallow Publisher, pp. 244, 315–16.
   References to Crane's life as an example of surrender to sensation, and to his relationship to Whitman in that they shared many of the same ideas.

                              1968

1 ANON. "Crane, (Harold) Hart." Bröckahause. Vol. 4, p. 194.
   In German. Typical entry.

2 ANON. "Two Worlds and at Once." Times Literary Supplement, no. 3542 (25 April), p. 114.
   Review of The Poetry of Hart Crane by R.W.B. Lewis and The Literary Manuscripts of Hart Crane by Kenneth A. Lohf. Lewis's book is dedicated, thoughtful, persuasive, tactful, and gracefully done. Nevertheless, raises serious objections to the reading of poetry. Did Crane defect from certain obligations towards balance and emotional truthfulness? Did he use his intuition and lyric gift as an escape from emotional actuality? "Can we really understand Crane without tackeling head-on the question of the bizarre poetic diction?" Regards Lohf's work as important. See 1967.19, 21.

3 ANON. Review of The Literary Manuscripts of Hart Crane by Kenneth A. Lohf. Papers of the Bibliographical Society of America 62, no. 1 (January–March):154.
   Brief mention. See 1967.21.

4 BERTHOFF, WARNER. "R.W.B. Lewis's Hart Crane." Massachusetts Review 9, no. 4 (Autumn):792–800.
   Reprinted as 1971.4 where the following are omitted: faults Lewis for evident lack of "revision and improvement," for

his faulty interpretations of words and grammatical constructions,
and for his "erratic analysis" of "Black Tambourine," "Voyages,"
and "Lachrymae Christi."

5   BOTTORF, WILLIAM K. Review of Hart Crane by Herbert A.
    Liebowitz, The Poetry of Hart Crane by R.W.B. Lewis, and The
    Literary Manuscripts of Hart Crane by Kenneth A. Lohf. Library
    Journal 93, no. 4 (15 February):753.
         Liebowitz provides the reader with "full and highly infor-
    mative analysis of Crane's poetic period." Lewis has written "a
    major study, quite likely the best study of this highly complex
    and subtle subject." Lohf's work "will save scholars and critics
    weeks of investigation." See 1967.19-21; 1968.22.

6   BOYLE, KAY, and McALMON, ROBERT. Being Geniuses Together.
    New York: Doubleday & Company, pp. 237, 247, 368, 371-72.
         Passing references to Crane, the most notable being Boyle's
    account of Crane's imprisonment in Paris. See 1968.24.

7   BROWN, SUSAN JENKINS. "Hart Crane: The End of the Harvest."
    Southern Review 4 (Autumn):945-1014.
         Contains Crane's letters to William Slater Brown and Susan
    Jenkins Brown, edited with an introduction and reminiscenes by
    Susan Jenkins Brown. The texts of the letters are unpublished
    except for the following numbers which appear in Weber's edition
    of The Letters of Hart Crane: 5, 6, 7, 9, 12, 13, 14, 15, 16,
    18, 21. The texts of the eleven previously published letters
    differ from those in The Letters of Hart Crane in that they are
    uncut and that the names of persons referred to are (with one
    exception) used in full instead of initials, except where Crane
    himself used initials as a shortcut. "Hart adopted me and a
    number of my friends as his family." The circle included William
    Slater Brown, the Tates, the Cowleys, the Josephsons, Bina Flynn
    and her husband Romolo Bobba, Eleanor Fitzgerald, and Emil Opffer.
    After the Browns were married, Crane joined them in remodeling
    their farmhouse. While the bright side of Crane was more apparent
    to Mrs. Brown, she does record that there was a darker side to
    his nature--especially after the bitter quarrel with his mother
    in 1928. She does, however, object to the biographers and com-
    mentators who have emphasized the dark side of Crane. Reprinted:
    1968.8.

8   _____. Robber Rocks: Letters and Memories of Hart Crane 1923-
    1932. Middletown, Conn.: Wesleyan University Press, 176 pp.
         Reprint of 1968.7 with the addition of a brief note by
    Malcolm Cowley, pp. 102-7, and a reprint of 1961.2. Reviewed in:
    1970.11, 24, 31; 1971.20.

9   CASPER, LEONARD. "Review." Thought 43 (Winter):613-15.
         Review of R.W.B. Lewis's The Poetry of Hart Crane. Lewis's
    explication of Crane's earlier poems is more significant than his

careful reading of The Bridge. The major weakness of the book is the identification of religious vision with romantic vision. "So facile an exchange of romantic for religious sentiment leaves one critically uncomfortable. . . ." See 1967.19.

10   CHENEY, FRANCIS N. Review of The Literary Manuscripts of Hart Crane by Kenneth Lohf. Wilson Library Bulletin 42, no. 10 (June):1045.
     A short, favorable review. See 1967.21.

11   COHEN, J.M. Poetry of This Age: 1908-1965. New York: Harper & Row, pp. 166-67.
     Brief comparisons of Crane with Rimbaud, Edith Sitwell, and Dylan Thomas. Although Crane and Sitwell are excellent small scale poets, when their words take command of sense, their rhetoric forces their poems to fail.

12   CONNOLLY, CYRIL. "Myth-Maker of the Jazz Age." Sunday Times (London), 15 September, p. 12.
     Review of Weber's The Complete Poems, Selected Letters and Prose of Hart Crane. Generally a negative tone focusing on his weaknesses: rhetorical, inflated, pretentious and unnecessarily obscure. "The Rimbaud of the Gatsby Era."

13   COWLEY, MALCOLM. "The Flower and the Leaf." Southern Review 4 (Autumn):1015-18.
     Verse appreciation. See 1968.14.

14   ____. "The Flower and the Leaf." In Blue Juanita: Collected Poems by Malcolm Cowley. New York: Viking Press, pp. 139-41.
     Verse appreciation. See 1968.13.

15   DEMBO, L[awrence].S. "Hart Crane's 'Verticalist' Poem." American Literature 40 (March):77-81.
     Verticalism emphasized the creative urge toward reconstructing the myth of voyage, flight, or ascent in all of its "romantic-mystic" manifestation. Crane was one of the signers of the verticalist manifesto entitled "The Revolution of the Word" which appeared in Transition in June 1929. Although Horton says that Crane in a more sober moment retracted his interest in the movement, Dembo feels that the manifesto is consistent with Crane's own esthetic theories. The Ideal expression of the doctrine of this movement is found in "Cape Hatteras."

16   FAIRCHILD, HOXIE NEALE. Religious Trends in English Poetry. New York: Columbia University Press, pp. 40, 48, 49, 56, 68, 73, 79, 80, 81, 86, 192, 193, 273, 287, 289, 303, 361, 363, 385, 414, 419.
     Many references in passing; some of more than passing interest. The poetry is autonomous, yet having too much private symbolism. Crane's difficulty in The Bridge is related to its

"non-existent roots in primitive Indian culture." The Bridge is
the "most ambitious attempt of the romantic spirit to derive
aesthetic and spiritual values from the machine age." Crane did
not want "communion with some life greater than his own; he
simply wanted his own life better than it was."

17 FIEDLER, LESLIE A. The Return of the Vanishing American. New
    York: Stein & Day, pp. 55-56, 63-64, 87-89.
        Described as the most ambitious modern exploiter of the
    myth of Rip Van Winkle. The Bridge is an attempt at a full-scale
    résumé of American mythology. Rip must embrace the Indian--the
    male preferably--and Crane must have understood this when he
    wrote The Bridge, although his own homosexuality apparently got
    in his way. The Bridge was doomed from the start because of the
    author's sexual problems and because of his ill-fated resolve to
    weave together the myth of Rip and the Indian with the stereotype
    of Priscilla and Captain Smith. His use of the Pocahontas material
    is dubious. "The Dance" constitutes the true center of The
    Bridge. This section celebrates not the legendary princess but
    her dusky Indian prince, his true lover. Crane named the dusky
    prince Maquokeeta because this was the middle name of one of his
    cab driver boyfriends. The myth becomes phallic rather than
    idyllic.

18 HAZO, SAMUEL. "The Last Minute of Hart Crane." In Blood
    Rights. Pittsburgh: University of Pittsburgh Press, pp. 16-
    17.
        Verse appreciation.

19 HIRSHFELD, SUSAN EVE, and PORTNER, RUTH. "A Voyage Through
    Two Voyages: A Study of Hart Crane's Voyages IV and V."
    Language and Style 1, no. 2:115-28.
        Linguistic approach to the poems. "Voyages V" is superior
    in its precision and definition; it embraces more, is more com-
    plex, and is more economical.

*20 HUTSON, RICHARD EUGENE. "The World Dimensional: A Study in
    Hart Crane's Poetry." Ph.D. dissertation, University of
    Illinois.

21 KRAMER, J. "Allen Ginsberg: Profile." New Yorker 44 (24
    August):86-87.
        Quotes Ginsberg as saying that Dylan Thomas and Crane were
    "killed by their own intentions." They were forced to drink, be-
    cause they attempted to recreate the unconscious through rational,
    conscious means. If Crane had lived in Haight-Ashbury and had
    had a chance "to goof around" he "never would have died. If he'd
    had enough boyfriends or girlfriends, or whatever it was he liked.
    And if somebody had turned him on, to get him off lush. Instead
    he had this heavy literary environment on his back." See 1968.18.

22 LEIBOWITZ, HERBERT A. Hart Crane: An Introduction to the
    Poetry. New York: Columbia University Press, 308 pp.
        Reading of the short poems. Crane's life is peculiarly
    American. Central to understanding Crane must be the reader's
    awareness of how faithful he was to the spirit of modernism.
    "The radical fact" about Crane is the abrupt maturation that took
    place; it is important to trace chronologically the development
    of his poetry. The turning point was marked by "Faustus and
    Helen." In it, he solemnized "his vocation as a visionary poet."
    "Voyages" is Crane's highest achievement, because it is the best
    expression of his lyric gift concerning a subject about which he
    could not fake. Crane's language is best understood by comparing
    it with the language and structure of the great romantic odes.
    His imagery is often tortured and complex because he was part of
    the mainstream of contemporary poetry. The tortured complexity
    of figurative languages is characteristic of the modern romantic.
    Compiles and analyzes a list of his most frequent images. From
    a metrical point of view, Crane was a traditional craftsman, only
    occasionally flirting with the new movements of his time. He
    "attempted to fuse Romantic and modern rhythms into a new rhet-
    oric." After chapter 1, four chapters are devoted to Crane's
    poems through "Voyages" in chronological fashion. The following
    five chapters deal with the technical characteristics of his
    poetry such as diction, imagery, syntax, etc. Reviewed in:
    1968.34; 1969.4, 7-8, 14, 30-31, 35, 37, 52, 58; 1970.5, 23;
    1971.20.

23 LUBBERS, KLAUS. Review of L'Universe poetique de Hart Crane
    by Jean Guiguet and To Brooklyn Bridge and Other Poems: Au
    Pont de Brooklyn et autre poemes. Translated by Jean Guiguet.
    Jahrbüch für Amerikastudien 13:328-30.
        In German. Guiguet's study rests mainly on the statistical
    frequency of words. He does not do justice to the peculiar func-
    tion each word has in his study of Crane's key words that are
    value-laden. The translation follows the original closely and
    functions well for the French reader.

24 McALMON, ROBERT, and BOYLE, KAY. Being Geniuses Together.
    New York: Doubleday & Co., pp. 237, 247, 369, 371-72.
        See 1968.6.

25 MUNSON, GORHAM. "A Comedy of Exiles." Literary Review 12,
    no. 1 (Autumn):41-75.
        Record of the difficulties encountered in the printing of
    "For the Marriage of Faustus and Helen."

26 _____. "Poetry: 1900 to the 1930's." In American Literary
    Scholarship: An Annual/1966. Edited by James Woodress.
    Durham, N.C.: Duke University Press, pp. 187-204.
        A notable advance in the criticism of Crane has been made
    by R.W.B. Lewis.

27   NASSAR, EUGENE PAUL. "Both God and Fake." Essays in Criti-
      cism 18 (October):448-53.
           Review of R.W.B. Lewis's The Poetry of Hart Crane, de-
      scribed as the best book yet written on Crane. Criticizes Lewis
      for ending in Emersonian transcendentalism, hence the book falls
      short of doing full justice to Crane. See 1967.19.

28   NILSSON, OLLE W. "Hart Crane och myten om Amerika" [Hart
      Crane and the Myth of America]. Finsk-Tidskrift, pp. 163-64,
      218-22.
           In Norwegian. Comments on Horton's Hart Crane, discusses
      Tate's criticism, provides a few biographical details, and then
      analyzes Crane's attempt to answer Eliot's position in The Waste
      Land. A discussion of Crane's romanticism, particularly the in-
      fluence of Whitman and the idea of an American myth.

29   PAUL, SHERMAN. "Reviews." Journal of English and Germanic
      Philology 67 (April):329-32.
           Review of R.W.B. Lewis's The Poetry of Hart Crane: A Crit-
      ical Study and a brief mention of The Literary Manuscripts of
      Hart Crane by Kenneth A. Lohf. Does not think that Crane is well
      served by Lewis's study. The book, rather, is a monument to con-
      temporary criticism, an interpretation, not a critical study. He
      makes no attempt to judge Crane's stature; he assumes it and de-
      clares it. "The essential limitations of this book are to be
      found, I think, in Mr. Lewis' failure to read the poems as he
      might have and in his unwillingness to follow his methods
      through." Lewis should have paid more attention to the criticism
      written about Crane, because Crane's vision is essentially a
      shared vision and his indebtedness to others should be recorded.
      This is far more important than his archetypal imagination.
      Lohf's work is praised. See 1967.19, 21.

30   PORTER, FRANK. "'Chaplinesque': An Explication." English
      Journal 57 (February):191-92.
           The poet identifies with Chaplin--the figure of the little
      tramp. The word "meek" indicates that the identification may
      also be with a Christ-figure. The little tramp figure provokes
      laughter so as to throw up a shield against the ever-threatening
      cruelty of society. Finally, the Christlike qualities of the
      poet and of the clown are fused.

31   RADHUBER, S[tanley].G[regory]. "Hart Crane: An Annotated
      Bibliography." Ph.D. dissertation, University of Michigan.
           Includes a seventy-three page introduction-survey of the
      criticism.

32   SIMPSON, WILLIAM T. "An Explication of Hart Crane's 'Black
      Tambourine.'" Xavier University Studies 7:5-7.
           A poem about the American Negro and the American Negro
      poets specifically, as well as about the destiny of poets generally

in the modern world. The universal quality of the poem is akin
to the image raised in Ralph Ellison's Invisible Man.

33   THOMPSON, LAWRENCE S. "Review." Papers of The Bibliographical
       Society of America 62 (First Quarter):154.
          Brief description of Lohf's The Literary Manuscripts of
   Hart Crane (1961.21).

34   UNTERECKER, JOHN. "Hart Crane." Yale Review 57 (Spring):
       455-60.
          Review of Lewis's The Poetry of Hart Crane: An Introduction
   to Poetry, Voelcker's The Hart Crane Voyages, Lohf's The Literary
   Manuscripts of Hart Crane, and Leibowitz's Hart Crane. The books
   of Lewis and Leibowitz are praised because they do the most to
   erase the "failure" label from Crane, and firmly establish him as
   a central figure in a dominant American literary tradition--the
   tradition of romantic writing. Although both books are superior,
   occasionally the authors confuse the materials of Crane's art
   with the finished product. Both authors insist on reading
   "Voyages" as if it were exclusively an anecdote about a homosexual love affair. If one must read the poem biographically,
   the only effective way to do it is as Voelcker has done in his
   book. "Voelcker's book offers us one man's version of another
   man's soul--for me, convincingly." See 1967.19, 21, 39; 1968.22.

35   Van NORSTRAND, A.D. "Hart Crane's Span of Consciousness." In
       Everyman His Own Poet: Romantic Gospels in American Litera-
       ture. New York: McGraw-Hill Book Co., pp. 63-81.
          Reprint of 1962.22.

36   WAGGONER, HYATT H[owe]. "Hart Crane." In American Poets:
       From the Puritans to the Present. Boston: Houghton Mifflin
       Co., pp. 494-511.
          Crane belongs to the nature mysticism tradition of Blake,
   Wordsworth, Emerson, and Whitman. He attempted to articulate his
   experience in the American, romantic, and transcendental manner.
   His aim as a poet is expressed in "The Broken Tower," where the
   visionary attempts to formulate a "cognate" vision. "Voyages VI"
   is "among the great poems of mystical experience in our literature." Although The Bridge is one of the finest long poems in
   literature, almost all readers are impressed with the unevenness
   of the poem. No poem could have achieved all that Crane said he
   intended to achieve in this poem. Whitman, Eliot, and Ouspensky
   are the great influences on The Bridge. "Cape Hatteras" is the
   key to the poem's intent. His borrowings from Whitman show that
   this particular poem is about union with God "achieved through
   sensing the imminence of deity in present experience." Traces
   the influence of P.D. Ouspensky's Tertium Organum on Crane. The
   tradition which Crane adopted did not sustain him; Whitman's
   example did more harm than good. "Crane had more in common with
   St. John of the Cross than with Whitman."

37 _____. "Hart Crane and the Visionary Tradition." <u>Virginia</u>
    <u>Quarterly Review</u> 44 (Spring):323-28.
        Review of Lewis's <u>The Poetry of Hart Crane</u>, the major
    modernist poet in the first half of this century. He acknowledged
    his indebtedness to Whitman, Melville, and Dickinson. The most
    valuable contribution of Lewis's book is his placing of Crane in
    the romantic visionary tradition of Blake, Emerson, and Whitman.
    Even though Crane got his Emersonianism chiefly through Whitman,
    the fact that he got it at all testifies to Emerson's centrality
    in the principal American poetic tradition. Another virtue of
    Lewis's book is that he takes into account not only the Emersonian
    tradition, but the British romantic tradition as well. The par-
    allels cited between Crane and Keats and Shelley, for instance,
    are helpful. The sense one gets from the book is that Northrup
    Frye is hovering over one of Lewis's shoulders as he writes, and
    the ghost of some New Critic over the other. Waggoner has some
    reservations about Lewis's claim of religious importance for
    Crane, since Lewis seems to equate religious vision with make-
    believe. See 1967.19.

38 WEBER, BROM. Review of <u>The Poetry of Hart Crane</u> by R.W.B.
    Lewis. <u>American Literature</u> 40 (May):252-54.
        Crane's indebtedness to Dante is a rich line of inquiry
    which Lewis might have followed, since he conceives of Crane as
    the foremost religious poet of his generation. Points out the
    materials available for studying the question of Crane's re-
    sponse to Dante. The positive monolithic critical structure
    erected by Lewis may be as damaging to Crane as the negative
    structure to which he is responding, since Lewis refuses to con-
    sider the contradiction, complexity, and inconsistency in Crane's
    life and work. Lewis's admirers "will be puzzled and disturbed"
    by this work. See 1967.19.

39 WHEELWRIGHT, PHILIP. <u>The Burning Fountain</u>. Bloomington:
    Indiana University Press, pp. 47, 82, 90, 120.
        Crane's theory of the "illogical impingements of words on
    the consciousness" can be made "more academically by saying that
    poetic meanings can, and deeply need to, overreach the raw datum
    of sensation in quite different ways, along quite different lines,
    and by quite different techniques from those which characterize
    logical literal meanings."

40 WOODRESS, JAMES. <u>Dissertations in American Literature, 1891-</u>
    <u>1966</u>. Durham, N.C.: Duke University Press, pp. 454-82, 483-
    513.
        A listing of twelve dissertations.

41 YANNELLA, PHILLIP R. "Toward Apotheosis: Hart Crane's
    Visionary Lyrics." <u>Criticism</u> 10 (Fall):313-33.
        "For the Marriage of Faustus and Helen" is not a reflection
    of the twenties or of anything particularly modern; it is simply

an expression of the poet's need to believe in something. The
Helen of the poem disappears from his later poetry, but the
imaginative Faust-figure who looks upward, bent on achieving the
Absolute, remains. The struggle of this figure is apparent in
several poems contained in White Buildings. Crane's visionary
poems are poems of process, which tend to capture the moments of
visionary experience and convey its quality. In "Voyages" we
are not left with the accomplishment of an ultimate vision, but
with the hope that such a vision will occur.

42   ZUKOFSKI, LOUIS. Prepositions. New York: Horizon Press, pp.
     129-33.
          Mentions Joyce's influence on Crane. Praises the poetry
     for energy, although it is often too "pseudo-musical," mystical,
     and filmy. Single words are rarely symbols for the things they
     represent, the result of being "a haze."

                              1969

1   ADAM, PHOEBE. "Short Reviews (Unterecker)." Atlantic 224
     (August):103.
          Brief review of Unterecker's life of Crane, Voyager
     (1969.46).

2   ANON. "Altering the Mode of Consciousness: The Ecstatic, In-
     definite Idealism of Hart Crane." Times Literary Supplement,
     no. 3527 (2 October), pp. 1117-19.
          Review of Weber's The Complete Poems and Selected Prose and
     Poetry of Hart Crane and Butterfield's The Broken Arc: A Study
     of Hart Crane. Weber's volume includes many important additions.
     Butterfield's work is painstaking and always sensible, the ap-
     proach being more exegetical than critical. See 1969.11.

3   ANON. "Bridges and Towers." Time 94, no. 3 (18 July):80.
          Review of Unterecker's life of Crane, Voyager, described as
     trying to put Crane in perspective and avoiding the eccentricities
     of Crane's instability. See 1969.46.

4   ANON. Review of Hart Crane: An Introduction to His Poetry
     by Herbert Leibowitz. Choice 6, no. 2 (April):216.
          An introduction to Crane's poetic theory; deals with the
     stylistic elements of his work, substantiates previous evaluations
     of Crane's virtues, and establishes Crane's link with the romantic
     tradition. Leibowitz "fails to answer questions of what kind of
     artistic wholes Crane characteristically constructed." There is
     a need for a new formal estimate of The Bridge. See 1968.22.

5   ANON. Review of Voyager: A Life of Hart Crane by John
     Unterecker. Kirkus Service 37, no. 9 (1 May):553-54.
          Praised as a landmark of literary scholarship because it is

                              154

meticulous and encompassing. However, it does not say the final word about its subject. See 1969.46.

6   ANON. Review of Voyager: The Life of Hart Crane by John Unterecker. Yale Review 59, no. 2 (December):xxx-xxxii.
        Gives a full view of Crane's life and illuminates some of the poetry in brief, pertinent and sympathetic comments. The weaknesses are an inclncation to be tender-minded toward people and ideas, leaving characters indistinct, and an unwillingness to make psychological judgments. See 1969.46.

7   AMACHER, RICHARD E. Review of Hart Crane: An Introduction to the Poetry by Herbert A. Leibowitz. American Quarterly 21, no. 2 (Summer):382-83.
        Praised for expertly tracing Crane's development and examining the influences on his style. See 1968.22.

8   BJORNSON, GERHILD. Review of Hart Crane: An Introduction to the Poetry by Herbert Leibowitz. Studia Neophilologica 41: 443-47.
        Compliments Leibowitz on his careful and meticulous analysis of Crane's language, imagery, verse form, and rhythm. Is criticized for employing vague terminology and for characterizing Crane's complex poetry with simple generalizations. See 1968.22.

9   BRYANT, J[oseph].A., Jr. "Hart Crane and the Illusory Abyss." Sewanee Review 77 (Winter):149-54.
        Essay review of Weber's 1966 edition of The Complete Poems, Lewis's The Poetry of Hart Crane and Hunce Voelcker's The Hart Crane Voyages. Although Weber has presented an adequate text, serious students will need the variorum edition, which Weber has promised for sometime. Lewis's study is "probably the most consistently useful explication of Crane's work that has appeared in two decades." But even more important is his vigorous defense of Crane's work which several of his distinguished contemporaries repudiated. Bryant connects Crane with Emerson and Whitman: "The world was good and the illusion of sin on it a flaw in the vision." Responding to Lewis's discussion of The Bridge as being concerned with "the birth of God," Bryant is disturbed by the possibility that "Crane's new deity was nothing more than Crane himself in the person of poet." Voelcker's work is a piece "of extravagant discourse only occasionally redeemed by the illumination of sparks." See 1967.19, 39.

10   BURKE, KENNETH. "The 'Christ-Dionysus Link.'" New Republic 161 (16 August):24-26.
        Review of Unterecker's life on Crane, Voyager. Crane's major poem is a bridge from his world to the world of an idealized "mythic" past which lives on in the present and infuses it with its essence. The book is painstakingly thorough. See 1969.46.

11   BUTTERFIELD, R.W. The Broken Arc: A Study of Hart Crane.
      Edinburgh: Oliver & Boyd, 276 pp.
           Regards Crane as a "central and absolutely crucial" figure
      in the history of American literature. Procedure is basically
      chronological, a discussion of the poety from 1916 to 1932.
      While two chapters are concerned with The Bridge, the emphasis,
      in contrast to many books on Crane, is on the shorter poems. One
      appendix is devoted to an analysis of the influences of Nietzsche
      and Plato on Crane. Aims at illustrating the special excellence
      of the poetry. Wishes to draw attention to the poems excluded
      from White Buildings and to the poems in Key West. Attempts to
      "isolate" the causes of his "poetic and personal disintegration,"
      and to demonstrate that such disintegration has a much wider than
      personal cultural significance. After analyzing the internal con-
      tradictions of The Bridge, concludes that the poem is not about
      America but about Crane and is "conceptually fractured." The de-
      fects of the poem, magnificent as are some of the parts, can be
      found in its plan. Reviewed in: 1969.2; 1972.12.

12   FAVERTY, FREDERICK E. "Discovering the 'True' Hart Crane."
      Chicago Sun Times Book Week, 20 July, sec. 3, p. 8.
           Unterecker in Voyager does a good job in recreating the
      atmosphere of the times. His main intent is to present Crane as
      a serious artist who was troubled by psychological, social, and
      financial problems. Taking no sides, he presents all of the
      views of Crane and allows the reader to form his own judgment.
      See 1969.46.

13   GLIDZEN, ALEX. "Hart Crane." Sumac 1 (Spring):67.
      Verse appreciation.

14   GREEN, MARTIN. Review of Hart Crane: An Introduction to the
      Poetry by Herbert A. Leibowitz. Critical Quarterly 11, no. 4
      (Winter):381-82.
           Does not use enough biographical evidence in reading the
      poetry. See 1968.22.

15   HALPERT, STEVEN, and JOHNS, RICHARD. A Return to Pagany: The
      History, Correspondence, and Selections from a Little Magazine
      1929-1932. Boston: Beacon Press, pp. 16, 22, 218.
           Reprints letter from Crane to Johns, and letters from
      Gorham Munson and Edward Dahlberg mentioning Crane as a possible
      contributor to Pagany.

16   HART, JEFFREY. "Divided Being." National Review 21 (4 Novem-
      ber):1119, 1121.
           Complimentary review of Unterecker's life of Crane,
      Voyager. Uses it to write a brief essay on the squalor and self-
      destructiveness of Crane's life as contrasted with the genius of
      his poetry. Scc 1969.46.

17 HARTLEY, LODWICK. "Stephen's Lost World: The Background of Katherine Anne Porter's 'Downward Path to Wisdom.'" <u>Studies in Short Fiction</u> 6, no. 5 (Fall):574-79.
    An attempt to trace the parallels between Porter's story and Phillip Horton's life of Hart Crane, indicating that the biography may have been the source of the story.

18 HAYMAN, RONALD. "From Hart Crane to Gary Snyder." <u>Encounter</u> 32 (February):72-79.
    Ostensibly a review of Weber's edition of <u>The Complete Poems and Selected Letters and Prose of Hart Crane</u>. Instead of making an evaluation of the edition, provides a comment on Crane's work. By bringing together references to unrelated concepts, he hoped to establish some relationship between them. "It is because of this total inability to synthesize" that the shorter poems are much more successful than the longer ones.

19 HAZO, SAMUEL. John Unterecker's <u>Voyager: A Life of Hart Crane</u>. <u>Commonweal</u> 90, no. 20 (5 September):545-46.
    Positive review praising Unterecker for his thoroughness and attention to detail. Although Crane's life was a disaster, "his poems were his salvation." See 1969.46.

20 HUBERMAN, ELIZABETH. "Hart Crane's Use of 'Symphonic Form.'" <u>American-Austrian: Bietrage Zur Amerikakunde</u> 2:15-29.
    Explications of "For the Marriage of Faustus and Helen" and <u>The Bridge</u>. Develops what Crane had to say about symphonic form weaving together the various strands of <u>The Bridge</u>. Attempts to show that the strands are prefigured, then stated, then evoked by repetition until they all "sound together." Concentrates on the Columbus theme in <u>The Bridge</u> to show how Crane does this.

21 HUTSON, RICHARD [Eugene]. "Exile Guise: Irony in Hart Crane." <u>Mosaic</u> 2, no. 4:771-86.
    Crane's use of the ironic mode, the diminished hero, was inevitable given his times, but the surprising thing is that it has been so little noted by his critics. "The attractions of negation were always powerful for Crane." It was only after he had grounded himself convincingly on the negations of T.S. Eliot that Crane was capable of risking affirmations. Particular attention is paid to "Chaplinesque" and "Lachrymae Christi."

22 KATZ, JOSEPH. "CALM Addendum No. 1: Hart Crane." <u>Papers of the Bibliographical Society of America</u> 63 (Second Quarter): 130.
    An amendment to section D of Kenneth Lohf's <u>The Literary Manuscripts of Hart Crane</u>, noting the appearance in <u>American Weave</u> 30 (December 1966):1, of a juvenile poem by Crane, "A Song for Happy Feast Days," inscribed on a preliminary leaf of <u>The Complete Poetical Works of Robert Burns</u>, dated December 1914. See 1966.5, 12; 1967.21.

23   KRAMER, AARON. Review of <u>Voyager: A Life of Hart Crane</u> by
      John Unterecker. <u>Library Journal</u> 94 (15 June):2462.
        Brief review. See 1969.46.

24   LEHMAN-HAUPT, CHRISTOPHER. "More Than One Can Hope to Know
      About Hart Crane." <u>New York Times</u>, 14 July, p. 33.
        Review of Unterecker's <u>Voyager</u>, charging that the design of
   the book is dull and repetitious, that it has no organization,
   and that the author is not selective enough in his use of details.
   See 1969.46.

25   LEIBOWITZ, HERBERT [A.]. "Remembering Paul Rosenfeld."
      <u>Salmagundi</u> 9 (Spring):3-27.
        Crane is mentioned in passing.

26   LEWIS, THOMAS S.W. "Hart Crane and His Mother: A Corres-
      pondence." <u>Salmagundi</u> 9 (Spring):61-87.
        Biographical article stressing the years 1917-1925. Prin-
   cipally a publication of letters between Crane, his mother, and
   his grandmother published here for the first time.

27   LOEB, HAROLD, ed. <u>The Broom Anthology</u>. Kennebunkport, Maine:
      Milford House, pp. xv, 345-46.
        Reference to Crane's appearance in his magazine.

28   LONG, ROBERT EMMET. "His Art Was His Obsession." <u>Christian</u>
      <u>Science Monitor</u>, 24 July, p. 7.
        Brief review of Unterecker's life of Crane, <u>Voyager</u>
   (1969.46).

29   LOVEMAN, SAMUEL. "Hart Crane." <u>New York Times Book Review</u> 74
      (10 August):22.
        Letter to the editor stating that he took the photograph of
   Crane that illustrated Helen Vendler's review of Unterecker's
   <u>Voyager</u>. See 1969.48.

30   MAZZARO, JEROME. Review of <u>Hart Crane: An Introduction to</u>
      <u>the Poetry</u> by Herbert Leibowitz. <u>Criticism</u> 11, no. 1 (Winter):
      104-6.
        Unfortunately this study does not come to grips with the
   larger problems of Crane's romanticism, his idealism, and his
   homosexuality. It lacks organization and coherence, developing
   no clear image of the poet. See 1968.22.

31   McSWEENEY, KERRY. Review of <u>Hart Crane: An Introduction to</u>
      <u>the Poetry</u> by Herbert Leibowitz. <u>Queen's Quarterly</u> 76:132-33.
        Complements the work of Lewis, restricting itself to a dis-
   cussion of Crane's style and technique. See 1968.22.

32   MUNSON, GORHAM. "Magazine Rack at the Washington Square Book-
      shop." <u>Studies in the Twentieth Century</u>, no. 4 (Fall):pp. 23,

24, 31, 32, 34, 39, 41.
    Miscellaneous information on various of the little maga-
zines available to Crane and his contemporaries.

33   _____. "Woodstock 1924." Hartford Studies in Literature 1,
    no. 3:169-80.
        Remembers Crane's initial plan for The Bridge, his relation-
ship with the painter, William Sommer, and compares William Carlos
Williams with Crane, particularly with reference to their differences with respect to Stieglitz, Whitman, and Ouspensky.

34   NASSAR, EUGENE PAUL. "Hart Crane: The Poem Before the Poet."
    Quartet 14 (Fall):32-33.
        Positive review of Unterecker's Voyager. Unterecker adopts
a laudatory attitude toward Crane and uses his poetry to illumine
his biography. See 1969.46.

35   PAUL, SHERMAN. Review of Hart Crane: An Introduction to the
    Poetry by Herbert A. Leibowitz. Journal of English and German
    Philology 68, no. 2 (April):324-26.
        While the book is modest, full of good sense, and accounts
for Crane's poetry with greater attention than before, it is
neither introductory nor conclusive. It lacks coverage and
range, does not deal with The Bridge nor with the thematic development of Crane's poetry; biographical details are neglected. See
1968.22.

36   POULIN, A. "Crane's Voyages II." Explicator 28 (October):
    Item 15.
        The poem is governed by the logic of its own imaginative
framework, realized in the opening and closing lines. Beginning
with eternity and ending with paradise, it develops the journey
from birth to death and the confusion of essential cruel experience. Only love raised to the intensity of religious faith saves
the speaker.

37   PRITCHARD, WILLIAM H. "A Fine Messed-Up Life." Hudson Review
    22, no. 4 (Winter);725-31.
        Review of Unterecker's Voyager and Leibowtiz's Hart Crane.
Both books need to make "more of the problematic nature of the
various rhetorical effects by bringing into play the hesitation,
uncertainties, exhilarations a reader feels in the presence of
these effects." Unterecker should have been less reverent when
dealing with Crane. He does too little interpretation and plays
down Crane's homosexuality. Leibowitz deals with syntax, diction,
and imagery sensitivity. Pritchard holds that the main difficulty with Crane's poetry is that it does not present much interesting variety in tone. See 1968.22; 1969.46.

38   PUKNAT, E.M., and PUKNAT, S.B. "Goethe and Modern American
    Poets." German Quarterly 13, no. 1 (January):21-36.

Because Crane was interested in Goethe's creation of Faust as a representative image of the artist, he used that concept for the scaffolding of "Faustus and Helen."

39   QUINN, VINCENT [Gerard]. Review of The Poetry of Hart Crane: A Critical Study by R.W.B. Lewis. English Language Notes 6, no. 3 (March):228-30.

While Lewis is astute and persuasive, he adds little to our appreciation of the poems that has not been previously suggested. His description of The Bridge as a religious poem seems unrealistic. Crane's religion was no more than an intuition of a transcendent power and a wish that human joys could last forever. Feels that Crane had strong religious impulses, but had only a partially developed mature religious consciousness. See 1967.19.

40   REITER, THOMAS. "Hart Crane." Discourse 12, no. 2 (Spring): 191.

Verse appreciation.

41   RUNDEN, JOHN P. "Whitman's 'The Sleepers' and 'The Indiana' Section of Crane's The Bridge." Walt Whitman Review 15, no. 4 (December):245-48.

Both poems deal with the relation of an Indian woman to a white youth in an attempt to reveal the spiritual continuity of aboriginal Indian culture and the world of the twentieth century. While working on "Indiana" and "Cape Hatteras," Crane probably came across "The Sleeper." Wanting to strengthen what he thought of as a weak section of the poem, he used Whitman. And by using the female character, Crane maintained his personification of America as feminine throughout The Bridge.

42   SCHWARTZ, JOSEPH. "An Elusive Genius Challenges his Third Biographer--and Eludes Again." Milwaukee Journal, 10 August, p. 3.

Review of Unterecker's Voyager. See 1969.46.

43   SIMPSON, LOUIS. "The Failure of a Poet Who Was False to His Feelings." Book World 3, no. 28 (13 July):1, 3.

Review of Unterecker's life of Crane, Voyager. After briefly reviewing Unterecker, Simpson provides his own negative criticism of The Bridge--a failure, "a pile of incipient junk." See 1969.46.

44   STEEN, MIKE. A Look at Tennessee Williams. New York: Hawthorne Books, p. xv.

A brief reference to Williams's having read the poetry of Crane.

45   TATE, ALLEN, ed. Introduction to Six American Poets from Emily Dickinson to the Present. Minnesota Library on American Writers. Minneapolis: University of Minnesota Press, pp. 3-8.

Crane's "problem," complicated by The Bridge, will never be resolved; there is always room for more work on him. See 1965.21.

46 UNTERECKER, JOHN. Voyager: The Life of Hart Crane. New York: Farrar, Straus & Giroux, 787 pp.
    The storehouse of factual information now available concerning Crane. Many reviewers complained that the detail overwhelmed the biography, that Unterecker had not been selective enough in using his sources. Avoids presenting a full critical discussion of the poetry, placing it rather within its historical setting. The overwhelming enumeration of facts is justified by his plea that we cannot now know where significance lies. Scientific in intent rather than artistic; a log from which another writer one day will select the materials for a valid portrait. The major difficulty in using the text is that the forty-two pages of notes are published separately in pamphlet form. Reviewed in: 1969.1, 3, 5-6, 10, 12, 16, 19, 23-24, 28, 34, 37, 42-43, 47-49, 53, 55, 57; 1970.2, 5, 7, 24, 32, 38; 1971.2, 20-22; 1972.12, 14; 1973.12.

47 UNTERMEYER, LOUIS. "Poet Stranded on a Bridge." Saturday Review 52 (19 July):27-29, 39.
    Unterecker's Voyager presents Crane in almost photographic detail, perhaps too full. Nevertheless his insights into Crane are so excellent that the book "merits continual applause." See 1969.46.

48 VENDLER, HELEN. "The Terrible Details of Hart Crane's Life." New York Times Book Review, 30 July, pp. 1, 18.
    Review of Unterecker's life of Crane, Voyager. The biographer remains true in spirit to Crane, resulting in a complex protrait. Unterecker resisted three temptations: writing a commentary on the poems, carrying on debate with unfriendly literary critics, and analyzing Crane's personality too simply. See 1969.46.

49 WEBER, BROM. "Hart Crane: Detail and Meaning." Virginia Quarterly Review 45, no. 4:697-700.
    In Voyager Unterecker lacks the discriminating intelligence to select the proper details and fuse them into some pattern. Says little about Crane's development as a poet and virtually nothing about his intellectual life and his significant artistic and personal associates. The biographer's task is to do more than merely accumulate and document the details of another's life. "Its subject has been compressed and trivialized." See 1969.46.

50 _____. "Hart Crane." In Fifteen Modern American Authors. Edited by Jackson R. Bryer. Durham, N.C.: Duke University Press, pp. 63-100.
    Along with the "Supplement" (1973.31), the indispensible starting point for any serious study of Crane. Various sections

devoted to bibliography, editions, manuscripts and letters, biography, and criticism. See 1973.31.

51   WEBER, BROM, and WOODRESS, JAMES. "Poetry: 1900 to the 1930's." In American Literary Scholarship: An Annual/1967. Edited by James Woodress. Durham, N.C.: Duke University Press, pp. 210-35.
       Survey of the year's work on Crane.

52   WEBER, BROM. Review of Hart Crane: An Introduction to the Poetry by Herbert A. Leibowitz. American Literature 41 (May): 295-96.
       "An admirable addition" to Crane criticism. Wisely focuses on the short poems and does not get entangled in The Bridge. The first extended, systematic scrutiny of Crane's diction, imagery, syntax, metrics. Occasionally fails to use authoritative versions of Crane's texts. See 1968.22.

53   WEINSTOCK, HERBERT. "Re-creating Crane." Chicago Daily News Panorama, 2 August, p. 4.
       Review of Unterecker's life of Crane, Voyager. While it may seem too long, its "unquestionable virtue" lies in its very inclusiveness. While avoiding most value judgments, it approaches as near as possible to presenting the whole, real Crane. See 1969.46.

54   WILBUR, RICHARD. "Poetry and Happiness." Shenandoah 20, no. 4 (Summer):3-23.
       Crane is mentioned in passing.

55   WOLFF, GEOFFREY. "Journey to Oblivion." Newsweek 74 (21 July):100-2.
       Review of Unterecker's Voyager, who "fails to do well by his subject" for a number of reasons. The documentation is published separately; characters are unidentified; barbarisms are frequent; the writing is at times embarrassingly florid. See 1969.46.

56   YANNELLA, PHILLIP R. Review of Hart Crane: An Introduction to the Poetry by Herbert A. Leibowitz. Modern Language Journal 53 (January):38-39.
       Described as "first rate and extremely valuable"; contains a penetrating analysis of Crane's imagery and diction. See 1968.22.

57   _____. Review of Voyager: Life of Hart Crane by John Unterecker. Modern Language Journal 54, no. 6:455-56.
       Presents a great mass of relevant and useful information about the poet. Although Unterecker does not usually permit himself to focus on exegesis or literary criticism, he makes a number of suggestions which serve to establish fresh approaches to the

poetry. See 1969.46.

<u>1970</u>

1   ALVAREZ, A[lfred]. "The Art of Suicide." <u>Partisan Review</u> 37,
     no. 3 (Spring):339-58.
         Crane's suicide was the result of his homosexuality, al-
coholism, and thinking himself a failure.

2   ATLAS, JAMES. "Voyager." <u>Poetry</u> 116, no. 4 (July):256-59.
         Review of Unterecker's life of Crane, called a triumph as
a biography, but later faulted for lapses into melodrama, jour-
nalese, and insensitivity of style. See 1969.46.

3   BEWLEY, MARIUS. "Hart Crane's Last Poem." In <u>Masks and</u>
     <u>Mirrors</u>. New York: Atheneum, pp. 324-38.
         Reprint of 1959.1.

4   BOGAN, LOUISE. <u>A Poet's Alphabet</u>. New York: McGraw-Hill
     Book Co., pp. 81-82, 129, 143.
         Identifies "surrealism-out-of-Rimbaud-out-of Victor Hugo"
as the primary influence on Crane.

5   BRYANT, J[oseph].A., Jr. "Hart Crane, Poet of the Sixties."
     <u>Journal of Modern Literature</u> 1, no. 2:283-88.
         Reviews of Leibowitz's study of Crane's poetry and
Unterecker's <u>Voyager</u>. Generally positive about Leibowitz, although the book is faulted for its style and lack of precision.
Positive view of Unterecker, although Bryant deals more with his
own view of Crane's life than with Unterecker's study. See
1968.22; 1969.46.

6   CLARK, DAVID R., ed. <u>The Merrill Studies in "The Bridge."</u>
     Columbus, Ohio: Merrill Publishing Co., 131 pp.
         A collection of essays on <u>The Bridge</u> which should prove
very useful in teaching the poem. Reprints of 1930.7-8, 11, 22;
1948.17, 19; 1949.2; 1951.4 1955.23; 1960.7; 1962.22; 1963.6;
1965.24.

7   COWLEY, MALCOLM. "Hart Crane: The Evidence in the Case."
     <u>Sewanee Review</u> 78, no. 1 (Winter):176-84.
         Begins with a favorable review of Unterecker's <u>Voyager</u>, and
then relates biographical anecdotes concerning his own relationship with Crane. See 1969.46.

8   CREELEY, ROBERT. "Hart Crane and the Private Judgment." In
     <u>A Quick Graph: Collected Notes and Essays</u>. Edited by Brom
     Weber. San Francisco: Four Seasons Foundation, pp. 75-87.
         Reprint of 1960.5.

9   _____. "The Letters of Hart Crane, Edited by Brom Weber." In
       A Quick Graph: Collected Notes and Essays. Edited by Brom
       Weber. San Francisco: Four Seasons Foundation, pp. 88-91.
          A general discussion of Crane with almost no attention paid
    to Weber's edition.

10   GILMER, WALKER. Horace Liveright: Publisher of the Twenties.
       New York: David Lewis Publisher, pp. vii, 22, 97, 101, 129-
       33.
          An account of Crane's dealing with Liveright and his firm.

11   GORDON, CAROLINE. "Robber Rocks: Letters and Memories of
       Hart Crane." Southern Review 6, no. 2 (Spring):481-87.
          Enthusiastic review of Robber Rocks by Susan Jenkins Brown,
    calling it a valuable source of information about his life and
    work. Calls attention to the religious tenor of Crane's poetry.
    See 1968.8.

12   GULLANS, CHARLES. "Poetry and Subject Matter: From Hart
       Crane to Turner Cassity." Southern Review 6, no. 2 (Spring):
       488-505.
          Review of The Complete Poems and Selective Letters and
    Prose of Hart Crane edited by Brom Weber. Is particularly con-
    cerned with Crane's obscurity which may be in part related to his
    failure to discover a subject matter. "That Crane has passed
    from a possession of the common reader to the professors in so
    short a time is in large measure the result of his own flawed
    talent and the principles of procedure in writing poems which
    have left the most patient and devoted reader not more informed
    as to his meaning after long contemplation than before."

13   HALL, DONALD. Marianne Moore: The Cage and the Animal. New
       York: Pegasus, pp. 28, 66, 67, 71.
          Relates the incident in which Moore changes considerably
    one of Crane's poems before publishing it.

14   HAMBURGER, MICHAEL. The Truth of Poetry: Tensions in Modern
       Poetry from Baudelaire to the Nineteen Sixties. New York:
       Harcourt, Brace & World, pp. 207-13, 323-24.
          Concerned with the parallels in Crane's work with T.S.
    Eliot and Garcia Lorca.

15   HOUSTON, ROBERT W. "Hart Crane and Arthur Rimbaud: A Com-
       parison." Essays in Honor of Richebourg Gaillard McWilliams.
       Edited by Howard Creed. The Birmingham Southern College
       Bulletin 63, no. 2:13-19.
          A comparison of Crane's "Voyages" with Rimbaud's "Le Bateau
    ivre" which are "journeys in search of a concept of the poet, and
    the source of his poetry." In the course of their journeys both
    must shed their illusions. Notes similarity of their images.

16   HUTSON, RICHARD [Eugene]. "Hart Crane's 'Black Tambourine.'"
      Literatur in Wissenschaft und Unterricht (Kiel) 3:31-36.
         A successful effort in transforming his humiliation and
      frustration in art by Crane's identification with the black man
      on a personal and mythic level. Uses a variation of his charac-
      teristic ironic mode, since the modern black man is "clearly a
      figure of irony."

17   ICKSTADT, HENRICK. Dichterische Erfahrung und Metaphern-
      struktur. Eine Untersuchung der Bildersprache Hart Crane.
      Ph.D. dissertation, Freie Universitat Berlin. Heidelberg:
      Carl Winter, 150 pp.
         In German. Crane's imagery interprets reality in the very
      act of experiencing it--dynamic rather than visual, abstract
      rather than concrete. "The organic experience of the lyrical
      self--the organic structure of metaphor culminates in the utopian
      idea of a deeper, more dynamic life in which the gap between self
      and society, fact and consciousness, between the work of art and
      the machine is bridged at last." Crane's transcendentalism is
      strictly his own, not like that of Whitman or Emerson. See
      1974.10.

18   JAFFE, IRMA. "Joseph Stella and Hart Crane: The Brooklyn
      Bridge." In Challenges in American Culture. Edited by Ray B.
      Browne, Lacy N. Landrum, and William Bottorff. Bowling Green,
      Ohio: Bowling Green University Press, pp. 29-39.
         Concerned with the alliance between painting and poetry,
      using Stella and Crane as his chief example. Traces the scholar-
      ship connecting the two. Crane's use of Brooklyn Bridge was
      primarily lyrical, while Stella's was heroic.

19   KAHN, SY. "Hart Crane and Harry Crosby: A Transit of Poets."
      Journal of Modern Literature 1, no. 1:45-56.
         Concerned with the personal and poetic relationship between
      Crane and Crosby. The important literary event connecting them
      was the completion and publication of The Bridge by the Black Sun
      Press. Compares the two poetically with respect to their vision,
      metaphor, and hope for America. Emphasizes that both sought
      death.

20   KELLER, DEAN H. "CALM Addenda No. 2: Hart Crane." Papers of
      the Bibliographical Society of America 64 (First Quarter):98-
      99.
         A listing of the Charles Harris collection of letters and
      manuscripts which are not in Lohf's The Literary Manuscripts of
      Hart Crane.

21   KESSLER, EDWARD. "Crane's 'Black Tambourine.'" Explicator
      29, no. 1 (September):Item 4.
         The central idea of the poem is the same idea that under-
      lies The Bridge--"the power of personal myth to transform a

chaotic--even antagonistic--world into meaningful order." Because the Black is alien, he embodies the imaginative conflict that persistently troubled Crane.

*22   KOSAWA, ATSUO. "Allusive Variation--Hashi Mo Hoho." Eigo Seinen (The Rising Generation) (Tokyo) 116, no. 4 (1 April): pp. 194-95.

23   LIEBERMAN, LAURENCE. "Poet--Critics and Scholar-Critics." Poetry 115, no. 5 (February):346-52.
     Review of Leibowitz's Hart Crane: An Introduction to the Poetry. "No modern poet has been more consistently misread and more scandalously undervalued by intelligent critics than Hart Crane. Leibowitz's outstanding book should help to correct this unfortunate state of affairs." See 1968.22.

24   MALOFF, SAUL. "The Fine Hart of Biography." Commonweal 91, 18 (6 February):513-15.
     Reviews of Unterecker's Voyager and Susan Jenkins Brown's Robber Rocks: Letter and Memories of Hart Crane. Suggests that Unterecker may have been overwhelmed by the abundance of his material. Crane emerges as less a man and less complex than he really was. Brown is not disinterested enough, writing as a loyal friend. While charming, it is not necessarily enlightening. See 1968.8; 1969.46.

25   McMICHAEL, JAMES. "Hart Crane." Southern Review 8, no. 2 (Spring):290-309.
     Concerned with the structure of The Bridge, emphasizing Crane's affirmation of the word's reality. Crane's doubts about the reality and value of the myth are explicit and implicit throughout; the poem is "little more than representation of these doubts." Emphasizes "The Dance" as central, Crane's "most ambitious and most successful piece of writing."

26   MIHAILA, RODICA. "Dincolo de ermetismul poeziei lui Hart Crane." Studii de literatura universala 15:133-42.
     In Romanian. "Beyond Hart Crane's Hermetism" interprets the metaphors and symbols of the poetry to get to the essence of its message. Examines "the logic of metaphor" as a method, since the logical structure is hidden. Concludes that Crane did not write a poetry of negation but sought instead eternal beauty, happiness, and fulfillment.

27   MINKOFF, GEORGE ROBERT. A Bibliography of the Black Sun Press. Great Neck, N.Y.: G.R. Minkoff, pp. 30-31.
     Bibliographical description of The Bridge (A-32).

28   MUNSON, GORHAM, and STANFORD, ANN. "Poetry: 1900 to the 1930's." American Literary Scholarship: An Annual/1968. Edited by J. Albert Robbins. Durham, N.C.: Duke University

Press, pp. 228–45.
A survey of the scholarship and criticism for 1968.

29   NASSAR, EUGENE PAUL. "Hart Crane's The Bridge and Its Critics."
In The Rape of Cinderella; Essays in Literary Continuity.
Bloomington: Indiana University Press, pp. 143–245.
Examines what other critics have said about the poem, especially the view that its purpose was to create a myth of America. Disagreeing with this, he asserts that the subject of the
poem is the greatness of myth itself and how the myth-making
power sustains man. Tate and Winters were wrong in their criticism of the poem, because as "metacritics" they used the poem as
a weapon in their battle with the age. Neither tanscendental nor
romantic, Crane affirmed the endless myth-making capacity of the
imagination which is man's way of satisfying his hunger for
vision. Summarizes and responds to most of the major readings of
the poem since its publication.

30   PACK ROBERT. "On Hart Crane." Today's Poets. McGraw-Hills
Sound Seminar Tapes, no. 78145 (reel-to-reel), no. 81646
(cassette). New York: McGraw-Hill Book Co.
A general introduction; could be of interest to those
teaching Crane to undergraduates or high school students.

31   PAUL, SHERMAN. Review of Robber Rocks: Letters and Memories
of Hart Crane, 1923-1932 by Susan Jenkins Brown. Journal of
English and Germanic Philology 69 (October):682-84.
A personal view of Crane, not concerned with scholarly
matters. "The book must be discounted--read carefully as a docu-
ment about Hart Crane's friends who, in devoting themselves to
him, are doing what the living always do, mediating the past."
See 1968.8.

32   _____. Review of Voyager: A Life of Hart Crane by John
Unterecker. Journal of English and Germanic Philology 69
(April):325-31.
"An inside biography distinguished more by sympathy than
criticism." Not much aid in helping one to understand the poems.
A "needlessly large" canvas; simple explanations for complex
matters. Overcome by his sources, Unterecker fails to see that
Crane's poetry was his life. Is evasive about the more spectacu-
lar parts of Crane's life. See 1969.46.

33   ROSENTHAL, M.L. "Dynamics of Form and Motive in Some Representative Twentieth-Century Lyric Poems." English Literary
History 37, no. 1 (March):136-51.
Brief reference to Crane. "The weak links in sequences
like The Bridge are less aesthetic failures than aspects of the
intransigence of certain necessary materials."

34   SCHWARTZ, JOSEPH. Hart Crane: An Annotated Critical Bibliog-

raphy. New York: David Lewis Publisher, 276 pp.
    An alphabetical listing by author of the writings about
Crane from 1921 to 1968.   See 1971.2; 1972.12.

35   SPEARS, MONROE K. <u>Dionysus and the City: Modernism in Twen-</u>
     <u>tieth-Century Poetry</u>. New York: Oxford University Press, pp.
     7, 51-52, 82, 165, 167, 169-70, 172-73, 203, 214-15, 267-68.
     Brief mentions of Crane.

36   SWEETKIND, MORRIS. "Poetry in a Scientific World." <u>English</u>
     <u>Journal</u> 59, no. 3 (March):359-66.
         Brief reference to Crane's poetry and its relation to
     technology and science.

37   THOMAS, F. RICHARD. "The Literary Admireres of Alfred
     Stieglitz, Photographer." Ph.D. dissertation, Indiana Univer-
     sity, pp. 89-113, 141-45.
         Examines relationship between Crane's poetry and Stieglitz's
     photography. Alike in their use of the machine, but Crane could
     never surrender to the machine culture as Stieglitz did.

38   TRACHTENBERG, ALAN. "Lost at Sea." <u>Nation</u> 16 (February):
     183-85.
         Review of Unterecker's <u>Voyager</u>, "an unflinching account of
     the wreckage of Crane's life." Book takes no perspective and is
     not systematically specific in discussing the poetry. "Crane's
     capacity for poetry lay crippled under the debris of his personal
     life." See 1969.46.

39   UROFF, MARGARET D. "Hart Crane's 'Recitative.'" <u>Concerning</u>
     <u>Poetry</u> 3:22-27.
         Deals with a theme crucial to Crane, "the restorative
     powers of the poet's vision in a dark and divided world." A de-
     tailed explication.

40   _____. "Hart Crane's 'Voyages VI,' Stanza 6." <u>English Lan-</u>
     <u>guage Notes</u> 8, no. 1 (September):46-48.
         Examines image of the goddess as Amphitrite, queen of the
     sea, and traces the development of the image in the other poems
     in the sequence.

41   Van CROMPHOUT, GUSTAFF. Review of <u>Hart Crane: An Introduction</u>
     <u>to the Poetry</u> by H.A. Leibowitz. <u>English Studies</u> 51, no. 3
     (June):272-73.
         Concentrates on Crane as a craftsman. "What saved Crane as
     a poet was a dedication to technical discipline that contrasted
     sharply with emotional and psychological instability." Study
     would have been clearer if organizing principles had been ex-
     plained more carefully early in the book.

42   WEBER, BROM. <u>Hart Crane: A Biographical and Critical Study</u>.

New York: Russell & Russell, 452 pp.
Reprint with minor corrections of 1948.21.

1971

1   ANON. "More Colour than Events." Times Literary Supplement,
       19 February, p. 2.
            Review of Unterecker's Voyager which presents "a narrow and
pedestrian" interpretation with little attempt to see Crane in a
wide cultural context. See 1969.46.

2   ANON. Review of Hart Crane: An Annotated Critical Bibliog-
       raphy by Joseph Schwartz. Choice 8, no. 4 (June):534.
            The successor to Rowe and Weber. See 1970.34.

3   ASHBERRY, JOHN. Introduction to The Collected Poems of John
       O'Hara. New York: Alfred A. Knopf, p. viii.
            Mentions Crane as a possible influence on O'Hara's earlier
poetry.

4   BERTHOFF, WARNER. Fictions and Events: Essays in Criticism
       and Literary History. New York: E.P. Dutton & Co., pp. 329-
       39.
            Review of The Poetry of Hart Crane by R.W.B. Lewis (1967.
19). Chatty, voluble, noisy, a critical "miscarriage" that fails
in its style. Includes surprisingly little discussion of Crane's
religiosity given its thesis. See 1968.4.

5   BEYER, WILLIAM. "Hart Crane." English Journal 60, no. 9
       (December):1213.
            Verse appreciation.

6   BLOOM, HAROLD. "Bacchus and Merlin: The Dialectic of Romantic
       Poetry in America." Southern Review n.s. 7, no. 1 (January):
       140-75.
            Crane's "furious synesthesia betrays an Emersonian uneasi-
ness with pure vision, yet Crane is tormented by particulars of
light, and testifies frequently to the eye's tyranny."

7   COMBS, RICHARD E. Authors: Critical and Biographical Refer-
       ences. Metuchen, N.J.: Scarecrow Press, pp. 39-40.
            Very limited bibliographical listing of works which discuss
Crane.

8   COWAN, JAMES. "The Theory of Relativity and The Bridge."
       Hartford Studies in Literature 3, no. 2:108-15.
            Images, symbols, and metaphors used in connection with
Brooklyn Bridge show "a significant parallel between Crane's
poetic statement . . . and relativity." Though he may not have
known Einstein's theory, the poem contains "as clear a poetic

statement as one could wish of the function of the general theory
of relativity."

9   CROWDER, RICHARD. "Poetry: 1900 to the 1930's." In American
    Literary Scholarship, An Annual/1969. Edited by J. Albert
    Robbins. Durham, N.C.: Duke University Press, pp. 252-77.
        A survey of the year's work on Crane.

10 DAHLBERG, EDWARD. The Confessions of Edward Dahlberg. New
    York: George Braziller, pp. 227-28.
        Remembers his approval of the as-yet-unpublished The Bridge
    when he read it at Crane's request.

11 FOLGER, MARY. "Hart Crane: Garrettsville's 'Magnificent
    Failure', One of the World's Top Poets." Ravenna and Kent
    (Ohio) Record-Courier, 14 August, pp. 10-11.
        Typical local newspaper feature, mostly biographical.

12 HAINES, ROBERT E. "Alfred Stieglitz and the New Order of Con-
    sciousness in American Literature." Pacific Coast Philology
    6:26-34.
        Crane saw philosophical optimism in Stieglitz's photographs,
    and appreciated his "apprehension of the spiritual essence of
    outwardly inanimate objects."

13 HAYMAN, RONALD. Arguing with Walt Whitman: An Essay on His
    Influence on 20th Century Verse. London: Covent Garden Press,
    pp. 20-23.
        Surprisingly brief mention of the influence of Whitman (as
    legend not poet) on Crane.

14 JOOST, NICHOLAS, and SULLIVAN, ALVIN. The Dial, Two Authors
    Indexes: Anonymous & Pseudonymous Contributors; Contributors
    in Clipsheets. Carbondale and Edwardsville: Southern Illinois
    University Press, pp. 15, 40, 41, 43.
        Bibliographical information on some of Crane's poems pub-
    lished in the Dial. Copy of "Praise for an Urn."

15 KAPLAN, PHILIP. "'Look for the Miracle!' Some Early Memories
    of William Sommer, From 1924 to 1936." Serif 8 (June):3-8.
        Mentions Crane in passing as a friend and admirer of litho-
    graph artist William Sommer.

16 KAYE, HOWARD. "The Post-Symbolist Poetry of Yvor Winters."
    Southern Review n.s. 7, no. 1 (January), 176-97.
        Crane mentioned in a discussion of Winters's poem "Orpheus,"
    which is about Crane, who Winters saw as writing "meaningless"
    poetry.

17 KNOX, GEORGE. "Crane and Stella: Conjunction of Painterly
    and Poetic Worlds." Texas Studies in Language and Literature

12, no. 4 (Winter):689-707.
   The relationship between Crane's and Stella's works, citing
some "specific" influences on The Bridge. "Considered together,
their works present a fascinating aspect of Taine's theory: how
various environmental forces in a milieu and current aesthetic
theories affect the production of different art forms. . . ."

18 _____. "'Sight, Sound, and Flesh': Synoptic View from Crane's
   Tower." Markham Review 3 (October):1-10.
      Explication of "The Broken Tower," showing how it is "the
last magical fusion" of "the sight, sound, and flesh imagery
which pervades" Crane's poetry. Traces this imagery in other
works, speaking of Crane's "visual-auditory conjunctions," "mixture of pagan and Christian implications," and concludes that, in
"The Broken Tower," "sight, sound, and flesh achieved mythic pre-
figuration of imminent death."

19 KUGEL, JAMES L. The Techniques of Strangeness in Symbolist
   Poetry. New Haven: Yale University Press, pp. 86-95, 100-4.
      Examines the similarities and differences between the works
of Crane and "Symbolist" poetry, saying that Crane was more a
"Modern" than a symbolist, and that Crane's generation no longer
shared many of the preoccupations of the symbolist aesthetic:
"anti-Positivism, the German idealistic thinkers, the inroads of
science and technology on the modern world." Examines "Black
Tambourine" for symbolist influences.

20 LaFRANCE, MARSTON. "The Bridge-Builder." Canadian Review of
   American Studies 2, no. 2 (Fall):106-13.
      Four reviews. Voyager by Unterecker is "complete," "honest,"
and overwhelming. Robber Rocks by Brown is "simultaneously af-
fectionate and not at all uncritical." The Poetry of Hart Crane
by Lewis is "a disappointment," full of misprints and misspellings,
scrambled metaphors, apologetic, with occasionally unreliable explications. Hart Crane: An Introduction to the Poetry by
Leibowitz is a "commonsense approach valuable to anyone interested
in Crane." See 1967.19; 1968.8, 22; 1969.46.

21 LITZ, A. WALSTON. Review of Voyager: A Life of Hart Crane
   by John Unterecker. American Literature 42, no. 4 (January):
   591-93.
      Praises Unterecker for all the information he amasses, but
faults him for the lack of coherent organization of the work as
a whole. Did not select the most significant facts for more in-
depth discussion, and he put in too much material to handle
properly. See 1969.46.

22 MARIANI, PAUL L. "Words for Hart Crane." Hartford Studies in
   Literature 3:150-53.
      Review of Voyager by John Unterecker. Unterecker is too
thorough and detailed. The biography is an "artificial tedium of

rhythms." Compliments Unterecker for his refusal to read Crane
in terms of a particular school of psychology, for balancing the
influences of Crane's parents, for rectifying the image of Crane
as "roaring boy," and for focusing on the reflectiveness of Crane.
The biography shows scholarship and sheds light on Crane's life,
but he wishes for a different kind of book because "Crane's
poetic reputation has not even yet been sufficiently established."
See 1969.46.

23   McCORMICK, JOHN. American Literature 1919-1932: A Comparative
      History. London: Routledge & Kegan Paul, pp. 136-44.
           Crane is a great twentieth century American poet and The
      Bridge is "successful" but not an "epic." Rebukes Crane's
      "friends" and early critics (especially Winters) for their two-
      faced criticism; praises Crane's use of diction and rhythm. Ad-
      mits the difficulty in understanding Crane's poetry. Discusses
      the nature of Crane's mysticism, and in general gives a broad
      outline of what Crane's poetry is like.

24   NILSEN, HELGE NORMAN. "Hart Crane's Indian Poem." Neuphil-
      ogische Mitteilungen (Modern Language Society of Helsinki) 50,
      no. 73:127-39.
           Discusses the various ancient Indian myths which Crane used
      in The Bridge: Pocahontas as fertility goddess, Pocahontas as
      universal mother, Maquokeeta's dance of death, worship of snakes,
      the myth of Quetzalcoatl. Accepted the Indian as the foremost
      guide to the land and guided by the spirit of the Indian, he would
      be able to recapture his mind and the promised land of America,
      and bridge the gap between the white man and the Indian.

25   O'HARA, FRANK. "Poem: Before Mario Schifano." In The Col-
      lected Poems of Frank O'Hara. Edited by Donald Allen. New
      York: Alfred A. Knopf, pp. 477-78.
           Verse appreciation.

26   PANIKER, K. AYYAPPA. "Myth and Machine in Hart Crane."
      Literary Criterion 9, no. 4:27-41.
           A general essay emphasizing Crane's major themes and their
      operation in The Bridge. "For the Marriage of Faustus and Helen"
      is an early example of his attempt at a fusion of the mythical
      vision of art and the mechanical civilization of his time. The
      Bridge represents his lifelong attempt to reconcile these two
      elements.

27   REXROTH, KENNETH. American Poetry in the Twentieth Century.
      New York: Herder & Herder, pp. 91-92.
           Crane's indebtedness to Poe, Rimbaud, Whitman, and Marlowe.

28   RIDING, LAURA, and GRAVES, ROBERT. A Survey of Modernist
      Poetry. Edinburgh: Folcroft Library Editions, pp. 47-49,
      289-91.

Reprint of 1927.15.

29   SCARLETT, JOHN R. "Crane's 'The Sad Indian.'" Explicator 29,
     no. 8 (April):Item 69.
        Knowing Crane's Mexican background reveals that the poem is
     a protest, the Indian being a symbol. The poem is also a strategy
     for helping Crane to find his own identity and purpose. Protests
     society's exploitation and corruption of the Indian and his art.
     Complains that Christianity repressed the Indian's relgion. De-
     spite this, the Indian has not lost his understanding of the need
     for being part of the organic process of life. Crane sees a com-
     parison between the plight of the Indian and his own suffering
     from the misunderstanding and rejection of a pragmatic and ir-
     religious world.

30   SHEEHAN, PETER J. "Hart Crane and the Contemporary Search."
     English Journal 60, no. 9 (December):1209-13.
        Crane's poetry lends itself to biographical interpretation.
     In teaching Crane, it is important to show how the problems he
     deals with are common to all men. He was a rebel in his attempt
     to go beyond the social limits of his time and find lasting
     values. Brief explications of "Black Tambourine," "Chaplinesque,"
     and "At Melville's Tomb."

31   SIMON, MARC. "Hart Crane and Samuel Greenberg: An Emblematic
     Interlude." Contemporary Literature 12, no. 2 (Spring):166-
     72.
        Greenberg's influence is seen most notably in "Emblems of
     Conduct." In addition to borrowing some lines directly from
     Greenberg, he also borrowed his da Capo technique of repetition.

32   SQUIRES, RADCLIFFE J. Allen Tate: A Literary Biography. New
     York: Pegasus, pp. 39, 44, 45, 50-53, 56-67, 72-77, 80, 183,
     204, 216-17.
        Many references in passing. Important because Tate was one
     of Crane's closest friends and had such remarkable insight into
     his poetry. Tate had hoped to learn "the way of vision" from
     Crane, but he learned instead that a personal vision could not
     weld together the split view of America. Crane's poetry could
     not find any equivalent universals, any support from a tradition
     of belief and feeling.

33   SUGG, RICHARD P. "The Imagination's White Buildings and
     'Quaker Hill.'" Erasmus Review 1:147-55.
        Beginning with a reference to his "architecture method,"
     Sugg shows how "Quaker Hill" fits into the major design of The
     Bridge. The clue to its function is found in its placement in
     the poem. The attempt to create an organic structure embodying
     the myth of God makes it necessary for the poet to move through
     various inadequate systems. The major contrast in the poem is
     between the Quaker's faith in Providence and the speaker's skep-

ticism. Both architectural meanings of the place have failed,
forcing the poet to recognize that he must find his own way in
the tension between ideal and real which is the contrast between
the dream of the Quakers and the reality of the materialistic
tourists.

34   UROFF, M.D. "The Imagery of Violence in Hart Crane's Poetry."
     American Literature 43, no. 2 (May):200-16.
        Images of violence, destruction, and suffering are central
     to Crane's work, especially those poems written about artistic
     creation, an intimate connection between art and violence. The
     pain of art was the pain of self-awareness. Some early poems
     picture the poet as destroyed and victimized: "Black Tambourine,"
     "Praise for An Urn," "Chaplinesque," "Possessions," "Lachrymae
     Christi," "Eternity," "Return." "Legend" is the central poem in
     describing Crane's artistic method. "The Broken Tower" shows the
     violence of poetic vision. Through poetry Crane heals himself.

35   VOGLER, THOMAS A. "Crane: A Myth to God." In Preludes to
     Vision: The Epic Venture in Blake, Wordsworth, Keats and Hart
     Crane. Berkeley and Los Angeles: University of California
     Press, pp. 143-96.
        An examination of the position which labels The Bridge a
     failure because Crane did not achieve his purpose. Contends that
     reasons for naming the poem a failure are the elements which give
     it its greatest significance: (1) the attempt to move from
     momentary lyric vision to "sustained and comprehensive vision";
     and (2) the lack of faith as the motivating force behind the com-
     position of the poem. The theme is a search for a mythic vision,
     not the fixed expression of a vision firmly in the poet's mind.
     The vision Crane seeks is one that would assure a positive future
     in the face of a pessimistic present, one that would be based on
     the knowledge of a glorious past providing a bridge from that
     past to a future of hope. Each poem in The Bridge highlights
     this theme, the process of coming to a mythical vision.

                              1972

1   ANDERSON, DAVID D. "Journey Through Time: The Poetic Vision
    of Hart Crane." Ohioana Quarterly 15 (Summer):59-64.
       Crane "attempted to fuse all of the American experience
    into a single statement of affirmation," making the most signifi-
    cant attempt of any modern American poet to "define the spiritual
    essence of the nation." As a mythic poet he was determined to
    explore transcendence. The most important fact is his being a
    transcendental romantic in the tradition of Emerson and Whitman,
    and, like them, finding that the ultimate unifying principle
    which he sought eluded him.

2   ANON. "KSU Libraries Mount Exhibit for Ohio Poet." Warren

(Ohio) <u>Tribune Chronicle</u>, 28 April, p. 18.
   An exhibition of publications and memorabilia mounted by
Kent State University Libraries to mark the fortieth anniversary
of Crane's death.

3   ANON. "Library Remembers Poet Hart Crane." Kent and Ravenna
    (Ohio) <u>Record-Courier</u>, 27 April, p. 4.
       Report on Kent State University Libraries exhibit to mark
the fortieth anniversary of Crane's death.

4   BASSOFF, BRUCE. "Rhetorical Pressures in 'For the Marriage of
    Faustus and Helen.'" <u>Concerning Poetry</u> 5 (Fall):40-48.
       Crane's ambition was to "promulgate an order for the world
through language," to create a new mythology, "free from his own
personality and legislating a new reality." A study of the
rhetoric of Part I demonstrates that by working against "personal
emotion and toward the anonymous impulse, Crane moves away from
the poet as person to the poet as priest, as pray-er."

5   BROWN, ANDREAS. <u>Hart Crane: The Catalogue of His Works</u>.
    New York: Gotham Bookmart & Gallery, 12 pp.
       An extension "in a logical manner" of the Schwartz and
Schweik descriptive bibliography. See 1972.28 and 1978.32.

6   BURKE, W[illiam].J., and HOWE, WILL D. "Crane, Hart." In
    <u>American Authors and Books: 1640 to The Present Day</u>. 3d ed.
    rev. Edited by Irving Weiss and Ann Weiss. New York: Crown
    Publishers, p. 142.
       Reprint of 1943.1.

7   CLARK, DAVID R. "Hart Crane's Technique." In <u>Lyric Resonance:
    Glosses on Some Poems of Yeats, Frost, Crane, Cummings, and
    Others</u>. Amherst: University of Massachusetts Press, pp. 137-
    84.
       Reprint of 1963.7.

8   CROWDER, RICHARD. "Poetry: 1900 to the 1930's." In <u>American
    Literary Scholarship, An Annual/1970</u>. Edited by J. Albert
    Robbins. Durham, N.C.: Duke University Press, pp. 280-307.
       A survey of the year's work on Crane.

9   DAVISON, RICHARD ALLAN. "Hart Crane, Louis Untermeyer and
    T.S. Eliot: A New Crane Letter." <u>American Literature</u> 44,
    no. 1 (March):143-46.
       A letter to Untermeyer (19 January 1923) commenting on <u>The
    Waste Land</u>, on Untermeyer's mention of Crane in "The New Patri-
cians" (1922.1) and on "For the Marriage of Faustus and Helen."

10 FLANNER, JANET (GENÊT). <u>Paris Was Yesterday, 1925-1939</u>.
    Edited by Irving Drutman. New York: Viking Press, p. xviii.
       "Hart Crane, whom I only met once at dinner, when he became

so intoxicated and created such a scene in the Montparnasse
Restaurant over a mislaid overcoat that I hoped never to see him
again, and did not, a squeamishness I later regretted."

11   GALPIN, ALFRED. "A Boat in the Tower: Rimbaud in Cleveland,
1922." Renaissance: Essays on Values and Literature 25, no.
1 (Autumn):3-13.
       A personal memory by one of the members of Crane's Cleveland
circle. In addition casts some light on Crane's knowledge of
French.

12   _____. "Hart Crane: Three Books." Contemporary Literature
13 (Winter):106-15.
       A complimentary review of Schwartz's critical bibliography.
Unterecker's Voyager and Butterfield's The Broken Arc. "Each
surpasses all previous works in its field and is likely to main-
tain a position of pre-eminence for some time to come." See
1969.11, 46; 1970.34.

13   HINZ, EVELYN J. "Hart Crane's 'Voyages' 'Reconsidered.'"
Contemporary Literature 13 (Summer):315-33.
       A study of the genesis of these poems reveals that the poet
may have begun with a traditional affirmation, but the sequence
ends with the speaker realizing "that the hand-me-down faith,
hand-me-down ideals, no matter what the professed content, is in
the end not only meaningless but vicious. It is vicious because,
as parody, it is the enemy of all faith." Particularly stresses
comparisons between "Voyages I" and the earlier "Poster" and
"Voyages VI" and the earlier "Belle Isle."

14   HUTSON, RICHARD [Eugene]. "A Life of Hart Crane." Southern
Review 108 (Winter):234-42.
       A complimentary review of Unterecker's Voyager, although
faulting him for not interpreting sufficiently the numerous facts
he includes. Should have been more aggressive in drawing connections between the poet's life and his works. See 1969.46.

15   LANE, GARY. A Concordance to the Poems of Hart Crane. New
York: Haskell House Publishers, 126 pp.
       Uses Weber's 1966 edition of The Complete Poems and Selected
Letters and Prose of Hart Crane. Lists each word, special character, and number in the poetry; gives a separate listing of the
components of hyphenated compounds; provides a table of word fre-
quencies. See 1973.15.

16   LOHF, KENNETH A. "The Prose Manuscripts of Hart Crane: An
Editorial Portfolio." In Proof: The Yearbook of American
Bibliography and Textual Studies. Edited by Joseph Katz.
Vol. 2. Columbia: University of South Carolina Press, pp.
1-61.
       Facsimiles of: (1) "Note of the Paintings of David

Siqueirous," (2) "A Pure Approach to Any Art," (3) Reviews, (4)
"Vocabulary," (5) "Title," (6) "Note Book"--all published prose
manuscripts.

17 _____. "Ten Unpublished Poems by Hart Crane." Antaeus 5
   (Spring):17-21.
        Ten poems and parts of poems written between 1920 and 1932
   not published elsewhere. Approximate dates of the composition of
   the poems given. From the Columbia University Library Hart Crane
   collection.

18 LUDWIG, RICHARD M. Bibliography Supplement II to Literary
   History of the United States. Edited by Robert E. Spiller et
   al. New York: Macmillan Co., pp. 132-34.
        Brief bibliography.

19 LYON, MELVIN E. The Centrality of Hart Crane's "The Broken
   Tower." Lincoln: University of Nebraska Press, 34 pp.
        "The Broken Tower" is climactic, a summary of Crane's
   earlier works and prophetic of the direction his later work would
   have taken had he lived. Focuses on the tower, God, Christ, the
   lady. Shows how each of these four are used in Crane's other
   work as well as their specific use in "The Broken Tower." Such
   an examination reveals the implied pattern of psychosexual
   development in Crane's work which reaches its climax in this
   poem. Homosexual consummation had been achieved in the "Voyages"
   and heterosexual consummation in "The Broken Tower." Consummation
   in "Voyages" meant spiritual fulfillment by platonic destruction
   of the flesh; in the later poem it is an implicit prelude to
   creative fulfillment of flesh and spirit together in completely
   realized humanity. "The Broken Tower" is "an attempt to achieve
   union not directly but through the elevation of spirit gained
   through human love."

20 MATTSON, FRANCIS O. "Hart Crane and Roy Campbell." Bulletin
   of the New York Public Library 76:17-18.
        A comment on Crane's visit with Roy Campbell at Martigues
   in southeast France. The source used for this incident in
   Unterecker's Voyager is Crane's 11 June 1929 letter to Tate. A
   different account is given by Campbell in his autobiography, Light
   on a Dark Horse (1951.2). Crane was not an easy guest to enter-
   tain, although charming when he was sober. "It is clear that
   Campbell's admiration and affection for his difficult guest continued in spite of Crane's erratic and apparently self-destructive
   behavior."

21 McCULLOUGH, DAVID. The Great Bridge. New York: Simon &
   Schuster, p. 549.
        Crane saw Brooklyn Bridge "as a shining symbol of affirma-
   tion at the end of an epic search through the American past."

22   OBERG, ARTHUR. "The Modern British and American Lyric: What
      Will Suffice." Papers on Language and Literature 8, no. 1
      (Winter):78-80.
         A brief contrast of The Bridge and William Carlos Williams's
      Paterson; each reaches toward a unity to be arrived at by a
      sequence of "lyrical imaged moments." Both poems are greatly
      concerned with language; the choice of metaphor shows that each
      poet was dissatisfied with the limitations of human language.
      Crane's dramatic use of images threatens the very integrity of
      the words used to build the image.

23   PAUL, SHERMAN. Hart's Bridge. Urbana: University of Illinois
      Press, 315 pp.
         A phenomenological study of Crane, with attention given to
      his biography, his milieu, and the connections of Crane with his
      time. Crane's principal problem is poetic growth beyond the
      limited self--"the risk of being." The early poems indicate a
      withdrawn poet, meditative and dreamy, not yet ready to "burst
      out." His experience and temperament did not make it easy for
      him to come to terms with the machine. Due to many influences in
      addition to his own introspection, "Crane's Romanticism becomes
      tragic." Features a very careful explication of the poems in
      White Buildings. His later poems show "how willing he has been,
      and how necessary it has become for him, to use poetry to ex-
      plore, to order, and to consolidate his experience." In the com-
      position of "Voyages" Crane found the creative assurance he needed
      to complete his "task," The Bridge. Exemplifies the kind of
      journey "the self must take in order to liberate the imagination
      and overcome the disassociations of self and world (space) and
      self and history (time)." The circular form of the poem "derives
      from the recurrence of natural process. So does the faith in
      vital renewal--the reverence for generative feminine force, the
      sacramental sense of the world." The longest chapter is a care-
      ful reading of The Bridge. Chapter 5 deals with the criticism
      of The Bridge, particularly that which reacted negatively to it.
      Reviewed in 1973.8; 1974.3, 6, 15; 1975.3.

24   _____. "Lyricism and Modernism: The Example of Hart Crane."
      In English Symposium Papers III, edited by Douglas Shepard.
      Fredonia: State University of New York, Fredonia, Department
      of English, pp. 47-107.
         See his "A Stab at Truth," Chapter 5, Hart's Bridge (1972.
      23). A new introduction and conclusion has been added, dealing
      with the question of the negative criticism of Crane because of
      his opposition to the values of T.S. Eliot.

25   PEMBERTON, VIVIAN H. "Poet Hart Crane Linked to Warren,
      Garrettsville." Warren (Ohio) Tribune Chronicle, 21 July,
      p. 5.
         General biographical information connecting Crane with the
      two Ohio towns.

26 SCHWARTZ, DELMORE. "'Primitivism and Decadence' by Yvor
    Winters." In Selected Essays of Delmore Schwartz. Edited by
    D.E. Dike and D.H. Suker. Chicago: University of Chicago
    Press, pp. 340-42.
      One of the structural methods of presenting subject matter
    given by Winters is "pseudo-reference," grammatical coherence in
    excess of, or in absence of, rational coherence. Illustrates
    one type of pseudo-reference by quoting a passage from "The
    Marriage of Faustus and Helen." Schwartz contends that he mis-
    uses the quotation; if he had quoted the whole poem or other
    appropriate parts, Winters's accusation would have no basis.
    Winters attacked The Bridge solely because he rejected the be-
    liefs upon which it was based.

27 SCHWARTZ, JOSEPH, and SCHWEIK, ROBERT C. "CALM Addendum No.
    3: The Literary Manuscripts of Hart Crane." Papers of the
    Bibliographical Society of America 66 (First Quarter):64-65.
      Two corrections of Lohf's work: (1) incorrectly identified
    the seven poems which Crane sent to the Church Head Press in
    Cleveland in 1918; and (2) a typewritten manuscript of "Voyages
    I-VI" is identified as a typescript of the sequence as published
    in the Little Review. Since it is a complete typescript of the
    poems as published in White Buildings, it should not be associated
    with the incomplete version published in the Little Review. See
    1967.21.

28 _____. Hart Crane: A Descriptive Bibliography. Pittsburgh
    Series in Bibliography, no. 1. Pittsburgh, Pa.: University
    of Pittsburgh Press, 168 pp.
      Includes everything written or drawn by Crane that appeared
    in any published form. Listed first are separate editions ar-
    ranged chronologically by date of publication. Followed by works
    not published separately, divided into poetry, prose, and letters.
    Drawings, translations, and adaptations are separately listed.
    Three appendixes. See 1972.5 and 1978.32.

29 TATE, ALLEN. The Translation of Poetry. Washington, D.C.:
    Library of Congress, p. 25.
      Although Crane tried, prematurely, to translate Rimbaud,
    and although he didn't ever understand Rimbaud at all, it made no
    difference. "He identified himself with Rimbaud in a certain
    way. So there the misunderstanding resulted in something quite
    remarkable."

30 VEZA, LAURETTA. "Hart Crane ou la chute du pont." La Poésie
    Américaine de 1910-1940. Paris: Didier, pp. 148-58.
      In French. Of the three types of epic poetry, The Bridge
    can be classified as the modern epic, speculative and philosophi-
    cal. Concerned with the promise of America and paradise lost, the
    nostalgia of lost innocence and the hope of some kind of eternal
    return through discovering a myth capable of compensating modern

man for his loss. Conceived as a protest against the corrosive
pessimism of T.S. Eliot's The Waste Land. Was concerned with
the labyrinth the poet must go through in order to reach the
triumphant note of "Atlantis."

1973

1   BASSOFF, BRUCE. "Crane's 'For the Marriage of Faustus and
    Helen,' III, 1-23." Explicator 31, no. 7 (March):Item 53.
      Attempts to determine the persons "addressed" in Part III
of the poem especially the referents of "we" and "you." Identifies the "religious gunman" as "the historical community or the
historically delimited Faustian seeker addressing himself in his
archetypal dimensions."

2   BROOKS, CLEANTH; LEWIS, R.W.B.; and WARREN, ROBERT PENN, eds.
    American Literature: The Makers and the Making. Vol. IV. New
    York: St. Martin's Press, pp. 2203-20.
      A discussion of Crane more interesting than the ordinary
textbook entry. Includes also a brief discussion of each of the
poems reprinted.

3   BRUNNER, EDWARD. "'Your Hands Within My Hands Are Deeds':
    Poems of Love in The Bridge." Iowa Review 4, no. 1 (Winter):
    105-26.
      The Bridge is most concerned with the poet's discovery of a
direction that will free him to write more poetry. It is the
mind of the poet that gives continuity to the poem, particularly
in his aim to achieve the kind of continuity that commits one to
the present.

4   COLEMAN, ARTHUR, ed. "Bridge (Crane)." In Epic and Romance
    Criticism: A Checklist of Interpretations 1940-1972 of Eng-
    lish and American Epics and Metrical Romances. Vol. 1. New
    York: Watermill Publishers, pp. 36-40.
      A bibliographical listing of various studies of The Bridge.

5   COWLEY, MALCOLM. A Second Flowering: Works and Days of the
    Lost Generation. New York: Viking Press, pp. 191-215.
      Probably his most personal and moving essay on Crane. Con-
tains material used before, but put in a new and more comprehensive setting. Knew Crane from 1923 to the bitter end. Tate
brought them together. Recalls the first meeting, the time when
Crane was living in the country with the Tates and near the
Browns, a reflection on his troubled life, and a record of their
last meeting before Crane went to Mexico. As to his life, "I
thought he was obeying the iron laws of another country than
ours. . . ."

6   CROFT, P.J., ed. Autograph Poetry in the English Language:

Facsimiles of Original Manuscripts from the 14th-20th Century. Vol. 2. London: Cassell, pp. 186-87.

   Because of his habit of extensive revisions, there are numerous typescripts of some of Crane's poetry. The worksheets for "Cape Hatteras" are reproduced, showing him actively engaged in expanding some passages.

7   CROWDER, RICHARD. "Poetry: 1900 to the 1930's." In American Literary Scholarship, An Annual/1971. Edited by J. Albert Robbins. Durham, N.C.: Duke University Press, pp. 277-98.
   A survey of the year's scholarship on Crane.

8   DEMBO, L[awrence].S. Review of Hart's Bridge by Sherman Paul. American Literature 45 (November):469-71.
   Generally a negative review. Being tedious is its principal fault. While Paul acknowledges previous major commentators on Crane's poetry, "he never engages them head-on nor makes clear what he has added to their insights." Some of his own readings are not wholly reliable. See 1972.23.

9   DICKINSON-BROWN, ROGER. "Crane's 'For the Marriage of Faustus and Helen,' II." Explicator 31, no. 8 (April):Item 66.
   An explication with particular reference to the cultural artifacts in Crane's experience.

10 FRANK, WALDO. "Two Faces or Hart Crane and Norbert Wiener." In Memoirs of Waldo Frank. Edited by Allan Trachtenberg. Amherst: University of Massachusetts Press, pp. 239-45.
   Calls Crane his "close and beloved friend." Since Crane had no politics and knew it was a serious omission, Frank gave him the reassurance that he needed. Most comments are biographical on the basis of their correspondence.

11 FUSSELL, EDWIN. "The Genesis of Hart Crane's The Bridge." In Lucifer in Harness: American Meter, Metaphor, and Diction. Princeton, N.J.: Princeton University Press, pp. 89-98, 151-56.
   The bridge itself is the consituting metaphor of the poem. "Because Crane wrote so many letters about it, The Bridge is the best documented example we have of at least one way in which a poem of constituting metaphor may come into being." The poem is uneven and fragmentary because somewhere between the beginning and the end it gets lost. "Ultimately Crane failed to perfect The Bridge because he was trying to write out of the wrong tradition." "Linguistic Lapses in Crane and Stevens" is an attack on Crane's language, metaphors, rhymes, words and the pretentiousness of "the logic of metaphor."

12 HAMILTON, IAN. "Hart Crane." In A Poetry Chronicle. London: Faber & Faber, pp. 151-53.
   A generally complimentary review of Unterecker's Voyager.

One weakness of the book is that it makes little attempt to relate the life to the poetry; another is that he does not explore
the sources of self-destruction in Crane's experience. See
1969.46.

13   HARDY, JOHN EDWARD. Katherine Anne Porter. New York:
      Frederick Ungar Publishing Co., pp. 6-8.
         A brief report on the period in Mexico when Crane lived
      near Porter and the strains this put on their friendship.

14   KINNELL, GALWAY. "Whitman's Indicative Words." American
      Poetry Review 2 (March/April):9-11.
         Whitman's influence is "barely visible" in Crane's work.

15   LANDRY, HILTON, and LANDRY, ELAINE. A Concordance to the
      Poems of Hart Crane. Metuchen, N.J.: Scarecrow Press, 379
      pp.
         Based on Weber's 1966 edition, The Complete Poems and
      Selected Letters and Prose of Hart Crane. See 1972.15.

16   LEGGETT, BERNIE. "Crane's 'The Mango Trees.'" Explicator 32,
      no. 3 (November):Item 18.
         A response to 1967.23. Though Crane did associate the
      mango with the tree of Eden he saw it as like a Christmas tree.
      The two allusions are mixed. "The mango guides the way to love,
      but the source behind its light remains mysterious."

17   LOHF, KENNETH A. "The Library of Hart Crane." In Proof: The
      Yearbook of American Bibliographical and Textual Studies.
      Edited by Joseph Katz. Vol. 3. Columbia: University of
      South Carolina Press, pp. 283-333.
         A descriptive bibliography of the 154 surviving titles of
      Crane's library at the Columbia University Library. Introduction
      to the descriptive bibliographical listing comments on the reading
      that Crane did, although many of the books referred to were not
      in his personal library.

18   MacNIVEN, IAN S. "Hart Crane and T.S. Eliot on the Modern
      City." Revista de la Universidad de Costa Rica 136:63-73.
         Twentieth century authors have had difficulty reconciling
      a positive philosophy and the conditions of urban life. The
      Bridge is Crane's attempt to do this by way of answering Eliot's
      The Waste Land. Although Crane had come to doubt the validity of
      his position by the time he finished The Bridge, he tried to see
      some justification for celebration in the life of the city.
      Crane admitted the shortcomings of his society, but held out hope
      "for salvation through pain and suffering, along the traditional
      Christian lines."

19   MIHAILIA, RODICA. "O abordare nigvistica a metaforei si
      definirea stilului poetic." Analele Universidatli Bucuresti

Literatura Universala Si Comparata 22, no. 1:145-52.
    In Romanian. A linguistic approach to metaphor and personal
poetic style, exemplified by Crane's poetry. Metaphor was the
fundamental, and often the only principle of organizing his
material. An analysis of his metaphors, using this method, proves
that his style uses the poetic devices of romanticism and symbolism, despite his wish to be "a modernist poet." Should never
have taken Eliot's The Waste Land as an example for The Bridge.

20   MOSHER, HAROLD F., Jr. "La Métamorphose des symboles chez
      Hart Crane et Arthur Rimbaud." Revue des langues vivantes 39
      (July-August):291-311.
    In French. Previous studies see the relationship between
Crane and Rimbaud from the point of view of both authors toward
the art of poetry, toward symbolism, and in their diction. It is
very difficult to prove that the poetry of Rimbaud actually influenced that of Crane; parallel or similar interests do not
necessarily demonstrate direct influence. It is in the metamorphosis of symbols that the relationship between Crane and Rimbaud
is best understood. They had like sensibilities, using the same
images to express like ideas.

21   NILSEN, HELGE N[orman]. "Hart Crane's 'Atlantis': An Analy-
      sis." Dutch Quarterly Review of Anglo-American Letters 3:145-
      58.
    "The aim of this essay is to investigate the strands of
[myth of America] as they occur in the preliminary drafts of
'Atlantis' as well as in the finished poem, and to provide an
analysis of the poem as a whole, using the myth as the frame of
reference." The poem's theme is a voyage to "Belle Isle" of the
imagination where the experience of the ultimate integration of
America will take place. Examines the first sketches of the
poem, tracing its development, investigating The Bridge as a symbol of the act of fusion of wildly desperate spheres, and the
development of the Atlantis myth.

22   POWNALL, DAVID. "Crane, Hart." In Articles on Twentieth
      Century Literature: An Annotated Bibliography 1954-1972. Vol.
      1. New York: Kraus-Thomson Organization, pp. 605-15.
    A short list for which the principle of selection is not
clear.

23   ROSENFELD, ALVIN [H.]. "The Examples of T.S. Eliot and Hart
      Crane." American Poetry Review, no. 2 (January/February),
      pp. 48-50.
    Part of the modern movement to completely liberate the
imagination. A great influence on Crane, Eliot was one of his
most threatening precursors because Crane was constantly tempted
to imitate him. The Bridge and "For the Marriage of Faustus and
Helen" were composed in reaction to The Waste Land. In reference
to Eliot, Crane wrote Tate that imitation leads to hatred of the

object imitated. "To undo the influence of Eliot, Crane had to
follow Eliot's lead and turn poetry into a form of cultural criticism spinning the thread of the modern back to its earliest un-
windings in mythology and American pre-history." Although Crane
sought the aid of Whitman in this task, Whitman's America was
radically different from Crane's.

24 SCHWARTZ, JOSEPH. "Technology and Personalism in the Poetry
    of Hart Crane." Proceedings of the 12th International Congress
    of the International Federation of Modern Languages and Liter-
    atures, Cambridge, England, Fall, pp. 218-20.
        An abstract of a paper delivered at the conference. Con-
    cerns itself with trying to answer the question as to why Crane
    undertook the task of becoming Whitman's successor and how this
    effort affected his poetry. Much is made of the influence of
    Waldo Frank in persuading Crane to adopt Whitman's vision.

25 SEXTON, RICHARD J. The Complex of Yvor Winters' Criticism.
    The Hague: Mouton, pp. 27-29, 36, 48, 51, 183, 215, 217-26.
        In addition to references in passing, there is a longer
    section on the relationship between Whitman and Crane. Since,
    however, Whitman is the heir of Emerson, the ultimate source is
    Emerson. The Bridge is obscure and disorganized; the pantheistic
    doctrine is an unsatisfying reduction. "Crane had failed because
    of his assuming the false and weak ideas of Emerson and Whitman."

26 SHEEHAN, PETER J. "Crane's 'Moment Fugue.'" Explicator 31,
    no. 9 (May):Item 78.
        The structure of the poem depicts the five impressions in
    the mind of the speaker when he sees the flower seller. The im-
    pressions are blended with their opposites (e.g., seller and
    buyer). An intensive examination of the figurative language.

27 SUTTON, WALTER. American Free Verse: The Modern Revolution
    and Poetry. New York: New Directions, p. 209.
        A brief reference to Crane's influence on Galway Kinnell.

28 UNTERECKER, JOHN. "Crane, Hart." In Collier's Encyclopedia.
    Edited by William D. Halsey. Vol. 7. New York: Crowell-
    Collier Educational Corporation, p. 418.
        Of more interest than a typical encyclopedia entry because
    it was written by Unterecker.

29 WEBER, BROM. "Hart Crane I." Modern American Poetry Criti-
    cism: Cassette Curriculum. Deland, Fla.: Everett/Edwards,
    33 minutes, cassette no. 882. LCCCN-72-750843.
        A general introduction to Crane's life and work of more
    than usual interest because it is by Weber. Of value as a peda-
    gogical device to those teaching Crane to undergraduates. See
    1973.30.

30 _____. "Hart Crane-Part II." Modern American Poetry Criticism: Cassette Curriculum. Deland, Fla." Everett/Edwards,
39 minutes, cassette no. 823. LCCN-72-750843.
      See 1973.29.

31 _____. "Hart Crane." In Sixteen Modern American Authors.
Edited by Jackson R. Bryer. New York: W.W. Norton, pp. 75-
122.
      Reprint of 1969.50 with a "Supplement" covering the years
from 1969 to 1973.

32 WINTERS, YVOR. The Uncollected Essays and Reviews of Yvor
Winters. Edited by Francis Murphy. Chicago: Swallow Press,
pp. xiv-xv, xviii, 61-62, 140-42, 245-47, 263-67.
      Various references to Crane's work in passing. The parallels
cited between Blake's "The Tyger" and Crane's "Repose of Rivers"
are especially interesting.

*33 ZECK, GREGORY R. "Hart Crane and the Logic of Metaphor."
Ph.D. dissertation, University of Texas at Austin.

                              1974

1 ANON. "Allen Tate Gives Southern Authors Vintage Insights."
Arkansas Gazette, 25 March, p. 14a.
      An interview with Tate in which he discusses some of his
personal memories of Crane.

2 ANON. In Memoriam: Hart Crane.
      The program for a concert given at the Blossom Festival
School of the Cleveland Orchestra and Kent State University.
Vance George, Conductor, with Richard Howard, poet. Recital Hall,
School of Music, Kent State University. Sunday, 21 July 1974.

3 BUTTERFIELD, HERBIE. Review of Sherman Paul's Hart's Bridge.
Journal of American Studies 8, no. 1 (April):127-28.
      Emphasizes the "superb final chapter" in which Paul takes
issue with those critics "who saw in the poet principally an
object-lesson in the failure of a neo-romantic aesthetics or in
a catastrophe of the Whitmanic heresy." The rest of the text is
not as valuable. There is not much new in perception, and he is
unable to put together the significance of the dual influence of
Eliot and Whitman on Crane. See 1972.23.

4 FURIA, PHILLIP. "Crane's 'At Melville's Tomb.'" Explicator
33, no. 9 (May):Item 73.
      "An important ambiguity in the last line . . . significantly
alters the way the poem is usually read. Instead of the sea
being the only repository large enough to hold the spirit of
Melville, the line means that only Melville's 'shadow' is in the

sea; his true spiritual presence resides elsewhere." This reading emphasizes "the elements of resurrection and transcendence" in the poem.

5   FAIN, JOHN T., and YOUNG, THOMAS DANIEL. The Literary Corres-
       pondence of Donald Davidson and Allen Tate. Athens: Univer-
       sity of Georgia Press, pp. 6, 8, 16–17, 26–27, 30, 71–72, 78,
       99–100, 119–21, 142, 144, 146, 157, 173, 175, 184, 193, 196–97.
       Brief references concerning Tate's personal and literary
relationships with Crane. Of special interest is Tate's interpretation of the "religious gunman" as "the symbol of the present
day American conquest of space. . . ."

6   FLINT, R.W. "Family Man." New York Times Book Review, 21
       July, pp. 4–5.
       Review of Sherman Paul's Hart's Bridge and Thomas S.W.
Lewis's Letters of Hart Crane and His Family. Praises the letters
but finds nothing new in Paul's work. See 1972.23.

7   GUILLORY, DANIEL L. "Hart Crane, Marianne Moore and Brooklyn
       Bridge." Ball State University Forum 15 (Summer):48–49.
       "To Brooklyn Bridge" is one of the major sources of inspir-
ation for Moore's "granite and steel." Her approach to the
bridge is the opposite of Crane's because she sees it as a real
bridge not as the "romantic passageway" found in Crane.

8   GUNN, D.W. American and British Writers in Mexico, 1556-1973.
       Austin: University of Texas Press, pp. 154–60.
       A recounting of some incidents of Crane's stay in Mexico.
Contributed to the legend of Mexico created by various visiting
writers, not by his life, but by his death.

9   HOWARD, RICHARD. Decades (For Hart Crane). Kent, Ohio:n.p.,
       21 July, unpaginated.
       Verse appreciation published as a seven page pamphlet in
an edition of 200 copies to mark the seventy-fifth anniversary of
Crane's birth.

10   ICKSTADT, HEINZ. "Hart Crane: 'The Broken Tower.'" In Die
       Amerikanisch Lyric. Edited by Klaus Lubbers. Dusseldorf:
       August Bagel Verlag, pp. 306–16.
       In German. A close explication of the poem by an analysis
of its structure as a dramatic monologue using the romantic
scheme of thesis, antithesis, and synthesis. Concerned with the
theme of the Incarnation of the Word in words, which illustrates
the influence of transcendentalism, especially Emerson, on Crane.
See 1970.17.

11   JASON, PHILIP K. "Wilbur Underwood: Hart Crane's Confidant."
       Markham Review 4 (October):66–68.
       Mostly about Underwood, Crane's friend, who was a part-time

poet and government employee in Washington, D.C.

12   KRAMER, VICTOR A. "The 'Mid-Kingdom' of Crane's 'Black Tam-
     bourine' and Toomer's Cane." College Language Association
     Journal 17 (June):486-97.
         Compares Cane and "Black Tambourine." Says both show the
     "black man" in a "mid-kingdom." Crane and Toomer were friends
     and could have been familiar with each other's work. Both works
     are autobiographical, and both "emphasize that imprisonment or
     denial can not suppress the strength of Black Americans."

13   LOADER, DANIELLE. "In His Native Garrettsville Poet Plaque
     Plans at Standstill." Ravenna and Kent (Ohio) Record-Courier,
     5 July, p. 22.
         Uses Unterecker's Voyager for biographical background on
     Crane and his family.

14   MILES, JOSEPHINE. Poetry and Change: Donne, Milton, Words-
     worth, and the Equilibrium of the Present. Berkeley and Los
     Angeles: University of California Press, pp. 39-43, 147-48.
         Brief references to Crane.

15   MORRISON, J.M. Review of Sherman Paul's Hart's Bridge. Books
     Abroad: An International Literary Quarterly 48, no. 4
     (Autumn):782.
         "A thoughtful, informative, but also rather wooden and paro-
     chial study." Two accusations: (1) Paul's assumption that The
     Bridge "is the cornerstone in an edifice that ranks him in the
     stars"; and (2) the use of many generalities. Skillfully portrays
     Crane's family, especially his mother. Too much emphasis is
     placed on the influence of the nineteenth century, and no con-
     sideration is given to the relevance of surrealist theory. See
     1972.23.

16   NASSAR, EUGENE P[aul]. "Illusions as Value: An Essay on a
     Modern Poetic Idea." Mosaic 7, no. 4:112-13, 114.
         The majority of The Bridge criticism is from extrinsic
     facts rather than the precise examination of the language. The
     language is a dramatization of complex attitudes that revolve
     around the idea of illusion as value. Explicates three sections
     labeled as incoherent by hostile criticism to illustrate his
     point: "Atlantis," "Cape Hatteras," and "The Dance."

17   PARKINSON, THOMAS. "The Hart Crane--Yvor Winters Correspon-
     dence." Ohio Review 16, no. 1 (Fall):5-24.
         Based on letters from Crane to Winters and Parkinson's in-
     terviews with Janet Lewis Winters. Despite the common prejudice
     of Crane and Winters as "almost allegorically antithetical fig-
     ures," their relationship was "not that of Winters the critic to
     Crane the poet but of two young student and writers of poetry who
     took serious interest in each other's work." And the writing of

letters was an important way of establishing their relationship, especially on Winters's part. "Winters was a demon letter writer. . . . His correspondence was immense and generous." The correspondence with Crane and Allen Tate was only part of Winters's way of maintaining his connections and extending them when he was young. "The professional utility of the correspondence helped Crane on a practical level and lifted him from the bog of his personal problems." The literary relationship was to stop after Winters had written a critical review of The Bridge. Reprinted: 1978.22.

18   ROSENFELD, ALVIN H.   "Poetry: 1900 to the 1930's."   In American Literary Scholarship, An Annual/1972. Edited by J. Albert Robbins. Durham, N.C.: Duke University Press, pp. 312-31.
      A survey of the year's work on Crane.

19   ROSENTHAL, M.L.   Poetry and the Common Life. New York: Oxford University Press, pp. 135-38.
      Cites a passage from Voyages to demonstrate how verbs bring us into the world of the poem.

20   RUECKERT, WILLIAM.   "Humanizing a Poet."   New Republic 171, no. 8 (24 August):28-29.
      Review of Letters of Hart Crane and His Family, edited by Thomas S.W. Lewis. Thoughtfully, intelligently and helpfully edited and commented on.

21   STANFORD, DONALD E.   "The Poetry of James Agee: The Art of Recovery." Southern Review 10, no. 2 (April):xvi-xix.
      Agee's work contains a rhetoric sometimes reminiscent of that of Crane and Allen Tate.

22   SIMON, MARC.   "CALM Addendum No. 4: Hart Crane." Papers of the Bibliographical Society of America 68:69.
      A supplement to Lohf's work regarding "For the Marriage of Faustus and Helen." See 1967.21.

23   STAUFFER, DONALD B.   A Short History of American Poetry. New York: E.P. Dutton, pp. 252, 271, 292, 325-33, 346, 349.
      General information on biographical background, biographical influences on his poetry, and listing individuals and movements which influenced him. Discussion of "The Wine Menagerie," "Voyages," and "For the Marriage of Faustus and Helen." Develops the symbol of the bridge and presents the accepted thematic interpretations of the individual poems of The Bridge. Crane embodies two aspects of the American romantic tradition: Poe-- the desire for pure poetry, and Whitman--the vision of spiritual fulfillment.

24   UROFF, M.D.   Hart Crane: The Patterns of His Poetry. Urbana: University of Illinois Press, 263 pp.

"Designed to examine not simply the connective links between Crane's two genres [lyric and epic] but the imaginative patterns that are repeated throughout his poetry and thus may be said to typify it." Attempts to correct the notion of Crane as "a poet of broken efforts, of varied creative aims," to show him rather as having written "a work of unusual continuity, of patterns recurring with obsessive frequency." First, there are two "separate and in some ways opposing patterns of impulses: the impulse to violence and the impulse to possession." As a creative writer, Crane had the urge to "violate the certainties of the world," but his violation also brought to him suffering of "self-expenditure as well as the torment of the world's scorn." Eventually, however, as Crane's poetic powers developed, he could have "confidence in the victory to be won from the violence of art." Crane came to see that the "suffering and self-expenditure of the poet lead . . . not to exhaustion and defeat but to a new vision." This pattern of violence is "intricately interwoven with a second pattern: the urge for possession." Violence is a means to possession. "To violate the world and thus possess it is one way of imaginative access to an otherwise resistant reality." Violation brings to the poet isolation as well as suffering, in which "he is tormented by a desire to possess the miraculous spirit that has the power to transform the ugliness and torpor of the quotidian world, perfect pure." This spirit is imagined in Crane's poetry as an elusive female figure. The pattern of flight appears in escape from all restrictions, pursuit, and the transportation of the modern mechanical world. At the same time Crane's poetry shows the pattern of stasis in which "he felt rooted in space, enclosed in a world of hardened forms, oppressed by the resistant bulk of the material world." "Violence and possession, flight and stasis, these are the alternating and inextricably intertwined patterns in Crane's poetry." In addition to these, there is the pattern of mastery, the "persistent effort to give direct expressive form to those moments of intense consciousness." Crane's poetry, from this perspective, is "a persistent and rigorous effort to give form to the furthest range of his imagination." It is "a sincere and continuing effort to make accessible" the intensity of consciousness and to "find words and patterns that would articulate it." See 1965.25. Reviewed in 1977.20.

25 WIGGINS, ALLEN. "KSU Orchestra Honor Hart Crane's Memory." Cleveland Plain Dealer, 22 July, p. 7.
    Report of a concert and poetry reading at Kent State University commemorating Crane's seventy-fifth anniversary of his birth.

26 YANNELLA, PHILIP R. "'Inventive Dust': The Metamorphoses of 'For the Marriage of Faustus and Helen.'" Contemporary Literature 15 (Winter):102-22.
    "For the Marriage of Faustus and Helen" sets forth "one of the characteristic dichotomies of 20th century American," the

diametrical opposition of Eliot and Blake. Instead of taking a side, he combines both. "One of the earliest American poets (after Whitman) to express a renewed hope in the American city." Identifies Helen's mythological meanings as insignificant, preferring to see her as a symbol of "the speed, intensity and dynamism of modern industrial-technological culture." Focuses on the development of images and the multilevel functioning of specific words. Discusses the influence of Waldo Frank and Gorham Munson who preached a "new art" which emphasized machinery in art. "Crane's poem can be seen as working out the same philosophical contention that serves as premise for Blake." "The crucial issue which emerges is the conflict between an aesthetic and metaphysic based on a Newtonian conception of the universe and an aesthetic and metaphysic which is probably best characterized as relativistic and atomist."

27   ZATKIN-DRESNER, Z. "Levels of Meaning in Hart Crane's 'Royal Palm.'" Thoth 15 (Winter):29-37.
        Begins by recounting Crane's travels to Cuba, illustrating the experiences and thoughts that form a background to "Royal Palm." It is part of the Key West group, "the consistent theme" of which "is alienation." The poem stands out among this group "because it seems to represent a positive synthesis of . . . contrasting island experiences." The poem is based on an experience of the object, and the poem's language and structure capture its grace and beauty. The symbol of the tree developed in the poem is "ultimately . . . Crane's tropical bridge, serving the same purpose in Crane's imagination as the bridge in 'Atlantis' and suggesting the same transcendence."

1975

1   ANON. "Hart Crane Letters." Bancroftiana, no. 60 (February), pp. 6-7.
        A report on the acquisition of Crane's letters to Yvor Winters by the Bancroft Library, University of California-Berkeley.

2   BLOOM, HAROLD. A Map of Misreading. New York: Oxford University Press, pp. 160, 162, 164, 178.
        Miscellaneous references.

3   BRYANT, JOSEPH A., Jr. Review of Sherman Paul's Hart's Bridge. English Language Notes 12, no. 3 (March):228-30.
        Paul is successful except when he attempts to defend Crane against the attacks of Tate, Winters, and Blackmur. Sees these attacks as the cause of the "inhibited" development "of an interest in Crane for a whole generation." See 1972.23.

4   CROWDER, RICHARD. "Poetry: 1900 to the 1930's." In American

Literary Scholarship, An Annual/1973. Edited by James Woodress.
Durham, N.C.: Duke University Press, pp. 304-28.
A survey of the year's work on Crane.

5   FURIA, PHILIP. "Crane's 'At Melville's Tomb.'" Explicator 33,
     no. 9 (May):Item 73.
     Mostly interested in the last line, which he sees as meaning
"The sea keeps only Melville's shadow--his spiritual presence resides elsewhere." Also notes references to "the Christian pattern of death and resurrection" in the poem.

6   FORD, HUGH. Published In Paris: American and British Writers,
     Printers, and Publishers in Paris, 1920-1939. New York:
     Macmillan Co., pp. 184-88, 198-99, 209-13, 218, 297.
     About the Crosbys' Black Sun Press in Paris, detailing the
publishing of The Bridge and other Black Sun editions. Anecdotes
about Crane's life in Paris and his dealings with the Crosbys.

7   HEWARDITH, RICHARD et al. "Figures in Gay Male Literature."
     Los Angeles, Calif.: Pacifica Audiotapes, BC 2146.01.
     Crane is called "the Christopher Fry" of American society,
who drowned himself when he could find no escape from neurosis
associated with chronic alcoholism.

8   IRWIN, JOHN T. "Naming Names: Hart Crane's 'Logic of Meta-
     phor.'" Southern Review 2, no. 2 (Spring):284-99.
     Deals with Crane's use of metaphor and discusses the "logic
of metaphor," "the dynamics of inferential mention," the "linguistic structure" of Crane's metaphors, and the "counterworld of
the poem." Says that "language in Crane's poetry attempts to
break a purely mimetic relationship to the external world and to
establish in its place a creative relationship wherein the conjunction or juxtaposition of words on the basis of wholly linguistic features enables us to build new realtions between the things
they name."

9   LENSING, GEORGE S. "Hart Crane's Tunnel from The Waste Land."
     Ariel: A Review of International English Literature 6, no. 3:
     20-35.
     In comparing Eliot's The Waste Land and The Bridge, notes
that "there are . . . numerous evidences of linkings between the
two poems--especially in the larger structural pattern wherein
characters within the poem share identities with other characters,
frequently through ironic associations. In addition, the poems
disclose remarkable similarities in imagery, in the use of fragmented conversations, and in prosodic variations." Recounts what
we know biographically of the link between Eliot and Crane,
pointing to several poems in which echoings appear, finally dealing at greatest length with "The Tunnel," the single section of
The Bridge that appears most indebted to Eliot's influence. "At
no point does the reader discern servitude on his part to the

model of Eliot."

10   MARDER, DANIEL. "Exiles at Home in American Literature."
      Mosaic 8, no. 3 (Spring):52-53.
           Crane's suicide is not attributed "to fears that his extra-
      ordinary sexual urges had dissipated his creative energies," but
      to the eternal return to the spiritual exile.

11   MARTIN, ROBERT K. "Crane's The Bridge, 'The Tunnel,' 58-60."
      Explicator 34, no. 2 (October):Item 16.
           Demonstrates "their meaning in the poem and their relation-
      ship to the larger body of Crane's imagistic language." Dissects
      the images of the three lines, coming to the conclusion that "the
      two apparently totally different metaphors of these lines are
      . . . closely linked."

12   NICHOLS, KENNETH. "The Akron Years." Akron Beacon Journal,
      13 April, pp. 9, 21-22.
           Suggests that his importance is still being established.
      Includes biographical information revealing his parental problems,
      tracing his employment and residences in Ohio, and giving brief
      details about his publications.

13   PARKINSON, THOMAS. "Hart Crane and Yvor Winters: A Meeting
      of Minds." Southern Review 2, no. 3 (July):491-512.
           A biographical study of the early relationship between
      Crane and Winters, based on letters from Crane to Winters.
      Largely concerned with how they began their correspondence, how
      Crane responded to the earlier high estimate by Winters of his
      poetry, and how Crane felt about Marianne Moore's revision of his
      "The Wine Menagerie." See 1978.22.

14   PAYNE, JOHN R. "Addenda to Rowe: Hart Crane's Collected
      Poems." Papers of the Bibliographical Society of America 69,
      no. 1 (First Quarter):120-21.
           Examination of eight copies of the 1933 Liveright edition
      at University of Texas Library indicates three printings of the
      first edition.

15   PEASE, DONALD. "The Bridge: Emotional Dynamics of an Epic of
      Consciousness." In The Twenties: Poetry, Fiction, Drama.
      Edited by Warren French. Deland, Fla.: Everett/Edwards, pp.
      387-403.
           "Crane intended to create . . . an 'epic of modern con-
      sciousness' motivated by and organized through the 'emotional
      dynamics' of individual lyrics." But The Bridge is different
      from other epics in that it requires "the reader to become a
      participant in the action" of the poem. Explicates each poem of
      The Bridge, emphasizing the linking transitions that unify the
      whole. The unifying themes not only serve to link poem to poem,
      but also provide the reader with the "connective experience" to

establish an awareness "of that spiritual home of which . . . America [is a] type."

16   PEMBERTON, VIVIAN. "Hart Crane's Heritage." In <u>Artful Thunder: Versions of the Romantic Tradition in American Literature in Honor of Howard P. Vincent</u>. Edited by Robert J. DeMott and Sanford E. Marovitz. Kent, Ohio: Kent State University, pp. 221-40.
        Considering Crane's limited education it is surprising that he became the poet he did. Such a career was established by more than his self-education; it was nurtured by the interest of his ancestors in literature. The clues to Crane's artistic development lie in his relation with his father's family. Discusses the poetry career of Hart's great uncle, Frederic Crane, and Alice Crane's influence. Shows how "The Fernery," formerly "Portrait of Aunty Climax" works in personal material referring to Aunt Alice.

17   PERRY, ROBERT L. "Critical Problems in Hart Crane's 'Chaplinesque.'" <u>Concerning Poetry</u> 8, no. 3 (Fall):23-27.
        "The poem is a portrait of the poet as clown, as spiritual exile in a hostile, frenetic, and uncomprehending world, surviving by virtue of his defensive self-irony and yet as more than a clown, for, with his Parsifal-like faith and purity, he has been granted a vision of a holy 'grail of laughter' and has discovered the riches of the human soul." Considers the problems that have concerned the critics of the poem: the sentimentality that is "the weakness of the kitten as symbol"; the identity of the "inevitable thumb" in the third stanza; and the explication of the fourth stanza, centering on the nature of the "collapses" of the first line and the "obsequies" of the third line.

18   _____. "Critical Problems in Hart Crane's 'Sunday Morning Apples.'" <u>Rendezvous</u> 10:23-27.
        The poem "celebrates the art of his close friend William Sommer, and in particular that artist's drawings and paintings of apples, and that it is also, at least implicitly, a statement about aesthetics." Mentions the opinions of the most prominent critics of the poem, focusing upon the work of R.W.B. Lewis and Sherman Paul. The connection that might appear between Crane and Wallace Stevens, in his poem titled "Sunday Morning," is considered. Deals with it in terms of some of Sommer's work, as it might illuminate and explain these problems.

19   SMOLLER, SANFORD J. <u>Adrift Among Geniuses: Robert McAlmon, Writer and Publisher of the Twenties</u>. University Park: Pennsylvania State University Press, pp. 4, 26, 46, 78, 207, 304, 359.
        Miscellaneous references.

20   STRANDBERG, VICTOR. "Hart Crane and William James: The

Psychology of Mysticism." <u>McNeese Review</u> 22:14–25.
James's <u>The Varieties of Religious Experience</u> provides a
valuable reference source for understanding many features of
Crane's poems: "Their relation to psychedelic stimuli, their
fire and water imagery, their mood of mingled fear and welcome
towards annihilation of the ego, and above all, their striving to
express monistic insight." Strandberg begins by citing Freudian
interpretations of Crane's life. In contrast, James's religious-
based theories seem to be more appropriate to Crane's themes.
Crane drew satisfaction from his reading in James's <u>Varieties</u> for
its "corroboration of several experiences in consciousness that I
have had." These "corroborations," though unidentified by Crane,
can be interpreted as "James's validation of the mystic's resort
to psychedelic stimuli and his clarification of several phases of
mystic consciousness."

21   STRIER, RICHARD. "The Poetics of Surrender: An Exposition
     and Critique of New Critical Poetics." <u>Critical Inquiry</u> 2:
     171–89.
         Begins with an analysis of the New Criticism, isolating its
     fundamental premise, that of a "belief in the ultimate intelli-
     gibility and potential cognitive content of (what seem to be)
     nonlogical connections between words." Applies his analysis to
     Crane, who "both shared the poetics of the New Criticism and con-
     sciously based his poetic practice upon this poetics." Crane
     "accepted the premise of 'explication as criticism,'" and felt
     any poem that he could not explicate to be deficient. Looks
     specifically at "At Melville's Tomb" and at "Voyages (II)." The
     "difficulty which Hart Crane felt in evaluating the success of
     his own poems relates quite directly to the difficulty with
     form."

22   TASHJIAM, DICKRAN. "Hart Crane and the Machine." In <u>Sky-</u>
     <u>scraper Primitives: Dada and the American Avant-Garde, 1910-</u>
     <u>1925</u>. Middletown, Conn.: Wesleyan University Press, pp. 143–
     64.
         The influences which led to Crane's treatment of modern
     mechanized society are developed: Josephson's enthusiasm for
     American technology; Munson's treatment of mechanization in his
     monograth of Waldo Frank; Eliot's negative response to mechaniza-
     tion in <u>The Waste Land</u> and his emphasis on the past; Whitman's
     spiritual affirmation. Crane wanted to "bring the machine within
     the ambience of art." The symbolic function of the bridge in the
     achievement of these goals is discussed.

23   TATE, ALLEN. <u>Memoirs and Opinions, 1926-1974</u>. Chicago:
     Swallow Press, pp. 110–14.
         Reprint of his 1926 foreword to <u>White Buildings</u> (1926.3).

24   TOMLINSON, CHARLES. "Destruction Begins at Home." <u>Times</u>
     <u>Literary Supplement</u>, 24 January, p. 78.

Review of Lewis's Letters of Hart Crane and His Family; praises the text as a complete collection of Crane's letters, not edited like Weber's.

25 ULLYATT, A.G. "Hart Crane: The Bridge." Unisa English Studies 13:24-30.

"The Bridge represents one of the most complex epic attempts within the American tradition." "Crane sought to portray the American experience in mystical and symbolic terms, and his work is characterized by its density of thought and complexity of imagery." The author notes that Crane considered this work to be "a symphony with an epic theme," but he would like to characterize it more accurately as a rhapsody, because of its looser structure and "irregularity of form." Ullyatt then traces some of the dominant imagery, analyzes the stylistic variations, and considers the fluctuations in tone from affirmative to pessimistic and back.

26 WELLEK, RENE. "Yvor Winters Rehearsed and Reconsidered." Denver Quarterly 10 (Autumn):1-27.

A brief review of the Crane-Winters relationship.

27 ZECK, GREGORY R. "The Logic of Metaphor: 'At Melville's Tomb.'" Texas Studies in Literature and Language 17, no. 3 (Fall):673-86.

The three letters that accompanied its original publication in Poetry are the primary object of his analysis. "Critics have thus far commented on [the exchange of letters] only superficially, usually attacking or defending either paraphrase or Crane's 'logic of metaphor.'" "At Melville's Tomb" does not fit into his stated theory. "Crane does not explain as much as he might have known, and Harriet Monroe does not probe as acutely as Crane tries to teach her to do."

1976

1 ASSILINEAU, ROGER. "From Whitman's Yawp to Ginsberg's Howl or The Poetry of Large Cities in American Literature." Revues des langues vivantes, U.S., Bicentennial Issue (Liège, Belgium), pp. 23-35.

In twentieth century European and American literature, the city has gradually been "naturalized" as writers have slowly come to terms with it. Hart Crane went into raptures over Brooklyn Bridge. It was "a confluence of water and air and fire, a meeting-place of sky and earth, or river and ocean, of man and metal . . . it is the acme of urban civilization."

2 BLOOM, HAROLD. Figures of Capable Imagination. New York: Seabury Press, pp. 85-86.

Crane is a failed Orphic; the most Orphic poem he wrote is

"Atlantis," the "prophecy of the Orphic poet's high spiritual failure." His poetic tradition prevented him from being "more rational and less enthusiastic in his glimpses of salvation."

3   CROWDER, RICHARD. "Poetry 1900 to the 1930's." In American Literary Scholarship, An Annual/1974. Edited by James Woodress. Durham, N.C.: Duke University Press, pp. 321-44.
        A survey of the year's work on Crane.

4   EDMISTON, SUSAN, and EDMISTON, CIRINO D. Literary New York: A History & Guide. Boston: Houghton Mifflin Co., pp. 62, 69-70, 72-73, 78-79, 89, 106, 108, 110, 156, 211, 251, 339, 355, 365.
        Brief references to Crane's places of residence in Greenwich Village, Cleveland, and New York. Brief details concerning Crane's social life.

5   HOMBERGER, ERIC. "Chicago and New York: Two Versions of American Modernism." In Modernism: 1890-1930. Edited by Malcolm Bradbury and James McFarlane. Pelican Guides to European Civilization. Atlantic Highlands, N.J.: Humanities Press, pp. 151-62.
        Crane's attraction to New York City is briefly discussed.

6   HYDE, B.M. "The Poetry of the City." In Modernism: 1890-1930. Edited by Malcolm Bradbury and James McFarlane. Pelican Guides to European Literature. Atlantic Highlands, N.J.: Humanities Press, pp. 337-48.
        Modern man is sterile in spirit and passion. The Waste Land is about sterility. The Bridge and For the Marriage of Faustus and Helen reply to The Waste Land with its idiom and imagery. Eliot uses a great cultural past to evaluate negatively the culture's present condition while Crane uses that of the past (Pocahontas and Helen) which can be made to serve an eclectic imagination celebrating an untrammelled future. The Waste Land shows a state of impurity for which atonement is needed. This challenges Crane to make good American optimism while using the city images Eliot did.

7   JENNINGS, MARGARET, C.S.J. "Parabola: Hart Crane and Existentialism." Markham Review 5 (Winter):31-34.
        Claims that there is a "correlation between Crane's poetic statement of existence and that of existentialist thinkers, particularly Jean Paul Sartre." Existentialism is rooted in Crane's boyhood, developed in his reading and study of Munson, Frank, and finally in his adherence to the writings of Ouspensky. Traces existentialism through several of the poems and concludes that it forced him to "trace the downward arc to self-destruction."

8   MARTIN, ROBERT K. "Hart Crane's 'For the Marriage of Faustus and Helen.'" Concerning Poetry 9, no. 1:59-62.

Readers have frequently been unclear about the specific meaning of the title. Finds that a close relationship exists with its sources. Finds symbolic references to Aphrodite, Hera, and Athena. The young man is then Paris. Faustus is recalled in the references to alchemy and in the role that Helen plays in the Faustus legend. By changing the Faustus legend, Crane produces "an alchemical marriage, which unites two opposed principles." This "poem is a celebration of the triumph of the imagination, which makes the unreal real, and the real unreal."

9   MAYNARD, REID. "A Defense of Hart Crane's Poetic License." Literatur in Wissenshaft und Unterricht (Kiel) 9:182-87.
        Crane's explications of parts of his "At Melville's Tomb" are defensible when it is seen how close they come to the allusions in Moby Dick.

10   McMILLAN, DOUGLAS. Transition 1927-1938. New York: Braziller, pp. 125-47.
        The magazine was sympathetic to Crane because the editor, Jolas, shared Crane's myth of America, countering the negative elements of technological society by realizing the spiritual perspectives of the machine. Jolas set the stage for the positive acceptance of much of Crane's poetry, helping to publicize the elements of his American myth and establish his symbols. Jolas is responsible for bringing Crane to Crosby and the Black Sun Press. Crane's signing of Jolas's proclamation stirred varied speculation on the motivation behind his action. Crane's connection with Transition reflected his ascending and then declining hopes for The Bridge.

11   O'BEIL, HEDY. "Joe Bascom." Arts Magazine 51 (December):32.
        "Dark and brooding, Bascom's paintings, an homage to his mentor Hart Crane, American poet, express his compassion and oneness with this tragic figure who took his life at thirty-two."

12   PARKINSON, THOMAS. "Hart Crane and Yvor Winters: White Buildings." Southern Review 12, no. 2 (April):232-45.
        Recounts the history of the publication of White Buildings, and traces the relationship of Crane and Winters through Crane's letters. Winters was quite enthusiastic over White Buildings, and "the praise from Winters was exhilarating" for Crane. See 1978.22.

13   PEMBERTON, VIVIAN. "Hart Crane's Ancestor, Ohio's Poet of Politics: Jason Streator." Ohioana Quarterly 19, no. 2 (Summer):62-66.
        Biographical details on Jason Streator, the great-great-grandfather of Crane, a writer of verse. With photograph.

14   _____. Icon Honors Poet Hart Crane." Icon 11 (Winter):13-18.
        Records the creation of a Hart Crane Memorial Poetry Award

at Kent State University--Trumbull. Includes some previously unpublished photographs.

15   PERKINS, DAVID. A History of Modern Poetry: From the 1890's
      to the High Modernist Mode. Cambridge, Mass.: Harvard Uni-
      versity Press, pp. 317, 326, 451.
          Brief references.

16   PERRY, ROBERT L. "Critical Problems in Hart Crane's 'The
      Fernery.'" Explicator 35, no. 1 (Fall):3-5.
          "The poem grapples with the philosophical problem of man's
      inability to attain absolute truth and in particular, the anxiety
      involved in the endless task of processing external reality."
      Points out reoccuring pattern of the aggressive, masculine world
      invading the dark, solemn feminine realm.

17   RAMSEY, PAUL. "The Biding Place: Reflections on Hart Crane."
      Parnassus 5 (Fall/Winter):187-99.
          "How very good a poet is Hart Crane?" An analysis of "O
      Carib Isle!" shows that in spite of its flaws of obscurity, im-
      precision, ellipses, etc., the poem is "one of the greatest
      visions in twentieth century poetry of moral and metaphysical
      evil." Crane's Voyages II, III, IV, and VI, "Repose of Rivers,"
      "To Brooklyn Bridge," "Possessions," and "The Broken Tower" are
      among the best "fused" lyrics in English. By Coleridge's defini-
      tion, where "the test of such a lyric, . . . is not whether the
      poem withstands close scrutiny but whether it has a profound,
      evocative, resonating, unifying effect." The Bridge is a "fused-
      lyric epic" with the same methods of development and reconcilia-
      tion as the lyrics, but the lack of transition between sections
      makes it seem greater as separate poems rather than a fulfilled
      poem.

18   SIMON, MARC. "Hart Crane's 'Greenberg MSS' and the Launching
      of 'Voyages II.'" Journal of Modern Literature 5 (September):
      522-29.
          In various phases of the composition of "Voyages II," Crane
      borrowed, adapted, sometimes retained or rejected elements from
      Samuel B. Greenberg. Examines Greenberg's influence on particular
      lines.

19   SUGG, RICHARD P. Hart Crane's "The Bridge": A Description of
      Its Life. Studies in the Humanities, no. 20. University:
      University of Alabama Press, 127 pp.
          Part I examines Crane's aesthetics and The Bridge as a
      whole--structure and style--with special attention to "Proem."
      Parts II, III, and IV are explications of each individual section
      of the poem. In contrast to the misreadings of Tate, Winters,
      and Blackmur, The Bridge "results from an organic process proper
      to man, a process that develops and integrates intellect and
      passion in the unitive life of the imagination." Emphasizes the

structure of the poem in the examination of each section. Tends
to be circular in argument. Takes little account of the many already existing interpretations of the poem. Reviewed in 1977.23;
1978.13.

20   UNTERECKER, JOHN. "Hart Crane As His Friends Remember Him."
      Los Angeles, Calif.: Pacifica Tape Library, cassette no.
      BB325.
          "Friends and the widow [sic] of the late poet discuss his
      short unhappy life and creative struggles in the anarchic bohe-
      mainism of the jazz-age and early depression era. Slata [sic]
      Brown, Nathan Ash, Peggy Baird, and Crane's biographer recall
      Crane's agonized hetero affairs, self-destructive homosexuality
      and alcoholism."

21   WOLFF, GEOFFREY. Black Sun: The Brief Transit and Violent
      Eclipse of Harry Crosby. New York: Random House, 405 pp.,
      passim.
          Majority of references are biographical.

1977

1   ANON. "A Drawing of Crane by William Sommer." Hart Crane
      Newsletter 1, no. 1 (Winter):31-33.
          Shared the view that mere sight is different from vision.
      An ink and matchstick drawing done around 1921-22 emphasizes
      Crane's eyes as his most notable physical feature.

2   ANON. "My Dear Father: A Crane Letter." Hart Crane News-
      letter 1, no. 1 (Winter):3-6.
          A previously unpublished letter, March 1917, attempting to
      persuade his father to allow him to remain in New York.

3   ANON. "'Sam Loveman from Hart Crane': A Drawing by Crane."
      Hart Crane Newsletter 1, no. 1 (Winter):15-17.
          Included among his drawings is one of Samuel Loveman, one
      of his closest friends. Loveman reports that "he just sat down
      and drew. He knew just what to do and what to make. And he made
      a likeness."

4   ANON. "An Unpublished Crane Poem." Hart Crane Newsletter 1,
      no. 1 (Winter):8-9.
          "What Nots?" is supposed to have been sent to Gorham Munson
      in a letter dated 20 December 1923. Crane described the poem as
      filled with melody and the act of composition as gleeful.

5   ASPEL, PAULINE. "Au Pont de Brooklyn." Hart Crane Newsletter
      1, no. 1 (Winter):30.
          The concluding stanzas of "To Brooklyn Bridge" translated
      into French.

6   BROWN, SLATER. "A Letter from Peter Blume." Hart Crane News-
     letter 1, no. 1 (Winter):10-14.
          Blume and Crane formed a strong friendship based on an
     interest in each other's work, and had several discussions. It
     is significant that when Crane published The Bridge, Blume ex-
     hibited a large canvas also entitled "The Bridge." Blume talks
     about Crane's interest in the arts. The letter is dated 6 Novem-
     ber 1976.

7   CAHEN, ALFRED B. "Hart Crane's Ghost Written Suicide Notes."
     Hart Crane Newsletter 1, no. 2 (Fall):11-16.
          The marks and underlinings in Hart Crane's copy of The Poems
     of John Donne, published by E.P. Dutton & Co. in 1931 shed light
     on the causes of his suicide in 1932. The underscored material
     in the book is characterized by the "conflict, guilt and despair"
     which Crane experienced during that time.

8   CARTER, EVERETT. The American Idea: The Literary Response to
     American Optimism. Chapel Hill: University of North Carolina
     Press, p. 249.
          Crane is listed among "poets of the glory of the common-
     place" along with Robert Frost and William Carlos Williams.

9   CROWDER, RICHARD. "Poetry: 1900 to the 1930's." In American
     Literary Scholarship, An Annual/1975. Edited by James
     Woodress. Durham, N.C.: Duke University Press, pp. 363-78.
          A survey of the year's work on Crane.

10   FIKE, FRANCIS. "Symbolic Strategy in 'Repose of Rivers.'"
     Hart Crane Newsletter 1, no. 1 (Winter):18-27.
          Symbolically, the poem exposes universal aspects of human
     existence, tracing the common journey of life from childhood
     through various experiences attended by pleasure and pain and
     finally through death.

11   GERMAIN, EDWARD, ed. Shadows of the Sun: The Diaries of Harry
     Crosby. Santa Barbara: Black Sparrow Press, pp. 7, 15, 193,
     218, 233, 234, 236-40, 257, 258, 260-62, 266, 287.
          Biographical references to Crane and to the Crosby's pub-
     lication of The Bridge by the Black Sun Press.

12   HAZO, SAMUEL. Smithereened Apart: A Critique of Hart Crane.
     Athens: Ohio University Press, 146 pp.
          Reprint of 1963.12 with an updated bibliography and a new
     preface. See 1977.26.

13   LEWIS, THOMAS S.W. "'O Thou Steeled Cognizance': The Brook-
     lyn Bridge, Lewis Mumford and Hart Crane." Hart Crane News-
     letter 1, no. 2 (Fall):17-26.
          The impact of Brooklyn Bridge on Crane and Lewis Mumford.

14   LIBMAN, V.A. American Literature in Russian Translations and
      Criticism: Bibliography 1776-1975. Academy of Sciences USSR/
      Institute of World Literature. Moscow: Naukee, pp. 138-39.
            In Russian. Listing of three reviews of studies of Crane.

15   LINDSAY, CLARENCE B. Hart Crane: An Introduction. Columbus:
      State Library of Ohio, 30 pp.
            Monograph published for the public libraries of Ohio. Biog-
      raphy based on John Unterecker's Voyager, introductory expositions
      of "For The Marriage of Faustus and Helen," "Voyages," and The
      Bridge. In "For The Marriage of Faustus and Helen" Crane "wrote
      not only what was immediately recognized as a major poem, but one
      that fulfilled his own demands of affirmation and reconciliation
      for modern poetry." But the "affirmative ecstasy that Crane was
      seeking exists merely as an ecstatic statement of the poet's will.
      The affirmation is not a reconciliation of the two worlds of body
      and spirit nor even a balance; it is instead a heightened vision
      that comes only at the demise of the material world." "Voyages"
      also introduces a quester for love and knowledge. "The poet
      discovers that time, the world of dissolution and change, will
      triumph over love." Defends the unity of The Bridge by pointing
      that there is a structure. The first part of the poem seeks the
      meaning of America's past, showing a movement toward the West and
      the past. The second part "seeks to reconcile the conflicts
      within America's present in order to provide a synthesis that will
      be the basis for a vision of America's future."

16   NILSEN, HELGE [Norman]. "Crane and Frank: Images of America."
      Hart Crane Newsletter 1, no. 1 (Winter):36-42.
            Frank saw The Bridge as "a complex artistic presentation of
      the consciousness of America" that he was trying in Our America,
      The Re-Discovery of America and Virgin Spain. "Both writers saw
      Columbus, the discoverer of America, as representing the original
      supreme aspirations of the white man in America, the quest for a
      new perfect world." Certain metaphors echo in Virgin Spain which
      Crane called "something of a prelude to my intentions for The
      Bridge." "The fundamental idea that Frank and Crane shared was
      that the ideal America is a state of mind, a revelation in the
      eyes of the beholder."

17   _____. "Hart Crane's The Bridge and the Poetics of Faith."
      Edda Nordisk Tiddskrift For Litteraturforskning 2, no. 1:237-
      42.
            Whereas poets like Eliot and Pound spoke of the chaos and
      decay of Western culture, Crane "believed it possible to create a
      harmonious synthesis out of modern reality by means of an effort
      of the poetic imagination." The Bridge is a result of this faith,
      the poem a metaphor for the creative process itself. "The very
      creation of a poetic image or phrase was for Crane an act of
      bridging, of fusion of diverse elements." Crane struggled to
      produce "the new 'word' of America, the revelation of a totally

new, mystic beauty in the environment." To capture the "timeless vision," Crane resorted to "the logic of metaphor." For Crane, "modern technology is inspired by a universal creative force that 'connects' rather than 'separates.'" The technique of linking sections of the poem by recurring images and references and the poetic method of fusing disparate elements by means of "dynamic metaphor" counterpoint each other.

18   ____. "The Modern Long Poem." Hart Crane Newsletter 1, no. 2 (Fall):34-35.
        The openness and flexibility of American long poems may reflect the desire of the America spirit to "experiment with forms and include very wide ranges of experience and history." The Bridge is perhaps the best example of the impulse to "synthesize experience and establish new and authentic harmonies."

19   PARKER, MARY A. "Hart Crane Seminar." Hart Crane Newsletter 1, no. 1 (Winter):43-46.
        Report on the seminar, "Hart Crane: Modern Poetics and The Bridge," held on 27 December 1976 at the MLA convention.

20   PARKINSON, THOMAS. "Hart Crane and some Critical Procedures." Southern Review 13 (Winter):217-20.
        Review of Uroff's Hart Crane: The Patterns of His Poetry. The chronological procedure is faulty because it emphasizes how small Crane's total output was and how he deteriorated in his later years. It raises the question of whether this deterioration was implicit in the thought and poetic methodology from the beginning. The biographical approach does not answer this question. Another way to look at Crane is from an "organizational design" point of view—to trace the recurring patterns in his poetry. Uroff is successful in treating both "Crane's sense of the poet's role and the world's shape." The second and third chapters examine Crane's view of the world as both in flight and in stasis. The style is clear and the work is in many ways superior to that of Butterfield or Lewis. The sixth chapter, on Crane's poetics, is the best. See 1974.24.

21   PEMBERTON, VIVIAN. "Poetry and Portraits: Reflections on Hart Crane." Hart Crane Newsletter 1, no. 2 (Fall):4-11.
        Crane was very close to his cousin Helen Hart Hulbert. They shared a love for literature, art, and music. After the death of his father, Crane spent some time in Ohio, and Helen described him at that time as being "more philosophical, less exuberant than usual."

22   ____. "The Roebling Response to Hart Crane's The Bridge: A New Letter." Ohioana Quarterly 20, no. 4 (Winter):155-57.
        A previously unpublished letter from Mrs. John Roebling, thanking Crane for sending a copy of The Bridge to her husband, the son of Washington Augustus Roebling, who, along with his

father, designed Brooklyn Bridge. With photograph.

23   QUINN, VINCENT [Gerard]. "Diminished Glory." Hart Crane
        Newsletter 1, no. 2 (Fall):29-33.
            Review of Sugg's Hart Crane's The Bridge: A Description of
    Its Life. The poem acts as a bridge, connecting Crane to what he
    had been seeking and offering him a liberating experience. A
    "poem about the creation of a poem." Pays no attention to the
    historical allusions. Certain sections like "To Brooklyn Bridge,"
    "Ave Maria," "The River," "Cutty Sark," and "Atlantis" are treated
    with insight but some parts are misread. Makes the fallacious
    claim that the imagination was "the only Absolute to which Crane
    ascribed." See 1976.19.

24   SHAWCROSS, JOHN T. "A Note on The Bridge." Hart Crane News-
        letter 1, no. 2 (Fall):29-33.
            Compares The Bridge with Whitman's "A Noiseless, Patient
    Spider." "The Spider's work of spanning a gap by its connective
    links and concentric circles is equated to the Soul's need to
    build a bridge over time and the wider world of the heavenly
    sphere and the numerous spheres of action in life." Crane in
    building his bridge "becomes a kind of spider, and his poem, a
    kind of web of intricate design." The bridge for Crane, as for
    Whitman, is "the means of commerce between souls."

25   STOKES, ERIC. "The Continental Harp and Band Report." Louis-
        ville Symphony Orchestra. First Edition Record Series. Con-
        ducted by Dennis Russell Davies.
            The first movement is titled "Brooklyn Bridge" and bears an
    inscription from Crane's poem. Composed in 1974-75 on a commis-
    sion from the Minneapolis Symphony to celebrate the opening of
    Ochestra Hall. Premiered there on 5, 6, and 7 March 1975, con-
    ducted by Stanislaw Skrowaczewski.

26   SUGG, RICHARD P. "Hart Crane's Fabulous Shadow." Hart Crane
        Newsletter 1, no. 2 (Fall):38-42.
            Review of Hazo's Smithereened Apart: A Critique of Hart
    Crane. Much Crane criticism sees the poetry in terms of the
    poet's life, resulting in a confusion between the man and his
    work. Hazo's criticism goes straight to the poetry itself. See
    1977.12.

27   SUNDQUIST, ERIC J. "Bringing Home the Word: Magic, Lies, and
        Silence in Hart Crane." English Literary History 44 (Summer):
        376-99.
            To redeem the fallen American community in which technology
    has usurped the poetic throne of belief, there is in all of
    Crane's work, emphatically in The Bridge, an attendant psycho-
    analytic inquiry into the problem of genealogy. "Such an inquiry
    is the economic record of a curious double movement which re-
    enacts the story of the sacrifice of ancestral fathers with one

eye toward sexual reunion with a maternal, <u>free</u> origin, the other
toward the <u>debt</u> aroused by the patricide necessary to an acquisi-
tion of power over that origin." Crane couched his pursuit of
the Word in a style whose "psychological <u>gaming</u> many have found
to be overwrought past the point of sense." As a reaction
against the pessimistic tradition of his age, Crane desired to
locate and stabilize tradition. Crane's task was to establish
America as a proper mythical and historical "home." Crane's
flights of poetic lunacy reveal a darker side of the sweet memories of childhood. "Crane's cultural psychoanalytic seeks that
which--in his recurrent metaphor--we are most blind to; but the
final horror of this buries blissful origin, this unblemished ego,
is that <u>it</u> is no longer, if ever, <u>there</u>: <u>there</u> are only words
about <u>it</u>."

28   THOMAS, RICHARD. "Hart Crane, Alfred Stieglitz, and Camera
      Photography." <u>Centennial Review</u> 21 (Summer):294-309.
          Crane's poetry was influenced by the photographs of Alfred
Stieglitz who "emphasized (by manipulating focus, vantage point,
detail, time, and frame within a photograph) that the illusion of
reality could be put at the service of allusion." After attending
an exhibition of Stieglitz's photographs, Crane began to define
his own poetry in terms of Stieglitz's photographic aesthetic.
In spite of all the parallels between Crane's poetry and
Steiglitz's photographs, Crane could not finally "surrender" to
the machine culture the way the photographer did. For instance,
"to secure its link with eternity, Crane had to abolish the
bridge's link with the opposite shores--to abolish exactly that
which made it a bridge!"

29   TOMLINSON, CHARLES. "Some American Poets: A Personal
      Record." <u>Contemporary Literature</u> 18 (Summer):279-304.
          Contains biographical information on author's personal
experience as an Englishman experiencing American poetry. Includes comments on Crane's "Voyages."

                              1978

1   ANON. "Hart Crane Honored." Ravenna and Kent (Ohio) <u>Record-
      Courier</u>, 22 October, p. 4.
          An editorial commenting on the dedication of a stone monu-
ment to Crane in Garrettsville where he was born.

2   ANON. "Marker Dedicated in Honor of Hart Crane." Garretts-
      ville (Ohio) <u>Newsletter News and Views</u>, 21 November, pp. 1, 3.
          News story on the dedication of the granite commemorative
marker to Crane in Garrettsville.

3   ANON. "An Unpublished Poetic Fragment." <u>Hart Crane News-
      letter</u> 2, no. 1 (September):6-7.

An unpublished poetic fragment, the manuscript of which is located in the Waldo Frank papers of the Rare Book Collection of the Charles Van Pelt Library at the University of Pennsylvania. As we see from the manuscript how the poem struggles towards form, we recall Crane's lines to Gorham Munson about the writing of poetry in which he talks about the necessity of soaking in words before "the right ones form themselves into the proper pattern at the right moment."

4   ANTHONY, DOROTHY. "Tribune Publisher Preserves Memory of Poet Hart Crane." Warren (Ohio) Tribune Chronicle, 21 Novmeber, pp. 1, 3.
    News story of Crane's being commemorated in Garrettsville by a rose quartz marker.

5   BLEICH, DAVID. "Symbolmaking and Suicide: Hart Crane (1899-1932)." Hartford Studies in Literature 10:70-102.
    A biographical and psychological study of Crane's life and poetry (especially The Bridge). Attempts to find an "underlying logic" in the poet's suicide and his symbolmaking process ("bridge") by discussing the basic patterns--"oral" and "holistic"--of his psychological disturbance, caused chiefly by his relationship with his mother.

6   BLUME, PETER. "A Letter from Peter Blume." Hart Crane Newsletter 2, no. 1 (September):17-19.
    Blume writes affectionately and intimately of his friend, Crane, describing him as volatile with a sense of humor and a weakness for alcohol. He was given to depressions but worked hard at his poetry and saw himself as a timeless and universal poet.

7   BROGUNIER, JOSEPH E. "The Two Cranes and 'Blind Baggage.'" Hart Crane Newsletter 2, no. 1 (September):33-35.
    "Blind baggage" in "The River" (line 33), also occurs in Ford Madox Ford's depiction of Stephen Crane in Portraits from Life in a passage Ford attributes to the novelist. The literal meaning of the phrase in "The River" is "a baggage or mail car lacking front end doors (thus providing a harbor between the cars for hidden riders)." "Crane then makes of the literal phrase a metonymy referring to the hobos." Both Stephen and Hart Crane associate "blind baggage" with exotically named places.

8   BROWN, JAMES F. "The Editor's View." Warren (Ohio) Tribune Chronicle, 22 November, p. 4.
    An editorial on the commemoration of Crane in Garrettsville.

9   COMBS, ROBERT. Vision of the Voyage: Hart Crane and the Psychology of Romanticism. Memphis: Memphis State University Press, 181 pp.
    Attempts to correct the traditional view that Crane was a

visionary poet whose main function was to redeem society. This
way of thinking "carries with it a predisposition toward dogma."
On the assumption that Crane was a visionary poet, they believed
that Crane's success or failure should be judged according to
"the efficacy of whatever vision the critic can find." This
evaluation has failed to see Crane's basic tendency as a romantic
who necessarily opposes any dogmatic way of thinking. Crane's
poetry does not "represent an attempt to reassert the religious
consciousness in an unreligious age." "What Crane discovered is
that the power of the mind never has depended on the absolute
truth of its beliefs. Instead, the flexibility of the mind, its
genius for disagreeing with itself, is its greatest strength."
After an introductory chapter dealing with the ideological meaning
of the romantic revolution (Kant and Hegel), Combs is concerned
with the quality of Crane's lyricism in White Buildings, and,
then, with The Bridge as the personal record of one man of the
struggles and suffering caused by the failure of "life-sources to
take on any permanently meaningful form." Reviewed in 1978.27;
1979.24.

10   COWLEY, MALCOLM. "A Response from Malcolm Cowley." Hart
     Crane Newsletter 2, no. 1 (September):15-16.
          In a letter to the editors, says that Crane's "Supplication
     to the Muses on a Trying Day" was meant as a frivolous poem
     written merely for the joy of putting words together.

11   CORMAN, CID. "Hart Crane." In At Their Word: Essays on the
     Arts of Language. Santa Barbara, Calif.: Black Sparrow Press,
     pp. 2, 53-66.
          Crane is the instance of American incoherence. Two quotes
     from his declaration suggest the direction he was taking. The
     quiet tense lyric of painful relation or gentle regard in "Garden
     Abstract" reveals one side of Crane. More typical of Crane is his
     "piled-up shifting" of metaphors, and a verbal gorgeousness out-
     running sense. Yet, he has a capacity for unusual concentration
     and density. Key West opens with less flourish than The Bridge
     or White Buildings. A larger world of sympathy in the face of
     obvious destruction and a sense of impotency appears while it is
     absent but not unpromised in his other works. In Key West and
     in the final poems, "the strain recedes, the scope nears a clear
     naked exact ache." His voice is now his own, as he no longer
     plays the epic poet and begins to "look on."

12   CROWDER, RICHARD. "Poetry: 1900 to the 1930's." In American
     Literary Scholarship, An Annual/1976. Edited by J. Albert
     Robbins. Durham, N.C.: Duke University Press, pp. 319-37.
          A survey of the year's work on Crane.

13   DUFFEY, BERNARD. Review of Hart Crane's The Bridge: A De-
     scription of Its Life by Richard P. Sugg. American Literature
     49 (January):667.

An effort to "explicate and interpret Hart Crane's most ambitious work with arguments spun out of Crane himself." Looks at the poems as manifestations of Crane's poetic theories but what results is a circular argument. Crane proclaimed that the effect of his work should be to give the reader "a single new word never before spoken," but Sugg's critique suggests that Crane's ambitious new word in The Bridge is a "successful word" by its own inner nature. See 1976.19.

14   FENDER, STEPHEN. "Ezra Pound and the Words Off the Page: Historical Allusions in Some American Long Poems." Yearbook of English Studies 8:95-108.
        How far should one search for poetic allusions outwards to the shared past and present of society in considering the allusions to American history in the poetry of Whitman, Pound, Crane, and Williams? Whitman's and Crane's allusions seem to refer to events and figures more public and of greater popular familiarity than those more subtle historic themes used by Pound and Williams. Crane used a readily available translation of an abstract of Columbus's journal of his first voyage and Irving's popular biography of Columbus for his "Ave Maria" section of The Bridge. He drew on the common image of Pocahontas preserved in popular tradition. Whitman and Crane restrict allusion to what they know is widely disseminated historical information. Pound and Williams make no immediate appeal to shared knowledge.

15   GARDNER, JOHN. On Moral Fiction. New York: Basic Books, p. 9.
        Crane is cited as one who "fractured poetry." Because his metaphysical system has broken down, "the forms of art which supported that system no longer feel true or adequate."

16   GRAHAM, CHAEL. "Hart Crane: 1899-1932." Hart Crane Newsletter 2 (Summer):36.
        Verse appreciation.

17   HAKALA, CATHY. "Crane's Life Was Like a Novel." Ravenna and Kent (Ohio) Record-Courier, 20 October, p. 9.
        Feature story on the granite monument to Crane in Garrettsville.

18   _____. "Crane Monument Dedication Adds Awareness." Ravenna and Kent (Ohio) Record-Courier, 21 November, p. 13.
        News story on dedication of granite marker to Crane in Garrettsville.

19   HENRY, NAT. "Crane's 'The Fernery.'" Explicator 27 (Summer): 7-9.
        An examination of the grammatical structure of the first two lines. If line 1 is not read as endstopped but as a runover, the reading shows a habitual state interrupted by a sudden light

of the lifted shade in line 3. This changes the connotation of
"But" in line 3 from "however" to "merely," which is more in line
with "as you may chance" in line 3.

20   MESSERLI, DOUGLAS. "'Out of the Square, the Circle': Vision
      in Nightmare in Crane's 'Tunnel.'" Four Decades of Poetry,
      1890-1930 1:201-17.
           Yvor Winters argued that "The Tunnel" was unjustified by
      Whitmanian optimism while it was a personal impression of des-
      pair. L.S. Dembo, Thomas A. Vogler, Herbert A. Leibowitz, and
      Sherman Paul defended the structural unity of the poem by arguing
      that the poem, in terms of structural, imagistic, or thematic
      patterns, is to be perceived as a presentation of an experience
      which stands in opposition to and/or apart from the experience
      of which the Bridge serves as symbol, thus, in spite of their in-
      tention, helping to confirm Winters's final evaluation of "The
      Tunnel" rather than refuting it. Messerli suggests that the poem
      is an expression of both despair and new found solutions. About
      the time he wrote the poem, Crane read Oswald Spengler's The De-
      cline of the West. "The Tunnel" is an expression of the despair
      he felt. The reader must, however, search "The Tunnel" for
      images which will stimulate his memory and permit him a moral
      vision. The vision must exist within the nightmare or the myth
      cannot be promised in "Atlantis."

21   NILSEN, HELGE NORMAN. "Memories of Hart Crane: A Talk with
      Emil Opffer." Hart Crane Newsletter 2, no. 1 (September):8-
      15.
           Emil Opffer, a Danish-American sailor, was a close friend
      of Crane's. Their relationship was strongest in the spring of
      1924 when both lived in the same apartment house in Brooklyn
      while Crane was working on "Voyages." He first told Opffer that
      the poem was about their relationship but after a temporary fall-
      ing out said the theme of the poem was entirely general in mean-
      ing. Opffer remembers Crane as a person of changing moods and a
      prankster. He throws a new light on Crane's death by regarding
      it not as a suicide but as an accident resulting from a prank
      aimed at attracting attention.

22   PARKINSON, THOMAS. Hart Crane and Yvor Winters: Their
      Literary Correspondence. Berkeley and Los Angeles: University
      of California Press, 173 pp.
           While attempting to correct a miscomprehension caused by
      the schematic sense that Crane and Winters are antithetical fig-
      ures, Parkinson concludes that "the relationship was not that of
      Winters the critic to Crane the poet but of two young students
      and writers of poetry who took serious interest in each other's
      work." Given the restriction of Winters's will, Parkinson relies
      largely on the letters from Crane to Winters, on his interview
      with Janet Lewis Winters, on Winters's letters to Allen Tate, on
      Winters's published work, and on the internal evidence of Crane's

letters to Winters. Chapter One provides a biographical study of
the early relationship. Chapter Two recounts the history of the
publication of White Buildings and Winters's enthusiasm for White
Buildings. Chapter Three deals with the "Emerging Differences"
between Crane and Winters. Chapter Four recounts the correspondence between Crane and Winters when Crane was writing The Bridge.
Chapter Five deals with "A Threatening Letter" from Crane to
Winters. When Edmund Wilson's review of White Buildings that
both praised and damned the style of Crane's poetry appeared,
Winters wrote a letter "casting gratuitous moral doubts on Crane's
private conduct." Chapter Six deals with "The Last Phase" of the
relationship, an unhappy one. Crane sent him a copy of the newly
published The Bridge, expecting a favorable review. But Winters
pointed out Crane's "lack of any 'adequate ideational background'"
even though he did not deny the brilliance of Crane. And this
ended their relationship. The "Epilogue" deals with Winters's
reaction toward Crane's suicide and his poetry. See 1974.17;
1975.13; 1976.12. Reviewed in 1979.6, 22, 24.

23　　PEMBERTON, VIVIAN H. "Hart Crane and Yvor Winters, Rebuttal
　　　and Review: A New Crane Letter." American Literature 50
　　　(May):276–81.
　　　　　The long lost reply of Crane to Yvor Winters's review of
　　The Bridge, dated 4 June 1930. See 1979.7.

24　　_____. "On the Side of Life: A 'Lost' Letter Fragment."
　　　Hart Crane Newsletter 2, no. 1 (Summer):2–6.
　　　　　Previously unpublished letter written to his stepmother two
　　months before his death.　In the second part of the letter, printed
　　here for the first time, "Crane discusses the possibility of
　　marriage to Peggy Cowley, confesses the feeling of futility he
　　has experienced, and reveals his fear of the destructive effects
　　of financial uncertainty on both himself and his creative powers."

25　　_____. "Three Obituaries--Bessie Crane Hise (1893–1977)."
　　　Hart Crane Newsletter 2, no. 1 (Summer):37–39.
　　　　　Crane's stepmother died on 22 April 1977 of a cerebral
　　hemorrage in her Hamlet Hills home in Chagrin Falls, Ohio. She
　　married C.A. Crane on 25 January 1930 and eventually became man-
　　ager of his restaurant "Canary Cottage." During her eighteen-
　　month marriage to Crane and until Hart Crane's own death in April
　　1932, she played an important role, at times providing him with
　　funds, always with encouragement and friendship, and helped ease
　　the tension in his relationship with his father.

26　　PICULIN, KARL T. "The Critics and Hart Crane's The Bridge:
　　　An Interview with John Unterecker." Hart Crane Newsletter 2,
　　　no. 1 (Summer):22–33.
　　　　　Prior to the 1959 interest in his poetry, Crane was con-
　　sidered a brilliant lyricist but The Bridge was regarded as a
　　"magnificent failure" because New Criticism which was in vogue at

the time could deal effectively only with small works. This
analytical approach resulted in "fragmented interpretations."
The correct way to read The Bridge is as several details con-
tributing to a larger structure. "The idea of a mythic structure
for America is parallel . . . to what Joyce was then doing in
Ulysses." Crane's friends misunderstood him in that they read
his acceptance of the present as a praise for it. The references
to his personal life in The Bridge serve "to infuse privacy into
a large work." Crane was very disappointed with the critical
reaction to The Bridge and the major opposition to it from his
friends who did not regard it as their idea of a unified poem.

27   QUINN, Sister [M.] BERNETTA. "Silence Beyond Method." Hart
      Crane Newsletter 2, no. (Summer):37-39.
           Robert Comb's aim in his Vision of the Voyage: Hart Crane
      and the Psychology of Romanticism is to establish "a sub-structure
      of idealism from Plato, through Kant, but chiefly through Hegel,
      as relevant to an understanding of Hart Crane." "Main Currents
      in Romantic Psychology" is interesting for readers who enjoy
      nonliterary philosophers but it does not shed any light on the
      verse itself. He also believes, quite wrongly, that Crane had
      nothing in common with American transcendentalism. His analysis
      of individual lyrics is very useful. The middle chapter stresses
      individual images rather than "reflexive reference, the logic of
      association of images." The chapter on The Bridge calls it a
      poem on suffering. See 1978.9.

28   RAMSEY, ROGER. "Crane's 'Twin Monoliths.'" Four Decades of
      Poetry 1890-1930 2, no. 1 (January):24-27.
           The first and final poems of The Bridge balance each other.
      Balance establishes the structural principle. "Proem" and
      "Atlantis" are the twin monoliths of The Bridge. Depends also on
      their balanced imageries. "Each set of images is archetypal and
      involves movement; since the movement, however, is completed and
      reinitiated in 'Atlantis,' there is the larger archetypal idea of
      circularity and perfection involved."

29   READ, DENNIS [M.]. "Additions to Lohf's Literary Manuscripts
      of Hart Crane." Papers of the Bibliographical Society of
      America 72:256-58.
           "In the files of the Little Review, now in the Special Col-
      lections of the University of Wisconsin-Milwaukee Library, are
      seven typescripts of poems by Hart Crane, none of which are listed
      in Literary Manuscripts of Hart Crane, comp. Kenneth A. Lohf
      (Columbia: Ohio State University Press, 1967). All seven poems
      were included in Crane's White Buildings (1926) and thus should
      appear under A. White Buildings: Individual Poems of Lohf's
      Literary Manuscripts." The poems are: "North Labrador,"
      "Chaplinesque," "Possessions," "Passage," "The Wine Menagerie,"
      "Recitative," and "Voyages I-IV."

30   RODGERS, AUDREY T.   "Hart Crane's 'Deathless Dance.'"   Four
     Decades of Poetry, 1890-1930 2, no. 1 (January):1-24.
          The image of the dance is crucial in Crane's poetry; it be-
     comes an equivalent for the kinetic energy of all living things
     as they "consummate their own rhythm; but it is also an emblem of
     harmony and synthesis, the inviolate activity of the gods, the
     gestures of orgiastic celebration, or the mimetic evocation of a
     primitive realtiy."   From the earliest lyrics to his later poems,
     the dance externalizes a broad spectrum of experiences.   The
     dance attempts to harmonize the duality in the mind of the poet
     for whom antithesis is the very nature of existence, and he seeks
     in the dance a means whereby the natural and supernatural conjoin.

31   ROWE, JOHN CARLOS.   "The 'Super-Historical' Sense of Hart
     Crane's The Bridge."   Genre 11:597-625.
          Critics frequently concluded that Crane expressed in The
     Bridge a desire for mythic vision that is never achieved and by
     its nature unrealizable.   This conclusion depends on interpre-
     tations that attempt to read the poem according to traditional
     models for a historical or mythic consciousness, and fails to
     "recognize that the poem itself is an extended attack on the very
     idea of American history, whose obsession with the past or future
     has exhausted the synergy of the present."   Rowe thus objects to
     the view that The Bridge is a failure for being insufficiently
     "historical," because he thinks that Crane's very effort to trans-
     form American history is also an attempt to destroy the hold of
     that history on contemporary man.   "Crane attacks modern America
     for its secret aversion to time, for its desire to escape the
     transience of the present in lust for the future or nostalgia
     for the past."   Therefore, The Bridge is "'unhistorical' in its
     effort to 'forget' the historical burden that compels man to hate
     his own existence; The Bridge is 'super-historical' in its effort
     to affirm human and natural transience as that becoming 'which
     gives existence an eternal and stable character.'"

32   SCHWARTZ, JOSEPH, and SCHWEIK, ROBERT C.   "A Supplement to
     Hart Crane: A Descriptive Bibliography."   Hart Crane News-
     letter 2, no. 1 (Summer):47-62.
          Follows and elaborates the number-letter-decimal system of
     their original (1972.28) and employs the same descriptive prac-
     tices.   Editions, impressions, and other publications which
     appeared after the original was published are listed as well as
     some corrections.   See 1972.5.

33   SIMON, MARC.   Samuel Greenberg, Hart Crane, and the Lost Manu-
     scripts.   Atlantic Highlands, N.J.: Humanities Press, 149 pp.
          A study of the influence of Greenberg on Crane by an in-
     quiry into the lost Greenberg manuscripts.   Contains a biographi-
     cal background of Greenberg, a tracing of the history of the
     manuscripts after his death, and their record to 1964.   Asserts
     that Crane made much more liberal use of the manuscripts than

previous critics have noted. See 1979.5.

34   VOELCKER, HUNCE. "The Case For Casque." In The Gay Academic.
     Edited by Louie Crew. Palm Springs, Calif.: ETC Publications,
     pp. 193-99.
          The spelling of "casque" in the "Ave Maria" section of The
     Bridge is proper for the word's usage there, and one can "gain an
     insight . . . into the potent meanings of the spelling . . . also
     into the secret strange divinity which . . . Crane attempts to
     share with us." Is used as a method for a reading of "Ave Maria."

35   WEBSTER, EMILY. "Plaque Is Unveiled in Garrettsville to Hart
     Crane, Town's Native Son." Youngstown (Ohio) Daily Vindicator,
     21 November, p. 6.
          News account of the commemorative granite memorial to Crane
     in Garrettsville.

36   WHITTING, JOHN H. "Crane, Chaplin, and the Kitten." Hart
     Crane Newsletter 2, no. 1 (Summer):21.
          Verse appreciation.

37   ZECK, GREGORY R. "Identity and Form in Hart Crane." Michigan
     Academician 11 (Summer):19-24.
          Crane wrote obscure poetry "as a much needed defense
     against doubts about his identity." Because Crane could not make
     an outright confession of his homosexuality, "he developed in his
     poetry a heavily symbolic form within whose protective confines
     he could work out the dilemma of his identity: his feeling that
     he was psychically feminine, while he inhabited a masculine body."
     Crane found a hiding place in poetry to express the feelings he
     could not "openly admit as a man in society." But Crane camou-
     flaged his feelings too much for his own good. When he felt him-
     self powerless before a ruthlessly competitive masculinity, he
     withdrew into the intellectual shell of his poetry. "The heavy
     intellectual machinery of the poems represses feeling too much
     and fails to synthesize the male and female elements of the human
     identity."

                              1979

1   ANON. "'In Homage to' the Roeblings: An Unpublished Letter."
     Hart Crane Newsletter 2, no. 2 (Spring):13-14.
          Previously unpublished letter to John A. Roebling, grandson
     of the designer of Brooklyn Bridge, written "in homage to your
     family as builders of the Brooklyn Bridge, to which the poem is
     dedicated." With the letter Crane sent Roebling a copy of The
     Bridge.

2   ANON. "A Last Letter from Mexico." Hart Crane Newsletter 2,
     no. 2 (Spring):3-4.

Previously unpublished letter to Wilbur Underwood, an older poet, whom he met in 1920 when representing his father's candy firm in Washington, D.C.

3   COWLEY, MALCOLM. And I Worked at the Writer's Trade: Chapters of Literary History, 1918-1978. Middlesex and New York: Penguin Books, pp. 3, 62, 64-68, 72-73, 76, 266.
          Miscellaneous biographical details and memories. Crane as well as Fitzgerald and Dylan Thomas had a course of conduct which "they recognized as self-destructive, but which they thought essential to the production of masterpieces."

4   CROWDER, RICHARD. "Poetry: 1900 to the 1930's." In American Literary Scholarship, An Annual/1977. Edited by James Woodress. Durham, N.C.: Duke University Press, pp. 343-64.
          A survey of the year's work on Crane.

5   DEMBO, L[awrence].S. "Less Than Kind." Hart Crane Newsletter 2, no. 2 (Spring):48-51.
          Review of Samuel Greenberg, Hart Crane and the Lost Manuscripts by Marc Simon. Although Dembo regrettably admits that Simon "succeeded admirably" in writing "the definitive work on the relations between Hart Crane and Samuel Greenberg," and in establishing a "conceptual framework for defining 'influence,'" he dismisses Simon's work simply as futile: "the pattern that he sees seems to be little more than a description of obvious similarities that need no exposition." Simon's whole business is "of so little consequence that we can only wonder at Simon's indefatigable efforts to take its measure." See 1978.33.

6   DONOGHUE, DENIS. "Literary Despots." New York Times Book Review, 4 February, pp. 12, 28, 30.
          Review of Parkinson's Hart Crane and Yvor Winters: Their Literary Correspondence. They met only once and their admiration-hate relationship came to an end in 1930 when Winters wrote an unfavorable review of The Bridge. Since only Crane's letters to Winters are contained in the book, the title is misleading. The letters, however, are accompanied by informative comments and Winters's replies can be conjectured quite reliably by reading between Crane's lines and by references to Winters's letters to Allen Tate. Winters maintained that in The Bridge Crane was attempting to imitate Whitman and that his poetry for the most part was loosely and incoherently structured. "Winters was a despot of order, knowledge, concept and restraint. Crane's despotism luxuriated in passion, instinct, genius." See 1978.22; 1979.7.

7   _____. "A Remarkable Letter." New York Times Book Review, 15 April, p. 33.
          A note added to his review (1979.6) of Parkinson's Hart Crane and Yvor Winters: Their Literary Correspondence. Crane

sent an angry letter to Winters when the latter published a review of The Bridge. Vivian H. Pemberton published the letter in
American Literature (1978.23). "And a remarkable letter it is,
a detailed rebuttal rather than a mere cry of rage."

8   GILDZEN, ALEX. "A Crane Memorial." Hart Crane Newsletter 2,
     no. 2 (Spring):57-58.
         A report on the unveiling of the memorial to Crane in
     Garrettsville. With photograph.

9   _____. "The Morning After the Storm." Hart Crane Newsletter
     2, no. 2 (Spring):61.
         Verse appreciation.

10   GUNN, GILES B. The Interpretation of Otherness: Literature,
     Religion, and the American Imagination. New York: Oxford
     University Press, pp. 22, 126.
         Two mentions of Crane and religion.

11   HAMILL, JANET. "The Lonesome Death of Hart Crane." Hart
     Crane Newsletter 2, no. 2 (Spring):56.
         Verse appreciation.

12   HERENDEEN, WARREN, and PARKER, DONALD G. "An Interview with
     Philip C. Horton." Hart Crane Newsletter 2, no. 2 (Spring):
     15-37.
         Horton was first introduced to the works of Crane in 1930
     when Willard Thorpe gave him copies of White Buildings and The
     Bridge. Warder and W.W. Norton suggested that he write a biog-
     raphy of Crane. He met Malcolm Cowley, Matty Josephson, Bill
     Brown, and others. In 1935, he met Grace Crane. She had "a lot
     of energy and courage," and that was the "side of her which one
     had to admire, but her attitude toward Hart was not very pleasant
     always." "She worshipped him, of course, but on the other hand
     she saw nothing wrong with trying to exploit his weaknesses."
     Horton regards his book as a young man's, but does not want to
     change anything except "a few matters of fact that were corrected
     by material that became available later on to Unterecker." He
     had no access to Clarence Crane's correspondence, but talked to
     Bess Crane, Clarence's second wife. Horton remembers Peggy Baird
     Cowley as a disorderly, "very bawdy creature." Horton does not
     think that she had any resemblance to Crane's mother.

13   JOSEPHS, LAURENCE. "Hart Crane: To A Young Poet Who Mis-
     judged Him." Hart Crane Newsletter 2, no. 2 (Spring):38.
         Verse appreciation.

14   MARTIN, ROBERT K. "Hart Crane." In The Homosexual Tradition
     in American Poetry. Austin: University of Texas Press, pp.
     115-63.
         His homosexuality has been discusses repeatedly, but the

discussions almost always assume that there is something wrong
about homosexuality, that Crane's "failure" is related to his
"neurosis." Crane's recognition of "his homosexuality meant a
recognition of himself as an outsider." The two strains found in
homosexual poetry influenced him: (1) the search for a poetry
that could express "a particularly American identity" (Whitman);
and (2) "an emphasis on hopeless love and the alienation of the
artist." Although the source of his Platonism cannot be traced
exclusively to his sexual preference, he was an ardent Platonist,
"seeking a return to the unity of body and soul." These ideas
dominate Martin's analysis of the poetry. The relationship with
Whitman is complex. "Crane both completes and, in so doing,
'misreads' [Harold Bloom] Whitman," turning him into Crane or
making him "into a patron for his art." While praising Whitman,
he "suggests his own superiority, for only Crane can make Whitman
whole, by becoming his perfect reader and lover. Once the relationship is established, it is Crane alone who journeys to
Atlantis."

15   PARKENDEEN, WARD [Herendeen, Warren, and Parker, Donald?].
      "Bright Logician." Hart Crane Newsletter 2, no. 2 (Spring):
      11.
          Verse appreciation with photograph of Crane's tombstone.

16   PEMBERTON, VIVIAN H. "The Composition of 'The Broken Tower.'"
      Hart Crane Newsletter 2, no. 2 (Spring):6-10.
          Concerns the date of the composition of "The Broken Tower."
      On 27 January 1932, Crane mailed two picture postcards to Chagrin
      Falls, Ohio, one to Bess Crane, the other to Ethel Clark, an em-
      ployee of Crane's Canary Cottage. The contents of the postcards
      suggest that "Crane wrote 'The Broken Tower' not five years be-
      fore his death, but within a few weeks of it."

17   POPE, ALAN L. "Last Voyage." Hart Crane Newsletter 2, no. 2
      (Spring):47.
          Verse appreciation.

18   READ, DENNIS M. "Hart Crane's Letters to The Little Review."
      Bulletin of Research in the Humanities 82:249-61.
          Crane's relationship with the Little Review and its editors,
      Margaret Anderson and Jane Heap, by examining primarily Crane's
      correspondence with them and other letters from the files, 1917-
      1926.

19   RODGERS, AUDREY T. "The Deathless Dance: Hart Crane." In
      The Universal Drum: Dance Imagery in the Poetry of Eliot,
      Crane, Roethke, and Williams. University Park: Pennsylvania
      State University Press, pp. 59-90.
          In Crane's poetry, dance stands for "the kinetic energy of
      all living things as they 'consumate their own internal rhythm.'"
      It is also an emblem of a fleeting harmony, a transcending syn-

thesis of the fragmented dualities of life. The "liberation of
language, the emphasis on dynamism, the concept of a many-faceted
image as a verbal equation of thought and emotion in constant
transformation, and the attempt to utilize spatial dimensions of
the poem" led Crane to use the dance metaphor. Author details
his life-long attraction to the dance as his "chief personal mode
of expression." To proclaim this vision, he chose to use a
spiritual American myth of transcendence (Whitman) and "ritual's
reassuring design." Traces evidences of the development of the
dance image throughout his poetry.

20   SCHWARTZ, JOSEPH. "A Divided Self: The Poetic Sensibility of
      Hart Crane with Respect to The Bridge." Modernist Studies 3:
      3-18.
          Considers the question of how Crane came to think of him-
      self as the kind of poet who could undertake the composition of
      The Bridge, since he was the worst equipped of poets to undertake
      an exhaustive meditation on the nature of modern, technological
      culture. He was by nature and temperament one kind of poet, and
      he undertook a willful shift because of the influence of Waldo
      Frank to become another kind of poet. Traces how the divided
      self came about by considering, first, the essential poetic sen-
      sibility of Crane, and, second, how he came to think of himself
      as Whitman's heir.

21   SIMON, MARC. "Carlyle, Samuel B. Greenberg, and Hart Crane:
      An Original Source." American Notes and Queries 17:103-6.
          William Murel Fisher, the only one to know both Samuel B.
      Greenberg and Crane, gave Greenberg Thomas Carlyle's On Heroes,
      Hero Worship, and the Heroic in History in 1915, the year
      Greenberg wrote "Conduct," which influenced "Emblems of Conduct."
      Carlyle influences Crane by influencing Greenberg.

22   _____. "More Than Kin." Hart Crane Newsletter 2, no. 2
      (Spring):51-54.
          Favorable review of Hart Crane and Yvor Winters: Their
      Literary Correspondence by Thomas Parkinson. Crane scholars are
      indebted to Parkinson for "preventing these materials from going
      astray and for making them readily available for research." See
      1978.22.

23   SMITH, WARE. "Strands of The Bridge." Hart Crane Newsletter
      2, no. 2 (Spring):39-47.
          Three points concerning The Bridge about which "critics
      have perpetuated misleading assumptions": (1) Crane does not
      speak directly through the narrator in the poem, but creates a
      first-person narrator; (2) the women in the poem have characteri-
      zations "more diverse and more important than previously thought";
      and (3) while critics have left the religious region of The
      Bridge unexplored, "Crane's vision comprises an intricate com-
      bination of the Christian and American Indian heritage."

24   STANFORD, DONALD E. Reviews of Hart Crane and Yvor Winters:
     Their Literary Correspondence by Thomas Parkinson and Vision
     of the Voyage: Hart Crane and the Psychology of Romanticism
     by Robert Combs. American Literature 51 (May):285-87.
          Parkinson's book is required reading for students of the
     period. Combs uses Crane's poetry as material for demonstrating
     a thesis and makes little or no attempt to evaluate the ideology
     of romanticism. His explications are, however, valuable. See
     1978.9, 22.

25   ZECK, GREGORY R. "Hart Crane's 'The Wine Menagerie': The
     Logic of Metaphor." American Imago: A Psychoanalytic Journal
     of Culture, Science, and the Arts 36:197-214.
          "The Wine Menagerie," dramatizes the family context of his
     struggle for identity and shows how his "logic of metaphor" and
     his whole poetic enterprise accommodates the ambivalence of his
     life--his wish to be dependent and independent, revealing and
     concealing, male and female, as a defense and achievement in his
     family and society.

                              1980

1   BROWN, JAMES F. "The View from Here." Warren (Ohio) Tribune
     Chronicle, 24 January, p. 4.
          "In November 1978, a special boulder and plaque, presented
     by [Helen Hurlbert] in tribute to and in memory of Hart Crane
     [her first cousin], was unveiled and dedicated at a special
     ceremony," in Garrettsville.

2   COWLEY, MALCOLM. The Dream of the Golden Mountain: Remember-
     ing the 1930's. New York: Viking Press, 328 pp.
          Reprint of 1964.5.

3   CROWDER, RICHARD. "Poetry: 1900 to the 1930's." In American
     Literary Scholarship, An Annual/1978. Edited by J. Albert
     Robbins. Durham, N.C.: Duke University Press, pp. 323-42.
          A survey of the year's work on Crane.

4   HERENDEEN, WARREN, and PARKER, DONALD G. "Wind-blown Flames:
     Letters of Hart Crane to Wilbur Underwood." Southern Review
     16 (April):339-76.
          Previously unpublished letters apart from brief passages
     quoted by Unterecker in Voyager. Deals with the circumstances
     which brought Crane to Washington in 1920 and describes the
     friendship with Underwood, who served as "surrogate college pro-
     fessor" for Crane, introduced him to nineteenth century poetry
     through his own poetry which Crane admired and which influenced
     him in diction, rhythm, subject matter and imagery. Correspon-
     dence reveals Crane in all his moods, his family troubles, his
     realtionship with Harry Candee, his literary education, his

                              217

efforts to promote the value of literature. The letters give "the point of view of a visionary passionately . . . absorbing sensations and ideas." The development of Crane's genius and of The Bridge are themes unifying the correspondence.

5   JOHNSON, CAROL. "Hart Crane's Unimproved Infancy." In The Disappearance of Literature. Atlantic Highlands, N.J.: Humanities Press, pp. 30-39.
      Crane was an extraordinarily open personality, utterly lacking in defenses. He was unwilling to convert the least bearable psychic burdens of his life into art. Instead, he used poetry in "the simplest romantic mode," to escape reality and pursue an abstract ideal of "absolute beauty." Does not mean to disparage his gifts; "he was at least Keats' equal." Attempts, rather, to explain why his great natural gifts did not produce more nearly perfect poems. His best work was in White Buildings.

6   NILSEN, HELGE NORMANN. Hart Crane's Divided Vision: An Analysis of The Bridge. Oslo: Universitetsforlaget, 202 pp.
      Using Crane's letters, manuscripts, and the text, examines the influence of Waldo Frank and Whitman on the poem, and analyzes it "as a whole in terms of its leading ideas." The national idealism expressed ("the destiny of America itself") is a central factor of the American character which is a continual challenge to the artist. In the poem there is a mystic, national symbolism—a mystique Crane was never wholly convinced of or comfortable with. The last poet "to reaffirm the grand attempt of American Romanticism," the poem expresses the fundamental principle of synthesis, "the unification and bridging of diversities." His America did not live up to his expectations. Poses the same problems as any liberal utopian literature. Its enduring importance is in its being a reminder to America to fulfill its destiny. It is an act of religious faith; the myth of America reveals God in the works of Americans. Crane was concerned with the spiritual element of life. The bridge of love is positive, affirmative. In his confronting experience headlong, however, a divided attitude becomes evident. "It consists of a wholly affirmative, loving attitude toward everything, . . . and a black pessimism, in which everything that looked so promising suddenly becomes transformed . . . and assumes all sorts of sinister and threatening forms and shapes." Both responses are equally real for Crane; The Bridge is a drama of his faith and doubt in relation to his vision of a mystic America.

7   PRITCHARD, WILLIAM H. "Hart Crane: A Fine Messed-Up Life." In Lives of the Modern Poets. New York: Oxford University Press, pp. 235-62.
      His admirers endorse his exciting effects, and his detractors remain unconvinced by the recent, large amount of work on him. Assorted biographical details, selected to show how Crane stands apart from the majority of modern poets. "But whatever

one says about the disintegration of Crane's life . . . his
poetry when it is successful . . . shows a distinctive individual
consciousness like no other modern poet's." Some poems from
White Buildings, especially "Voyages," and The Bridge are discussed. In the latter, he had nothing to "say" beyond repeated
appeals "for moving onward and upward" toward some ill-defined
end. What Allen Tate said about him cannot be bettered.

8   RAMSEY, ROGER. "A Poetics for The Bridge." Twentieth Century
    Literature 26 (1980):278-93.
        Instead of looking for myth, story, and catharsis, the
    critic should look for "points of expanding apprehension" when
    poem, poet, and reader are unified. The experience for the
    reader is subjective ecstasies. The Bridge is an associative
    rhetorical process, mostly below consciousness, a chaos of para-
    nomasia, sound-links, ambiguous sense-links, and memory-links
    like in a dream. It is religious in that it involves ritualized
    ecstasy. To judge it one must participate in the ecstatic
    moments.

Undated

1   WIENRES, JOHN. Untitled Poem. Broadside B No. 2. Detroit,
    Mich.: Workshop Press, n.p.
        Verse appreciation.

2   WILLIAMS, TENNESSEE. The Poems of Hart Crane. Altanta, Ga.:
    Houghton Mifflin-Caedomon Records, TC 1206.
        Reads the following Crane poems: "To Brooklyn Bridge,"
    "Powhatan's Daughter," "Cutty Sark," "Three Songs," "Legend," "My
    Grandmother's Love Letters," "Praise for an Urn," "Voyages III,"
    "Voyages V," "O Carib Isle," "Royal Palm," "The Hurricane,"
    "The Broken Tower," "The Phantom Bark," and "Eternity."

Index

Holder, Alan, 1966.13
Höllerer, Walter, 1965.12
Holmes, John, 1937.12
Holton, Milne, 1967.14
Homberger, Eric, 1976.5
Honig, Edwin, 1948.8; 1960.11
Hopkins, Gerard Manley
-as subject, 1931.15
Hopkins, Konrad, 1955.8
Horace Liveright: Publisher of
    the Twenties, 1970.10
Horton, Philip
-as author, 1936.5-6; 1937.13;
    1938.2; 1942.3
-as subject, 1979.11
Horton, Rod W., 1952.9
Hound and Horn: The History of a
    Literary Quarterly, The,
    1966.10
Houston, Robert W., 1970.15
Howard, N.R., 1962.12
Howard, Richard, 1974.9
Howe, Will D., 1943.1; 1962.2;
    1972.6
"How Wide Is the Atlantic? or Do
    You Believe in America?,"
    1938.4; 1966.30
Huberman, Elizabeth, 1969.20
"Humanizing a Poet," 1974.20
Hurner, Joy A., 1966.14
"Hurricane, The"
-as subject, 1935.4
Hurwitz, Leo, 1966.15
Hutchinson New Twentieth Century
    Encyclopedia, 1964.3
Hutchinson, Percy, 1930.14
Hutson, Richard Eugene, 1968.20;
    1969.21; 1970.16; 1972.14
Hyde, B.M., 1976.6

Ickstadt, Heinz, 1974.10
Ickstadt, Henrick, 1970.17
"Icon Honors Poet Hart Crane,"
    1976.14
"Identity and Form in Hart
    Crane," 1978.37
"Identity of S.B. Greenberg,"
    1936.6
"Ideology and Irrationalism,
    1930-51," 1951.1
"Il 'Bridge' di Hart Crane arco

voltaico della poesia amer-
    icana," 1955.4
"Illusions as Value: An Essay
    on a Modern Poetic Idea,"
    1974.16
Il Ponte di Brooklyn: "The
    Bridge" di Hart Crane e la
    poesia americana degli anni
    benti, 1966.26
"Image and Idea in 'Voyages II,'"
    1965.4
"Imagemes and Allo-images in a
    Poem by Hart Crane," 1958.16
"Imagery of Violence in Hart
    Crane's Poetry, The," 1971.34
"Imagination's White Buildings
    and 'Quaker Hill,' The,"
    1971.33
Imagism, 1951.3
"Imagist in Amber, An," 1927.16
"In Another Direction," 1951.7
"In Brandywine (Hart Crane),"
    1962.6
In Defense of Ignorance, 1952.18
"Indiana"
-as subject, 1969.42; 1971.24;
    1975.20
Influence of Ezra Pound, The,
    1966.9
"Influence of the Metaphysicals
    on Modern Poetry, The,"
    1948.10
Ingalls, Jeremy, 1964.9
"In His Native Garrettsville Poet
    Plaque Plans at Standstill,"
    1974.13
"'In Homage to' the Roeblings:
    An Unpublished Letter,"
    1979.1
"In Memoriam," 1942.4
"In Memoriam: Hart Crane,"
    1932.24
"In Memoriam: Hart Crane,"
    1974.2
Interpretation of Otherness:
    Literature, Religion, and the
    American Imagination, 1979.10
"Interview with Donald Hall,"
    1961.18
"Interview With Melvin B. Tolson,
    An," 1966.31

McHugh, Vincent, 1930.15
MacIntyre, C.F., 1937.14
McLaughlin, John C., 1958.16
McMahon, William E., 1964.12
McManis, Jack, 1946.4; 1947.4
McMichael, James, 1970.25
McMillan, Douglas, 1976.10
MacNiven, Ian S., 1973.18
McSweeney, Kerry, 1969.31

"Magazine Rack at the Washington
    Square Bookshop," 1969.32
Major Adjectives in English
    Poetry: From Wyatt to Auden,
    1946.5
Major Poems of Hart Crane, The,
    1965.20
"Make the Dark Poems Light: A
    Study of Hart Crane's White
    Buildings," 1955.8
Maloff, Saul, 1970.24
"Man and Animals in Recent
    Poetry," 1936.1
"Mango Tree, The"
-as subject, 1967.23; 1973.16
Man of Letters in the Modern
    World, The, 1955.20
"Man: Rimbaud and Hart Crane,"
    1965.7
"Many Poets of the Past Found
    Success Here," 1965.13
Map of Misreading, A, 1975.2
Marder, Daniel, 1975.10
Mariani, Paul L., 1971.22
Marianne Moore: The Cage and the
    Animal, 1970.13
Marichalar, Antonio, 1927.13
Maritain, Jacques
-as author, 1953.15
-as subject, 1963.18
"Marker Dedicated in Honor of
    Hart Crane," 1978.2
"Market Report: Poetry," 1931.11
Martey, Herbert, 1952.11
Martin, Robert K., 1975.11;
    1976.8; 1979.14
"Mary Hirshfeld Hears. . . ,"
    1966.12
Matthiessen, F.O., 1937.15; 1947.
    7; 1952.12; 1958.15
Mattson, Francis O., 1972.20

Maynard, Reid, 1976.9
Mazzaro, Jerome, 1969.30
Meaker, M.J., 1964.13
"Meaning of the Discarded Poem,
    The," 1948.17
"Meditation Out of Hart Crane,"
    1967.8
Melville, Herman
-as subject, 1956.2
Memoirs and Opinions, 1926-1974,
    1975.23
"Memories of a Friendship,"
    1959.8
"Memories of Hart Crane: A Talk
    with Emil Opffer," 1978.21
Menken, H.L., 1931.11
"Merman, The"
-as subject, 1962.17
Merrill Studies in "The Bridge,"
    The, 1970.6
Messerli, Douglas, 1978.20
"Metamorphosis in American
    Poetry," 1952.14
Metaphor and Reality, 1962.24
"Metaphor in Contemporary
    Poetry," 1931.9
Metaphysical Passion, The,
    1952.15
"Metaphysical Tradition in Three
    Modern Poets, The," 1939.7
Metzger, Deena Posy, 1964.14
Meyer, Gerard Previn, 1948.9
"'Mid-Kingdom' of Crane's 'Black
    Tambourine' and Tomer's Cane,
    The," 1974.12
Mihaila, Rodica, 1970.26; 1973.19
Miles, Josephine, 1946.5; 1961.
    17; 1964.15; 1974.14
Miller, James E., Jr., 1957.7;
    1959.13
Millet, Frederick B., 1940.5;
    1949.7
"Millionaire's Son Is Clerk in
    Akron Store," 1919.1
Minkoff, George Robert, 1970.27
Modern American Poetry and Modern
    British Poetry, 1930.19
"Modern British and American
    Lyric: What Will Suffice,
    The," 1972.22
Modern English and American

"Note on Hart Crane," 1956.6
"Note on Hart Crane As Discussed
    by Yvor Winters and Allen
    Tate, A," 1940.7
"Note on The Bridge, A," 1977.24
"Note on White Buildings by Hart
    Crane, A," 1928.5
"Notes on the Concrete as Method
    in Criticism," 1931.12
"Not Even Important or The Case
    of the Embryo Rimbaud,"
    1961.20
Nyren, Dorothy, 1964.16

"O abordare nigvistica a meta-
    forei si definierea stilului
    poetic," 1973.19
O'Biel, Hedy, 1976.11
Oberg, Arthur, 1972.22
"Obituary Notice: Hart Crane,"
    1932.7
Obsessive Images, 1966.2
"O Carib Isle"
-as subject, 1956.8; 1976.17
O'Connor, William Van, 1948.10-
    12; 1953.24
"Of Prayer and Praise: The
    Poetry of Hart Crane,"
    1966.20
"Of Resolution," 1942.3
O'Hara, Frank, 1971.25
"Old Thresholds, Old Anatomies:
    A New Approach to the
    'Voyages' of Hart Crane,"
    1966.14
O'Neill, 1962.7
"On Finding a Hart Crane Poem,"
    1966.5
Ong, Walter J., 1966.23; 1967.27
"On Hart Crane," 1958.5, 7;
    1970.30
On Moral Fiction, 1978.15
"On My Own Work," 1966.36
"On Poets and Poetry," 1953.17
On the Limits of Poetry, 1948.19
"On the Side of Life: A 'Lost'
    Letter Fragment," 1978.24
Opffer, Emil
-as subject, 1978.15
Opinions of Oliver Allston,
    1941.1

Oppenheimer, Joel, 1961.20
"Optimism Lost," 1967.11
"Order Wrested from Chaos,"
    1960.16
"Orpheus, in Memory of Hart
    Crane," 1960.23
"'O Thou Steeled Cognizance':
    The Brooklyn Bridge, Lewis
    Mumford and Hart Crane,"
    1977.13
"Our Almost Forgotten Poet,"
    1961.14
"Our Modern Sensibility," 1962.5
Our Singing Strength: An Outline
    of American Poetry (1620-
    1930), 1929.4
Ouspensky, P.D.
-as subject, 1947.12; 1950.9
"'Out of the Square, the Circle':
    Vision in Nightmare in
    Crane's 'Tunnel,'" 1978.20
Oxford Companion to American
    Literature, 1965.11; 1966.16

Pack, Robert, 1970.30
Pagan, The
-as subject, 1962.16
Pagany
-as subject, 1969.15
Paniker, K. Ayyappa, 1971.26
"Parabola: Hart Crane and Exis-
    tentialism," 1976.7
"Paraphrase"
-as subject, 1954.6
Paris Was Our Mistress, 1947.9
Paris Was Yesterday, 1925-1939,
    1972.10
Parkendeen, Ward [Herendeen,
    Warren, and Parker, Donald?],
    1979.15
Parker, Donald G., 1979.12;
    1980.4
Parker, Mary A., 1977.19
Parkinson, Thomas, 1974.17;
    1975.13; 1976.12; 1977.20;
    1978.22
Parry, Albert, 1933.12
"Passage"
-as subject, 1949.4; 1955.9, 13,
    25; 1966.21
"Passenger Notifies Hart Crane's

Uncle Here," 1931.4

Passionate Years, The, 1953.8

Paul, Sherman, 1968.29; 1969.35;
1970.31-32; 1972.23-24

Payne, John R., 1975.14

Pearce, Roy Harvey, 1961.21

Pease, Donald, 1975.15

Pemberton, Vivian H., 1972.25;
1975.16; 1976.13-14; 1977.21-
22; 1978.23-25; 1979.16

Penguin Book of Modern American
Verse, The, 1954.8

Perkins, David, 1976.15

Perlmutter, Ruth, 1960.9

Perry, Robert L., 1966.24; 1975.
17-18; 1976.16

Personal Principle, The, 1944.2

Peyre, Henri, 1947.8; 1948.13

"Phelps Putnam and America,"
1932.27

"Photographs in the First Edition of The Bridge, The,"
1962.8

Piculin, Karl T., 1978.26

"Piece of Pure Invention, A,"
1966.32; 1967.38

Pierce, Frederick E., 1927.14

"Plaque Is Unveiled in Garrettsville to Hart Crane, Town's
Native Son," 1978.35

"Plight of Romanticism, The,"
1967.37

"Poem: Before Mario Schifano,"
1971.25

Poems for Study, 1953.24

"Poesia è platonismo," 1947.10

"Poet and His Life, A," 1937.19

Poet and the Machine, The,
1961.11

"Poet-Critics and Scholar-
Critics," 1970.23

"Poète Maudit," 1948.9

"Poet from Oblivion," 1946.4

"Poet Hart Crane Linked to Warren,
Garrettsville," 1972.25

"Poetics of Hart Crane, The,"
1951.12

"Poetics for The Bridge, A,"
1980.8

"Poetics of Surrender: An Exposition and Critique of New

Critical Poetics, The,"
1975.21

"Poet in the Machine Age, The,"
1949.12; 1953.25

"Poet Leaped into Sea Ship Reports," 1931.5

"Poet Lost at Sea Is Air Report,"
1931.6

"Poet of a Mystical Atlantis,"
1948.4

Poetry: A Critical and Historical
Introduction, 1962.16

Poetry: A Modern Guide to Its
Understanding and Enjoyment,
1959.6

Poetry and Change: Donne,
Milton, Wordsworth, and the
Equilibrium of the Present,
1974.14

"Poetry and Happiness," 1969.54

"Poetry and Portraits: Reflections on Hart Crane," 1977.21

Poetry and Prayer, 1967.26

"Poetry and Subject Matter: From
Hart Crane to Turner Cassity,"
1970.12

Poetry and the Common Life,
1974.19

"Poetry Corner," 1935.4

"Poetry in a Scientific World,"
1970.36

Poetry in Our Time, 1952.5

"Poetry, Morality, and Criticism,"
1930.21

"Poetry: 1900 to the 1930's,"
1968.26; 1969.51; 1970.28;
1971.9; 1972.8; 1973.7; 1974.
18; 1975.4; 1976.3; 1977.9;
1978.12; 1979.4; 1980.3

"Poetry: 1910-1930," 1965.5;
1966.27; 1967.33

"Poetry of Hart Crane, The,"
1927.10; 1955.5

Poetry of Hart Crane, The,
1961.23

Poetry of Hart Crane: A Critical
Study, The, 1967.19

"Poetry of James Agee: The Art
of Recovery, The," 1974.21

Poetry of Our Time, 1965.6

"Poetry of Praise, The," 1961.17

"Poetry of the City, The," 1976.6

Poetry of This Age: 1908-1965, 1968.11

"Poetry Out of Chaos," 1933.5

Poet's Alphabet, A, 1970.4

"Poet's Death Linked with Loss of Father," 1932.8

"Poet Seized on 'Left Bank': Now You Must Stay Dry," 1929.1

"Poet's Progress," 1937.4

"Poet's Suicide and Some Reflections, A," 1932.20

"Poets Talking to Themselves," 1931.8

"Poet Stranded on a Bridge," 1969.48

Poore, Charles, 1937.17

Pope, Alan L., 1979.17

Porter, Frank, 1968.30

Porter, Katherine Anne

-as author, 1952.13; 1965.17

-as subject, 1952.13; 1963.13; 1965.17; 1969.17; 1973.13

Portner, Ruth, 1968.19

"Portrait of the Artist as American," 1948.22

"Possibility of a Western Poetics, The," 1966.11

"Post-Symbolist Poetry of Yvor Winters, The," 1971.16

Poulin, A., 1969.36

Pound, Ezra

-as subject, 1966.9

Pownall, David, 1973.22

"Praise for an Urn"

-as subject, 1951.15

"Preface"

-in, Poems by Samuel Greenberg, 1947.11

-to, The Hart Crane Voyages, 1967.22

"Preface to Hart Crane, A," 1930.8

"Preludes to Vision: The Epic Venture in Blake, Wordsworth, Keats, and Hart Crane," 1964.20

Prepositions, 1968.42

Press, John, 1955.13

Primitivism and Decadence, 1937.21

"'Primitivism and Decadence' by Yvor Winters," 1972.26

Pritchard, William H., 1969.37; 1980.7

"Progress of Hart Crane, The," 1930.22

"Prophetic Rhapsody," 1939.8

"Prose Manuscripts of Hart Crane: An Editorial Portfolio, The," 1972.16

Published in Paris: American and British Writers, Printers, and Publishers in Paris, 1920-1939, 1975.6

Puknat, E.M., 1969.38

Puknat, S.B., 1969.38

Putnam, Samuel, 1947.9

"Quaker Hill"

-as subject, 1971.33

Quinn, Arthur Hobson, ed., 1951.11

Quinn, Sister M. Bernatta, 1951.12; 1952.14; 1955.14; 1978.27

Quinn, Vincent Gerard, 1959.14; 1963.18; 1969.39; 1977.23

Radhuber, Stanley Gregory, 1968.31; 1969.40

Rago, Henry, 1948.14; 1967.28-29

"Rainbow and the Grid, The," 1964.19

Raiziss, Sonia, 1944.1; 1952.15

Ramsey, Paul, 1976.17

Ramsey, Roger, 1978.28; 1980.8

Ramsey, Warren, 1947.10; 1950.6; 1953.16; 1964.17

"Rationale of Hart Crane, The," 1964.15

"Raw Genius, Self-delusion, and Incantation," 1948.16

Read, Dennis M., 1978.29; 1979.18

Reader's Guide to Dylan Thomas, A, 1962.20

"Reading of Hart Crane's 'For the Marriage of Faustus and Helen,' A," 1967.24

Realismo e simbolismo: saggi di letteratura americana contemporanea, 1957.6

"Recitative"

-as subject, 1970.39

"Recollections of Hart Crane,"
1934.4
"Re-creating Crane," 1969.53
"Rediscovery of America," 1930.13
Re-discovery of America, The,
1947.2
"Reflections on American Poetry,
1900-1950," 1957.9
Reiter, Thomas, 1969.40
"Relation of Certain Modern
Poets to the Metaphysical
Poets of the Seventeenth Cen-
tury, The," 1944.1
"Religious Elements in Modern
Poetry," 1941.4
"Religious Poet in America,"
1953.6
Religious Trends in English
Poetry, 1968.16
"Remarkable, Letter, A," 1979.7
"Remembering Hart Crane,"
1934.8; 1941.3
"Remembering Paul Rosenfeld,"
1969.25
"Report Hart Crane Lost from
Ship," 1932.9
"Repose of Rivers"
-as subject, 1963.24; 1977.10
"Response from Malcolm Cowley,
A," 1978.10
"Return, The"
-as subject, 1951.13
"Return of the Vanishing Ameri-
can, The," 1968.17
Return to Pagany: The History,
Correspondence, and Selec-
tions from a Little Magazine
1929-1932, A, 1969.15
"Review," 1948.8, 14, 20; 1962.
14; 1964.21-22; 1968.9, 33
"Review of Horton's Hart Crane,"
1937.5; 1958.3
"Reviews," 1968.29
Rexroth, Kenneth, 1949.8; 1961.
22; 1971.27
"Rhetorical Pressures in 'For the
Marriage of Faustus and
Helen,'" 1972.4
"Rhetoric of Motives, A," 1955.3
Ribner, Irving, 1962.16
Rice, Philip Blair, 1933.13

Richards, I.A., 1950.9
Richman, Sidney, 1962.17
Riddel, Joseph, 1966.25
Ridge, Lola, 1934.5
Riding, Laura, 1927.15; 1928.5
"Rimbaud and Hart Crane: A Com-
parative Essay," 1950.5
Rimbaud, Arthur
-as subject, 1940.4; 1943.2;
1950.3, 5; 1953.5; 1965.7;
1970.4, 15; 1973.20
"Rimbaud et Hart Crane," 1950.3
Ritchey, John, 1937.18
"River, The"
-as subject, 1949.2; 1965.2;
1966.11
"Roaring Boy, The," 1937.8;
1964.13
"Robbed from Pain and Existence,"
1947.3
Robber Rocks: Letters and Memor-
ies of Hart Crane 1923-1932,
1968.8
"Robber Rocks: Letters and Mem-
ories of Hart Crane," 1970.11
Roberts, Michael, 1932.21; 1934.6
"Robinson Jeffers and Hart Crane:
A Study in Social Irony,"
1934.7
Robinson, Jethro, 1955.15
Rodgers, Audrey T., 1978.30;
1979.19
Rodman, Selden, 1952.16
Roebling, John A.
-as subject, 1977.22; 1979.1
"Roebling Response to Hart
Crane's The Bridge: A New
Letter, The," 1977.22
"Romantic Heritage of Dylan
Thomas, The," 1954.5
"Romantic Image in the Poetry of
Hart Crane, The," 1965.19
Romantic Rebels: An Informal
History of Bohemianism in
America, 1967.12
Romantic Survival, The, 1964.3
Rosenfeld, Alvin H., 1973.23;
1974.18
Rosenfeld, Paul, 1927.7
Rosenthal, M.L., 1955.16; 1958.
17; 1960.17; 1970.33; 1974.19